THE REVEL

Former general editors
Clifford Leech, F. David Hoeniger
and E. A. J. Honigmann

General editors
David Bevington, Richard Dutton,
J. R. Mulryne and Eugene M. Waith

LOVE'S SACRIFICE

THE REVELS PLAYS

BEAUMONT *The Knight of the Burning Pestle*
CHAPMAN *Bussy d'Ambois*
CHAPMAN, JONSON, MARSTON *Eastward Ho*
DEKKER *The Shoemaker's Holiday*
FORD *Love's Sacrifice* *'Tis Pity She's a Whore*
JONSON *The Alchemist* *The Devil Is an Ass* *Every Man In His Humour* *Every Man Out of His Humour* *Poetaster* *The Magnetic Lady* *Sejanus: His Fall* *The Staple of News*
LYLY *Campaspe* and *Sappho and Phao* *Endymion* *Galatea* and *Midas*
MARLOWE *Doctor Faustus* *Edward the Second* *The Jew of Malta* *Tamburlaine the Great*
MARSTON *Antonio's Revenge* *The Malcontent*
MIDDLETON *A Game at Chess* *Michaelmas Term* *Women Beware Women*
MIDDLETON AND DEKKER *The Roaring Girl*
MIDDLETON AND ROWLEY *The Changeling*
WEBSTER *The Duchess of Malfi* *The White Devil*

THE REVELS PLAYS

LOVE'S SACRIFICE

JOHN FORD

edited by A. T. Moore

MANCHESTER
UNIVERSITY PRESS
Manchester and New York

Distributed exclusively in the USA
by Palgrave

Published by Manchester University Press
Oxford Road, Manchester M13 9NR, UK
and Room 400, 175 Fifth Avenue, New York, NY 10010, USA
www.manchesteruniversitypress.co.uk

Distributed exclusively in the USA by
Palgrave, 175 Fifth Avenue, New York NY 10010, USA

Distributed exclusively in Canada by
UBC Press, University of British Columbia, 2029 West Mall,
Vancouver, BC, Canada V6T 1Z2

British Library Cataloguing-in-Publication Data
A catalogue record for this book is available from the British Library

Library of Congress Cataloging-in-Publication Data
A catalog record for this book is available from the Library of Congress

ISBN: 978 0 7190 7828 6

First published in hardback 2002 by Manchester University Press

First digital paperback edition 2008

Printed by Lightning Source

FOR MY MOTHER
AND IN MEMORY OF MY FATHER

Contents

List of Illustrations

General Editors' Preface

Clifford Leech conceived of the Revels Plays as a series in the mid-1950s, modelling the project on the New Arden Shakespeare. The aim, as he wrote in 1958, was 'to apply to Shakespeare's predecessors, contemporaries and successors the methods that are now used in Shakespeare's editing'. The plays chosen were to include well-known works from the early Tudor period to about 1700, as well as others less familiar but of literary and theatrical merit: 'the plays included', Leech wrote, 'should be such as to deserve and indeed demand performance'. We owe it to Clifford Leech that the idea became reality. He set the high standards of the series, ensuring that editors of individual volumes produced work of lasting merit, equally useful for teachers and students, theatre directors and actors. Clifford Leech remained General Editor until 1971, and was succeeded by F. David Hoeniger, who retired in 1985.

Since 1985 the Revels Plays have been under the direction of four General Editors: initially David Bevington, E. A. J. Honigmann, J. R. Mulryne and E. M. Waith. E. A. J. Honigmann retired in 2000 and was succeeded by Richard Dutton. Published originally by Methuen, the series is now published by Manchester University Press, embodying essentially the same format, scholarly character and high editorial standards of the series as first conceived. The series concentrates on plays from the period 1558–1642, and includes a small number of non-dramatic works of interest to students of drama. Some slight changes have been made: for example, in editions from 1978, notes to the introduction are placed together at the end, not at the foot of the page. Collation and commentary notes continue, however, to appear on the relevant pages.

The text of each Revels play, in accordance with established practice in the series, is edited afresh from the original text of best authority (in a few instances, texts), but spelling and punctuation are modernised and speech headings are silently made consistent. Elisions in the original are also silently regularised, except where metre would be affected by the change; since 1968 the '-ed' form is used for non-syllabic terminations in past tenses and past participles ('-'d' earlier), and '-èd' for syllabic ('-ed' earlier). The editor emends, as distinct from modernises, the original only in instances where error is patent, or at least very probable, and correction persuasive. Act divisions are given only if they appear in the original or if the structure of the play clearly points to them. Those act and scene divisions not in the original are provided in small type. Square brackets are also used for any other additions to or changes in the stage directions of the original.

Revels Plays do not provide a variorum collation, but only those variants which require the critical attention of serious textual students. All departures of substance from 'copy-text' are listed, including any relineation and those changes in punctuation which involve to any degree a decision between alternative interpretations; but not such accidentals as turned letters, nor necessary additions to stage directions whose editorial nature is already made clear by the use of brackets. Press corrections in the 'copy-text' are likewise collated. Of later emendations of the text, only those are given which as alternative readings still deserve attention.

One of the hallmarks of the Revels Plays is the thoroughness of their annotations. Besides explaining the meaning of difficult words and passages, the editor provides comments on customs or usage, text or stage-business—indeed, on anything judged pertinent and helpful. Each volume contains an Index to the Commentary, in which particular attention is drawn to meanings for words not listed in *OED*, and (starting in 1996) an indexing of proper names and topics in the Introduction and Commentary.

The introduction to a Revels play assesses the authority of the 'copy-text' on which it is based, and discusses the editorial methods employed in dealing with it; the editor also considers the play's date and (where relevant) sources, together with its place in the work of the author and in the theatre of its time. Stage history is offered, and in the case of a play by an author not previously represented in the series a brief biography is given.

It is our hope that plays edited in this fashion will promote further scholarly and theatrical investigation of one of the richest periods in theatrical history.

DAVID BEVINGTON
RICHARD DUTTON
J. R. MULRYNE
E. M. WAITH

Preface

Among the host of people who have helped me in preparing this edition, I am especially indebted to Stanley Wells, who supervised my studies for a thesis edition of the play at the Shakespeare Institute in Stratford-upon-Avon, and Ernst Honigmann, the general editor of the present volume. I could not have got by without the expert guidance (not to mention patience) of these two scholars.

I should also like to thank Tom Craik, whose advice and support have been invaluable, and Joost Daalder, who supervised me with exemplary care in the early stages of work on my thesis edition at the Flinders University of South Australia. Martin White generously provided information about his production of *Love's Sacrifice* at Bristol University and shared his thoughts about the play in performance. Michael Neill, whose critical writings on Ford and Renaissance drama have much influenced my interpretation of *Love's Sacrifice*, made incisive comments on my discussion of the masque and the final scene. Andrew Gurr assessed my discussion of the play's date; Martin Butler supplied me with information about the production of the play at Leeds University; and John Jowett saved me from many errors in my analysis of the Quarto. Susan Brock, Librarian at the Shakespeare Institute during my years in Stratford, gave scrupulous advice on many aspects of my research. Sergio Mazzarelli assisted with the translation of materials in Italian. My sister-in-law, Angelika Nebel, translated research materials in German. My wife, Regina Levkovitch, checked several parts of the typescript. Goran Stanivuković, Warren Hudson and Katsuhiko Nogami all helped on numerous occasions over the years. I am also grateful to Lorna Flint, Lisa Hopkins, Mark Thornton Burnett, Philip Hobsbaum, R. N. Wills, Colin Harris at the Bodleian Library, Oxford, Erich Schleier of the Gemäldegalerie in Berlin, Alexander E. Lucas at the Newberry Library, Chicago, Lorise C. Topliffe, Sub-librarian at Exeter College, Oxford, Christopher Stevens, Superintendent of the Royal Collection, Hampton Court Palace, Costantino Sardella and Francesco Scaringia of the Avellino Tourist Board, and M. M. Rowe, County Archivist at the Devon Record Office in Exeter.

My debts to the staff of libraries in Britain and the United States are too numerous to mention here in full, but I should like to give special thanks to the librarians at the Bodleian Library, the British Library, the Victoria & Albert Museum, John Rylands University Library of Manchester, the National Library of Scotland, the Folger Shakespeare Library, Washington, D.C., and the libraries of the University of Liverpool, Eton College, Magdalen and Worcester Colleges, Oxford, and Trinity College, Cambridge. The illustrations in this book are reproduced by permission of the Bodleian Library, the Provost and Fellows of Worcester College, the Staatliche Museen zu Berlin and the Dulwich Picture Gallery.

I should also like to express my gratitude to the British Council and the Association of Commonwealth Universities, by means of whose support, in the form of a Commonwealth Scholarship, I was able to study at the Shakespeare Institute.

Finally, this edition would have remained a mere will-o'-the-wisp if not for the kindness, love and good sense of my wife Regina, my mother Marie and my late father Eric.

A. T. MOORE
COLES BAY, TASMANIA

Abbreviations and References

ABBREVIATIONS

App. Appendix
Coll. Collation
corr. corrected reading
Ep. Epistle Dedicatory
F Folio
fig. figurative
Lat. Latin
LN Longer Note
MS, MSS manuscript, manuscripts
Prol. Prologue
Q quarto (often refers to the 1633 Quarto of *LS*)
r recto
repr. reprinted
rev. review, revised
Revels The Revels Plays series
SD stage direction
this edn (reading adopted for the first time in) this edition
transl. translated (by)
v verso

FORD'S WORKS

References include collaborations and works of doubtful authorship. (Editions marked with an asterisk have been collated for the present text.)

Bang W. Bang, ed., *John Fordes Dramatische Werke*, in *Materialien zur Kunde des älteren Englischen Dramas*, vol. 13, *The Queen* (Louvain: Uystpruyst, 1906); vol. 23, *The Lover's Melancholy* and *Love's Sacrifice* (1908).
Barker John Ford, *'Tis Pity She's a Whore*, ed. Simon Barker (London and New York: Routledge, 1997).
BH *The Broken Heart*, ed. T. J. B. Spencer, Revels (Manchester: Manchester University Press, 1980).
Candy *The Laws of* Candy, in *The Works of Francis Beaumont and John Fletcher*, ed. Arnold Glover and A. R. Waller, 10 vols (Cambridge: Cambridge University Press, 1905–12), vol. III.
*Coleridge (C) *The Dramatic Works of Massinger and Ford*, ed. Hartley Coleridge (London: Moxon, 1839–40).
Darling *The Sun's Darling*, in *The Dramatic Works of Thomas Dekker*, ed. Fredson Bowers, 4 vols (Cambridge: Cambridge University Press, 1953–61), vol. IV.

Edmonton *The Witch of Edmonton*, in Peter Corbin and Douglas Sedge, eds, *Three Jacobean Witchcraft Plays*, Revels Plays Companion Library (Manchester: Manchester University Press, 1986).

*Ellis (E) *John Ford*, ed. Havelock Ellis, Mermaid series (London: Fisher Unwin, 1888).

Fancies *The Fancies Chaste and Noble*, in Henry de Vocht, ed., *John Ford's Dramatic Works* (*Materials for the Study of Old English Drama*, n.s., vol. I; Louvain: Librarie Universitaire, 1927).

*Gifford (G) *The Dramatic Works of John Ford*, ed. William Gifford, 2 vols (London: Murray, 1827).

*Gifford and Dyce (GD) *The Works of John Ford, with Notes . . . by William Gifford, Esq. A New Edition, carefully Revised . . . by the Rev. Alexander Dyce*, 3 vols (London, 1869).

Gypsy *The Spanish Gypsy*, in *The Works of Thomas Middleton*, ed. A. H. Bullen, 8 vols (London, 1885–6; repr. New York: AMS Press, 1964), vol. VI.

*Hoskins (H) 'A Critical Edition of *Love's Sacrifice* by John Ford', ed. Herbert Wilson Hoskins, unpublished Ph.D. dissertation, Columbia University, 1963.

*Lamb (L) Selection from *LS*, 2.4, in Charles Lamb, *Specimens of English Dramatic Poets, who lived about the Time of Shakspeare* (London: for Longman, Hurst Rees & Orme, 1808).

LM *The Lover's Melancholy*, ed. R. F. Hill, Revels (Manchester: Manchester University Press, 1985).

Lomax, ed., *Plays* John Ford, *'Tis Pity She's a Whore and Other Plays*, ed. Marion Lomax, World's Classics (Oxford: Oxford University Press, 1995).

LS *Love's Sacrifice* (this edition unless otherwise specified).

PW *The Chronicle History of Perkin Warbeck: A Strange Truth*, ed. Peter Ure, Revels (London: Methuen, 1968).

*Quarto (Q) *LOUES Sacrifice. A TRAGEDIE* . . . (London: Hugh Beeston, 1633).

Queen *The Queen*, in W. Bang, ed., *John Fordes Dramatische Werke* (*Materialien zur Kunde des älteren Englischen Dramas*), vol. 13 (Louvain: Uystpruyst, 1906).

*Sutfin (S) 'Ford's *Love's Sacrifice*, *The Lady's Trial*, and *The Queen*, Critical Old Spelling Editions of the Texts of the Original Quartos', ed. Joe Andrew Sutfin, unpublished Ph.D. dissertation, Vanderbilt University, 1964.

'Tis Pity *'Tis Pity She's a Whore*, ed. Derek Roper, Revels (London: Methuen, 1975).

Trial *The Lady's Trial*, in *John Ford's Dramatic Works*, vol. I, ed. Henry de Vocht.

*Weber (W) *The Dramatic Works of John Ford*, ed. Henry Weber, 2 vols (Edinburgh. G. Ramsay, 1811).

Quotations from Ford's non-dramatic works are taken from: L. E. Stock, Gilles D. Monsarrat, Judith M. Kennedy and Dennis Danielson, eds, *The Nondramatic Works of John Ford* (Binghamton, New York: Medieval & Renaissance Texts & Studies, in conjunction with the Renaissance English Text

Society, 1991)—abbreviated as *Nondram. Wks.* The titles of the non-dramatic works are abbreviated as follows:

CBS *Christes Bloodie Sweat*
'Contract' 'A Contract of Love and Trueth'
FM *Fames Memoriall or The Earle of Devonshire Deceased*
GM *The Golden Meane*
HT *Honour Triumphant*
LOL *A Line of Life*
'A Memoriall' 'A Memoriall, Offered to that man of virtue, Sir Thomas Overburie'
Jonson Elegy 'On the best of English *Poets*, BEN: JONSON, *Deceased*'

OTHER WRITERS (EDITIONS OF COLLECTED WORKS)

Quotations of writers other than Ford are generally taken from the following editions of collected works. Where editions of individual works have been preferred (e.g. volumes in the Revels Plays series), details of these are given in the next section.

Beaumont, Francis and John Fletcher *The Dramatic Works in the Beaumont and Fletcher Canon*, gen. ed. Fredson Bowers, 10 vols to date (Cambridge: Cambridge University Press, 1966–). If a play has not yet appeared in this edition, I refer to *The Works of Francis Beaumont and John Fletcher*, ed. Arnold Glover and A. R. Waller, 10 vols (Cambridge: Cambridge University Press, 1905–12).
Chapman, George *The Plays: The Comedies*, gen. ed. Allan Holaday (Urbana: University of Illinois Press, 1970).
Crashaw, Richard *The Poems English Latin and Greek*, ed. L. C. Martin, 2nd edn (Oxford: Clarendon Press, 1957).
Day, John *The Works . . . Reprinted from the Collected Edition by A. H. Bullen* (1881), ed. Robin Jeffs (London: Holland Press, 1963).
Dekker, Thomas Plays: *The Dramatic Works of Thomas Dekker*, ed. Fredson Bowers, 4 vols (Cambridge: Cambridge University Press, 1953–61). Other works: *Thomas Dekker* (Selected Prose Writings), ed. E. D. Pendry, The Stratford-upon-Avon Library, vol. 4 (London: Arnold, 1967).
Donne, John *The Poems*, ed. Herbert J. C. Grierson, 2 vols (Oxford: Clarendon Press, 1912).
Greene, Robert *The Life and Complete Works in Prose and Verse*, ed. A. B. Grosart, 15 vols (London, 1881–6; repr. New York: Russell, 1964).
Heywood, Thomas *The Dramatic Works*, ed. R. H. Shepherd, 6 vols (London: Pearson, 1874).
Jonson, Ben *Ben Jonson*, ed. C. H. Herford and Percy and Evelyn Simpson, 11 vols (Oxford: Clarendon Press, 1925–52).
Lyly, John *The Complete Works*, ed. R. Warwick Bond, 3 vols (Oxford: Clarendon Press, 1902).
Marlowe, Christopher *The Complete Works*, ed. Fredson Bowers, 2 vols (Cambridge: Cambridge University Press, 1973).

Marston, John *The Selected Plays of John Marston*, ed. MacDonald P. Jackson and Michael Neill (Cambridge: Cambridge University Press, 1986).

Massinger, Philip *The Plays and Poems of Philip Massinger*, ed. Philip Edwards and Colin Gibson, 5 vols (Oxford: Clarendon Press, 1976).

Middleton, Thomas *The Works of Thomas Middleton*, ed. A. H. Bullen, 8 vols (London, 1885–6; repr. New York: AMS Press, 1964).

Montaigne, Michel Eyquem de *The Essayes of Michael Lord of Montaigne Done into English by John Florio*, intro. Thomas Seccombe, 3 vols (first publ. 1603; London: Grant Richards, 1908).

Nashe, Thomas *The Works*. ed. R. B. McKerrow, 2nd edn, rev. by F. P. Wilson, 5 vols (Oxford: Oxford University Press, 1958).

Peele, George *The Life and Works*, gen. ed. Charles Tyler Prouty, 3 vols (New Haven: Yale University Press, 1952–70).

Petrarch *Petrarch's Lyric Poems*, transl. and ed. Robert M. Durling (Cambridge, Massachusetts: Harvard University Press, 1976).

Plato *The Dialogues of Plato*, transl. B. Jowett, 5 vols, 3rd edn (Oxford: Clarendon, 1892).

Shakespeare, William *The Complete Works* (The Oxford Shakespeare), gen. eds Stanley Wells and Gary Taylor (Oxford: Clarendon Press, 1988). The following abbreviations are used for Shakespeare's works: *A&C* (*Antony and Cleopatra*), *AWW* (*All's Well that Ends Well*), *AYL* (*As You Like It*), *Cor.* (*Coriolanus*), *Err.* (*The Comedy of Errors*), *Haml.* (*Hamlet*), *1/2H4* (*1/2 Henry IV*), *H5* (*Henry V*), *1/2/3H6* (*1/2/3 Henry VI*), *JC* (*Julius Caesar*), *John* (*King John*), *Lear* (*King Lear*; also *History of King Lear* (Quarto text); *Tragedy of King Lear* (Folio text), *LLL* (*Love's Labour's Lost*), *Luc.* (*The Rape of Lucrece*), *Mac.* (*Macbeth*), *MAdo* (*Much Ado About Nothing*), *Meas.* (*Measure for Measure*), *MerVen.* (*The Merchant of Venice*), *MND* (*A Midsummer Night's Dream*), *MWW* (*The Merry Wives of Windsor*), *Oth.* (*Othello*), *Per.* (*Pericles*), *R&J* (*Romeo and Juliet*), *R2* (*King Richard II*), *R3* (*King Richard III*), *Shrew* (*The Taming of the Shrew*), *Son.* (*Sonnets*), *T&C* (*Troilus and Cressida*), *Temp.* (*The Tempest*), *Tim.* (*Timon of Athens*), *Tit.* (*Titus Andronicus*), *TwN* (*Twelfth Night*), *VA* (*Venus and Adonis*), *WT* (*The Winter's Tale*).

Shirley, James *The Dramatic Works and Poems . . .*, ed. William Gifford and Alexander Dyce, 6 vols (London: Murray, 1833).

Sidney, Sir Philip *The Countess of Pembroke's Arcadia, The New Arcadia*: ed. Victor Skretkowicz (Oxford: Clarendon Press, 1987). *The Old Arcadia*: ed. Jean Robertson (Oxford: Clarendon Press, 1973). *Poems*: ed. William A. Ringler, Jr (Oxford: Clarendon Press, 1962).

Webster, John *The Complete Works*, ed. F. L. Lucas, 4 vols (London: Chatto & Windus, 1927).

Wyatt, Sir Thomas *Collected Poems*, ed. Joost Daalder (London: Oxford University Press, 1975).

OTHER REFERENCES

A&M John Marston, *Antonio and Mellida*, in Jackson and Neill, eds, *Selected Plays*.

Abbott E. A. Abbott, *A Shakespearean Grammar* (London: Macmillan, 1883).

Adams Joseph Quincy Adams, *The Dramatic Records of Sir Henry Herbert* (New Haven, 1917).

Alchemist Ben Jonson, *The Alchemist*, ed. F. H. Mares, Revels (London: Methuen, 1971).

Alciati Andreas Alciati [Alciatus], *The Latin Emblems*, ed. Peter M. Daly, Virginia W. Callahan and Simon Cuttler (Toronto: University of Toronto Press, 1985).

Ali Florence Ali, *Opposing Absolutes: Conviction and Convention in John Ford's Plays*, Salzburg Studies in English Literature; Jacobean Drama Studies (Institut für Englische Sprache und Literatur, Universität Salzburg, 1974).

Anatomy Robert Burton, *The Anatomy of Melancholy* (1621), ed. Holbrook Jackson (London: Dent, 1936).

Antipodes Richard Brome, *The Antipodes*, in *Three Renaissance Travel Plays*, ed. Anthony Parr, Revels Plays Companion Library (Manchester: Manchester University Press, 1995).

Antonio's Rev John Marston, *Antonio's Revenge*, in Jackson and Neill, eds, *Selected Plays*.

Arber Edward Arber, *A Transcript of the Registers of the Company of Stationers of London 1554–1640*, 5 vols (London and Birmingham, 1875–94).

Attwater Donald Attwater, *A Dictionary of Saints*, 2nd edn (London: Burns, Oates & Washbourne, 1948).

B. Fair Ben Jonson, *Bartholomew Fair*, ed. E. A. Horsman, Revels (London: Methuen, 1960).

Babb Lawrence Babb, *The Elizabethan Malady* (East Lansing: Michigan State College Press, 1951).

Bawcutt *The Control and Censorship of Caroline Drama: The Records of Sir Henry Herbert, Master of the Revels 1623–73*, ed. N. W. Bawcutt (Oxford: Clarendon Press, 1996).

BCP *The Book of Common Prayer.*

Belsey Catherine Belsey, *The Subject of Tragedy: Identity and Difference in Renaissance Drama* (London and New York: Routledge, repr. 1991).

Bible The Authorized Version (1611), unless otherwise indicated.

Brand John Brand, *Observations on Popular Antiquities* (London: Chatto & Windus, 1900).

Brewer *Brewer's Dictionary of Phrase and Fable*, 14th edn, rev. Ivor H. Evans (London: Cassell, 1989).

Brockbank Philip Brockbank, *On Shakespeare: Jesus, Shakespeare and Karl Marx, and Other Essays* (Oxford: Blackwell, 1989).

Bryson Anna Bryson, *From Courtesy to Civility: Changing Codes of Conduct in Early Modern England* (Oxford: Clarendon Press, 1998).

Burning Pestle Francis Beaumont, *The Knight of the Burning Pestle*, ed. Michael Hattaway, New Mermaids (London: Benn, 1969).

Bussy George Chapman, *Bussy D'Ambois*, ed. Nicholas Brooke, Revels (Manchester: Manchester University Press, 1964).

Butler Martin Butler, '*Love's Sacrifice*: Ford's Metatheatrical Tragedy', in *Critical Re-Visions*, 201–32.

Butler, *Crisis* Martin Butler, *Theatre and Crisis 1632–1642* (Cambridge: Cambridge University Press, 1984).

Camb. Comp. A. R. Braunmuller and Michael Hattaway, eds, *The Cambridge*

Companion to English Renaissance Drama (Cambridge: Cambridge University Press, 1990).

Cardinal James Shirley, *The Cardinal*, ed. E. M. Yearling, Revels (Manchester: Manchester University Press, 1986).

Cercignani Fausto Cercignani, *Shakespeare's Works and Elizabethan Pronunciation* (Oxford: Clarendon Press, 1981).

Chambers, *WS* E. K. Chambers, *William Shakespeare, A Study of Facts and Problems*, 2 vols (Oxford: Clarendon Press, 1930).

Changeling Thomas Middleton and William Rowley, *The Changeling*, ed. Joost Daalder, New Mermaids (London: Black, 1990).

Chaste Maid Thomas Middleton, *A Chaste Maid in Cheapside*, ed. R. B. Parker, Revels (Manchester: Manchester University Press, 1969).

CHEL *The Cambridge History of English Literature*, ed. A. W. Ward and A. R. Waller (Cambridge: Cambridge University Press, 1910).

Chess Thomas Middleton, *A Game at Chess*, ed. J. W. Harper, New Mermaids (London: Benn, 1966).

Clare Janet Clare, *'Art made tongue-tied by authority': Elizabethan and Jacobean Dramatic Censorship*, Revels Plays Companion Library (Manchester: Manchester University Press, 1990).

Cockeram Henry Cockeram, *The English Dictionarie; or, An Interpreter of Hard English Words . . .* (1623).

Coles Elisha Coles, *An English Dictionary* (1676).

Colman E. A. M. Colman, *The Dramatic Use of Bawdy in Shakespeare* (London: Longman, 1974).

Concord in Discord Donald K. Anderson, ed., *'Concord in Discord': The Plays of John Ford, 1586–1986* (New York: AMS, 1986).

Conspiracy/Tragedy of Byron George Chapman, *The Conspiracy and Tragedy of Charles Duke of Byron*, ed. John Margeson, Revels (Manchester: Manchester University Press, 1988).

Countess John Marston and others, *The Insatiate Countess*, ed. Giorgio Melchiori, Revels (Manchester: Manchester University Press, 1984).

Courtier Baldassare Castiglione, *The Book of the Courtier*, translated by Sir Thomas Hoby, 1561 (London: Dent, 1975).

Critical Re-Visions Michael Neill, ed., *John Ford: Critical Re-Visions* (Cambridge: Cambridge University Press, 1988).

Cropper Elizabeth Cropper, 'The Beauty of Woman: Problems in the Rhetoric of Renaissance Portraiture', in Margaret W. Ferguson, Maureen Quilligan and Nancy J. Vickers, eds, *Rewriting the Renaissance: The Discourses of Sexual Difference in Early Modern Europe* (Chicago and London: University of Chicago Press, 1986).

Daalder See *Changeling*.

Daniel, *Delia* Samuel Daniel, *Sonnets to Delia* (London, 1592).

Davril Robert Davril, *Le Drame de John Ford* (Paris: Didier, 1954).

Dent[1] R. W. Dent, *Shakespeare's Proverbial Language: An Index* (Berkeley: University of California Press, 1981).

Dent[2] R. W. Dent, *Proverbial Language in English Drama Exclusive of Shakespeare, 1495–1616* (Berkeley: University of California Press, 1984).

Dessen, *Conventions* Alan C. Dessen, *Elizabethan Stage Conventions and Modern Interpreters* (Cambridge: Cambridge University Press, 1984).

Dessen, *Recovering* Alan C. Dessen, *Recovering Shakespeare's Theatrical Vocabulary* (Cambridge: Cambridge University Press, 1995).

Dessen and Thomson Alan C. Dessen and Leslie Thomson, *A Dictionary of Stage Directions in English Drama, 1580–1642* (Cambridge: Cambridge University Press, 1999).

Dido Christopher Marlowe, *Dido Queen of Carthage* and *The Massacre at Paris*, ed. H. J. Oliver, Revels (London: Methuen, 1968).

Diehl Huston Diehl, 'Iconography and Characterization in English Tragedy 1585–1642', *Comparative Drama* 12, 2 (Summer 1978), 113–22.

DNB *The Dictionary of National Biography*, eds Leslie Stephen and Sidney Lee, 21 vols (London, 1908–9; Oxford: Oxford University Press, 1917–).

Doueihi Milad Doueihi, *A Perverse History of the Human Heart* (Cambridge, Massachusetts: Harvard University Press, 1997).

Duncan-Jones Katherine Duncan-Jones, *Sir Philip Sidney: Courtier Poet* (London: Hamish Hamilton, 1991).

EDD J. Wright, *The English Dialect Dictionary*, 6 vols (London and New York: H. Frowde, G. P. Putnam's Sons, 1898–1905).

Edw. II Christopher Marlowe, *Edward the Second*, ed. Charles R. Forker, Revels (Manchester: Manchester University Press, 1994).

Edwards and Gibson Philip Massinger, *The Plays and Poems*, ed. Philip Edwards and Colin Gibson, 5 vols (Oxford: Clarendon Press, 1976).

Elegy by WS Anon., *A Funeral Elegy In Memory of the Late Virtuous Master William Peter . . .* in Donald W. Foster, *Elegy by W.S.: A Study in Attribution* (Newark: University of Delaware Press, 1989).

ELR *English Literary Renaissance.*

Eng. Trav. *The English Traveller*, in Thomas Heywood, *Three Marriage Plays*, ed. Paul Merchant, Revels Plays Companion Library (Manchester: Manchester University Press, 1996).

ES E. K. Chambers, *The Elizabethan Stage*, 4 vols (Oxford: Clarendon Press, 1923).

Faret Nicholas Faret, *The Honest Man; or, The Art to Please in Court* (1632).

Farr Dorothy M. Farr, *John Ford and the Caroline Theatre* (London: Macmillan, 1979).

Faustus Christopher Marlowe and his collaborators and revisers, *Doctor Faustus*, ed. David Bevington and Eric Rasmussen, Revels (Manchester: Manchester University Press, 1995).

Faversham Anon., *Arden of Faversham*, ed. Martin White, New Mermaids (London: Benn, 1982).

Fawn John Marston, *Parasitaster, or The Fawn*, ed. David A. Blostein, Revels (Manchester: Manchester University Press, 1978).

Fehrenbach R. J. Fehrenbach, 'Typographical Variation in Ford's Texts: Accidentals or Substantives?', in *Concord in Discord*, 265–94.

Ficino, *Commentary* *Marsilio Ficino's Commentary on Plato's Symposium*, ed. and translated by S. R. Jayne (Columbia: University of Missouri Press, 1944).

Florio John Florio, *A Worlde of Wordes, or Most Copious and Exact Dictionarie in Italian and English* (London, 1598).

Foakes, *Illustrations* R. A. Foakes, *Illustrations of the English Stage 1580–1642* (London: Scolar Press, 1985).

Fraunce Abraham Fraunce, *The Arcadian Rhetorike* (London, 1588).
Gardiner Samuel Rawlinson Gardiner, ed., *Documents Relating to the Proceedings Against William Prynne in 1634 and 1637*, Camden Society, 1877; repr. Johnson Reprint Corporation (New York and London, 1965).
Gayton Edmund Gayton, *Pleasant Notes upon Don Quixot* (London, 1654).
Gilchrist Octavius Gilchrist, *A Letter to William Gifford, Esq. on the Late Edition of Ford's Plays* (London: Murray, 1811).
Gittings Clare Gittings, *Death, Burial and the Individual in Early Modern England* (London and Sydney: Croom Helm, 1984).
Golden Ass Lucius Apuleius, *The Transformations of Lucius, Otherwise Known as The Golden Ass*, translated by Robert Graves (Harmondsworth: Penguin, 1950).
Gowing Laura Gowing, *Domestic Dangers: Women, Words and Sex in Early Modern England* (Oxford: Clarendon Press, 1996).
Gray and Heseltine Cecil Gray and Philip Heseltine, *Carlo Gesualdo, Prince of Venosa, Musician and Murderer* (London: Kegan, 1926).
Greg W. W. Greg, *A Bibliography of the English Printed Drama to the Restoration*, 4 vols (London: Oxford University Press, 1939–59).
Gurr, *Companies* Andrew Gurr, *The Shakespearean Playing Companies* (Oxford: Clarendon Press, 1996).
Gurr, *Playgoing* Andrew Gurr, *Playgoing in Shakespeare's London* (Cambridge: Cambridge University Press, 2nd edn, 1996).
Gurr, *Sh. Stage* Andrew Gurr, *The Shakespearean Stage* (Cambridge: Cambridge University Press, 3rd edn, 1992).
Gurr, 'Singing' Andrew Gurr, 'Singing Through the Chatter: Ford and Contemporary Theatrical Fashion', in *Critical Re-Visions*, 81–96.
Gurr, 'Strutted' Andrew Gurr, 'Who Strutted and Bellowed?', *SS* 16 (1963), 95–102.
Halliwell James O. Halliwell, *A Dictionary of Archaic and Provincial Words, Obsolete Phrases, Proverbs, and Ancient Customs* . . . (London: J. R. Smith, 1847).
Harbage Alfred Harbage, *Cavalier Drama* (New York and London: Modern Language Association of America, 1936).
Herford and Simpson See Jonson, in previous section.
Hervey Mary F. S. Hervey, *The Life, Correspondence and Collections of Thomas Howard, Earl of Arundel* (Cambridge: Cambridge University Press, 1921).
Hilliard Nicholas Hilliard, *Art of Limning: A New Edition of 'A Treatise Concerning the Arte of Limning' Writ by N. Hilliard*, ed. Arthur F. Kinney, Linda Bradley Salamon, Sir John Pope-Hennessy (Boston: Northeastern University Press, 1983).
Hoeniger F. David Hoeniger, *Medicine and Shakespeare in the English Renaissance* (Newark: University of Delaware Press, 1992).
Holland Peter Holland, *The Ornament of Action: Text and Performance in Restoration Comedy* (Cambridge: Cambridge University Press, 1979).
Hopkins, 'Coterie Values' Lisa Cronin [later Hopkins], 'John Ford and His Circle: Coterie Values and the Language of Ford's Theatre', unpublished Ph.D. dissertation, Graduate School of Renaissance Studies, Warwick University, 1986.
Hopkins, *Political Theatre* Lisa Hopkins, *John Ford's Political Theatre*, Revels

Plays Companion Library (Manchester: Manchester University Press, 1994).

Hopkins, 'A Source' Lisa Cronin [later Hopkins], 'A Source for John Ford's *Love's Sacrifice*: The Story of Carlo Gesualdo', *N&Q*, n.s., 35, 1 (March 1988), 66–7.

Houlbrooke Ralph Houlbrooke, *Death, Religion, and the Family in England, 1480–1750* (Oxford: Clarendon Press, 1998).

Howarth David Howarth, *Lord Arundel and his Circle* (New Haven and London: Yale University Press, 1985).

Howe Elizabeth Howe, *The First English Actresses: Women and Drama 1660–1700* (Cambridge: Cambridge University Press, 1992).

Huebert, *Baroque* Ronald Huebert, *John Ford: Baroque English Dramatist* (Montreal and London: McGill-Queen's University Press, 1977).

Huebert, 'Staging' Ronald Huebert, 'The Staging of Shirley's *The Lady of Pleasure*', *The Elizabethan Theatre* IX (1981), 41–59.

Jackson and Neill *The Selected Plays of John Marston*, ed. MacDonald P. Jackson and Michael Neill (Cambridge: Cambridge University Press, 1986).

J. Malta Christopher Marlowe, *The Jew of Malta*, ed. N. W. Bawcutt, Revels (Manchester: Manchester University Press, 1979).

JCS Gerald Eades Bentley, *The Jacobean and Caroline Stage*, 7 vols (Oxford: Clarendon Press, 1941–68).

Kaufmann R. J. Kaufmann, 'Ford's Tragic Perspective', in *Elizabethan Drama: Modern Essays in Criticism*, ed. R. J. Kaufmann (New York: Oxford University Press, 1961), 356–72; first publ. in *Texas Studies in Literature and Language* I (Winter 1960), 522–37.

Kiefer Frederick Kiefer, *Writing on the Renaissance Stage: Written Words, Printed Pages, Metaphoric Books* (Newark: University of Delaware Press, 1996).

A King Francis Beaumont and John Fletcher, *A King and No King*, ed. Robert K. Turner, Jr, Regents Renaissance Drama Series (London: Arnold, 1964).

King, *Casting* T. J. King, *Casting Shakespeare's Plays: London Actors and their Roles, 1590–1642* (Cambridge: Cambridge University Press, 1992).

King, 'Staging' T. J. King, 'Staging of Plays at the Phoenix in Drury Lane, 1617–42', *Theatre Notebook* XIX, 4 (1965), 146–66.

Kökeritz Helge Kökeritz, *Shakespeare's Pronunciation* (New Haven: Yale University Press, 1953).

L. Stage *The London Stage 1660–1800; A Calendar of Plays, Entertainments & Afterpieces, together with Casts, Box-Receipts and Contemporary Comment*, 5 parts, ed. William Van Lennep, Emmett L. Avery, Arthur H. Scouten, George Winchester Stone, Jr and Charles Beecher Hogan (Carbondale, Illinois: Southern Illinois University Press, 1960–8); Part 1: 1660–1700, ed. Van Lennep.

Lady of Pleasure James Shirley, *The Lady of Pleasure*, ed. Ronald Huebert, Revels (Manchester: Manchester University Press, 1986).

Lanham Richard A. Lanham, *A Handlist of Rhetorical Terms* (Berkeley: University of California Press, 1991).

Lawrence W. J. Lawrence, *The Elizabethan Playhouse and Other Studies* [Volume I] (Stratford-upon-Avon, 1912).

Leech Clifford Leech, *John Ford and the Drama of his Time* (London: Chatto and Windus, 1957).

Lerma *The Great Favourite; or, The Duke of Lerma*, attrib. to Sir Robert Howard, ed. Margaret Elizabeth Shewring (unpublished thesis edn, Shakespeare Institute, University of Birmingham, 1977).

Linthicum M. Channing Linthicum, *Costume in the Drama of Shakespeare and his Contemporaries* (Oxford: Clarendon Press, 1936).

Lomax, *Stage Images* Marion Lomax, *Stage Images and Traditions: Shakespeare to Ford* (Cambridge: Cambridge University Press, 1987).

MacDonald and Murphy Michael MacDonald and Terence R. Murphy, *Sleepless Souls: Suicide in Early Modern England* (Oxford: Clarendon, 1990).

McLuskie, 'Language' Kathleen McLuskie, '"Language and Matter with a Fit of Mirth": Dramatic Construction in the Plays of John Ford', in *Critical Re-Visions*, 97–127.

McLuskie, *Ren. D.* Kathleen McLuskie, *Renaissance Dramatists* (London: Harvester Wheatsheaf, 1989).

McMaster Juliet McMaster, 'Love, Lust, and Sham: Structural Pattern in the Plays of John Ford', *RenD* 2 (1969), 157–66.

Madelaine Richard Madelaine, '"Sensationalism" and "Melodrama" in Ford's Plays', in *Critical Re-Visions*, 29–53.

Maid's Trag. Francis Beaumont and John Fletcher, *The Maid's Tragedy*, ed. T. W. Craik, Revels (Manchester: Manchester University Press, 1988).

Malcontent John Marston, *The Malcontent*, ed. George K. Hunter, Revels (London: Methuen, 1975).

Malfi John Webster, *The Duchess of Malfi*, ed. John Russell Brown, Revels (Manchester and New York: Manchester University Press, 1990; first publ. 1964).

Mariam Lady Elizabeth Cary, Lady Falkland, *The Tragedy of Mariam the Fair Queen of Jewry*, ed. Barry Weller and Margaret W. Ferguson (Berkeley: University of California Press, 1994).

Markward William B. Markward, 'A Study of the Phoenix Theatre in Drury Lane, 1617–38', unpublished Ph.D. dissertation, University of Birmingham, 1953.

Massacre *The Massacre at Paris*, in Christopher Marlowe, *Dido Queen of Carthage* and *The Massacre at Paris*, ed. H. J. Oliver, Revels (London: Methuen, 1968).

Mendelson and Crawford Sara Mendelson and Patricia Crawford, *Women in Early Modern England, 1550–1720* (Oxford: Clarendon Press, 1998).

Metamorphoses Ovid, *Metamorphoses*, transl. Frank Justus Miller, Loeb Classical Library, 3rd edn (Cambridge, Massachusetts: Harvard University Press, 1977).

Milan Philip Massinger, *The Duke of Milan*, in Edwards and Gibson, vol. I.

Mincoff Marco Mincoff, 'Shakespeare, Fletcher and Baroque Tragedy', *SS* 20 (1967), 1–15.

Minta Stephen Minta, *Petrarch and Petrarchism: The English and French Traditions* (Manchester: Manchester University Press, 1980).

Mirandola Barry Cornwall (pseud. of Bryan Waller Procter), *Mirandola, a Tragedy*, 2nd edn (London: Warren, 1821).

MLQ *Modern Language Quarterly*.

Monsieur Thomas John Fletcher, *Monsieur Thomas*, in *The Works of Beaumont & Fletcher*, ed. Alexander Dyce, 11 vols (Freeport: Books for Library Press, 1843–6; 1970), vol. VII.

Moryson, *Itinerary* Fines Moryson, *An Itinerary: Containing His Ten Yeeres Travell Through the Twelve Dominions of Germany . . . Italy, Turky, France, England, Scotland, and Ireland*, 3 parts (London, 1617).

MSR Malone Society Reprint.

N&Q *Notes and Queries*.

Neill, 'Feasts' Michael Neill, ' "Feasts put down funerals": Death and Ritual in Renaissance Comedy', in *True Rites and Maimed Rites: Ritual and Anti-ritual in Shakespeare and His Age*, ed. Linda Woodbridge and Edward Berry (Urbana: University of Illinois Press, 1992), 47–74.

Neill, *Issues* Michael Neill, *Issues of Death: Mortality and Identity in English Renaissance Tragedy* (Oxford: Clarendon Press, 1997).

Neill, 'Neo-stoicism' Michael Neill, 'Neo-stoicism and Mannerism in the Drama of John Ford', unpublished Ph.D. dissertation, Trinity College, Cambridge, 1974.

Neill, 'Riddle' Michael Neill, ' "What strange riddle's this?": Deciphering *'Tis Pity She's a Whore*', in *Critical Re-Visions*, 153–80.

Neill, 'Wits' Michael Neill, ' "Wits most accomplished Senate": The Audience of the Caroline Private Theaters', *SEL* XVIII, 1 (Winter 1978), 341–60.

New Inn Ben Jonson, *The New Inn*, ed. Michael Hattaway, Revels (Manchester: Manchester University Press, 1984).

Nicoll Allardyce Nicoll, *A History of English Drama 1660–1900*, 6 vols (Cambridge: Cambridge University Press, 1952–9); vol. I, 'Restoration Drama 1660–1700' (1952); vol. IV, 'Early Nineteenth Century Drama 1800–1850' (1955).

OCEL *The Oxford Companion to English Literature*, 5th edn, ed. Margaret Drabble (Oxford: Oxford University Press, 1985).

ODEP F. P. Wilson, rev., *The Oxford Dictionary of English Proverbs*, 3rd edn (Oxford: Clarendon Press, 1970).

Odyssey Homer, *The Odyssey*, transl. A. T. Murray, Loeb Classical Library (Cambridge, Massachusetts: Harvard University Press, 1966).

OED *The Oxford English Dictionary*, 2nd edn (Oxford: Oxford University Press, 1989).

Oliver H. J. Oliver, *The Problem of John Ford* (Melbourne: Melbourne University Press, 1955).

Opie Brian Opie, ' "Being All One": Ford's Analysis of Love and Friendship in *Loues Sacrifice* and *The Ladies Triall*', in *Critical Re-Visions*, 233–60.

Orbison Theodore Tucker Orbison, 'The Tragic Vision of John Ford', unpublished Ph.D. dissertation, Boston University Graduate School, 1963. (Later published in Salzburg Studies in English Literature, no. 21, Institut für Englische Sprache und Literatur, Universität Salzburg, 1974.)

Orrell, 'Inigo Jones' John Orrell, 'Inigo Jones at the Cockpit', *SS* 30 (1977), 157–68.

Orrell, *Theatres* John Orrell, *The Theatres of Inigo Jones and John Webb* (Cambridge: Cambridge University Press, 1985).

Parr, *Travel Plays* Anthony Parr, ed., *Three Renaissance Travel Plays*, Revels Plays Companion Library (Manchester: Manchester University Press, 1995).

Partridge Eric Partridge, *Shakespeare's Bawdy* (London and New York: Routledge, 1968).

Pepys, *Diary* *The Diary of Samuel Pepys*, ed. Robert Latham and William Matthews, 11 vols (London: Bell, 1970–83).

Philaster Francis Beaumont and John Fletcher, *Philaster, or Love Lies-a-Bleeding*, ed. Andrew Gurr, Revels (London: Methuen, 1969).

Phillips Edward Phillips, *The New World of English Words; or, A General Dictionary* (London, 1658).

'Philomusus' 'Philomusus' (John Gough?), *The Academy of Complements* (London, 1639).

Poetaster Ben Jonson, *Poetaster*, ed. Tom Cain, Revels (Manchester: Manchester University Press, 1995).

'Printing' Antony Telford Moore, 'The Printing of John Ford's *Love's Sacrifice*', *The Library* (Transactions of the Bibliographical Society), 6th series, 14, 4 (December 1992), 299–336.

Private Life Philippe Ariès and George Duby, gen. eds, *A History of Private Life*, vol. 3: *Passions of the Renaissance*, ed. Roger Chartier, translated by Arthur Goldhammer (Cambridge, Massachusetts and London: Belknap, Harvard University Press, 1989).

Puttenham Attrib. George Puttenham, *The Arte of English Poesie* (London, 1589).

Rebuilding Andrew Gurr and John Orrell, *Rebuilding Shakespeare's Globe* (London: Weidenfeld and Nicolson, 1989).

RenD *Renaissance Drama*.

RES *Review of English Studies*.

Rev. Trag. Cyril Tourneur (?), *The Revenger's Tragedy*, ed. R. A. Foakes, Revels (London: Methuen, 1966).

Revels History, III, IV, V *The Revels History of Drama in English*, vol. III, 1576–1613, gen. eds Clifford Leech and T. W. Craik (London: Methuen, 1975); vol. IV, 1613–1660, gen. ed. Lois Potter (1981); vol. V, 1660–1750, gen. ed. T. W. Craik (1976).

Ringler See Sidney in previous section.

Robson Ian Robson, *The Moral World of John Ford's Drama*, Salzburg Studies in English Literature; Jacobean Drama Studies (Institut für Anglistik und Amerikanistik, Universität Salzburg, 1983).

Rom. Actor Philip Massinger, *The Roman Actor*, in Edwards and Gibson, vol. III.

RORD *Research Opportunities in Renaissance Drama*.

Rowan[1] D. F. Rowan, 'A Neglected Jones/Webb Theatre Project: Barber-Surgeons' Hall Writ Large', *New Theatre Magazine* IX, 3 (Summer 1969), 6–15.

Rowan[2] D. F. Rowan, 'A Neglected Jones/Webb Theatre Project, Part II: A Theatrical Missing Link', *The Elizabethan Theatre* II (1970), 60–73.

Rowan[3] D. F. Rowan, 'A Neglected Jones/Webb Theatre Project: "Barber-Surgeons' Hall Writ Large"', *SS* 23 (1970), 125–9.

Sargeaunt M. Joan Sargeaunt, *John Ford* (Oxford: Blackwell, 1935).

Schmidt Alexander Schmidt, *Shakespeare Lexicon and Quotation Dictionary*, rev. Gregor Sarrazin (New York: Dover, 1971).

SE Sidney Lee and C. T. Onions, eds, *Shakespeare's England: An Account of the Life & Manners of his Age*, 2 vols (Oxford: Clarendon Press, 1916).

Sea Voyage John Fletcher and Philip Massinger, *The Sea Voyage*, in Parr, *Travel Plays*.

Sejanus Ben Jonson, *Sejanus*, ed. Philip J. Ayres, Revels (Manchester: Manchester University Press, 1990).

SEL *Studies in English Literature 1500–1900*.

Skretkowicz See Sidney in previous section.

Smallwood R. L. Smallwood, '*'Tis Pity She's a Whore* and *Romeo and Juliet*', *Cahiers Elisabéthains* 20 (Oct. 1981), 49–70.

SMT *The Second Maiden's Tragedy*, ed. Anne Lancashire, Revels (Manchester: Manchester University Press, 1978).

Sophonisba John Marston, *Sophonisba*, in Jackson and Neill, eds, *Selected Plays*.

SP *Studies in Philology*.

Span. Trag. Thomas Kyd, *The Spanish Tragedy*, ed. Philip Edwards, Revels (Manchester: Manchester University Press, 1977; first publ. 1959).

SQ *Shakespeare Quarterly*.

SR (*Stationers' Register*) See Arber.

SS *Shakespeare Survey*.

Staple Ben Jonson, *The Staple of News*, ed. Anthony Parr, Revels (Manchester: Manchester University Press, 1988).

Stavig Mark Stavig, *John Ford and the Traditional Moral Order* (Madison: University of Wisconsin Press, 1968).

Sturgess Keith Sturgess, *Jacobean Private Theatre* (London: Routledge & Kegan Paul, 1987).

Styan J. L. Styan, *The English Stage: A History of Drama and Performance* (Cambridge: Cambridge University Press, 1996).

Sugden E. H. Sugden, *A Topographical Dictionary to the Works of Shakespeare and His Fellow-Dramatists* (Manchester: Manchester University Press, 1925).

1 & 2 Tamb. Christopher Marlowe, *Tamburlaine the Great*, ed. J. S. Cunningham, Revels (Manchester: Manchester University Press, 1981).

Telford Moore Antony Telford Moore, 'A Critical Edition of John Ford's *Love's Sacrifice*', unpublished Ph.D. dissertation, The Shakespeare Institute, University of Birmingham, 1993.

Tilley M. P. Tilley, *A Dictionary of the Proverbs in England in the Sixteenth and Seventeenth Centuries* (Ann Arbor, Michigan: University of Michigan Press, 1950).

Ure Peter Ure, 'Cult and Initiates in Ford's *Love's Sacrifice*', in *Elizabethan and Jacobean Drama, Critical Essays by Peter Ure*, ed. J. C. Maxwell (Liverpool University Press, 1974); first publ. in *MLQ* XI (1950), 298–306.

Volpone Ben Jonson, *Volpone; or, The Fox*, ed. R. B. Parker, Revels (Manchester: Manchester University Press, 1983).

W. Devil John Webster, *The White Devil*, ed. John Russell Brown, Revels (Manchester: Manchester University Press, 1960).

Waith, 'Exaltation' Eugene M. Waith, 'John Ford and the Final Exaltation of Love', in *Concord in Discord*, 49–60.

Watkins Glenn Watkins, *Gesualdo: The Man and His Music* (London: Oxford University Press, 1973).

WBW Thomas Middleton, *Women Beware Women*, ed. J. R. Mulryne, Revels (Manchester: Manchester University Press, 1981; first publ. 1975).

Webb J. Barry Webb, *Shakespeare's Erotic Word Usage* (Hastings: Cornwallis Press, 1989).

Wedding *A Critical, Modern-spelling Edition of the 1629 Quarto of* The Wedding *by James Shirley*, ed. Sister Martin Flavin (New York: Garland, 1980).

White Martin White, *Renaissance Drama in Action: An Introduction to Aspects of Theatre Practice and Performance* (London: Routledge, 1998).

Whitney Geffrey Whitney, *A Choice of Emblemes a. Other Deuises* (Leyden, 1586).

Widow's Tears George Chapman, *The Widow's Tears*, ed. A. Yamada, Revels (London: Methuen, 1975).

Williams Gordon Williams, *A Dictionary of Sexual Language and Imagery in Shakespearean and Stuart Literature*, 3 vols (London and Atlantic Highlands: Athlone, 1994).

Wilson John Harold Wilson, *All the King's Ladies: Actresses of the Restoration* (Chicago: University of Chicago Press, 1958).

Woman Killed Thomas Heywood, *A Woman Killed with Kindness*, ed. R. W. Van Fossen, Revels (London: Methuen, 1961).

Wonderful Year Thomas Dekker, *The Wonderful Year* (London, 1603).

Wymer Roland Wymer, *Webster and Ford*, 'English Dramatists' series (Basingstoke: Macmillan, 1995).

Zarrella Michele Zarrella, *Il principe madrigalista: Carlo Gesualdo, l'albero genealogico e la sua città* (Gesualdo: Pro Loco, 1996).

Introduction

One afternoon more than a decade ago, when I was living in Adelaide, in South Australia, I picked up my rather fragile copy of Havelock Ellis's 1888 collection of John Ford's plays, and, having already read *The Broken Heart* and *'Tis Pity She's a Whore*, I decided to have a look at *Love's Sacrifice*. I was curious to know what Ford's other tragedy was like: why it was so little known, and why it was so often excluded from collections of his drama. By the time I had finished turning the foxed pages of Ellis's edition, I thought I understood some of the reasons for the play's neglect. *Love's Sacrifice* is an unusual, perplexing work, disconcertingly replete with echoes of Shakespeare and other dramatists of the period. The tone of its scenes (tragic? heroic? burlesque?) is often hard to identify; its climax, in particular, evades straightforward classification. And at the heart of the tragedy is Bianca, the Duchess of Pavia, who begins the play as a paradigm of virtue but later engages in a 'Platonic' relationship with the courtier Fernando which teeters on the verge of passionate abandon. In her final scene, before she is murdered by her husband, Bianca speaks openly of her overwhelming desire for Fernando. Yet at her funeral, husband and lover alike acclaim her as a glorious martyr.

It was precisely because of these peculiarities that I found—and continue to find—the play so appealing. Here, it seems to me, is a highly distinctive tragedy: no masterpiece, but an awkward, ambiguous, daring creation for the theatre. In this introduction I want to try to appraise *Love's Sacrifice* in the light of its own shaping concerns, and to identify the idiosyncratic ways in which it may speak to an audience. One of my critical assumptions is that the play 'speaks' most eloquently, and most idiosyncratically, through the *effects* of its moment-to-moment action and dialogue. Later in this introduction, therefore, in the section entitled 'The play', I shall describe and discuss a hypothetical performance of *Love's Sacrifice* in what was probably its original setting, the Phoenix Theatre. My main purpose in that section is to attend to what Ford seems to be 'doing or making happen with words and action'.[1]

I shall begin, though, by looking at the immediate circumstances of the play's origin: its date of composition and the playhouse and theatre company for which it seems to have been composed. Then, after examining evidence for a possible Restoration production of the play, I shall consider the important matter of its sources. Ford's choice and handling of his sources may well be the crux for interpretation of *Love's Sacrifice*, for this tragedy is profoundly allusive. A survey of the principal borrowings is given in the section on 'Sources', but this matter is also treated in the following section on 'The play'. In the next section, 'Responses', I present a review of critical reactions to *Love's Sacrifice*. As will be seen, the majority of responses to the play have been 'critical' in both senses of the word, many commentators dismissing the play for its lack of 'consistency' or formal coherence. But *Love's Sacrifice* seems a better play if we can be less proscriptive about its radical indeterminacy. It also grows in appeal when it is treated more carefully as a work for the stage. Of course, a theatrical approach offers no cure-all for the play's undoubted flaws, but it does appear that appreciation of this tragedy has often been hampered by disregard for theatrical perspectives. This is hardly surprising, given that, until June 1980, there had been no production of the play since the seventeenth century. Happily, the last twenty years have seen several productions, details of which are given later in the Introduction.

The text of *Love's Sacrifice* presented in this edition is only *a* text, reflecting in various ways my own practices and priorities as editor. I explain my editorial approach in Appendix 1, where readers will also find an account of the play's textual history.

FORD'S CAREER AND THE DATE OF *LOVE'S SACRIFICE*

Love's Sacrifice is difficult to date precisely, and may be a Jacobean or a Caroline work. It was certainly composed between 1621 and 1633, and internal evidence of uncertain import suggests that it may have been written in the shorter period between about 1626 and 1631.

Many Ford scholars now seem to have reached a consensus that *Love's Sacrifice*, *'Tis Pity* and *The Broken Heart* were composed in the three or four years before the publication of all three plays, in separate quarto editions, in 1633, with *Love's Sacrifice* usually assigned to 1632.[2] However, this widely held view lacks a firm basis, and a date for *Love's Sacrifice* in the year or two before its publication, though not impossible, cannot be assumed. The essential problem here is the dearth of hard evidence relating to Ford's theatrical career. About his life we have a moderate amount of information, no more or less than for many comparable figures of the time.[3] The second son of Thomas and Elizabeth Ford of Ilsington, Devon, he was christened at Ilsington on 12 April 1586,[4] and came from an old and well-to-do Devonshire family. His father owned substantial land in Ilsington and neighbouring parishes. His mother was the niece of Sir John Popham, Lord Chief Justice, who officiated at Ralegh's trial in 1603. A 'John Ford Devon, gen.' matriculated at Exeter College, Oxford, on 26 March 1601. This may have been the dramatist, although the surname is common in Devonshire. Ford was admitted on 16 November 1602 to the Middle Temple, where he seems to have remained until at least 1638.[5] Many of his relatives had preceded him at the Temple, most notably Sir John Popham. Ford was never called to the Bar, and for all we know may not have even studied law. Derek Roper notes that 'At this period the Inns of Court were esteemed not only for the legal training they slowly and unmethodically gave but as town residences for young gentlemen, centres of fashion and culture, where members might stay on indefinitely so long as they kept the rules and paid their dues'.[6] In fact, Ford was suspended from the Temple in early 1606 for failing to pay his buttery bill, and not reinstated until 10 June 1608. His first published works, *Fame's Memorial*, an elegy for the Earl of Devonshire, and *Honour Triumphant*, a prose pamphlet, appeared in the year of his expulsion.

In early 1610 Ford's father died. Thomas Ford left his estate to his wife, to revert to the eldest son, Henry, upon the widow's death, while the youngest sons, Thomas and Edward, received an annual allowance of £10, to be increased to £20 after the death of their mother. John, however, received a total bequest of only £10.[7] In May 1617, Ford was admonished by the Masters of the Bench at the Middle Temple for taking part in a protest by 'dyvers gentlemen of this Fellowship' against the 'auncient custom' of wearing lawyers' caps.[8]

As was common for writers in the period, Ford dedicated many of his works to noble patrons, including Penelope Devereux; Thomas Howard, Earl of Arundel; William and Mary Herbert, Earl and Countess of Pembroke; John Mordaunt, Earl of Peterborough; and William Cavendish, Earl of Newcastle. Partly on the basis of these dedications, Lisa Hopkins has argued that Ford was a member of 'a coterie with strong literary affiliations and markedly Catholic leanings'.[9] Not surprisingly, many of his friends were either writers, members of the Inns of Court (particularly Gray's Inn) or both.[10]

He seems to have been especially close to his cousin, John Ford of Gray's Inn, to whom he dedicated *Love's Sacrifice*, addressing him as '*my truest friend, my worthiest kinsman*'. Most commentators on Ford's life seize on the lines about him in William Heminges's *Elegy on Randolph's Finger* (c. 1632)—'Deep In a dumpe Iacke forde alone was gott / Wth folded Armes and Melancholye hatt'.[11] But whether this tells us anything about Ford's character or is merely 'a conventional portrait of the melancholy man in allusion to Ford's authorship of *The Lover's Melancholy*'[12] it is impossible to be sure. The date of Ford's death is unknown, although it was probably not before the 1639 publication of *The Lady's Trial*, for which he provided a dedicatory epistle.

In contrast to this biographical outline, the record of Ford's theatrical career is threadbare; there is little to help us dovetail the life with the dramatic work. In essence all we know is that, as well as a number of plays written with other dramatists in the period between about 1621 and 1625,[13] Ford wrote several independent works for the stage, the first of which to be published was *The Lover's Melancholy*, in 1629. Most of the independent plays (including *Love's Sacrifice*) were performed by Christopher Beeston's troupes at the Phoenix, or Cockpit, Theatre in Drury Lane, though *The Broken Heart* was staged by the King's Men at the Blackfriars playhouse. These few established facts led G. E. Bentley to order the independent plays according to the acting companies to which their title-pages assign them. 'Possibly', Bentley suggested in *The Jacobean and Caroline Stage* (*JCS*), 'Ford wrote for the King's Men in the first four or five years of Charles's reign and for Beeston thereafter' (III, 437). According to this hypothetical scheme, the period at Blackfriars produced *The Lover's Melancholy* (licensed for the stage in November 1628), *The Broken Heart* (dated by Bentley as 'c. 1627–31?'), and the lost play *Beauty in a Trance*. Then, after transferring to the Phoenix in about 1630, Ford is presumed to have written *'Tis Pity She's a Whore* ('1629?–33'), *Love's Sacrifice* ('1632?'), *Perkin Warbeck* ('1622–32?'), and *The Fancies Chaste and Noble* ('1631?, 1635–6?') for Queen Henrietta's Company, and *The Lady's Trial* ('1638') for the succeeding company at the same playhouse (*JCS* III, 433–64). Bentley never presented this theory as anything more than that—a theory—and even expressed reservations about it:

> Ford collaborated on four plays in 1624; three of his five best plays were in print in 1633, and the fourth in 1634. Given these facts, it is rather unlikely that he wrote none of his considerable plays in 1625, 1626, 1627,

> or early 1628, and then wrote his five best between 1628, when *The Lover's Melancholy* was licensed for the stage, and February 1633/4, when *Perkin Warbeck* was licensed for the press. (*JCS* III, 449)

Yet in the years since the publication of *The Jacobean and Caroline Stage* Bentley's hypothesis has assumed the status of accepted fact. Derek Roper is one of the few dissenters. He points out that Bentley's grouping of the plays into a Blackfriars and a Phoenix period ignores the fact 'that Ford had already written for Beeston and the Phoenix during the period 1621–4': 'We have no very strong grounds for supposing that Ford had successive regular engagements with these theatres: but if we are to suppose this, we may as easily suppose that he wrote *'Tis Pity*, *Love's Sacrifice* and *Perkin Warbeck* during what might be called his early Phoenix period, *before* writing anything for Blackfriars' (*'Tis Pity*, xxv).

The evidence that *Love's Sacrifice* was composed a year or two before its publication in 1633 is similarly open to challenge. In his discussion of the date of the play (*JCS* III, 451–3), Bentley cites internal evidence which he believes points to a composition date around 1632. He argues that Fernando's proposal of an entertainment for the Abbot's visit, featuring 'women antics' (3.2.14–22), 'was intended to remind the Phoenix audience of the Queen and the ladies of her court, who had acted in court performances like the one proposed' (III, 453). Bentley concludes that the lines—and presumably the play—were composed after there had been some talk about the Queen's proposed performance of Walter Montague's *The Shepherd's Paradise* 'in the late summer or early autumn of 1632' (453). In support of this conjecture, Bentley notes the close relationship between Ford's company and the court, as well as the 'polite tone of Ford's allusion' (453). However, it is not at all clear that Fernando's proposal involving 'women antics' can be used to date the play to the period shortly before its publication. To begin with, Bentley passes over the consequences of Fernando's proposal: a masque is indeed presented before the court, during which the profligate Ferentes is stabbed to death by the female performers, who also happen to be his rejected lovers. 'I am slain in jest,' Ferentes cries, 'A pox upon your outlandish feminine antics' (3.4.18–19). The dramatic context of Fernando's proposal, then—what was actually seen and heard on stage during this raucous, bloody episode—would surely have cast a strange light on any intention of a 'polite' allusion to the patron of Ford's company. Tucker Orbison doubts, too, that Ford would have referred to a play which was yet to be performed, for, as Orbison points out, *Love's Sacrifice* was entered in the Stationers' Register only eleven days after Montague's spectacular production was staged.[14]

But there is an even more serious difficulty with Bentley's theory. Even if the passage is accepted as an allusion to Queen Henrietta and her ladies, it cannot assist in dating *Love's Sacrifice* as precisely as he suggests. Henrietta's enthusiasm for courtly theatricals came to the fore after William Prynne's apparent attack on her in *Histriomastix*, which was published in late 1632, shortly after the Queen had performed in *The Shepherd's Paradise*.[15] But the storm which broke over Prynne's 'fower fould offence against the ladyes, magistrates, Kinge, and Queene'[16] has tended to obscure the fact that Henrietta had acted as early as January 1626/7 'in a beautiful pastoral of her own composition, assisted by twelve of her ladies'.[17] This performance at Somerset House was itself the subject of a great deal of comment, not all favourable.[18] It follows that any allusion to Henrietta's theatrical activities in Fernando's speech cannot be limited to the period of preparation for *The Shepherd's Paradise*. As far as Bentley's evidence is concerned, *Love's Sacrifice* could have been written as early as 1626, when Henrietta's theatrical interests first became known.

As it happens, Ford is very likely thinking of *Histriomastix* when he refers in the Epistle Dedicatory for *Love's Sacrifice* to 'the contempt thrown on studies of this kind by such as dote on their own singularity' (ll. 17–19). And James Shirley almost certainly has the long-winded Prynne in mind in his congratulatory verses for the play (see ll. 5–8). Since the proceedings against Prynne began in January 1632/3, soon after the publication of *Histriomastix*, it may be supposed that Ford and Shirley added their voices to the chorus of protest in the early months of that year. As Bentley observes, Shirley's violence 'suggests that he wrote at a time when he was aware of the probability of severe punishment for Prynne' (*JCS* III, 452), and his verses may well have been composed after Prynne was taken to the Tower in February 1633. But these allusions can serve only to date the *prefatory matter* of *Love's Sacrifice*, which we would expect to have been prepared shortly before the play was printed. The text of the play itself may have been much older.[19]

H. J. Oliver[20] presents other evidence that *Love's Sacrifice* was written close to the time of its publication. Having argued that *The Broken Heart* was composed in 1631–2, Oliver cites Crashaw's well-known couplet from *The Delights of the Muses* (1646): 'Thou cheat'st us Ford, mak'st one seeme two by Art. / What is *Loves Sacrifice*, but *the broken Heart*?'.[21] In Oliver's view, this 'surely implies' that *The Broken Heart* was written before *Love's Sacrifice* (48). But Bentley, who is otherwise in favour of a date close to publication, notes that the couplet may only tell us the order in which Crashaw had read the plays, or perhaps the order in which they were published (*JCS* III, 441). There must be a suspicion, too, that Crashaw was merely toying with the plays' titles. As T. J. B. Spencer remarks, 'it seems unlikely that one who had read the plays or seen them performed would have indulged himself in such an inapposite epigram'.[22]

Clearly, then, these attempts to date *Love's Sacrifice* close to the time of its publication are far from persuasive. Moreover, although the play itself does contain reliable evidence concerning its date, this evidence does not preclude a date prior to 1632. As I show in the section on 'Sources', below, *Love's Sacrifice* incorporates borrowings from Massinger's *The Duke of Milan* (datable to about 1621 or 1622[23]), Middleton and Rowley's *The Changeling* (licensed for performance by the Lady Elizabeth's Men at the Phoenix on 7 May 1622)[24] and Middleton's *Women Beware Women* (written between about 1621 and 1625–6[25]). These loans establish a *terminus post quem* of no later than 1621 or 1622, but this date can be pushed a few years later if, as I suspect, Ford borrowed from *The Roman Actor*. Massinger's tragedy was licensed for the stage on 11 October 1626, and was probably completed within the twelve months preceding that date (*JCS* IV, 815–16). Ford wrote commendatory verses for the 1629 edition of Massinger's play, commenting on Caesar's 'pride' and Domitia's 'lust vnabated' (9)—both features which may have influenced the depiction of Caraffa and Bianca. The close parallel with the discovery scene in *The Roman Actor*, 4.2.99ff, is discussed below, p. 63. For other parallels between the plays, see notes to 5.1.43–5, 96–7, 166, 5.2.60, 5.3.86.

One passage already referred to deserves reconsideration for the evidence it may provide on the play's date. In arguing that the 'women antics' passage in *Love's Sacrifice*, 3.2.14–22, was a reference to Queen Henrietta's involvement in the staging of Walter Montague's *The Shepherd's Paradise* in 1632, Bentley rejected an earlier interpretation of the passage by Frederick Gard Fleay, who suggested that the passage may be an allusion to a troupe of French actresses who visited London in 1629.[26] It is very likely that Ford had heard of this French company. They played in London at least three times in November and December 1629 (at Blackfriars, the

Red Bull and the Fortune),[27] and besides being 'the first of their kind to bring with them women players', they were also the first such company 'to make appeal to the ordinary playgoer'.[28] It is even more likely that Ford knew of their fate, for the unfortunate troupe were 'hissed, hooted, and pippen-pelted from the stage',[29] and later attacked by Prynne for their 'impudent, shamefull, unwomanish, gracelesse, if not more then whorish attempt'.[30] Perhaps, then, Ford's recollection of these ill-fated French actresses led to the idea of employing 'women antics' in Fernando's calamitous masque. It may even be possible that, when the dying Ferentes exclaimed against 'outlandish feminine antics' (3.4.18–19), spectators at the Phoenix recognised a play on 'outlandish', which could mean 'foreign' as well as 'bizarre' (*OED outlandish* 1).

Finally, James Shirley's apparent imitation of *Love's Sacrifice* in his similarly named *Love's Cruelty* (see 5.1.174n) suggests that Ford's play *may* have been completed before late 1631. *Love's Cruelty* was written for Queen Henrietta's Company at the Phoenix, and, although it was not printed until 1640, it was licensed for the stage on 14 November 1631 (*JCS* V, 1129).

To summarise: On the basis of the evidence currently available, it is not impossible that one or more of Ford's tragedies (including *Love's Sacrifice*) were written before 1628, perhaps even in the period of the datable collaborations with Dekker, Rowley and Webster (1621–5/6). As we have seen, Bentley's influential hypothesis, which dated *Love's Sacrifice* and the other 'Phoenix plays' to the early 1630s, cannot be substantiated. Bentley himself acknowledged the frailty of his theory, and warned of the possible folly of 'huddling' Ford's major plays into the years between the known date of the licensing of *The Lover's Melancholy* and the publication of the 1633 triplets (*JCS* III, 449). When one looks closely at the 'evidence' supporting a date for *Love's Sacrifice* near to the time of its publication, it evaporates. We can be confident, however, that *Love's Sacrifice* was composed during or after 1621—the earliest possible date for *The Duke of Milan*, *The Changeling* and *Women Beware Women*, three plays from which Ford definitely borrowed. We can further limit the period of composition if it is accepted that *Love's Sacrifice* influenced *Love's Cruelty* and was influenced by *The Roman Actor*. If so, then Ford's play must have been written between about 11 October 1626 (the licensing date of *The Roman Actor*) and 14 November 1631 (the licensing date of *Love's Cruelty*). If—and it is a weighty 'if'—the visiting French actresses of 1629 were the inspiration for Fernando's 'women antics' speech in 3.2, as Fleay suspected, then *Love's Sacrifice* could be dated even more precisely to the period between about November 1629 and November 1631. But overall it seems best to settle for 1626–31 as the likely period of composition.[31]

EARLY PERFORMANCES

The Phoenix Theatre

The title-page of the 1633 quarto of *Love's Sacrifice* (Figure 4) states that the play was 'Acted by the QVEENES Majesties Seruants at the *Phœnix* in *Drury-lane*'. The company referred to, Queen Henrietta's Men, performed at the Phoenix Theatre from late 1625 or early 1626 until 1637 (*JCS* I, 218–45). Since, as we have seen, *Love's Sacrifice* was probably not written before 1626, Queen Henrietta's may have been the first company to perform Ford's tragedy. The title-page statement receives external support from the inclusion of *Love's Sacrifice* in a list of forty-five plays protected for Beeston's Boys at the Phoenix by the Lord Chamberlain on 10 August 1639 (*JCS* I, 330–1). This proclamation shows that *Love's Sacrifice* remained in the Phoenix repertory for at least two years after the dissolution of Queen Henrietta's Men—testimony, perhaps, to the play's early commercial viability.

From the time of its opening in 1616 until the closure of the theatres in 1642, the Phoenix was London's chief private playhouse after Blackfriars.[32] Indeed, during the 1630s it very nearly matched Blackfriars in prestige and popularity.[33] After the interregnum, the Phoenix continued its important role in London's theatrical life, providing many of the actors and a good part of the repertory of the Restoration stage. The theatre's beginnings were rather less distinguished than its subsequent history might suggest. It was built in 1609 as a cockpit, and was converted to a playhouse only in 1616. This conversion was undertaken by the theatre entrepreneur Christopher Beeston.[34] The astute Beeston had no doubt remarked the success of the King's Men at Blackfriars (*JCS* VI, 48), and would have been well aware of the profits to be made from a private theatre. Certainly, his decision to move his troupe, Queen Anne's Company, from the Red Bull at Clerkenwell to the new theatre in the rapidly expanding western suburbs would prove to be one of his sharpest business moves (see 'The Phoenix audiences', below). The specific idea of converting a cockpit into a playhouse may have been prompted by Beeston's knowledge of the Cockpit-in-Court, where occasional theatrical performances had been staged for a decade or more.[35]

Not long after the opening of the Phoenix, on Shrove Tuesday, 4 March 1617, rioting apprentices attacked the new playhouse, ruining furniture and apparel and burning the actors' playbooks.[36] Despite their efforts, however, Beeston was able to renovate the theatre within about three months (*JCS* VI, 56). It is unclear whether the name 'the Phoenix' derived from this rebirth from the flames or from Beeston's initial conversion of the old gaming house.

As with other theatres of this period, our knowledge of the design of the Phoenix has always been hazy. But certain drawings by Inigo Jones in the Jones/Webb collection at Worcester College, Oxford, may well help to remedy the dearth of reliable information about Beeston's theatre. These drawings show the interior and exterior designs for a small indoor theatre built within a curious building with partly rounded walls and a conical roof (see Figure 1). Thanks to the research of D. F. Rowan, John Orrell and others, it now seems probable that these drawings represent the (or a) design for the Phoenix.[37] First published by D. F. Rowan in 1969, the two pages of sketches and plans in Jones's hand have only recently come to be connected with the Phoenix. It is true, too, that, even if their connection with the Phoenix were wholly secure, we would not know to what extent Jones's plans were followed in the actual construction of Beeston's theatre. Still, the intriguing, and very real, possibility remains that what we have in these drawings is the design for the theatre where not only *Love's Sacrifice*, but *The Changeling*, *A New Way to Pay Old Debts*, *'Tis Pity She's a Whore* and many other plays of the period were performed. In the following discussion, and in the later introductory section on 'The play', I wish to entertain that possibility. (The evidence for connecting the drawings with the Phoenix Theatre is summarised in Appendix 2.)

Jones's drawings have been used as the basis for the construction of the so-called Inigo Jones playhouse at the International Shakespeare Globe Centre in London. There is also a reconstruction of Jones's interior in the Wickham Theatre at the University of Bristol—the setting for a production of *Love's Sacrifice*, directed by Martin White, in March 1997 (see p. 86, below). The exterior view in the drawings shows a rather austere brick building with prominent buttresses, high windows and stair turrets possibly based on those at the open-air playhouses.[38] Keith Sturgess comments on the church-like appearance of the building,[39] but the overall impression

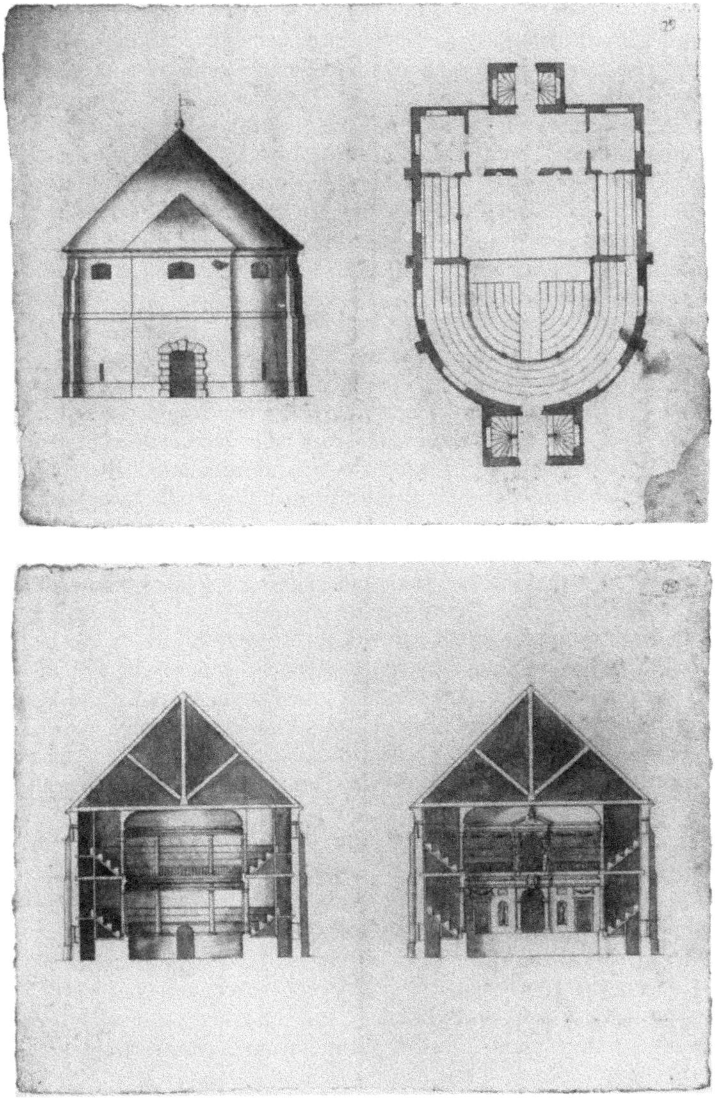

1. Inigo Jones's design for a hall playhouse, possibly the Phoenix.

from the front, at least, is of a modified cockpit. If we are looking here at the Phoenix Theatre, it is not surprising that many theatre patrons continued to refer to the building as the Cockpit even after its re-christening. Inside, perhaps the most immediately noticeable feature of the auditorium would have been its small size. The interior dimensions are 52 feet by 37; the height to the ceiling is 26 feet, 9 inches.[40] Estimates of the audience capacity vary between 500 and 750.[41] D. F. Rowan calculates that 120 people could be seated in the pit, 240 in the galleries at the house-end, 112 in the stage-end galleries, and about twenty-four over the stage.[42] John Orrell thinks there is a real chance that this theatre would have been cramped. He points out that the gallery seats have only 18 inches of leg-room.[43]

Nevertheless, the small auditorium is likely to have been a pleasing sight for the audience as they filed in before a performance. Orrell's tentative recreation of the interior finishing suggests that the woodwork of the stage façade and upper gallery would have been painted in pale yellow 'stone colour' to give an impression of carved stone. The wooden posts supporting the galleries would have been finished to resemble marble, and perhaps decorated with gilt. Metalwork would also have been gilded. The stage would probably have been covered with stretched green baize, and the seating may have been russet. The coved ceiling would very likely have been painted sky-blue, with the section above the stage decorated with representations of clouds and possibly the planets or signs of the zodiac. Orrell comments: 'with its russet and green lower surfaces and its stone-coloured structural elements, the interior will have borne more than a passing resemblance to the open-air theatres of antiquity, an allusion continued in the sky-like treatment of the ceiling and upper walls'.[44]

Lighting, for which there is no provision in the drawings, would probably have been provided by two or more candelabra suspended from the ceiling, perhaps over the orchestra or the stage, as in the title-page illustration from Marsh and Kirkman's *The Wits* (1662, 1673). (There are no references to footlights before the Restoration.) Candles may also have been mounted on brackets attached to the columns around the auditorium.[45] The Phoenix was used for command performances at night, but the usual playing time was in the afternoon. Even on a fine day, however, the stage area in Jones's theatre would have remained in semi-darkness without the aid of flame-light. This seems to indicate a deliberate reliance on artificial lighting. Keith Sturgess suggests that 'If both auditorium and stage were candlelit, then the auditorium was probably noticeably darker than the stage, giving something of the stage emphasis that today's lighting regularly and markedly creates'.[46] In Act 2, Scene 3 of *Love's Sacrifice*, a scene which takes place at 'night' (1), there are a number of suggestive references to lighting; see pp. 50–1 below.

The stage in Jones's design is 4 feet high, 23 feet 6 inches wide and 15 feet deep: a surprisingly generous playing area for a theatre of this size. However, valuable acting space must have been taken up (during some performances, at least) by the 'magistrates of wit' who, according to the preface of the Shakespeare First Folio (1623), sat on stage at the Cockpit as well as Blackfriars to 'arraigne Playes dailie'. Even three or four pipe-smoking gallants on either side of the stage would have occupied several feet of the actors' territory. Nevertheless, Sturgess thinks that, on a stage of these proportions, an actor could still use the depth of the stage as well as the width. The stage-pictures, he says, would still be three-dimensional, while the oblong shape of the stage would create an 'end-stage effect' favouring tableaux.[47] There is no sign of a stage-trap, and it is uncertain whether Jones's design includes a stage-rail. Andrew Gurr does not see a rail, but John Orrell interprets the scored line along the front of the stage in the plan as an indication of a balustered rail similar to that shown in the title-page vignette of Nathanael Richards's *Messallina* (1640).[48]

The most notable feature of Jones's stage façade is its three entrances. Scholars have tended to underrate evidence indicating three stage doors at the Phoenix, but the drawings entitle us to reconsider that evidence in terms of its most obvious interpretation.[49] William B. Markward cites a number of plays in the Phoenix repertory in which a discovery space also appears to have served as a stage entrance. This leads him to suggest that the 'inner stage' (as he calls it) was furnished with its own door.[50] Here in Jones's drawings we find a simpler explanation. The central stage door would have served equally well as an entrance *or* a discovery space—perhaps even both within a single scene. The central entrance is 4 feet wide and 8 feet high: wide enough to permit the entrance of the funeral procession and pall-bearers in William Heminges's *The Fatal Contract* (1653, 2.2, E3v), and high enough to allow Tom Lurcher to enter with his boy on his shoulders in Fletcher's *The Night-Walker*

(1640, D2v). But equipped with curtains or hangings, this central doorway would readily have served as a discovery space for the many scenes requiring such presentations in the Phoenix repertory.[51] In Act 2, Scene 4 of *Love's Sacrifice*, in which Bianca ventures to Fernando's bedside, and at the opening of Act 5, in which (according to the Quarto's stage direction) a curtain is drawn back to '*discover*' Bianca and Fernando engaged in love-talk (4.1), the central entrance may have been employed in just this way. Later, in 5.3.35.1, the same entrance may have served as Bianca's tomb.[52]

Above the central entrance is another interesting feature of Jones's design: a small, window-like opening which could have been used as an upper playing area. This feature also fits the evidence from plays performed at the Phoenix. Characters in Phoenix plays refer to the upper area in many ways: as a balcony, a turret, a mountain, the walls of a castle, but most often as a window.[53] Moreover, no play has more than four speaking characters in the upper area at one time, and, as T. J. King notes, 'in all scenes the action above is limited in scope and could have been performed on a small platform'.[54] In 2.1.13.1–2 of *Love's Sacrifice*, for example, the Quarto calls for the '*Duke, Lords and Ladies*' to enter '*above*' and watch Mauruccio's absurd romantic posturing on the main stage below. But despite the vague reference to the '*Lords and Ladies*', the only characters with lines here are Caraffa, Bianca, Fiormonda and Fernando.[55] Small though the upper station may be, however, I can imagine that actors standing on the balcony, framed by sculptures and an imposing pedimented arch, would tend to dominate the overall stage picture, even when action continued on the platform below. Indeed, many scenes from Phoenix plays feature characters above watching over the proceedings on the main stage.[56] There is one such scene at the opening of the final act of *Love's Sacrifice*, in which Fiormonda, 'ensphered above' (2), comments on Bianca and Fernando's behaviour below. Music—such as that which accompanies the procession to Bianca's tomb at the beginning of Act 5, Scene 3—was perhaps provided by musicians placed in a curtained area behind the balcony in Jones's design.[57]

The Palladian influence of the design is particularly evident in the semi-circular seating plan and in the stage façade with its arched central opening, square-headed side doors and statue niches.[58] But Jones manages to blend neoclassicism with the practical concerns of the Jacobean theatre.[59] The boxes on either side of the stage and the above-stage gallery, for example, derive from the playhouses of his own place and time. Perhaps related to this wedding of neoclassicism and Jacobean theatre design is the tension between intimacy and 'alienation' which John Orrell detects in Jones's plan. The small size of the auditorium (with no spectator more than about 32 feet from centre-stage), the theatre-in-the-round effect of the encircling galleries, the steep incline of the gallery seating and the thrust of the stage towards the middle of the pit would all have encouraged involvement with the action on stage. But, as Orrell remarks, that intimacy is counteracted by the way in which the stage is fenced in, not only by the rails of the audience boxes on either side but by the putative stage rail, which may have blocked sight-lines from the pit.[60] Even more disruptive to the theatre-in-the-round effect are the brick walls between the boxes and the auditorium. These would probably have reached to the ceiling, creating a split between the two ends of the theatre. Orrell thinks this division would have continued right across the middle of the auditorium in an architrave joining the two halves of the ceiling. Together with the supporting brick walls, this may have given an impression of a rudimentary proscenium arch.[61]

Observing the possible 'alienating' effect of such features in Jones's design, Orrell remarks that 'We should be unwise . . . to think of the Jones theatre . . . as simply arranging the closest possible contact between actor and audience':

> In matters of scale and physical disposition it does offer such intimacy; but what it gives with one hand it takes away with the other, setting up barriers that serve to distance the stage from the auditorium . . . Anyone having the least acquaintance with the dynamics of Shakespeare's acting texts will recognize this tension between the 'pull' of empathy and the 'push' of alienation, their exploitation from moment to moment of the diverse possibilities of the physical stage. (*Rebuilding*, 134)

That tension between imaginative involvement and detached observation is acutely important in *Love's Sacrifice*, a tragedy which probably contains as many references to other plays as any theatrical work of the period. One effect of these numerous overt allusions is surely to reinforce the audience's awareness that they are, after all, watching a piece of dramatic fiction. And yet, through the frequent subtlety of its dialogue and the skill of its staging, the play is fully capable of engaging the spectator in its illusion. In its combination of naturalistic and non-naturalistic elements, *Love's Sacrifice* would appear to be ideally suited to the theatre depicted in Inigo Jones's fascinating drawings.

The Phoenix audiences

The Phoenix Theatre was situated close to the expensive new residences along the Strand and in Westminster and Covent Garden, and within a short distance of Whitehall, Denmark House and the Inns of Court. Benchers, students at the Inns, members of the gentry, aristocrats, MPs, courtiers and the occasional foreign dignitary all patronised Beeston's playhouse. In the Epilogue to Richard Brome's Phoenix play, *The Court Beggar* (1639–40; publ. 1653), Swaynwit addresses the audience as 'Ladies . . . Cavaliers and Gentry'. The Duke of Buckingham saw Heywood's *The Rape of Lucrece* at the Phoenix only weeks before his murder in 1628; and in 1634, the year after the publication of *Love's Sacrifice*, King Charles and Queen Henrietta Maria probably attended the Phoenix for a performance of Heywood's masque, *Love's Mistress* (*JCS* I, 232–3; IV, 582). Not surprisingly, the lowest admission charge at the Phoenix was probably six times the basic one-penny fee at the amphitheatres. An extra sixpence bought a stool on the stage, while a box at the side of the stage cost half a crown (Gurr, *Sh. Stage*, 214).

It would be mistaken, however, to think of those attending a performance of *Love's Sacrifice* at the Phoenix as a 'cavalier audience'. Rather, as Martin Butler has demonstrated, the hall playhouses became the focus for an embryonic 'fashionable society' which, 'though partly overlapping with the court, was also definitely distinct from it'.[62] Butler characterises the audience of the Caroline private theatres as 'a distinctively *gentry* audience that is unlike both the wider early-Jacobean and narrower Restoration audiences': 'The audiences were societies still only in the process of developing towards a condition of greater exclusiveness, and the most striking demonstrations of this are the strong provincial ties which still bound many theatre-goers, and the surprising presence of spectators who had close connections with commercial or mercantile families' (130). London's 'semi-independent *beau monde*' provided 'elite' theatres like the Phoenix with 'an audience of active taste, critical, discriminating and alert' (108–9). Dramatists writing for these theatres were safe in assuming a sophisticated audience 'already conversant with the stage repertoire' (107).

Conspicuous amongst this audience, especially from about 1630, were gentlewomen. Dramatists at the hall playhouses 'paid attention to them, giving their plays titles like *The Lady's Privilege* or *The*

Lady's Trial' (Gurr, *Sh. Stage*, 222). *Love's Sacrifice* itself sounds like a title designed to appeal to female patrons (Gurr, *Companies*, 419). Jean E. Howard suggests that 'To be part of urban public life as spectator, consumer, and judge' moved the gentlewoman beyond the 'domestic enclosure' of the home. Howard argues, further, that 'the practice of female theatergoing . . . was part of a larger process of cultural change altering social relations within urban London and putting pressure on the gender positions and definitions upon which masculine dominance rested'.[63] With its sympathetic portrayal—even exaltation—of a woman who harbours an adulterous passion, *Love's Sacrifice* registers such social changes in a peculiarly eye-catching manner. Male auditors at the Phoenix, no less than the increasing numbers of female spectators, are likely to have found topical and compelling subject-matter in a play which has so many parallels with the records of contemporary adultery cases.[64]

Queen Henrietta's Men

Since *Love's Sacrifice* was probably written no earlier than 1626 (see the discussion of the play's date, above), Ford very likely prepared his tragedy for the company known as Queen Henrietta's Men, the troupe referred to on the title-page of the 1633 edition. The original patent for this company has not been found, but Bentley suggests that Christopher Beeston formed the troupe during the long plague-enforced closure of May to November 1625 (*JCS* I, 218–19; II, 654–7). As Bentley notes, the marriage of Charles and Henrietta Maria on 1 May in that year would have provided an auspicious occasion to organise a company under the new theatre-loving Queen's patronage, and the first patent for Queen Henrietta's Men—if indeed one was prepared—may have been issued around the same time as the new licence for the King's Men, which is dated 24 June 1625 (*JCS* I, 219; cf. Gurr, *Companies*, 417).

In assembling the company, Beeston took only Anthony Turner, William Sherlock and possibly William Allen from Lady Elizabeth's Men, the previous company at the Phoenix (*JCS* I, 220). Two other players, John Blaney and William Robbins, came from the old Queen Anne-Revels company, although Blaney seems to have left Queen Henrietta's within a year or two of its formation (*JCS* I, 221–2). The most prominent actor in the new troupe, Richard Perkins, had also been associated with Queen Anne's, though he had probably acted with the King's Men since then (*JCS* II, 526). The origins of the rest of the company are unclear. Bentley suspects that Beeston drew more extensively on Queen Anne's and Lady Elizabeth's companies than the surviving records show (*JCS* I, 220).

Cast lists are extant for five plays performed by Queen Henrietta's company: Massinger's *The Renegado* (printed 1630, first acted by Queen Henrietta's 1625–6), Shirley's *The Wedding* (1629, acted 1626), Heywood's *The Fair Maid of the West* (1631, acted c. 1630), Davenport's *King John and Matilda* (1655, acted c. 1628–34), and Nabbes's *Hannibal and Scipio* (1637, acted 1635).[65] The list for *The Renegado*, the first extant cast for Queen Henrietta's Men, names only nine actors, and appears to represent a temporary organisation of the company within a few months of its inception.[66] Since what concerns us here is the regular constitution of the troupe during the period from 1626 to 1633—that is, from the earliest likely date of the composition of *Love's Sacrifice* to the time of its publication—it is the cast list for *The Wedding* which appears to be our most important source of information. Bentley states that this list 'represents the company as it existed in 1626 and substantially as it continued to exist until it was broken in 1636' (*JCS* I, 222). It is plausible, then, that the fourteen actors mentioned in the list for Shirley's play provided the core of the company that performed in *Love's Sacrifice*.

In all, twenty-three actors can be connected with Queen Henrietta's Men at some point between 1626 and 1641. Six of these can be ruled out as being unlikely to have performed with the company between 1626 and 1632–3.[67] This leaves a total of seventeen players.[68] In fact, the text of *Love's Sacrifice* as it has been preserved suggests that at least sixteen or seventeen actors are required for the play's performance.[69] Perhaps the seventeen players linked to Queen Henrietta's between 1626 and 1632–3 were all involved in performance of Ford's tragedy. The seventeen are as follows:

Richard Perkins	Hugh Clark	John Dobson (?)
Michael Bowyer	William Robbins	Edward Rogers (?)
John Sumner	John Page	Timothy Reade (?)
William Sherlock	John Young	Robert Axen (?)
Anthony Turner	Theophilus Bird	Christopher Goad (?)
William Allen	William Wilbraham (?)	

The first eleven actors in this list were associated with Queen Henrietta's company continuously from 1626 until at least 1633. They are therefore very likely to have been available for performances of *Love's Sacrifice* in that period. The last six actors were members of the company for at least some of the period. William Wilbraham was a Queen's man from about 1626 until at least 1630, since his name appears in the cast lists for *The Wedding* and *The Fair Maid of the West* (*JCS* II, 619). John Dobson and Timothy Reade were members of the company for at least some of the performances of *The Wedding* (*JCS* II, 423, 540–1). Edward Rogers appears in the cast lists for *The Renegado* and *The Wedding*, but it is not known how long he remained with the company after the performances of Shirley's play (*JCS* II, 553). Robert Axen and Christopher Goad were associated with Queen Henrietta's from about 1630, when their names appeared in the cast for *The Fair Maid of the West* (*JCS* II, 353, 444–5). In the absence of evidence to the contrary, it is likely that some, or all, of these six actors made up the other members of the company of sixteen or seventeen required for *Love's Sacrifice*.

Richard Perkins appears to have been the leading actor in Queen Henrietta's company. He was certainly the longest-serving member, remaining with the troupe from about 1626 until its dissolution in 1636 (*JCS* II, 526). The few surviving remarks on the qualities of Perkins's acting suggest a versatile, self-possessed and graceful actor whose skills would have been well suited to a private theatre such as the Phoenix.[70] His known roles—Barabas in a revival of Marlowe's *The Jew of Malta*; the dignified Sir John Belfare in Shirley's *The Wedding*; the erring but ultimately dependable Captain Goodlack in the first (and probably the second[71]) part of Heywood's *The Fair Maid of the West*; Fitzwater in Davenport's *King John and Matilda*; Hanno in Nabbes's *Hannibal and Scipio*; and (according to Ronald Huebert) the tolerant, good-humoured Sir Thomas Bornwell in *The Lady of Pleasure*[72]—suggest a player of considerable diversity, but with a special talent for men of high standing.[73] As the leading tragic actor in the company, Perkins seems the obvious choice for the part of the Duke in *Love's Sacrifice*. Caraffa's quicksilver changes of mood, rendered with skilful modulations of phrasing (see for example 4.1.55–9), would have been relished by this experienced, adaptable player. Assuming that he was born in 1585, as Ronald Huebert suggests ('Staging', 50), Perkins must have been in his forties during the period 1626–33, when *Love's Sacrifice* was probably first performed. This would be an ideal age to play a husband who discovers that his wife craves 'variety of youth' (5.1.69). The anonymous portrait of '*Mr Perkins y^e^ actour*' at Dulwich Picture Gallery (Figure 2) probably dates from the late 1630s,[74]

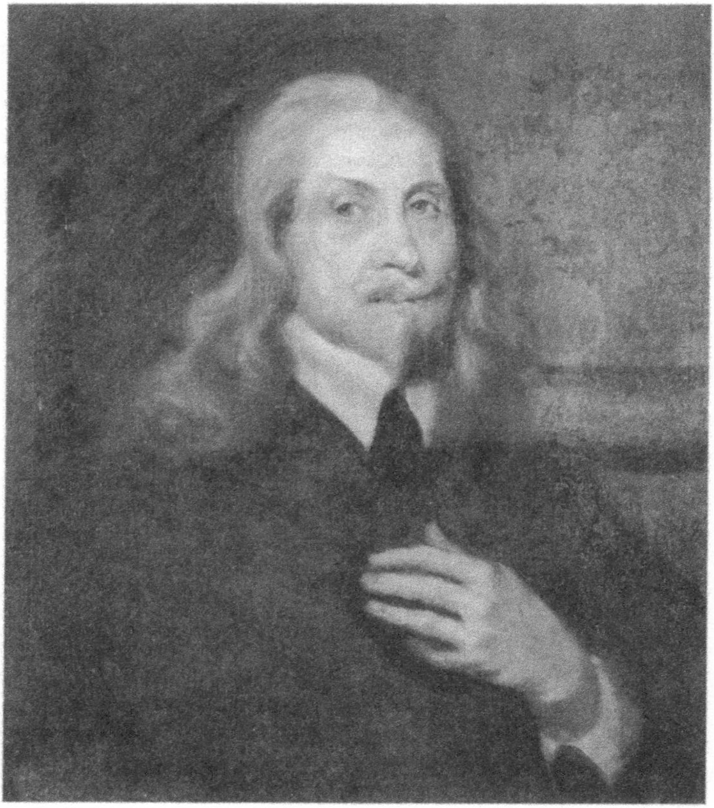

2. Richard Perkins. An anonymous portrait (late 1630s?).

when Perkins was in his early fifties. Since *Love's Sacrifice* seems to have remained in the Queen Henrietta's repertory until the dissolution of the company in 1636, the painting may have been executed while Perkins was still playing the part of Caraffa.

Edward Rogers, John Page, Timothy Reade, Hugh Clark and Theophilus Bird are all known to have taken female roles in plays produced by Queen Henrietta's company. It is tempting to think that the five female characters in *Love's Sacrifice*—Bianca, Fiormonda, Julia, Colona, and Morona—were played by these five actors. There is no obvious reason why this may not have been the case, but of course we cannot be sure. Of the five, Clark and Bird seem the strongest candidates for the important roles of Bianca and Fiormonda; the other three appear to have specialised in small or moderate-sized female roles.[75] Hugh Clark seems to have gained sufficient experience to play leading female roles by about 1626, when he took the part of the idealistic Gratiana in *The Wedding* (*JCS* II, 516). Clark evidently had an aptitude for playing unsullied heroines, for as well as Gratiana he played the true, intrepid Bess in Heywood's *The Fair Maid of the West*. The evidence is obviously slender, but his performances in these roles suggests that he may have been seen as a suitable player for the alternately saintly and defiant Bianca. Of course, it should not be assumed that Bianca's part would necessarily have been reserved for an experienced player of female roles. The dearth of extended speeches in the part could point to the inexperience of the actor playing the Duchess. But on the available evidence, Hugh Clark seems the most likely actor to have played Ford's heroine.

Theophilus Bird, born in 1608, played Paulina in *The Renegado* in about 1625. He was still taking female roles five years later, when, at the age of about twenty-two, he played the lascivious Toota, Queen of Fesse, in Part II of *The Fair Maid of the West*. The latter role, in particular, suggests that Bird would have been well cast as the brazen, unscrupulous Fiormonda. His comparatively advanced age (seventeen in 1625, the earliest likely date for *Love's Sacrifice*) may also have helped him to achieve the 'weight' required for the formidable widow.[76] This would leave the three subordinate female roles of Julia, Colona and Morona to be shared among Edward Rogers, John Page and Timothy Reade.

There are, I think, two especially likely contenders for the role of Fernando: John Sumner and Michael Bowyer. Sumner remained with Queen Henrietta's throughout the company's tenancy at the Phoenix, before being relocated with the new troupe of the same name at Salisbury Court (*JCS* II, 583). Although there is no surviving record of his playing a leading part, his known roles are all substantial, and James Wright refers to him as one of those 'of principal Note at the Cockpit'.[77] Ronald Huebert comments that Sumner 'seems to have played roles demanding sexual charisma, like that of Marwood in *The Wedding* or Mustapha in *The Renegado*'. He quotes Beauford's description of Marwood as evidence of the nature of Sumner's acting: 'He has a handsome presence and discourse, / Two subtle charms to tempt a woman's frailty' (2.2.56–7; 'Staging',

51). Beauford's description puts one in mind of what is said about Fernando in *Love's Sacrifice*. Fiormonda comments repeatedly on Fernando's suave eloquence (1.1.151–3, 174–5; 1.2.97–9, 110), and Bianca taunts Caraffa with rapturous praise of his friend's handsome form (5.1.98–100).

Michael Bowyer, who spoke the lines describing Marwood's 'handsome presence and discourse' in *The Wedding*, may also have been considered for the part of Fernando. Bowyer joined Queen Henrietta's company soon after its commencement in 1625. He played the leading role 'in five of the six casts in which his roles are identified'.[78] Bentley believes that his leading romantic roles with Queen Henrietta's 'offer strong evidence that he was both an experienced and a successful actor when he came to the troupe' (*JCS* II, 386). Bentley's comment raises the only real objection to the notion that Bowyer played Fernando: he may have been too old for the part. If he did not play Fernando, perhaps he took the part of the seducer Ferentes. Like Fernando, Ferentes is possessed of romantic charm and a 'smooth tongue', as Julia, Colona and Morona discover to their cost (1.2.17–19, 47).

William Robbins is very likely to have performed as Roseilli. Robbins was one of the earliest members of Queen Henrietta's Men, and seems to have continued with the company until its dissolution in 1636 (*JCS* II, 547–9). As the company's principal comedian he would almost certainly have taken a part with some opportunity for comic relief, but his popular performances as Antonio in *The Changeling* indicate a capacity for mixing comedy with romantic seriousness. Both qualities are required for the part of Roseilli. It would also make good theatrical sense to cast Robbins in a part which is such an obvious throw-back to that of Antonio (see p. 50, below). Ford may even have written the part to enable Robbins to capitalise on his success in *The Changeling*. Since Middleton and Rowley's tragedy seems to have remained a property of the Phoenix from the time of its first performance at the theatre in 1622 until at least 1639 (*JCS* I, 330–1), it is not unlikely to have played in repertory with *Love's Sacrifice* at some point between 1625–6 and 1636. Perhaps audiences were able to see Robbins in his two 'Changeling' roles within a single season.[79]

William Sherlock, the company's other leading comic actor, may have played the clown Mauruccio. In *The Wedding* Sherlock took the part of Lodam, 'a fat Gentleman' with a penchant for utterances like 'I have no stomach, sir, to your acquaintance' (2.3.143). In *The Fair*

Maid of the West he played 'Mr. Ruffman, a swaggering Gentleman' (*JCS* II, 572–3). Judging by the evidence of these two roles, Mauruccio would have been well within Sherlock's range. Ford's clown has the egotism of Ruffman, and moves 'stalkingly' around the stage in a grotesque parody of courtly manners (2.1.22). Dialogue at 2.2.266–72 suggests, also, that Mauruccio may be fat. The remaining lead role, D'Avolos, may have been taken by William Allen. Allen was one of the company's principal players. His portrayal of King Mullisheg in *The Fair Maid of the West* (in Part II, at least) and his depiction of Grimaldi, the desperate outlaw in Massinger's *The Renegado* indicate some skill in personating evil.

Ascription of the remaining roles is far more uncertain.[80] And in general, the above findings are no more than supposition drawn from scattered evidence and guided by the somewhat tenuous assumption that type-casting was a consistent feature of the allocation of parts in *Love's Sacrifice*.[81] But the task of assigning actors to particular roles is made a little easier by the fact that there could not have been very much doubling of parts in this play. In fact, if the Quarto's directions for appearances on stage are to be relied upon, doubling could have involved only two of the minor roles. The actor of Giacopo may have taken an additional part as either the Abbot, Colona or Julia, but all other speaking parts—including those of Mauruccio, Ferentes and Morona—could not have been doubled.

A Restoration production?

After the closure of the theatres in 1642, no performance of *Love's Sacrifice* is known to have taken place for more than three centuries. However, a copy of the 1633 quarto in the Folger Shakespeare Library, Washington, D.C., contains what appears to be a Restoration cast list for the play (Copy 2, A2v). Accompanying the names of 'The Speakers in this TRAGEDY' on page A2v are two handwritten lists of actors, presented in much the same way (and in a similar hand) as the two lists added to the dramatis personae in a copy of the 1637 edition of Heywood's *The Royal King and the Loyal Subject*.[82] The actors in the *Love's Sacrifice* lists, like those in the lists for Heywood's play, can be identified as members of the King's Company, one of the two patent companies established by Charles II in late 1660. Managed by Sir Thomas Killigrew, the King's Company played at the Vere Street Theatre from 1660 until 1663, and at the Theatre Royal, Bridges Street, from 1663 until 1672. It is not surprising to find Ford's play in their possession after the interregnum, for Killigrew had secured a virtual monopoly of pre-Restoration drama.[83] There is no definite evidence, however, that the company ever presented *Love's Sacrifice* before the public. For all we know, the plans for the production may have been abandoned after the preparation of the cast lists.

Study of the records of the King's Company indicates that the lists were prepared between late 1660 and 1664, possibly in the latter half of that period. The lists give the names of actresses for at least four of the five female parts, but no English actress is known to have appeared on the professional stage before the King's Company performance of *Othello* at the Vere Street Theatre on 8 December, 1660.[84] The lists also include the name of Walter Clun, who was murdered on 2 August 1664.[85] Additionally, if Beck (Rebecca) Marshall—assigned the part of Colona in the lists—did not join the King's Company until about 1663, as John Harold Wilson suggests, the lists must date from the 1662–3 or 1663–4 seasons; but the evidence is not very clear on this point.[86]

For a reproduction and further discussion of these cast lists, see Telford Moore, 181–4.

SOURCES

This section presents a short survey and discussion of the principal sources of *Love's Sacrifice*. Ford's creative use of his dramatic source-material is considered in more detail in the later section on 'The play'.

In his preface to *The White Devil*, John Webster praises the 'worthy labours' of his fellow dramatists, Chapman, Jonson, Beaumont, Fletcher, Shakespeare, Dekker and Heywood, and expresses the wish that 'what I write may be read by their light' (ll. 35, 42–3).[87] Surveying *Love's Sacrifice*, with its myriad borrowings and modifications of other writers' work (including that of Webster himself), it is difficult not to believe that Ford had similar ambitions. Written for a theatre with a 'fairly conservative' repertory (Gurr, *Companies*, 419)—and at a time when revivals were much in vogue—this tragedy may be seen as a witty act of homage to earlier drama. But Ford's use of borrowed material in *Love's Sacrifice* is also a large factor in the difficult interpretative problems posed by his play.

In its preoccupation with the conflicting pressures of love and friendship, its partly ironic, partly melodramatic treatment of sexual passion, its dizzying reversals and revelations, its self-conscious theatricality, and its uneasy juxtaposition of tragedy and farce, *Love's Sacrifice* betrays a profound debt to the drama of John Fletcher. Apart from a handful of close parallels, however—particularly with *Monsieur Thomas* (see LN to 2.4) and the Fletcher and Beaumont collaboration *The Maid's Tragedy* (see note to 5.1.52)—Fletcher's influence remains diffuse. The principal source of Ford's main plot is *Othello*. Many of the borrowings from Shakespeare's tragedy provide material for the depiction of the relationship between Duke Caraffa and his wife Bianca, but the presentation of Bianca's chaste love affair with the courtier Fernando appears to be inspired by *Romeo and Juliet*. The tension between these two conflicting dramatic influences proves to be crucial. The main plot also incorporates important elements of Philip Massinger's *The Duke of Milan*; and there are tantalising hints of a connection between the events of *Love's Sacrifice* and the real-life tragedy of the Italian 'prince, murderer and musician', Carlo Gesualdo.

Ford took the sub-plot involving Ferentes and his lovers from an episode in Sir Philip Sidney's *Arcadia*, but rounded off the tale with a different ending, a revenge masque. He interlaced these major borrowings with smaller but none the less significant loans from *The Duchess of Malfi*, *The White Devil*, *The Changeling*, *Women Beware Women*, *Antonio and Mellida*, *The Roman Actor* and other plays of the period.

Othello

E. A. J. Honigmann has recently argued that *Othello* was first performed in 1602.[88] If this is correct, Shakespeare's tragedy would have been amongst London's newest plays when the sixteen-year-old John Ford was admitted to the Middle Temple on 16 November of that year.[89] The first recorded staging of Shakespeare's play was by the King's Men at Whitehall on 1 November 1604, and there are records of other performances at the Globe and in Oxford in 1610, at court in 1612/13 and at Blackfriars in 1629.[90] Pepys saw *Othello* at the Phoenix on 11 October, 1660, and it would be interesting to know if the play had been performed at Ford's own playhouse before the closure of the theatres. In any case, it is clear that Ford would have had ample opportunity to view and re-view one of the most popular plays of the age.[91] The many echoes of *Othello* in *Love's Sac-*

rifice are a further testament to that popularity. Indeed, such is the extent of Ford's debt that his tragedy can too easily seem like a mere hodgepodge of words and stage images from Shakespeare's play. But *Love's Sacrifice* is more than an elaborate compliment to Shakespeare's art: it responds to *Othello* with its own creative devices.

Ford's borrowings from *Othello* are more numerous than has hitherto been realised, and are apparent from the very first scene of *Love's Sacrifice*. Like Othello, Philippo Caraffa, Duke of Pavia, has recently married. Like Othello, Caraffa is disturbed in his bliss by a subordinate, his secretary D'Avolos, who encourages the Duke's jealous imaginings about his new wife. Caraffa is a passionate, self-indulgent man, given to dramatising his own emotions—another similarity with Othello, if one agrees with T. S. Eliot's and F. R. Leavis's accounts of Shakespeare's Moor.[92] The most striking difference between the plays is Ford's depiction of his Desdemona figure, the Duchess Bianca. Bianca ultimately suffers the same fate as Desdemona, but is so ambiguous a figure that by the end of the play, when the repentant Caraffa eulogises her as 'the life of innocence and beauty' (5.3.48), it is difficult, if not impossible, to know whether he is supposed to be inspired or beguiled. On more than one occasion, Bianca and the young courtier Fernando (the counterpart of Cassio) are shown indulging in amorous dalliance (e.g. 2.4.59ff, 3.2.43–8, 5.1.4.1–3). Fernando himself is given more prominence than Cassio, and he too is a somewhat more complex figure, buffeted to and fro by feelings of loyalty to his friend the Duke and overwhelming passion for the Duchess.

Ford reflects seventeenth-century taste by paying special heed to Shakespeare's temptation scenes (3.3 and 4.1),[93] many details of which reappear in 3.2, 3.3 and 4.1 of *Love's Sacrifice*. There are also numerous minor similarities in plot, character, dialogue and stage movements. These sometimes superficial loans should not obscure the deeper and more expansive resemblances in the tone, style and thematic concerns of the two plays. Ford dwells on *Othello* imaginatively and analytically, and to a much greater extent than an exclusively formalist approach to *Love's Sacrifice* will allow.[94] Most obviously, he makes good dramatic use of the mode of domestic tragedy employed in *Othello*, establishing a similarly claustrophobic atmosphere and confining the audience's attention to the central characters and their private drama with a near-obsessive rigour.[95] In episodes such as the chess game (2.3) and the bedchamber scene (2.4) he provides visual parallels to *Othello*'s 'Rembrandtian' world of small lighted scenes enclosed by great areas of darkness.[96] These scenes also demonstrate his alertness to the sexually charged atmosphere of Shakespeare's tragedy.

Brian Opie observes that the emphasis in *Love's Sacrifice* on interpretation, on 'social knowledge and feeling which count as true representations of others or of oneself', has the effect of 'bringing all signifying behaviour, whether visual or verbal, under scrutiny'.[97] It is worth considering to what extent this feature may be due to the influence of *Othello*. As Norman Sanders points out, Shakespeare, too, can be observed blurring and inverting distinctions between good and bad, honesty and chastity, illusion and reality: 'The whole play', Sanders writes, 'is founded on the different ways a single object may be viewed because of divergent human perspectives'.[98] *Love's Sacrifice* presents an extreme variation of this semiotic instability. In 2.3.53.1–103, for example, D'Avolos is seen '*jeering and listening*' to a private conversation between Fernando and Bianca, which he interprets as nothing but a mating ritual. The episode seems to parallel the scene in Shakespeare's play (4.1.98–165) in which Othello eavesdrops on the conversation between Iago and Cassio, taking Cassio's remarks about his mistress Bianca for references to Desdemona. However, D'Avolos's interpretation of Bianca and Fernando's encounter is at even greater variance with what the audience witnesses, for the encounter does not appear to be an amorous tryst at all, but a re-enactment of the stock situation of Chastity rebuffing Passion. D'Avolos's version differs so wildly from the apparent truth that the villain's seeming misconstructions could easily be played as comedy. In the very next scene, though, Ford turns the tables on the audience by showing Bianca offer herself at Fernando's bedside. The reversal is genuinely startling, and likely to arouse in the audience a sceptical alertness to the action presented before them: Was D'Avolos mistaken in his cynicism and only 'made' right, in retrospect, by a real change in Bianca? Or did D'Avolos see (or hear)[99] something that we, in our naivety, did not? Such adaptations (others are discussed on pp. 50, 55, below) suggest that Ford was concerned, at a cognitive as well as a creative level, with the infectious sense of indeterminacy that permeates *Othello*. Overall, they give an impression of Ford meditating on his principal source rather than simply capitalising on its theatrical potential.

Finally, it is worth noting that Ford seems to have been familiar with a version of *Othello* that was closer to the First Folio than the First Quarto. The Pontic Sea speech, for example, echoed by Caraffa at 3.3.57–9, does not appear in the Quarto version of Shakespeare's play (*Oth.* 3.3.456–63). See 5.1.136n for further evidence on this point.

The Duke of Milan

We have no evidence that Ford and Shakespeare were personally acquainted, but Ford certainly knew Philip Massinger. He provided commendatory verses for the 1629 edition of *The Roman Actor* and the 1636 edition of *The Great Duke of Florence* (addressing Massinger as 'friend' in the former verses), and he may have collaborated with Massinger on *The Fair Maid of the Inn* (c. 1624–5).[100] Both dramatists also wrote plays for Christopher Beeston's companies at the Phoenix between 1621 and 1625.[101] *The Duke of Milan*, a Blackfriars play, seems to have been written towards the beginning of that period, perhaps in 1621 or 1622,[102] so it is possible that Ford first became familiar with the play during a time of personal association with its author. His imitation of Massinger's tragedy in *Love's Sacrifice* can be regarded, with the two early seventeenth-century editions of *The Duke of Milan* (1623 and 1638) and the (admittedly conventional) title-page references to its frequent performances at Blackfriars, as evidence that Massinger's play achieved some success.

Ford's debt to *The Duke of Milan* is most obvious in the depiction of four of his principal characters. Caraffa's rash, intemperate nature owes something to that of Massinger's Sforza (cf. *LS* 1.1.91–6, 108–20, 127ff, 177–97, *Milan* 1.1.102–6, 1.3.76–9). Caraffa's fierce sister, Fiormonda, is in important respects an amalgam of Massinger's 'somewhat sketchy envious princesses':[103] like these women, Fiormonda is given to making resentful comments about her brother's wife (*LS* 1.1.163, *Milan* 1.2), and she too raises doubts about the authenticity of her sister-in-law's love (*LS* 1.1.160–6; *Milan* 1.3.75–6). Caraffa's favourite, Fernando, plays a similar role to Massinger's Francisco. While Sforza tells Francisco that he has 'in my Dukedome made you next my selfe' (1.3.279), Caraffa acclaims Fernando as the 'partner in my dukedom' (1.1.141; cf. 132–4, *Milan* 3.1.267–9). Both favourites are shown making protestations of love to their patron's wife, although that in itself is hardly unusual behaviour in seventeenth-century drama. Like Ford's play, *The Duke of Milan* is greatly indebted to *Othello*, but Francisco, Massinger's Cassio figure, differs from Ford's in that he also takes on an Iago-like role, wooing Sforza's wife Marcelia as well as plotting the Duke and Duchess's downfall. Marcelia and Bianca provide the most interesting comparison between the plays. Both duchesses initially repulse the advances of the Duke's favourites (*LS* 2.3.68–82, *Milan* 2.1.301–13). And both women unknowingly assist the villain's designs, as does Desdemona. Marcelia rejects Francisco's advances, but, outraged by her husband's plan to have her murdered, resolves to greet him coldly upon his return from the emperor's court (3.3.58–66). Her subsequent aloofness and praise of Francisco (3.3.120–31), her bold confrontation of her husband (4.3.261–76) and her pretence that Francisco was indeed her lover (281–6) all seem to have influenced the behaviour of Bianca (cf. *LS* 5.1.52ff). Members of Ford's audience who were aware of the parallel with Massinger's story of an undoubtedly chaste Duchess and a courtly tempter may have been surprised when, in the scene following her rejection of Fernando's advances, Bianca presents herself at his bedside (2.4).

Romeo and Juliet

If *Othello* furnished a model of domestic tragedy for *Love's Sacrifice*, *Romeo and Juliet* (c. 1594) seems to have contributed to the play's problematic strands of romantic tragedy. As Martin Butler notes, *Love's Sacrifice* and *Romeo and Juliet* are alike in structure.[104] Both plays begin with 'basically comic actions' but gradually move towards tragedy. In both plays the change of direction is marked by 'the unexpected third-act death of a hitherto comic character' (Mercutio and the similarly profane figure of Ferentes, who dies echoing Mercutio's 'grim jesting and oaths'; *LS* 3.4.48–54, *R&J* 3.1.97–100).[105] In the final scenes of each play, romantic rivals confront each other before the tomb of their beloved (cf. *LS* 5.3.56.1ff, *R&J* 5.3.20.1ff) and a despairing lover drinks off a vial of poison (*LS*, ll. 85.1–2, *R&J*, ll. 108–20).[106] In general, Ford's finale, with its stage image of a young man arising from the tomb of his beloved, derives part of its effect from the same 'submerged resonance' of 'love consummated in deathly union' that Robert Smallwood finds in the last scene of *Romeo and Juliet*.[107]

Butler remarks that the allusions to *Romeo and Juliet* 'give definition but also puzzle':

> Fernando and Bianca are no Romeo and Juliet, yet their story happens within a dramatic space defined by reminiscences of that play which elicit

> from the spectator a consciousness of contrary perspectives on their tragedy. The link flatters their pretensions but its inappropriateness cannot be ignored, though if it is intended as a criticism of two less than perfect lovers Ford never makes this fully explicit.[108]

The references to *Romeo and Juliet* thus encourage the audience to see Bianca and Fernando as they themselves might prefer to be viewed: as romantic rebels, as another Romeo and Juliet, destined to become 'poor sacrifices', not to the 'enmity' of two warring families (*R&J* 5.3.303) but to the 'iron laws of ceremony' that govern love (*LS* 5.1.6). The strongly defined parallels with *Othello* and *The Duke of Milan*, on the other hand, reinforce the more conventional apprehension of Bianca and Fernando as betrayers of the Duke's love and trust.

The Gesualdo story

One of the more surprising notions expressed in Philip Heseltine and Cecil Gray's study of the Italian prince, musician and murderer Carlo Gesualdo is Cecil Gray's suggestion that 'the murderer needs the poet or the dramatist to complete his work, in the same way that the composer needs the executant to give life to his conception'. Gray laments the fact that Gesualdo's 'great achievement . . . in the field of murder' has never found 'a Shelley or a Webster to make a *Cenci* or a *Duchess of Malfi* out of him, and he is equally ignored and neglected by our choirs and choral societies'.[109] Gesualdo's music has achieved somewhat wider recognition in the seventy-odd years since Gray and Heseltine's idiosyncratic study. More remarkably, the Prince of Venosa's murderous deeds may in fact have attracted the attention of an important writer, and a contemporary of John Webster, at that. As Lisa Hopkins argues in her article 'A Source for John Ford's *Love's Sacrifice*: The Story of Carlo Gesualdo' and in her doctoral thesis, 'John Ford and his Circle: Coterie Values and the Language of Ford's Theatre', the Gesualdo story may be an important non-dramatic source for *Love's Sacrifice*.[110]

Don Carlo Gesualdo was born in 1566 of a noble and distinguished Neapolitan family.[111] From an early age he was known for his musical accomplishments. His father, Fabrizio, maintained a group of musicians in his house, and Carlo seems to have expanded this into a private academy, or *camerata*, of composers, musicians and poets. The most notable of Gesualdo's artist friends was

Torquato Tasso, some of whose lyrics Gesualdo set to music. In 1585, Don Carlo's elder brother died, leaving him as the sole male heir to the family's title and estates. It was therefore important for him to find a wife. In 1586 a marriage was arranged with his first cousin, Maria D'Avalos, a daughter from the marriage of Carlo's aunt, Donna Sveva, and Don Carlo D'Avalos. At twenty-five, Donna Maria was already a widow twice over. She was renowned for her beauty. The two were married in the church of San Domenico Maggiore in Naples, and the celebrations, held in the Palazzo San Severo next to the church, lasted for several days.

Initially the marriage seems to have been happy. Donna Maria gave birth to a son, Don Emanuele. But after three or four years the Princess began an affair with Fabrizio Carafa, third Duke of Andria. According to Ford's most likely source for this story, the *Successi tragici et amorosi di Silvio et Ascanio Corona*, or Corona Manuscript, 'one of the most colourful of the *chroniques scandaleuses* of the period',[112] Gesualdo soon grew suspicious of his wife's activities. He arranged for the locks of the palace doors to be removed or damaged, and spread word that he was going hunting and would not return until the following day (Corona MS, ll. 180–6).[113] Leaving secret instructions with his servants, he then hid himself in a relative's house (ll. 191–7). This was on 26 October 1590.[114] Don Fabrizio, aware of the Prince's departure, 'betook himself at four hours of the night to his accustomed pleasures' (ll. 200–1). Around midnight, the Corona Manuscript continues, 'the Prince returned to the palace accompanied by a troop of armed cavalieri'. Gesualdo hurried to Donna Maria's bedroom and broke down the door with his foot. Entering 'ablaze with anger', and supported by the cavalieri, he 'found his wife lying naked in bed in the arms of the Duke'. Shaking himself out of his 'stunned state', he 'slew the sleepy lovers with many dagger thrusts before they could catch their breath' (ll. 206–27).

Stories of husbands discovering their wives in adulterous liaisons are at least as old as the tale of Venus, Mars and Vulcan. But certain details of Ford's play—for example, the names D'Avolos and Caraffa, and the Duke's feigned trip to Lucca (4.2.67)—indicate that *Love's Sacrifice* may have roots in this Italian tragedy. A full translation of the relevant section of the Corona Manuscript, together with a more detailed comparison of manuscript and play, is provided in Appendix 3.

The Pamphilus story in the Arcadia

It was first noted by W. A. Neilson that Ford borrowed the sub-plot concerning Ferentes and his lovers from the story of Pamphilus in Book II of Sir Philip Sidney's *The Countess of Pembroke's Arcadia.*[115] Twenty or more years before writing *Love's Sacrifice*, Ford had dedicated *Fame's Memorial* (printed 1606) to Penelope Devereux, the 'Stella' of Sidney's *Astrophel and Stella*. Mary, the Countess of Pembroke, was mother of the Earl of Montgomery (co-dedicatee of Ford's *Honour Triumphant*, 1606) and the Earl of Pembroke (co-dedicatee of *Honour Triumphant* and sole dedicatee of *Christ's Bloody Sweat*, 1613).[116] Versions of the so-called *Old Arcadia* had existed in manuscript for nearly a decade when, in 1590, there appeared a printed edition of the expanded and revised *New Arcadia*. This edition of the new work, however, comprised only Books I and II and part of Book III of the projected five books, Sidney never having completed his revision. A further edition of 1593 reproduced the *New Arcadia* material together with Books III, IV and V of the *Old Arcadia*, and numerous other editions in the late sixteenth and early seventeenth centuries presented variations of this complete but composite work.[117] The story of the inconstant Pamphilus, the forebear of Ferentes in *Love's Sacrifice*, occurs only in the *New Arcadia*.

In Book II of the *New Arcadia*, Pyrocles relates how he once chanced upon a man lying by a tree, bound hand and foot, and beset by ten gentlewomen. 'Each of them held bodkins in their hands wherewith they continually pricked him . . . so as the poor man wept and bled, cried and prayed, while they sported themselves in his pain, and delighted in his prayers as the arguments of their victory' (236).[118] After Pyrocles had fought off a band of knights serving the women and put all but one of the women themselves to flight, he was able to obtain from the one who remained an explanation of the bizarre scene. She told him that the captive man, Pamphilus, had flattered and connived his way into the favour of each of the women, and broken their hearts with his treachery. Moreover, 'he thought the fresh colours of his beauty were painted in nothing so well as in the ruins of his lovers' (238–9). At length, she said, Pamphilus betrothed himself to a woman, 'leaving us nothing but remorse for what was past . . . Then indeed the common injury made us all join in fellowship, who till that time had employed our endeavour one against the other':

> And when we began in courteous manner one after the other to lay his unkindness unto him, he seeing himself confronted by so many, like a resolute orator went not to denial, but to justify his cruel falsehood, and all with such jests and disdainful passages that, if the injury could not be made greater, yet were our conceits made the apter to apprehend it . . .
>
> And so, in this jolly scoffing bravery he went over us all, saying he left one because she was over-wayward, another because she was too soon won, a third because she was not merry enough, a fourth because she was over-gamesome, the fifth because she was grown with grief subject to sickness, the sixt because she was so foolish as to be jealous of him, the seventh because she had refused to carry a letter for him to another that he loved, the eight because she was not secret, the ninth because she was not liberal; but to me (who am named Dido—and indeed have met with a false Aeneas!), to me, I say (oh, the ungrateful villain!), he could find no other fault to object but that, pardie, he met with many fairer! (239–40)

With the help of the band of knights, Dido continued, the women had laid hold of Pamphilus, 'beginning at first but that trifling revenge in which you found us busy—but meaning afterwards to have mangled him so, as should have lost his credit for ever abusing more' (240). At the conclusion of her narrative, Dido again recalled her own scornful treatment at the hands of Pamphilus, and 'surely would have put out his eyes' if Pyrocles had not leapt from his horse and restrained her (240–1).

The rest of the story, including Pyrocles' negotiation of a peace and Pamphilus's attempt to rape and murder Dido, has no connection with the narrative of *Love's Sacrifice*. But it is clear that Ford drew heavily on the first part of the Pamphilus story for the plot centring on Ferentes and his lovers. Ferentes' murder (3.4.17.1–55) represents a brutal re-enactment—and revision—of the scene in which Pamphilus's lovers torment him with their bodkins. Ford even echoes snatches of dialogue, with Julia playing the part of the outraged Dido: 'Not fair enough! O scorn! Not fair enough!' (44). Earlier, Ferentes had rejected the women in much the same way as Sidney's libertine, happily confessing his 'cruel falsehood' and mocking his lovers with 'jests and disdainful passages' (239; cf. *LS* 3.1.126–34, 138–49). Like Pamphilus, too, Ferentes scornfully enumerates his reasons for rejecting his mistresses (3.1.138–44). Particularly notable in Ford's adaptation is the care with which he has reproduced the character of Pamphilus: his 'infinite' vows and cunning flattery (cf. *LS* 1.2.10–16), his shamelessness (*New Arcadia*, 239; *LS* 1.1.97–8), his pride (*NA*, 239; *LS* 3.1.144–6), his wit and apparent merry simplicity (*NA*, 237; *LS* 2.2.122–7), and the heartlessness of his rejections (*NA*, 238; *LS* 3.1.98–106). Yet Ferentes is far more distasteful than Pamphilus, mainly because Ford utilises the dramatic medium to show him in close-up, as it were, and in the midst of his 'sin' (1.2.41). While Pamphilus always remains a rather distant figure in a story within a story, permitted direct speech on only one occasion, Ferentes looms all too close to the picture plane, revealing his iniquity in hypocritical discourse with others as well as in solitary moments of gloating and lecherous anticipation. In general, Ford's adaptation of Sidney's tale is marked with a savage directness which may help to account for earlier objections to the coarseness and depravity of the Ferentes episodes.[119]

Astrophel and Stella

From 1598 onwards, editions of the *Arcadia* included Sidney's *Astrophel and Stella*. Thomas Marc Parrott and Robert Hamilton Ball have suggested that Ford was 'brooding' on the story presented in these poems when he wrote *Love's Sacrifice*.[120] Sidney's poems tell of the love of a courtier for a married woman. The lady, Stella, eventually betrays her feelings for her young lover (Sonnets 66, 67). 'Of her high heart', he proclaims, she has 'giv'n me the monarchie' (cf. *LS* 2.4.18–19), but only 'while vertuous course I take' (69, ll. 10–14).[121] Astrophel steals a kiss from her as she sleeps (Second Song), and courts her at her bedroom window (Fourth Song), but she adheres to her resolution. Finally, she tells him they must part, reassuring him that 'Tyrant honour doth thus use thee, / Stella's selfe might not refuse thee' (Eighth Song, ll. 95–6). The sequence ends with Astrophel overwhelmed by sorrow. Parrott and Ball suggest that

> Ford's answer to the question whether [Stella] had still retained her honor would surely have been in the affirmative. Suppose, however, that the situation had developed beyond the point where it was dropped in Sidney's poem: suppose that Stella's husband had given way to jealous rage, had laid violent hands on the lovers, and in so doing had brought about their deaths and his own. What then would have been the final verdict? Ford's answer is given in the denouement of the play. (245)

As mentioned above, Ford had dedicated *Fame's Memorial* (1606) to Penelope Devereux, the Stella of Sidney's poems. Penelope was the eldest sister of Robert Devereux, the second Earl of Essex.[122] In

November 1581 she was married to Robert, the third Lord Rich. Sidney had become acquainted with her in the months before the marriage, but had 'loved not' (Sonnet 2, l. 5), and it was probably not until after the marriage that he found cause to write *Astrophel and Stella*.[123] Penelope's marriage to Lord Rich was not happy, and in 1588 she began a much-publicised affair with Sir Charles Blount, who succeeded as Lord Mountjoy in 1594 and became Earl of Devonshire in 1604. Penelope bore children to both husband and lover. In November 1605, she was granted a divorce from Lord Rich. Her subsequent marriage to Blount was certainly illegal, though the degree of official opposition to the match is unclear.[124] In the following April, Mountjoy died of fever. He was commemorated by Ford in *Fame's Memorial*, which describes Penelope and Charles as 'Linck't, in the gracefull bonds of dearest life / Unjustly term'd, dis-gracefull' (631–2). H. J. Oliver observes that Ford 'could not speak otherwise than approvingly in a poem dedicated to the Countess herself', and Mark Stavig argues that Ford's eulogy to Mountjoy and Penelope 'should not be taken as indicating his instinctive sympathy for passionate lovers and rebels against the moral order'.[125] Stavig suggests that the pair 'should be seen less as daring illicit lovers than as two basically moral people trying to live with outmoded divorce laws' (5), and he finds support for this view in the conventionality of the poem's praise for Mountjoy's exemplary virtue. Nevertheless, Ford's sympathetic portrayal of an adulterous love affair in this early poem is bound to be of interest to students of *Love's Sacrifice*, whose own heroine, a married woman, exclaims against the 'iron laws of ceremony' and exchanges kisses and vows of undying love with her devoted courtier (5.1.5–28). As Stavig concedes, *Fame's Memorial* reveals, at the least, a 'liberal' view of marriage (7). Whether *Love's Sacrifice* reflects an interest in Penelope Rich that extended beyond her life within the poems of *Astrophel and Stella* is therefore an interesting, but possibly unanswerable, question.

Other theatrical borrowings

Love's Sacrifice contains many small-scale but none the less significant borrowings from contemporary plays. The opening, for example, echoes *The White Devil* (first performed in 1612) and *The Duchess of Malfi* (first performed 1613–14, but revived in 1619 and 1630),[126] the two major tragedies of Ford's friend, one-time collaborator and possible colleague at the Middle Temple, John Webster.[127] Ford begins *Love's Sacrifice* with a banishment and a homecoming, thus combining the openings of both of Webster's plays (cf. *LS* 1.1.1–2, *W. Devil* 1.1.1–2; *LS* 1.1.26–83, *Malfi* 1.1.1–22). *Malfi* also provided the exemplar for Fiormonda's courting of Fernando (*LS* 1.2.94–167; *Malfi* 1.1.361ff),[128] while the Duchess of Malfi herself may have influenced Ford's presentation of Bianca. Both duchesses elicit contradictory judgements from other (usually male) characters, and both are rebels; though Mrs Frankford in Thomas Heywood's *A Woman Killed with Kindness* (performed 1603[129]), Evadne in Beaumont and Fletcher's *The Maid's Tragedy* (c. 1610–11) and Marcelia in *The Duke of Milan* all seem more obvious models for Bianca's rebellion against the bonds of marriage.[130]

Among the borrowings from other plays, Ford's chess scene (2.3) recalls the similar episode in Act 2, Scene 2 of Thomas Middleton's *Women Beware Women* (c. 1621–6; see n. 25). Ford's debt to Middleton is confirmed by the similar sexual quibbles on chess terms (*LS*, ll. 1–17, *WBW*, ll. 262–315, 388–93, 410–19), and by a handful of other verbal parallels.[131] Ford took the idea of Roseilli's disguise from the ploy used by Antonio in *The Changeling*. Middleton and Rowley's tragedy was licensed for the stage in 1622. It was performed by the Lady Elizabeth's Company and later by Queen Henrietta's Men at the Phoenix, and was still in the theatre's repertory in 1639, when, along with *Love's Sacrifice* and forty-three other plays, it was protected for Beeston's Boys by the Lord Chamberlain (*JCS* IV, 862–3; I, 330–1). As suggested above (p. 22), Ford may have written the part of Roseilli to enable William Robbins, the principal comic actor in Queen Henrietta's company, to capitalise on his success in the very similar role of Antonio in *The Changeling*. The scene in which Caraffa spies on and then breaks in upon the amorous Bianca and Fernando (5.1.29.1–37) has notable similarities with the episode in Massinger's *The Roman Actor* (c. 1625–6) in which Caesar discovers his wife Domitia with the actor Paris (4.2.99ff); see p. 63, below.

In both theme and content, the sub-plot of Thomas Heywood's *The English Traveller* (printed 1633; c. 1621–4?[132]) resembles the principal narrative of *Love's Sacrifice*. Both plays open with young men (Fernando, Young Geraldine) discussing the relative merits of foreign nations. Both travellers are the favourites of older men (Caraffa, Old Wincott), who encourage a close relationship between their friends and wives (*LS* 1.1.144–9, *Eng. Trav.* 1.1.84–96). Both young men must contend with the unwanted advances of forward women (Fiormonda, sister to Caraffa; Prudentilla, sister to Mistress Wincott), and both wives eventually reveal their love for the younger friend. Like Ford's lovers, Mistress Wincott and Young Geraldine exchange vows of chaste love (2.1.246ff); and Mistress Wincott shows some of Bianca's unpredictability in conducting an affair, not with Young Geraldine but with the villainous Delavil. In Heywood's play, however, friendship triumphs over romantic love. The wife dies overwhelmed by her sins (5.1.223ff), and Old Wincott reaffirms his allegiance to Young Geraldine (252ff).

The title-page of the 1633 edition of *The English Traveller* states that it was performed, like *Love's Sacrifice*, by Queen Henrietta's Company at the Phoenix Theatre. This increases the likelihood that Heywood's play had an influence on Ford's tragedy, but the similarities between the plays are broad and may simply be a matter of shared dramatic conventions.

Ford's 'old antic', Mauruccio, has a diverse theatrical pedigree. In the opening of Act 2 of *Love's Sacrifice*, Mauruccio practises his courtship in a careful reworking of Act 3, Scene 2 of John Marston's *Antonio and Mellida* (printed 1602). Marston's scene presents the similarly absurd posturings of Balurdo, a character who has much in common with the magniloquent Mauruccio.[133] In 2.1.94, Mauruccio quotes Orlando in Robert Greene's *The Historie of Orlando Furioso* (c. 1591), 1.1.134–5, while at 118–19 he leaves the stage with a parody of the hero of Christopher Marlowe's *1 Tamburlaine* (1587–8), 2.5.48–54. Both parts had been played by Edward Alleyn, which may indicate that Mauruccio's comic appeal depended, to some extent, on a satire of Alleyn's acting style (see 'The play', below, for further comment). Herbert Wilson Hoskins has argued that Mauruccio's descent may also be traced to two Shakespearian characters, Malvolio and Pistol.[134]

It is surely no accident that many of these theatrical borrowings are taken from other plays' most distinctive or celebrated episodes: the temptation scene in *Othello*, Marcelia's defiance of her husband in *The Duke of Milan*, the discovery scene in *The Roman Actor*, the wooing of Antonio in *The Duchess of Malfi*, the tomb scene in *Romeo and Juliet*, Antonio's disguise as a fool in *The Changeling*. Very often the borrowings are visual rather than verbal, as a result of which *Love's Sacrifice* can seem at times like an elaborate, dreamlike procession of scenes and tableaux from other plays. Yet the action rarely seems predictable, for the play regularly exploits the expectations aroused by the more familiar of the borrowed stage situations—the chess game from *Women Beware Women*, the widow-wooing-man trope of *The Duchess of Malfi*—to work a range of comic and ironic surprises. Similarly, verbal borrowings are often played off against the dramatic situation to achieve a new, usually ironic or parodic, perception of the borrowed utterance. This particular practice contributes much to the anti-heroic tenor of *Love's Sacrifice*. A comic example is the pathetic Mauruccio's quotation of the fearsome Tamburlaine (2.1.118–19). But Caraffa is likewise deflated by the loans from *Othello*. The Duke clearly follows Othello's trajectory from complacency to suspicion, jealousy, obsession and violence, but his Othello-like utterances, as well as the numerous other Shakespearian reminiscences in his role, only emphasise the disparity between his muddled fate and the 'glorious' Othello-like destiny (5.3.73) to which he evidently aspires.

Ford's borrowings do not always have such a diminishing effect, however. The multiple references to other plays also help to enhance the expressive potency of *Love's Sacrifice*, enduing it with a sophisticated and thought-provoking allusiveness. The borrowings enrich the play's characterisation, in particular. At different moments of her last scene, for example, Bianca is a wanton Domitia courting her Paris, a justly defiant Marcelia railing against her husband's tyrannical behaviour, and a Juliet, martyred for love. This role, with its complex range of dramatic influences, would ask much of any actor striving to 'personate' a living character on the stage.

In performances of *Love's Sacrifice* at the Phoenix Theatre, the actors' choice of gesture, expression, movement, vocal inflexion and timing may have rendered the play's borrowings amusing, or ironic, or moving, or simply intelligible to the audience in ways that can no longer be recaptured. Occasionally there are glimpses of this lost ghost-language of intimation and emphasis. The actor of Mauruccio, for example, may have 'settled his countenance' (2.1.24) in a manner which recalled the '*setting of faces*' employed by the players of Balurdo and Rossaline in *Antonio and Mellida* (3.2.123.7–8). For the most part, though, all that remains is the bare textual bones of Ford's appropriations. How much of the original experience of the play is therefore closed to us, it is impossible to know. Martin Butler has argued that *Love's Sacrifice* is 'designed to exploit the possibilities of collusion with, or teasing of, an informed, critically alert audience'. But Roland Wymer reminds us of 'the particular problems of the tragic writer who needs to make an audience *feel* rather than simply feel clever. Ford's self-conscious reworkings of previous plays are part of a continuing struggle to achieve authentic emotional expression despite the suffocating pressure of the "already written." '[135] How Ford's theatrical borrowings might work upon an audience's thoughts *and* feelings is a principal concern of the following section.

Many of the play's other borrowings, not cited above, are identified in the commentary; see especially the notes to 2.4 and 5.1.27, and the Longer Notes to 2.2.31.2, 3.2.31, 4.1.143.[136]

THE PLAY

As we have just seen, part of the interest of *Love's Sacrifice* derives from Ford's efforts to 'engage with and surpass' the work of his predecessors: Webster, Massinger, Marston, Middleton and Rowley, and especially Shakespeare.[137] In this section, then, I shall describe a conjectural performance of the play in which I shall pay special heed to Ford's transformation of his sources and influences into new and distinctive drama. I want to imagine this performance of *Love's Sacrifice* in what was very likely its original theatrical setting, the Phoenix playhouse, created by Christopher Beeston out of the old cockpit in Drury Lane. I shall refer to Inigo Jones's Worcester College drawings as a guide to playing conditions at this theatre, since these drawings are now widely believed to represent the design for Beeston's Phoenix. (The drawings are discussed on pp. 10–15 and reproduced as Figure 1.)

Let us imagine an afternoon's performance of *Love's Sacrifice* at the Phoenix some time between about 1626 and 1633. There, in the candlelit gloom and sparkle of Beeston's playhouse, the audience would have witnessed a skilfully written romantic tragedy whose major characters are clearly individuated by their speech, and in which the action is unfolded by means of an artful, triple-layered narrative. They would have found spectacle to occupy their attention and matter to engage their minds: romantic scenes touching on fashionable (possibly Neoplatonic) ideas about love, displays of courtly wit laced with a hint of intrigue, private confessions of overwhelming passion, scenes of rich pageantry featuring the entire cast, episodes of villainy, clowning and violence. On this particular afternoon, the stage may have been draped in black, for in this period the décor of tragedy often seems to have been determined by 'the conventions of funeral'.[138] A solemn backcloth would have seemed especially appropriate in the last scene of *Love's Sacrifice*, which presents an elaborate funerary ritual.

The audience would have felt encouraged to enjoy the play as a performance, recognising Ford's verbal and visual quotations from some of the best-known drama of the age. Indeed, this tragedy is a labyrinth of borrowed scenes, appropriated dialogue and resurrected stage images. But if this welter of allusions enhanced the audience's consciousness of theatrical illusion, the play's seamless progression of deftly constructed scenes would have engaged their imagination and borne them along on the story of friendship, love and betrayal—a story which begins with a handsome courtier conversing with friends about his experience of foreign lands, and ends with the same man emerging from a tomb in his shroud. For all its self-consciousness, *Love's Sacrifice* has the capacity to 'lead on your thought / Through subtle paths and workings of a plot' (Shirley, Prologue to *The Cardinal*, 7–8).

Act 1

We are plunged in mid-conversation. The very first lines of the play—'*Roseilli.* Depart the court? *D'Avolos.* Such was the Duke's command.'—explicitly recall the first words of Webster's *The White Devil* (c. 1612):[139] '[*Lodovico.*] Banish'd? [*Antonelli.*] It griev'd me much to hear the sentence' (1.1.1). The next episode, the homecoming of Fernando and his discussion with Roseilli and Petruccio of the characteristics of other nations (1.1.26–83), harks back to the opening of *The Duchess of Malfi* (first performed 1613 or 1614), in which Antonio is welcomed home by Delio and gives an account of developments at the French court (1.1.1–22). Ford's second Websterian allusion is coloured by the first, the apparent ease of Fernando's discourse on the traits of the Spanish, French and English undermined by the initial glimpse of machinations and hidden resentment, giving an immediate impression of 'a society of surfaces, gallant, glib and dangerous'.[140] This impression is strengthened when, after Roseilli's hurried departure under threat of death (90.1), Petruccio and Fernando resume their frank conversation about the excesses of Pavia's pleasure-loving duke (91–120). The play's setting is instantly recognisable as the Italy of Marston, Massinger and Webster: a realm of intriguers, passionate individualists and petty-minded, egocentric rulers.

These first episodes are part of a long sequence of expository encounters acted out on the main platform. The Websterian tensions of Roseilli and D'Avolos's initial exchange, the strained, almost menacing, pleasantry of Roseilli's meeting with Fernando (1.1.26–90), Petruccio's descriptions of the Duke's intemperate character and impetuous marriage (91–7, 108–20), with their strong echoes of the passion of Sforza in Massinger's *The Duke of Milan,*[141] and Caraffa's first appearance with his beautiful wife and strangely discontented sister (127ff) are all presented with a minimum of theatrical ostentation, allowing spectators to familiarise themselves with the principal characters and to enter imaginatively into the social byways of the Pavian court. With the entrance of the Duke and his train (perhaps through Jones's central doorway), the stage suddenly swells with the number of actors. But after a strained presence scene in which the courtly masquerade is very nearly punctured by the Duke's manic apostrophes to Bianca's beauty and worth—'They shall be strangers to my heart / That envy thee thy fortunes' (194–5)—the stage is quickly cleared of all but Fernando and D'Avolos, who circle round each other in another verbal fencing match (201–53). It is a brilliant opening. When one begins to imagine *Love's Sacrifice* in a theatrical setting, it is easy to understand why the play was still a part of the Phoenix repertory in 1639, as much as fourteen years after Ford wrote it (see p. 9, above).

Ronald Huebert notes that a lack of critical attention to Ford's language has resulted in the currency of a 'vague notion of Ford's stillness, calm, and restraint'.[142] Huebert calls this 'the quietness theory' (208), a critical commonplace which may reflect an overemphasis of the mood and dominant verbal texture of *The Broken Heart.* This preconception has 'discouraged critics from digging for subtleties of language', writes Huebert, and 'as a result, the poetry of a play like *Love's Sacrifice* has been virtually ignored' (209). Even a cursory examination of *Love's Sacrifice* shows that Ford's handling of his verbal medium is dynamic and versatile. He reserves some of his most colourful verbal devices for the speeches of the hapless, melancholy Duke, whose very first lines announce the arrival of a distinctive personality: 'Come, my Bianca, revel in mine arms, / Whiles I, rapt in my admiration, view / Lilies and roses growing in thy cheeks' (1.1.127–9). In this opening paean to Bianca's beauty (and Caraffa's own 'admiration'), subtle metrical variation creates an effect comparable to the tonal modulations of a song. The first line begins with a trochaic stress on the grandiloquent 'Come', then pauses before the ecstatic release of 'revel' (with its suggestive emphasis of Bianca's own capacity for sensual pleasure). The conventional 'Lilies and roses' is then followed by a suitably 'rapt' lyric caesura.

As Caraffa's first lines indicate, other characters may dominate the dialogue, but Bianca is often the real centre of attention. Caraffa's young and beautiful bride is the talk of the court (105–24) and the seemingly demure focus of various passions, from Fiormonda's resentment (160–6) to Caraffa's infatuation and Fernando's guilty desire (127–9, 171–3). Her speeches, when they come, are decidedly cautious, and are closely scrutinised by others:

Bianca. Sister, I should too much bewray my weakness
To give a resolution on a passion
I never felt nor feared.
Nibrassa. A modest answer.

(1.1.168–70)

Later, when this 'modest' statue finally resolves into flesh and blood and speaks her mind, she will have 'much to say' (2.4.12), her account of her 'swelling' sorrows (11) bursting from her under pressure of 'shame and passion' (17). But Bianca always waits for private dialogue or the opportunity of an aside to vent her feelings.

Similarities with *Othello* are already apparent. The opening sequence of Shakespeare's play—Iago and Roderigo's taunts at Brabanzio's window (1.1.78–142), Brabanzio's anxious reaction (142ff) and subsequent accusation of Othello (1.2.53ff, 1.3.47ff)—sharpens the audience's awareness of the social pressures on the unconventional match between the Moor and the Venetian lady. Similarly, in the first scene of *Love's Sacrifice*, the audience learns of opposition to Caraffa's union with Bianca (110–11, 120), and Caraffa himself speaks resentfully of the 'grey-headed senate in the laws', who wish to 'tie the limits' of his 'free affects' (179–81). Later in the play, the jealous Caraffa will reveal that he has internalised society's doubts about his marriage: 'Bianca?', he says in response to D'Avolos's Iago-like goading, 'Why, I took her / From lower than a bondage' (3.3.69–70). Likewise, when Iago suggests that Desdemona 'May fall to match you with her country forms / And happily repent' (3.3.242–3), Othello retorts with the commonplace view of his marriage: 'Haply for I am black, / And have not those soft parts of conversation / That chamberers have . . .' (267–9).

With the entrance of Ferentes in 1.2, Ford introduces the second thread of his triple-stranded drama. As Juliet McMaster has shown,[143] *Love's Sacrifice* is typical of Ford's plays in its incorporation of three interrelated plots, each presenting its own treatment of love. The main story, unfolding the fate of Caraffa, Bianca and Fernando, constitutes a serious treatment of love. The secondary plot, showing the dealings of Ferentes and his lovers, presents a comic-serious treatment of lust. The tertiary plot, concerning Mauruccio, is essentially a comic treatment of 'sham love' intended as 'a satire on the love convention', but probably also 'designed to set off the reality of the love in the main plot by presenting a love that is merely appearance' (158–9). As suggested earlier (p. 22), the role of Ferentes may have been taken by one of the two principal romantic actors in the company, Michael Bowyer. There is certainly scope for charm in the part, but whoever played Ferentes would have had to mingle it with less pleasant qualities. In 1.2, for example, Ferentes may have got laughs with his overworked gigolo routine—' 'Sfoot, I wonder about what time of the year I was begot' (71)—but the sourness in his character is never long in surfacing: 'Chastity? I am an eunuch if I think there be any such thing' (75–6).

Again the staging has a potent simplicity. For most of his time on stage in this scene—as he is shown talking with Colona, soliloquising on his 'sweet sin' (41), assuring Julia of his love (67–70), and meditating once more on his lascivious good fortune (71–5)—Ferentes is the principal focus of attention. With the entry of Fernando (79.1), however, interest shifts from the comic to the tragic character. Ferentes immediately becomes subservient, both in his social bearing (86) and in his dramatic status, and within eight lines he has left the stage to Fernando. This exchange of places encourages the audience to compare the speech and behaviour of these two men. That such a comparison is valid becomes apparent as soon as Fernando is left alone, for he immediately turns to thoughts of his overpowering passion for Bianca, lamenting 'the unruly faction in my blood' (90; cf. his confession of 'lust' in 5.3.65).[144] The audience may also recall Caraffa, in the previous scene, 'rapt' in admiration for his young wife (1.1.128) and patronising Ferentes to 'soothe him in his pleasures' (96–7). Eros appears to have wide powers at the Pavian court.

Like Ferentes, Fernando is interrupted in his reveries by the unwelcome overtures of a female admirer. The conduct of Fiormonda, Fernando's 'other plague' (93), does nothing to undermine prevailing stereotypes about lustful, calculating widows (see

1.1.23n). Together, courtier and noblewoman play out a scene (94–167) which in many of its verbal and visual details is a re-enactment of the episode in *The Duchess of Malfi* in which the Duchess reveals her love to Antonio (1.1). Fiormonda's offer of the ring (145.1) and even her kiss (156.1) are echoes of business from a play which may still have been in performance at the time *Love's Sacrifice* was first produced (cf. *Malfi* 1.1.404–15, 453–5).[145] Fernando's reaction to Fiormonda's advances—'What means the virtuous Marquess?' (157)—is in sharp contrast, however, to Antonio's willing acceptance of the Duchess's suit, and draws attention to the profound differences between the two situations. Malfi's frankness has been translated into Fiormonda's lubricity, Antonio's hesitance into Fernando's barely concealed repugnance, and a suit that is happily embraced becomes a sophisticated exercise in fending off unwelcome advances. The inversion is so extreme that it could be played as comedy. But in this instance the parallel has a serious point, too, exposing 'the gap between the courtly veneer of words and the half-spoken passions which they mask'.[146]

Fiormonda's manoeuvres are cut short by the entrance of Bianca (167.1), who seeks Fernando's support in her efforts to restore Roseilli to his place at court. The interruption gives theatrical expression to the seemingly fateful opposition between the two women. Not only is Bianca the real object of Fernando's love, but she comes to rectify an injustice which Fiormonda herself had engineered (see 1.1.21–4). Bianca's attempt to have Roseilli returned to court is also reminiscent of Desdemona's efforts on behalf of Cassio (*Oth.* 3.3.41–90), though the echo is partial, altered. Unlike Cassio, Roseilli is not the cause of his superior's jealousy. Moreover, while Desdemona's efforts serve only to inflame her husband's jealousy, Bianca's endeavours result in Fiormonda and D'Avolos's deception being exposed, and it is D'Avolos, not Bianca, who must face the Duke's wrath (241–70). Given the obvious similarities here, the reprimand which follows for D'Avolos appears to be a deliberate reversal of the *Othello* plot: Ford shows his Iago-figure foiled, rather than aided, by the lady's efforts to reinstate the discredited courtier.

In fact, this early mishap proves to be fairly representative of the efforts of D'Avolos, who sometimes seems more of a Monsieur Hulot than a Shakespearean hell-hound. Iago can of course be a comedian in his own right,[147] but when, near the end of *Love's Sacrifice*, Caraffa calls D'Avolos an 'arch-arch-devil' (5.2.105), the echo of Othello's 'demi-devil' (5.2.307) seems barely justified. For D'Avolos, as Roseilli recognises at the outset, is merely a 'politician' (1.1.21), and a rather inept one at that. It is true that there is a strong resemblance between the two characters. D'Avolos exhibits some of Iago's menacing watchfulness (e.g. at 2.2.32–46), a degree of his perceptiveness of others' weaknesses (2.2.91–101) and a measure of his powers of persuasion (2.2.80ff). He uses some of Iago's stratagems in arousing his superior's jealousy (see especially 3.2.50ff, 3.3.1ff), and assumes fragments of his darkly comic persona (e.g. 3.3.90–1). He shows, too, an Iago-like tendency to be 'vicious' in his 'guess' and to shape 'faults that are not' (*Oth.* 3.3.150–3). This last trait is especially evident in the scene in which he gives a cynical reading of the encounter between Bianca and Fernando after the chess game (2.3.54ff), his comments—'Ay, marry, the match is made, clap hands and to't, ho!' (92–3)—recalling Iago's distorted interpretation of the scene in which Desdemona and Cassio 'paddle palms' and exchange courtesies (*Oth.* 2.1.170–80). But on the whole, these partial similarities result in making D'Avolos seem unsavoury rather than downright evil. Above all, and in contrast to the ever-plausible Iago, D'Avolos's villainy is often quite transparent. He lacks Iago's consummate ability to blend into the social setting and to usurp other characters' modes of discourse. (He never attempts to trick up his knavery in verse, for example.) As early as the end of Act 1, when the wrongful banishment of Roseilli has been uncovered, Caraffa denounces him as a 'smooth officious agent' (1.2.270). The Duke's lack of trust in his right-hand man is another marked divergence from the plot of *Othello*, and one of several indications that D'Avolos should not be read as a simple clone of Iago.

Caraffa makes his second entrance in the company of Ferentes (1.2.222.1ff), a stage image which confirms Petruccio's earlier concern about the Duke's patronage of this voluptuary (1.1.97). The instability of the Pavian court becomes even more apparent as the Duke's 'intempestive laughing' (as Burton might have called it[148]) turns to anger upon his discovery of the ruse to banish Roseilli (236ff). The play provides many such mood-changes for the leading actor, perhaps encouraging the player to demonstrate his virtuosity in the portrayal of a dangerously capricious mind (see especially 4.1.31–2, 45–59, 4.2.51, 62–3).

In the final moments of the act, as the other courtiers leave Fernando and Petruccio on the platform (271.1), the audience is once again able to observe that ebb and flow of characters across the stage which contributes so much to the air of skittishness and apprehension at the Pavian court. Another, related pattern observable throughout the play is the alternation between group scenes and episodes involving only one or two characters. This is an ordinary enough feature of a play, but in *Love's Sacrifice*—a tragedy galvanised by the tensions between intimacy and civility[149]—it helps to point up the disjunction between public and private spheres of activity. The two kinds of scene even employ different types of language, the public scenes adhering for the most part to the courtly terms and ceremonial 'form' ridiculed by Fiormonda (1.1.151–3, 160), while the private scenes draw on a subjective language of sexual obsession and death. Here at the end of the first act, for example, when the Duke and his court have left the stage, Fernando summons images of extinction to express his desire for Bianca (273–6). His reference to his beloved as a sepulchre creates an ominous discord after the elegant converse of the foregoing presence scene, and underscores the hypocrisy of those displays of 'form'. Fernando's image of his 'heart entombed' within Bianca also figures love and passion as a necessarily fatal 'incorporation' in the body of the beloved (see 2.2.93–4n), foreshadowing his own final occupation of Bianca's crypt (5.3.56.1–4).

Act 2

Act 2 commences with the first appearance of the 'old antic' Mauruccio, in an episode modelled on Marston's *Antonio and Mellida*, 3.2.123.1–187. Ford's variations on the older play seem as significant as his imitation. While Marston shows both Balurdo and Rossaline '*setting of faces*' before a mirror (123.7–8), Ford has only Mauruccio '*looking in a glass*' and 'settling' his countenance (2.1.0.1, 24). And whereas in Marston's scene only Feliche is present to comment on the vanity of the two strutting fools, Ford places the Duke and several members of his court in the balcony to observe Mauruccio's buffoonery (13.1–2). As a result of these changes, Mauruccio's conduct comes to seem like the performance of an egotistical actor, an impression reinforced by his preoccupation with the 'harmony' of his voice (11), the 'moving' quality of his 'countenance' (10) and the courtliness of his gait (23).[150] These theatrical overtones also underline the mimetic quality of his behaviour, and indeed, in his self-consciousness, his pathetic desire to fashion a stylish new persona and his crude attempt to distinguish himself through a display of good taste,[151] Mauruccio is both an apish imitator and a grotesque parody of the Pavian elite, some of whom watch him now from the balcony.

Despite such parodic resonances, however, Mauruccio's role is to a large extent a self-contained comic routine, rather like that of Lance in *The Two Gentlemen of Verona*. I imagine him as a Quixote-like figure, using the extravagant gestures and over-wrought vocal mannerisms of a decaying thespian. There are, in fact, several theatrical allusions in Mauruccio's lines, particularly from roles associated with the great actor Edward Alleyn. In the present scene, for instance, he describes himself as moving 'stalkingly' (22), a word which often seems to have been used in connection with Marlowe's Tamburlaine, one of Alleyn's best-known roles.[152] A little later in this scene, Mauruccio actually quotes Tamburlaine (see 118–19n). At line 94, he echoes one of the hero's lines from Robert Greene's *The Historie of Orlando Furioso*, another role taken by Alleyn (see note). Perhaps, then, the comedy of Mauruccio's role derived in part from exaggeration of Alleyn's stately and vigorous style of performance, a style which may have come to seem old-fashioned by the 1620s and 1630s.[153] On at least two occasions, Mauruccio also echoes Pistol, and in his ludicrous attempt to win a lady far above his station he bears a resemblance to Malvolio.[154] Such allusions, and the repertoire of poses, gestures and expressions presumably used to signal them, would further enhance the musty theatricality of Mauruccio's behaviour.

The Quarto is uncharacteristically vague about the constitution of Mauruccio's audience. The stage direction reads simply, '*Enter Duke, Lords and Ladies above*' (D1v, 2.1.13.1–2), and the dialogue shows that in addition to Caraffa, at least Bianca, Fiormonda and Fernando must be present in the upper playing area. But a little later in the scene Giacopo speaks of 'The Duke's grace, and the Duchess' grace, and my lord Fernando's grace, with all the rabble of courtiers' as being witnesses to Mauruccio's exhibition (84–5). This tallies with T. J. King's findings that the upper stage at the Phoenix could accommodate four speaking characters as well as a few mutes.[155] The balcony in Inigo Jones's design is 4 feet wide, and would perhaps have been large enough for four persons to stand at the balustrade, possibly with two or three '*Lords and Ladies*' (Petruccio and Nibrassa? Colona and Julia? Ferentes?) visible behind them. But, as Martin White remarks to me, one need not take Giacopo's lines too literally. White's production in the reconstruction of the

Jones theatre at Bristol University in 1997 featured only Caraffa, Bianca, Fiormonda and Fernando above.

Looking at Inigo Jones's drawings (Figure 1), one can imagine that the Duke and the other watchers would occupy a marginal position between the provinces of the stage and the auditorium. On the one hand, they would be safely within the upper stage area, as conspicuously framed by Jones's pedimented arch and sculpted figures as the title of a book in a neoclassical title-page design. On the other hand, they would be flanked by real members of the audience who would also be looking down, like them, at the comic action below. From the latter perspective it might seem that Mauruccio's audience (and those whom he was aping) were disposed in an unbroken circle around the auditorium.

While the comic entertainment proceeds on the platform below, the serious plot advances in the upper playing area. Fiormonda and Bianca clash (41–8), Fiormonda departs in anger (79), and, when the Duke and the others leave Fernando and Bianca alone on the balcony, Fernando confesses his love to the Duchess—evidently the third time he has done so (140–2). The number of shared lines in the ensuing exchange (e.g. 122, 127, 132) may reflect the pace of this tense dialogue. Yet Fernando's suit seems strangely insubstantial, and not only because of its tissue of stock Petrarchan conceits (e.g. 128–9). For Fernando is a stagy romantic hero who seems at times to labour under an awkward awareness of his own staginess. Moments after Mauruccio and Giacopo have made their exits, for example, he implores Bianca to 'let not the passage of a jest / Make slight a sadder subject, who hath placed / All happiness in your diviner eyes' (124–6). In 'a sadder subject', Fernando, self-consciously adopting the third person, presents himself as a theatrical or literary type, a figure suitable for Bianca's sympathetic contemplation (see 125n). In the terms of his own remark, the sad lover and the amorous clown are accorded comparable dramatic status as they compete for the Duchess's attention (cf. 2.2.237 and 2.3.43).

The pictures scene (2.2.14–121)

The likeness between clown and courtier is further emphasized in the following scene, as Fernando soliloquises on his unrequited love (14–31). Like Mauruccio, Fernando favours literary expression of his feelings ('if I must not speak, I'll write', 28; cf. Mauruccio's poem, 2.1.28–33). And, as with Mauruccio, there is an unknown audience for his demonstration of passion (i.e. D'Avolos, who enters at 31.2). Again, too, Fernando's conduct seems distinctly melodramatic. Martin Butler, commenting on the 'tendency in *Love's Sacrifice* to foreground our consciousness of the characters as players in a play', remarks that Fernando's conventional representation of 'the frustrated stage lover' and D'Avolos's explicitly theatrical description of his behaviour (32–8) have the combined effect of reducing Fernando to 'little more than a performer' beset with the 'puppet-like jerkiness' of the clown Mauruccio.[156]

It is interesting in this connection that Fernando's 'So, now I am alone' (15) recalls the first line of Hamlet's Hecuba speech (*Haml.* 2.2.551)[157]—a speech in which the Prince draws an ironic distinction between the player's 'dream of passion' (554) and his own real 'motive' and 'cue for passion' (563). D'Avolos actually uses that last, crucial term to describe Fernando's behaviour—'Passion, by all the hopes of my life, plain passion' (34–5)—his choice of word highlighting the distinction which Hamlet himself makes between two contrasting definitions of the term: an actor's feigned emotion (often conventionally rendered), and authentic feeling or suffering.[158] The player, says Hamlet, 'Could force his soul so to his whole conceit / That from her working all his visage wanned, / Tears in his eyes, distraction in 's aspect, / A broken voice, and his whole function suiting / With forms to his conceit' (555–9). D'Avolos gives a briefer enumeration of histrionic devices: 'How now, striking his breast? . . . Tearing his hair?' (33–4). But the main difference, of course, is that Hamlet is recalling an actor's performance, while D'Avolos's description accompanies a 'real-life' manifestation of feeling. Ford's superimposition of a Hamlet-like metatheatrical commentary over Fernando's supposedly real display of high emotion is a potent innovation: it prompts the common perception that real men and women are, indeed, merely players, provokes doubts about this character's predilection for theatricality, and reminds the audience that, in any case, 'Fernando' is only an actor feigning emotion for his own imaginary beloved.

D'Avolos's introduction of the 'pictures' (at the Phoenix they may have been miniatures rather than larger portraits[159]) initiates one of the play's most distinctive episodes. D'Avolos's periphrastic description of the portrait of Bianca (80–101) reflects both his intentions as agent provocateur and the 'rapture' (98) he succeeds in producing in Fernando. His impromptu critique of Bianca's picture presents the painting as an image of dazzling beauty and actuality, encouraging Fernando to mistake the image for the original form:

'I verily almost was of a mind that this was her very lip' (88–9). The scene makes for an intriguing comparison with the episode in *Othello* in which Iago ensnares the Moor with a verbal picture of Cassio and Desdemona 'lying' together (4.1.24–46). Like Othello, Fernando is susceptible to 'what you will' (*Oth.* 33).

In the following episode, Roseilli makes his first appearance as a fool (2.2.179.1). At the Phoenix, he probably wore the long coat of the natural fool, as seen in the woodcut of Robert Armin on the title-page of *The History of the Two Maids of More-clacke* (1609) and in the depiction of the '*Changling*' in the frontispiece to Marsh and Kirkman's *The Wits* (1662, 1673). The illustration of Armin shows him in the role of 'John of the Hospital', a character apparently drawn from real life, and some features of his costume and bearing—the flat cap and beard, the lolling head, the hand pressed to the side, the limp—may refer specifically to that role.[160] The *Wits* illustration is likely to give a better idea of Roseilli's original appearance, for, as mentioned earlier (p. 22), the courtier's disguise is a manifest borrowing from *The Changeling*, the part of Roseilli perhaps having been devised to give the comedian William Robbins an opportunity to revisit his successful portrayal of Middleton and Rowley's Antonio. However, little is known about the relation between the '*Changling*' figure in the *Wits* frontispiece and representations of the character in performances of Middleton and Rowley's play.[161]

Una Ellis-Fermor objects that Roseilli's disguise is 'without proportionate motive or results', but, as Martin Butler points out, Roseilli is 'another courtier who has (literally) run fool for love'. Further, 'Roseilli's disguise allows him to mark time without being either too dominant or grossly implausible to an audience accustomed to similar conventions. The fact that he recollects a character from the comic part of an otherwise tragic play may lead us incidentally to expect that his will be the one part to work out happily'.[162] The spectacle of Robbins revisiting his earlier part would also have emphasised the fact that Roseilli is another of Ford's role-players.

The chess scene (2.3)

Thomas Middleton remains a prominent influence in the following scene, as Ford stages his own version of the chess game in *Women Beware Women* 2.2 (see p. 36, above). The scene opens with one of Ford's careful stage directions: '*Enter* COLONA *with lights,* BIANCA, FIORMONDA, JULIA, FERNANDO *and* D'AVOLOS. COLONA *placeth the lights on a table, and sets down a chess-board* (0.1–3). The 'lights' (probably candles) establish when the scene takes place. Perhaps the table and seating (for at least Bianca and Fernando) were brought on by stage-hands before the commencement of the scene. The chess-board is a noteworthy prop, with connotations extending far beyond remembrance of Middleton's scene. Most obviously, chess was a familiar metaphor for amorous strife, as is seen, for example, in the many illustrations of young lovers playing the game in a garden of love.[163] Similar overtones are detectable in Lucas van Leyden's early genre painting *The Game of Chess* (c. 1508, Figure 3), a work which provides a suggestive analogue for Ford's scene. As Jan Kelch observes, the painting is 'as carefully composed as an elaborately staged play' (170). The onlookers, each of their faces 'highly individual' (170), crowd into the scene like actors on a tiny stage. Although only one of the spectators is looking directly at the chess-board, the game remains the obvious focus of the painting, the onlookers' scattered glances suggesting, paradoxically, that the game is indeed of great—perhaps inordinate—interest to them. Van Leyden's two central spectators, who seem to whisper conspiratorially about the progress of the match, or about the chess-players, remind me of Fiormonda and D'Avolos. In both painting and play-scene, the chess-board is a powerful focal point, an ambiguous symbol at the heart of an enigmatic tableau.

In what follows, the play initially panders to the obvious expectations. Fiormonda pleads ill-health (18–20) and instructs D'Avolos to spy on 'their courtship' (23). She and the others then make their exits (27.1–2), leaving Bianca and Fernando alone on a stage that may have been noticeably darker after the removal of one or more of the lights (20).[164] The subsequent dialogue between Bianca and Fernando (28–36) may feature a number of pauses as they study the game: silences filled with sexual tension. Fernando '*often looks about*', I suppose (32.1), because he is checking that the coast is clear. But this would hardly seem like 'studious' behaviour (33). Perhaps in describing it as such, Bianca fails to notice Fernando's restlessness, or—since she must know what his behaviour portends (see 2.1.122ff)—ignores it.

Or perhaps she is being ironic. If so, it is not the only humorous moment in this scene, most of the comedy being provided by D'Avolos, who enters secretly, '*jeering and listening*' to Bianca and Fernando (53.1). Upon the completion of Bianca's ferocious fifteen-line denunciation of Fernando's 'baseness' and 'bestial dalliance'

3. Lucas van Leyden, *The Game of Chess*, c. 1508.

(68–82), D'Avolos is convinced that 'the game is afoot' (83). The contrast between his cynical, Iagoesque commentary (cf. *Oth.* 2.1.170–80) and the scene of high-flown passion and noble self-denial witnessed by the audience could hardly be more extreme. Yet the play constantly gives spectators cause to doubt straightforward judgements of its action. Here, the similarities between Bianca and Fernando's movements and those in other wooing scenes (especially *Malfi* 1.1)[165] seem to accentuate a certain theatricality in their conduct. It is also worth recalling that a woman's role in courtship was, indeed, 'to scorn, jeer, and generally discourage the advances of a suitor'.[166] Perhaps the point of D'Avolos's misogynist joke, then (assuming that he does actually '*listen*' to the conversation here—see 53.1n), is that women can hardly be expected to say what they really feel in such situations. Sure enough, in the very next scene the audience will hear Bianca confess to Fernando that 'how e'er my tongue / Did often chide thy love, each word thou spak'st / Was music to my ear' (2.4.23–5), a reversal which is sure to raise retrospective doubts about her conduct in the present scene.

Fernando embraces platonic restraint with religious fervour, promising never to 'make a repetition of my griefs', yet assuring Bianca: 'If, when I am dead, you rip / This coffin of my heart, there shall you read, / With constant eyes, what now my tongue defines: / Bianca's name carved out in bloody lines' (94–101). As so often in Ford, intense personal disclosure is expressed in the language of ritual.[167] Here, the body is seen as a repository of secrets, the imagined dissection becoming an act of dramatic revelation.[168] It is typical of this play, however, that Fernando's fervid image comes soon after Mauruccio's absurd idea of having a portrait made of himself in which his heart would be represented by a mirror, allowing Fiormonda to view herself 'as it were, in my heart' (2.1.76–7). In *Love's Sacrifice*, scepticism is constantly at war with romantic mysticism.

The discovery scene (2.4)

After the departure of the attendants with lights near the end of the previous scene (103.2–3), Act 2, Scene 4 begins in comparative darkness, and in silence (0.1–4). In the theatre designed by Inigo Jones, a convenient way to stage Bianca's entry and discovery of the sleeping Fernando would have been to position the bed just inside the central entrance, behind a drawn curtain. Bianca would then enter from one of the smaller side doors. In the Bristol University production, however, the bed was pushed out on to the stage, a common practice in the Renaissance theatre (see *ES* III, 113–14). The scene is evidently meant to puzzle and excite. The audience sees the Duchess of Pavia, no longer wearing a splendid gown but dressed only in her 'night-mantle', stealing through what is presumably the ducal palace late at night. Her hair is '*about her ears*', a conventional sign of passion, shame or grief.[169] As Bianca 'discovers' Fernando lying in bed, she simultaneously reveals a remarkably well-kept secret, for until this moment the audience has been given no clear indication that the Duchess loves her husband's friend. The revelation is enhanced by the texture of the theatrical moment: the wordless tension, the imagined darkness, the eroticism, the hint of the devotional in Bianca's placement of the candle '*before*' Fernando's bed. There are also strong reminiscences of the mythical moment when Psyche first viewed her mysterious lover.[170] Of course, Bianca and Fernando are not already lovers, like Cupid and Psyche, and Fernando is far from angry at the disturbance. But there is a similar conjunction of imagery and erotic interest which may have added to knowing spectators' enjoyment of the scene. Bianca's revelation of her love, like Psyche's revelation of Love himself, is a dangerous affair, and Ford, a master-manipulator of stage imagery, is well aware that danger and delight grow both upon the one stalk. This is not to suggest that Ford sacrifices narrative consistency for the sake of titillation, or that he wastes his energy on effects that are merely theatrical. Rather, he employs all the dramatic means at his disposal to unfold a sudden turn in the narrative.

Visual effects are combined in this episode with a strong emphasis on speech, with its capacity to express the heart's 'truth' (28). The very sound of Bianca's voice is given prominence (interestingly, her first words to Fernando are italicised in the Quarto; see 5–6n). When Fernando fails to recognise her voice at his bedside, the Duchess gently reprimands him: 'Have you forgot my voice? Or is your ear / But useful to your eye?' (8–9)—as if Fernando has never really listened to her speech before, but has always let her beautiful appearance occlude his sense of her as a living, articulate being. Indeed, this act has already shown Fernando 'dazzled' by the image of Bianca in the portrait: 'All sense of providence was in mine eye' (2.2.109, 121; cf. 1.2.273–4). Here, in the discovery scene, dialogue and stage business—the emphasis on 'breath as it is formed into syllable' (2.1.12–13), the soundless, tense opening—help to sustain the impression that the play's principal female character is breaking out of a spiritual silence and disturbing Fernando from his 'happy' (3) but unknowing sleep with the sound of her true voice: 'Sit up and listen' (16). (Similarly, when Bianca later reveals to Caraffa that she is in love with Fernando, she tells him: 'Unless you be mistook, you are now awaked', 5.1.54.) Commenting on Bianca's confession at Fernando's bedside, Brian Opie argues that identity, 'of the kind that concerns Ford, is known and expressed through hearing and speaking rather than sight'.[171] In Ford, says Opie, access to and revelation of another's heart is 'principally discursive' (249). Yet here in the discovery scene, Bianca's very presence is as much of a revelation as her words: '*Fernando.* Madam the Duchess! *Bianca.* She, 'tis she' (10; cf. 29, 47, 64–5).

Fernando and Bianca's determination to 'master passion' (85) and content themselves with 'chaste' kisses (78) has led some critics to suspect the influence of the Platonic love cult associated with Queen Henrietta Maria (see pp. 81–2 below). Such readings tend to overlook the everpresent tension between Bianca and Fernando's view of their love and the audience's awareness of the adulterous nature of their feelings.[172] Bianca's simultaneous suicide threat and surrender to Fernando—'I'll kill myself . . . Do what thou wilt, 'tis in thy choice' (56–7)—is an eruption of the formidable moral pressures underlying their romantic dream.

Act 3

Much of Act 3 is devoted to Ford's bold dramatisation of the Pamphilus story from Sidney's *New Arcadia* (see 'Sources', above). The plans for a masque to entertain the Abbot (3.2.10ff) follow neatly after Ferentes' scornful refusal to acknowledge his obligations to his lovers (3.1.87–149), for the women will, by the end of the act, use the masque to achieve a brutal revenge (3.4).

Meanwhile, the main plot advances with some prominent allusions to *Othello*. The audience could hardly have missed the references to Shakespeare's temptation scenes in the two encounters between Caraffa and D'Avolos (3.2.49–72, 3.3.1–77; cf. *Oth.* 3.3.91ff, 4.1.1–207). Shakespeare's play may still have been in performance at the time *Love's Sacrifice* was staged,[173] and part of spectators' enjoyment of the exchanges between the Duke and D'Avolos may have derived from their recognition of the skill with which Ford had remoulded two of Shakespeare's most celebrated episodes. Richard Perkins, who, as I have argued, is likely to have played Caraffa, seems to have been a member of the King's Men for two or three years before joining Queen Henrietta's Company (*JCS* II, 526–8), and it is not inconceivable that he was involved in performances of *Othello*. However that may be, as an actor whose career began in the early years of the century, he would surely have had recollections of Richard Burbage's portrayal of Othello, and perhaps savoured the opportunity to enact a role so closely related to Shakespeare's renowned Moor.

Allusions to *Othello* continue in Ford's handkerchief scene (3.2.43–55), in which Bianca, in full view of her husband and members of the court, wipes Fernando's lip with her handkerchief and whispers to the courtier that she longs to 'steal a kiss' (47). The Duchess's distinctly unplatonic flirting provides convenient matter for D'Avolos's Iago-like mutterings (50; cf. *Oth.* 3.2.33–5), but the business with the handkerchief also seems to be a transmuted version of Shakespeare's own handkerchief scene, in which Desdemona offers to bind her husband's forehead with her napkin (3.3.287–92). What is most striking here is the recurrence of the handkerchief, token of intimacy and principal emblem of misapprehension in *Othello*. Ford incorporates this crucial property into a very similar stage movement, and he makes both handkerchief and movement the focus of the kind of obsessive surveillance so common in Shakespeare's tragedy. This is not so much imitation as creative metamorphosis, a perceptive and imaginative refashioning of selected elements from Shakespeare's scene.

There are problems here, however, and they seem to arise from Ford's practice of reworking isolated episodes, tableaux and stage images from his sources. Unlike Iago, D'Avolos fully believes that the Desdemona figure is guilty of adultery (see 2.3.104ff). What is more, Fiormonda's aside to him after he has fended off Caraffa's first challenge—'Well put off, secretary' (55)—suggests that at this point, at least, he is making a real effort to avert the Duke's suspicions. But Fiormonda's remark does not quite accord with our expectations. It surprises because D'Avolos is also meant to be playing the Iago role of deceitful tempter (as is verified by Roseilli's later comment on his behaviour at this point: 'I observed / Even now a kind of dangerous pretence / In an unjointed phrase from D'Avolos', 3.2.140–2). D'Avolos, then, is required to act on the one hand as a man who does not wish to reveal his conviction that Bianca has been unfaithful, and on the other as an Iago who tempts his superior with a picture of infidelity which he himself does not wholly believe. The disjunction flares up with Fiormonda's remark, and it becomes evident that Ford's inclusion of disparate elements from *Othello* has forced D'Avolos into a contradictory position.

The more one examines Ford's second temptation scene (3.3.1–77), the more similarities one sees with Shakespeare's (*Oth.* 3.3). Both scenes feature avowals of love and loyalty by the tempters (*LS* 27–9, 37–8; *Oth.* 121). In both scenes, the tempted party challenges the tempter to substantiate his claims: 'Take heed you prove this true', warns Caraffa; 'See that you make it good' (67, 71), while Othello tells Iago, 'be sure thou prove my love a whore . . . Give me the ocular proof' (364–5). In both scenes, too, the tempter makes considerable capital out of the demand for proof (*LS* 72–4; *Oth.* 399–401), for Caraffa is as susceptible to an 'easy forgetting of the postulative for the assertive' as Othello.[174] Ford's scene even includes a truncated, and rather garbled, version of Othello's 'Pontic Sea' speech (*Oth.* 456–63, *LS* 57–9), a passage found only in the Folio text of Shakespeare's play.[175]

As a prelude to the masque, the Abbot is greeted with a stately reception (3.3.89.1–7). Fulfilling the Duke's resolution to 'meet our uncle in a solemn grace / Of zealous presence, as becomes the church' (3.2.38–9), the encounter is rendered in careful detail, Ford's stage direction specifying the salutations given and received (89.4–6), the 'ranking' of the Pavian party according to social degree (89.6), the provision of friars and attendants to accompany the Abbot (89.3–4), and apparent variation in musical accompaniment, from the '*loud*' (and presumably ceremonial) music at the beginning to the choral singing as the dignitaries and courtiers depart (89.1, 6–7). (Vocal music, incidentally, played a conspicuous part in theatrical entertainments at the Phoenix,[176] but I am unaware of any other Phoenix play requiring a choral performance.) Typically, Ford arranges for the ritual to be observed by an ironic commentator. 'On to your vittailes', D'Avolos exclaims as the procession leaves the stage, 'some of ye, I know, feed upon wormwood' (90–1). After the civilised speeches heard during the Abbot's reception, 'vittailes' sounds harshly colloquial.

The masque (3.4)

The final scene of Act 3 begins with a suggestion of the hurried arrangements for the masque. Petruccio and Nibrassa enter '*with napkins, as from supper*' (0.1–2)—a conventional shorthand signal of the kind analysed by Alan C. Dessen[177]—and steel themselves for the approaching trial (3–6). Then attendants '*with lights*' usher in the Duke and his party (6.1–2). Caraffa and Baglione exchange compliments (7–17), and the courtly audience settles itself to watch the entertainment. (As before, seating may have been brought on to the stage before the commencement of the scene, perhaps by the 'blue-coated Stage-Keepers' mentioned by Thomas Nabbes.[178]) Nibrassa and Petruccio's last-minute instructions, the almost ceremonial entrance of the noble audience and the careful observance of protocol all add to the sense of occasion. The tension may be heightened, too, by what looks like a brusque response from Caraffa to the Abbot's promise of 'an indulgence / Both large and general': 'Our humble duty', replies Caraffa. 'Seat you, my lords. Now let the masquers enter' (13–17). The three short sentences are perfectly expressive of the Duke's 'scanted' mind (7).

The murder of Ferentes (17.1–12) is a sudden outbreak of savagery in the midst of courtly rites. The dance—itself the 'quintessential social art', presenting the individual body 'as part of a group, governed by its norms'[179]—is brought to chaos by the body's anarchic passions. Ford choreographs the episode with fastidious attention to detail. He observes the conventions of the masque—the surprise entrances (17.3), the fantastic costumes and visors (17.4, 21), the dancing, the dumbshow (17.6–10)—and he makes good use of the entire performance area, bringing the men in at '*several doors*' (17.2), and extending the revelry over the whole platform by directing Mauruccio and Roseilli to stand '*at several ends of the stage*' as the women '*close* FERENTES *in*' (17.6–9). Like many an English court masque, the entertainment given before the Pavian nobles is a carefully prescribed arrangement of dance, gesture and tableau which encourages viewers to interpret it as a psychomachia. At first, Roseilli, Mauruccio and Ferentes '*gaze*' at the women, who seem like death-figures in a brief *Danse Macabre*. Invited to the dance (17.5–6), each man is perhaps paired with his own deathly partner. When Mauruccio and Roseilli are 'shaken off' by the women (17.7–8), they again fall to '*gazing*' (17.9), seemingly bewildered, or bewitched, by these figures in their strange costumes. Mauruccio and Roseilli, of course, are not the objects of the women's revenge, although both men are besotted with the same death-hungry female, Fiormonda. The women's '*diverse complimental offers of courtship*' are both a scandalous mimicry of the 'form' observed at the Pavian court and a precise mockery of Ferentes' charming deceptions. In the fifteenth-century Basel *Totentanz*, observes Michael Neill, 'the Cardinal's Death wears a cardinal's hat and the Abbot's a mitre', while 'the Jester is swept into the Dance by a mocking partner whose costume almost exactly mimics his belted jerkin, cap, and bells'.[180] In his own final scene, the suave lecher Ferentes encounters a death that was always immanent in his 'codpiece extravagancy' (48; cf. 51n).[181]

The murder of Ferentes—carefully choreographed, self-consciously theatrical, performed and witnessed by people who, like Ferentes himself, are thralls to sexual passion—has the air of a ritual sacrifice. But it brings no sense of wider culpability, let alone atonement. On the contrary, the murderesses are congratulated for their act ('O well done, girls!', exclaims Nibrassa; 58), and later pardoned (4.1.135–8). Only the Abbot seems to fear the 'fatal sad presages' of this sudden death (62). Like the killing of Mercutio (whose last words Ferentes echoes at 48–54; cf. *R&J* 3.1.97–100), the death of Ford's lecherous courtier marks a sudden exclusion of lighter moods and emphasises the violence inherent in unchecked passion.[182] But the play's subsequent action makes it clear that the Pavian court is too lost in sin to derive any spiritual benefit from the lecher's sacrifice. Moments after the murder, in the opening scene of Act 4, Fiormonda and D'Avolos are seen urging Caraffa to take much the same course as Ferentes' amorous assassins.

Act 4

One of the reasons why D'Avolos is never as frightening a villain as Iago is that he must share the villain's role with Fiormonda. This division of culpability is especially evident in 4.1, in which Fiormonda taunts her brother about his sullied honour while D'Avolos paints obsessive pictures of imagined adulterous scenes between Bianca and Fernando. The imitation of *Othello* here is closely observed (cf. *Oth.* 3.3.333ff and 4.1.1–207). Like Othello, Caraffa vows upon his knees to avenge his cuckoldom, and both D'Avolos and Fiormonda mirror Iago's movements in joining him (108.1). All rise 'friends' (111), and the Duke declares that 'some that are safe shall bleed' (112). In Shakespeare, Othello arises greeting Iago's 'love', both men united in their commitment to 'what bloody business ever' (*Oth.* 3.3.456–82).

There are further echoes of *Othello* later in this scene when Bianca and Fernando ask the Duke to pardon Mauruccio for his role in the masque (113ff). The request comes at precisely the wrong time for Caraffa, who has just vowed to pursue a 'royal revenge' for his supposed cuckoldom (106). This encounter is particularly interesting for its reworking of the episode in *Othello* in which Iago's attempt to arouse the Moor's jealousy is interrupted by the entrance of Desdemona (4.1.209.1). Desdemona proceeds with some ill-timed words in support of Cassio, her defence of the former lieutenant doing much to aggravate her husband's suspicions. When she tells Lodovico that there has fallen an 'unkind breach' between Othello and Cassio, 'But you shall make all well', Othello retorts:

> Are you sure of that?
> *Desdemona.* My lord.
> *Othello.* (*reads*) 'This fail you not to do as you will'—
> *Lodovico.* He did not call, he's busy in the paper.
> Is there division 'twixt my lord and Cassio?
> *Desdemona.* A most unhappy one. I would do much
> T'atone them, for the love I bear to Cassio.

Othello. Fire and brimstone!
Desdemona. My lord?
Othello. Are you wise?

(222–31)

Caraffa's confrontation with his wife (119–31) has the same air of tension and misapprehension. As in Shakespeare's scene, there is an interrupted speech (121), a passionate outburst (128–31) and a divorce between the speakers' intentions which is so radical that it verges on the comic. But feelings quite distinct from Desdemona's charitable 'love' for a friend of her husband's lurk behind Bianca's eagerness to 'join' with Fernando on Mauruccio's behalf (121). Shakespeare's ingredients are reformulated and given a new, acerbic complexity.

Worse is to come for Caraffa when he frees Mauruccio and allows him to marry Morona, whom the audience have just seen assisting at the murder of Ferentes. The Duke finds himself witness to a brief 'spousal' or 'handfasting' ceremony (see 167–75n) in which Fernando and Bianca bring the bride and bridegroom together (167–70) and '*join their hands*' (175.1). What Caraffa sees, in effect, is not the tainted union of Mauruccio and Morona but the mock marriage of Bianca and Fernando, a proceeding from which his wife seems to derive a genuine *frisson*: 'Yes, do, my lord, bring you the bridegroom hither' (169). D'Avolos, revealing some of Iago's perspicacity, recognises that this bit of play-acting is 'argument to jealousy as good as drink to the dropsy' (171–2). His comment emphasises the fact that Caraffa, like Othello, is corrupted by seeing. The psychological turning-point for the Duke is tellingly figured by a short, silent ritual and his own single utterance: ' 'Tis enough' (175). The arrangement of the (generally reliable) Quarto text indicates that the two unadorned words are spoken just as Fernando and Bianca are linking the hands of the older couple (H4v). It is one of the most memorable moments in the play, a compelling fusion of word and stage image. When Caraffa then proceeds to banish Mauruccio from the court, it is easy to see the old buffoon as a guileless victim of sacrifice, a scapegoat expelled by the Duke in a futile attempt to remove a claustrophobic awareness of sin: 'We'll have no servile slavery of lust / Shall breathe near us' (181–2).

With both of the principal comic characters now removed, events move swiftly towards the catastrophe. Fiormonda makes one last desperate appeal for Fernando's affections (4.1.217–62), and D'Avolos for once seems genuinely threatening as he plies Julia for information about the affair between the Duchess and Fernando (4.2.1–19). The scene in which Caraffa tells Bianca of his 'ominous vision' (4.2.56, 20–72) is steeped in foreboding, and gives the actor playing Caraffa plenty of scope for histrionic virtuosity, as the Duke lurches between love, sorrow, fear, rage and pitiful delusion: 'Still methinks / I dream and dream anew' (63–4). This is essentially Othello's gamut of feeling, and the dream itself (evidently Ford's invention) accords very well with the portrait of psychic disorder presented in Shakespeare's Moor. Burton's observation might stand as an epigram for both characters: 'Some ascribe all vices to a false and corrupt imagination.'[183]

Caraffa, of course, is no hero. Neither a great soldier nor a figure from the realm of romance, the languishing, distracted Duke of Pavia is most distinctive in his tormented ineffectuality. His pride and possessiveness, however, may well owe something to Othello. Othello's passion, says F. R. Leavis, 'may be love, but it can be only in an oddly qualified sense love of [Desdemona]: it must be much more a matter of self-centred and self-regarding satisfaction—pride, sensual possessiveness, appetite, love of loving—than he suspects'.[184] If this does not fully comprehend the scope of Othello's affection or character, it would do better justice applied to Caraffa. In his dream, the Duke tells Bianca, he saw himself 'in glorious pomp' sitting on his throne, 'whiles I had hemmed / My best beloved Bianca in mine arms' (4.2.33–5)—an egotistical fantasy which recalls his very first lines (1.1.127–9). Three hundred years before Leavis, Ford may have detected traces of self-absorption, pride and 'sensual possessiveness' in Othello, and lent them stronger colouring in his own portrait of a narcissistic Italian duke.

Act 5

The last act begins with Fiormonda, 'ensphered above' (2), commanding Revenge to 'wound the lower earth' and enable her to 'triumph' over the graves of those who have scorned her love (1–4). She is presumably speaking from the balcony, a position that would emphasise her goddess-like imperiousness. What is described next—'*A curtain drawn, below are discovered* BIANCA, *in her night attire, leaning on a cushion at a table, holding* FERNANDO *by the hand*'

(4.1–3)—may, like the earlier 'discovery' of Fernando in his bed (2.4.0.1–4), have been presented within the central opening of Inigo Jones's stage façade. It is true that Fiormonda would then have great difficulty actually seeing Bianca and Fernando from her place in the balcony, but that objection may be too literalistic. The initial sight of Fiormonda positioned above Bianca and Fernando would stress the degree of her control over the pair's fate; and, as Martin White has suggested to me, the action below may break out on to the main stage soon after the opening of the scene. The emblematic details of the tableau shown below are carefully specified: Bianca's 'night attire' and informal pose, the cushion (a symbol of *voluptas*?[185]), the clasped hands. The curtain may have been opened by a stage attendant by the simple means of a string passed through the curtain rings.[186]

Bianca's declaration of passion for Fernando (5–14) seems to confirm the impression created by the stage imagery. Her assertion that she would 'change my life / With any waiting-woman in the land / To purchase one night's rest with thee' (11–13) is a cry of shackled desire, a preferment of love over rank which seems to glance at the comparative sexual and matrimonial freedom of women in lower social orders (see 5.1.12n). But despite her provocation of moral authority ('What's a vow?', 7), the Duchess's speech makes two things clear: that she has *not* enjoyed 'one night's rest' with Fernando, and that at this point in the scene, at least, she considers such an indulgence to be impossible. Those pleasures would be attainable only, she says, 'Could I / As well dispense with conscience as renounce / The outside of my titles' (8–10). At this instant, then, Bianca cannot be called an 'adulteress in intention'.[187] Typically, the play immediately produces fresh complications: within moments, Bianca seems to have thrown over her circumspection as she engages in love-talk and kisses with Fernando (23–8). Whether this shows her finally 'dispensing' with 'conscience', however, is open to interpretation by performers, spectators and readers alike: the text gives no definite indication one way or the other. It may, of course, be theatrically effective to show Bianca and Fernando on the verge —or seemingly on the verge—of complete abandon at the very moment that Caraffa breaks in upon them. And to be sure, the exchanged kisses (23, 25) and the banter about swearing and forswearing oaths (24–8), by underscoring the erotic pleasure to be derived from knowing transgression, seem to support the view that their flirtation is meant in earnest. But the experience of the play would count for little if such arguments did not remind one of D'Avolos in the chess scene: 'Ay, marry, the match is made' (2.3.92).

Richard Madelaine notes the similarities between this and the earlier discovery scene (2.4), and argues that 'the repetition of the basic situation suggests that Ford is trying, rather unimaginatively, to gratify the audience with erotic sensations'.[188] I do not think it would appear that way in performance. To begin with, this is only the second 'love scene' in the play. And, as Madelaine recognises (45), there are significant variations. Most obviously, there has been a marked advance in relations between Bianca and Fernando since the Duchess's first visit to Fernando's bedchamber. Fiormonda's presence in the balcony also lends this scene a very different complexion. Fiormonda gives predictable, moralising responses to Bianca's scandalous behaviour—'This would make you swear' (15), 'Ignoble strumpet!' (23)—and encourages the audience's romantic (or lubricious) expectations: 'Here's fast and loose, / Which, for a ducat, now the game's on foot' (28–9). Her presence and her comments thus point up the exhibitionist tendency in both Fernando's mannered declaration of eternal love (16–23) and Bianca's show of bravado.[189]

The strong resemblance of the action here to an episode in Massinger's *The Roman Actor* deepens the tinge of theatricality. While Bianca and Fernando are kissing, the Duke and his supporters enter and pause at a distance to observe the scene before them (29.1–3), momentarily forming another of the play's on-stage audiences (cf. 2.1.13.1–2, 2.3.54ff). Bianca and Fernando are then disturbed by Colona's cries from within (30–1), and the Duke comes forward to confront the pair (36), who may by now have moved out of the central recess.[190] In *The Roman Actor* 4.2, Caesar's wife, Domitia, is shown lasciviously courting her husband's favourite, the actor Paris. At first, the actor's attempts to fend off Domitia's advances seem rather similar to the scene in *Love's Sacrifice* in which Fernando tries to avert the attentions of Fiormonda (1.2.94–167; cf. especially *Rom. Actor*, ll. 52–65). But with Caesar's entrance the episode turns into what looks like a model for the discovery scene in *Love's Sacrifice*:

[*Domitia*.] Thinke who 'tis sues to thee.
Denie not that yet which a brother may
Grant to his sister: as a testimonie

CAESAR, ARETINUS, IULIA, DOMITILLA, CAENIS *aboue.*

I am not scorn'd. Kisse me. Kisse me againe.
Kisse closer. Thou art now my *Troyan Paris*
And I thy *Helen.*
Paris. Since it is your will.
Caesar. And I am *Menelaus.* But I shall be
Something I know not yet. CAESAR *descends.*
Domitia. Why lose we time
And opportunitie? These are but sallads
To sharpen appetite. Let vs to the feast.
Courting PARIS *wantonly.*
Where I shall wish that thou wert *Iupiter*
And I *Alcmena*, and that I had power
To lengthen out one short night into three,
And so beget a *Hercules.*

[*Enter* CAESAR *and Guard.*]

Caesar. While *Amphitrio*
Stands by, and drawes the curtaines.
Paris. Oh?— *Falls on his face.*
Domitia. Betrai'd?
(*Rom. Actor* 4.2.99–113)

Ford adds comments by D'Avolos and Fiormonda, and cries from Colona, and he shows Fernando to be a far more willing amorist than Paris; but in terms of stage movement and imagery the two scenes are virtually identical.[191]

The succeeding action is hardly less allusive. After Fernando has been escorted away by Caraffa's guards (48.1), Bianca confronts the Duke with a show of defiance which is strongly reminiscent of Marcelia's spirited confrontation of her jealous husband in *The Duke of Milan*:

Marcelia. Where is this Monster?
This walking tree of Iealousie, this dreamer,
This horned beast that would be? O are you here Sir?
Is it by your commandement or allowance,
I am thus basely vs'd?
[. . .]
Sforza. Impudence,
How vgly thou appear'st now! Thy intent
To be a whore, leaues thee not blood enough
To make an honest blush; what had the act done?

Marcelia. Return'd thee the dishonor thou deseruest
Though willingly I had giuen vp my selfe
To euerie common letcher.

(*Milan* 4.3.261–76)

Bianca finds herself in a similar situation, and expresses kindred sentiments. But the language of her defiance is distinctive, her speech at ll. 87–107 demonstrating the adaptability of Ford's verse to the local requirements of mood and dramatic pulse. The rapid everyday speech-rhythm of 'I know what you would say now. / You would fain tell me how exceeding much' (88–9), as Bianca anticipates Caraffa's indignant response; the sing-song mockery of 'a símple géntlewóman's pláce' (91); the precise fall of the ictus on the sarcastic 'hónour' in 'honour of your bed' (92); the reflective stopped caesura between the (significantly stressed) 'bed' and the admission ''Tis true, you did' (92); the resumption of a strong, on-going rhythm in ''Twas but because' (93), suggesting a renewal of purpose—all of this provides useful verbal ammunition for the speaker of these lines.

Bianca's sacrifice (5.1.48ff)

There is a point in the murder scene at which it looks as though the play might be deflected from its tragic course. As Bianca pleads for the life of Caraffa's 'noble friend', the Duke '*casts away his sword*', declaring, 'Not this, I'll none of this, 'tis not so fit. / Why should I kill her? She may live and change' (166–7).[192] The last sentence gives a plausible psychological motivation for Caraffa's momentary doubt, but, in a scene in which both characters are playing roles from other plays (Marcelia and Sforza, Desdemona and Othello, Domitia and Caesar), this sudden lapse in the Duke's determination has the awkwardness of an actor breaking from his rehearsed lines. It is as if Caraffa wants to alter the script. Fiormonda, keen for the 'black', 'brave' tragedy she has orchestrated to follow its proper course (2.3.127),[193] prompts her brother with his part (169–71), and Caraffa, again revealing the power his sister has had over him from the outset (cf. 1.1.155ff), murders Bianca while delivering a couplet resounding with the tragic inevitability of their appointed roles:

[*Duke.*] Give me thy hand, Bianca.
Bianca. Here.
Duke. Farewell.

Thus go in everlasting sleep to dwell.

Draws his poniard and stabs her.

Here's blood for lust and sacrifice for wrong.

(172–4)

The action and dialogue here—the joining of hands, the rhyming couplet, the drawing of the dagger, the incantatory rhythm of the culminating line, the denomination of Bianca's blood—lend the murder the aspect of a ritual sacrifice. Caraffa's clasping of Bianca's hand is an especially potent gesture, mirroring both the marriage ceremony (cf. 4.1.175.1) and ancient sacrificial rituals such as the sin-offering described in Leviticus. In this ritual, the sacrificer is directed to 'lay his hand upon the head of the goat, and kill it in the place where they kill the burnt-offering before the Lord' (4:24). Before the release of the scapegoat, too, the high priest placed his hand upon the animal's head, confessing all the sins of the people and 'putting them upon the head of the goat' (Leviticus 16:21). In preparing to murder his wife, Caraffa has already assumed 'the role of confessor and priest', [194] insisting that Bianca tell him 'what could move / Thy heart to crave variety of youth' (68–9), encouraging her to admit her supposed guilt (113–18), enjoining her to 'confess / What witchcraft' Fernando used to corrupt her (133–6), and reminding her of the indissoluble nature of her 'guilt' (144–6). Fiormonda, for her part, might be seen here as a cruel inversion of the angel who prevented Abraham's sacrifice of Isaac (Genesis 22:11–12)—especially since only Caraffa is aware of her presence in the upper acting area.[195] Her warning to her brother that he risks 'blemishing' his 'glorious ancestors' if he fails to avenge himself hints at the notion of a disease requiring purgation (170; see note).

Many in Ford's audience would have read of ritual sacrifice in the Bible. Indeed, sacrifice is one of the principal themes of the Old Testament, as well as a vital thread linking the teachings of the Old Testament with those of the New.[196] In the offerings of Noah, Abraham, Jacob and Job, in the sacrifices of the Passover and the inauguration of the Covenant of Sinai, and in the dictates of the Law of Leviticus, sacrifice is perceived as an act which transcends human reasoning, expressing a desire for a renewal of communion with God; but it is also an expiatory act, an attempt to cleanse disease and purge sinfulness. Moreover, the three principal forms of sacrifice described in the Old Testament—the expiatory, the self-dedicatory and the eucharistic forms—were seen as typifying the ordained Atonement of Christ, which was itself a sacrifice rendered necessary by the sins of humanity. Christ himself is said to have been 'sacrificed for us', to liberate human beings and renew our bond with God (1 Corinthians 5:7; cf. Isaiah 53). The altar of sacrifice is directly compared to his Passion in Hebrews 13:10. As Rajiva Verma comments, 'Since the liturgy was organized around the crucifixion, the idea of sacrifice had a special place in the Elizabethan consciousness'.[197] Ford's own play *The Broken Heart* is one of many texts showing that there was also considerable knowledge of other forms of sacrifice.[198]

The murder of Bianca, with its strong sacrificial overtones, depends for part of its effect on the responses of an audience steeped in sacrificial lore. Some members of Ford's audience may have felt that the Duchess, like Ferentes, 'answers' the 'forfeit' in her blood (3.4.51–2). For those spectators, her insistence on Fernando's loyalty to Caraffa (105ff) may have been nothing more than the efforts of a compromised woman to protect her lover.[199] For other auditors, there may have been a moving sense that the victim comes willingly to the sacrificial altar, and that she translates Caraffa's ritual exaction of 'blood for lust' into her own sacrifice for love.

'My love to him that owes it, / My tragedy to thee' (177–8): that last impassioned cry is a further humiliation for Caraffa, and a confirmation of his diminished role in the drama.[200] Whenever Bianca has spoken at length in the play, it has been to confess socially disruptive feelings: scorn for her husband, sexual desire for another man, frustration at the constraints of marriage. On each of these points, her troublesome words find many parallels in the records of contemporary adultery suits, where special moral import was attributed to the words with which women confessed—or were alleged to confess—their adulterous passions.[201] What happens after Bianca's murder might be described as a process of normalisation, in which her contentious voice, now stifled, is overlaid by safer definitions of her identity: definitions founded on the widely held belief that 'sexual fidelity' was 'the core of women's honour and virtue'.[202] The script for the two last scenes certainly seems to encourage this ironic view of the play's concluding action, as Fernando and Caraffa seek to enshrine their 'last duchess' in overwrought tributes to her 'beauty' and 'innocence'. But these last scenes also convey, if only in fragmentary form, a loftier view of the relationship between Bianca and Fernando. The result is an odd mixture of irony and exaltation which is likely to present a considerable challenge to performers.

Act 5, Scene 2

The middle scene of Act 5 further undermines Caraffa's pretensions to being a tragic hero. First, Fernando convinces Petruccio and Nibrassa that Bianca's favours to him have extended no further than a kiss (2–5). Nibrassa condemns the Duke as a 'jealous madman' (9), an epithet swiftly borne out by Caraffa's entrance, '*his sword in one hand, and in the other a bloody dagger*' (25.1–2). The image is reminiscent of Giovanni's famous last entrance with his sister's heart upon his dagger in *'Tis Pity* 5.6.9.1, but, if Caraffa seems for a moment to possess some of that character's obsessive concentration of purpose, this soon collapses under the strain of Fernando's insistence on Bianca's 'martyrdom' (73). Caraffa's subsequent rapid shifts from one desperate pose to another—a botched suicide attempt (84.1–2), agonised self-condemnation (86–93), whispered vows or prayers (93.1–2), a sudden reaffirmation of his affection for Fernando (94–6), rejection of D'Avolos (103–6), hurried instructions for Bianca's burial (106–11)—are expressive, not only of his ignominy and confusion but of his uncertain role in this hybrid drama.

Fernando's descriptions of Bianca as a 'martyr' (73) and a paragon of 'innocence' and 'purity' (54, 58) could be played as part of a natural emotional response to the news of her death. But they also accord with his earlier tendency to indulge in idealising rhetoric (cf. 2.3.46ff). If neither he nor Caraffa is capable of truthful recollection, how is the audience to judge the play's remarkable climax, in which the two men stage competing tributes to the dead Duchess?

The final scene (5.3)

Similar questions of interpretation arise at the very beginning of the last scene, when Fiormonda accepts the suit of the long-suffering Roseilli, who has '*discovered*' (0.1) his identity to her. (He may retain part of his fool's costume, since D'Avolos recognises him as 'the supposed fool' at 17–18.) The language of magic and change—'Wonder not' (1), 'metamorphosèd' (2), 'shape' (3), 'Strange miracle' (8)—suggests that Roseilli's revelation may work a genuine alteration in Fiormonda, and her response sounds truthful enough: 'If my heart can entertain / Another thought of love, it shall be thine' (13–14). The problem, of course, is that Fiormonda is one of the two villains of the piece, and was last seen inciting a murder. The validity of such misgivings is shown by the play's final moments, in which Roseilli banishes Fiormonda from their marriage bed on account of her 'uneven' life and enjoins her to make her peace 'with heaven' (156–60). How, then, to perform the moment of Roseilli's 'discovery', in which 'wonder' and black comedy seem to jostle for the upper hand?

The final spectacle is constructed with scrupulous care (35.1–8). Music establishes the mood before the tomb is '*discovered*' (35.1), the monument immediately becoming the focus of the audience's attention.[203] William B. Markward suggests that this scene requires a property tomb such as was apparently used in a scene from Joseph Rutter's Phoenix play *The Shepheards Holy-Day* (printed 1635).[204] But it is evident later in the scene (56.3, 85.1) that the Duke and guards are able to walk into the tomb, which indicates that it was represented—or imagined—as a vault. (At 5.2.108–10, the Duke gives instructions that Bianca's body be 'interred . . . i'th' college church / Amongst Caraffa's ancient monuments'.) Inigo Jones's central entrance, with its marbled pillars, cartouche and pedimented arch, would have served very well for this purpose, and could have been 'discovered' simply by opening the curtains referred to in the two earlier discovery scenes (2.4, 5.1). Thus an area of the stage which may have represented a bedchamber in a previous scene would be translated into the 'sepulchre that holds / [Bianca's] coffin' (5.1.21–2). Perhaps Caraffa '*lays his hand*' on some part of this entrance, or on a door affixed to it (if there was one), before commencing his speech (33.8). It is conceivable that a property tomb such as Markward imagines was visible within the opening of the vault: a wooden structure painted and designed to resemble the funerary monuments seen in many English churches would have been quite appropriate for Bianca's sepulchre. But the difficulty with all such conjectures is that we do not know how realistically the tomb was represented on the Phoenix stage. Evidently *some* kind of physical structure was used since, as Alan C. Dessen observes, the tomb here is 'something that can be discovered, knelt before, touched, then opened so that a figure can arise in a winding sheet'.[205] But, as Dessen points out, 'tomb' is 'a slippery term that (in the original theatrical vocabulary as revealed in stage directions) can refer to something verisimilar or, even more likely, to something to be partly or wholly imagined' (188–9). In the final scene of *Love's Sacrifice*, Dessen argues,

> An elaborate verisimilar structure is possible, but equally possible (and very efficient) would be a closed coffin discovered behind a curtain or door that either remains in this upstage 'within' position or is thrust forward to become a more visible focus for the action (eventually to be opened). In this latter interpretation of the theatrical vocabulary, the *fiction* of a tomb would be set up and sustained, but the playgoer would actually *see* a single coffin. (179)

This 'minimalist' staging, requiring only a coffin and a curtain or doorway, is entirely plausible, and satisfies the requirement for Fernando to 'arise' from the tomb (56.1). But I suspect that, if *Love's Sacrifice* was indeed performed in the Inigo Jones theatre, there would have been a strong temptation to make more sustained use of Jones's imposing central doorway.

According to Ford's detailed stage direction, '*Four with torches*' lead the carefully ranked mourners on to the stage, presumably through one of Jones's side doors (35.2). Perhaps the members of the procession measure their steps to the '*sad*' music (35.1).[206] The torchbearers are followed by '*two Friars*' (35.2), the light of the flames illuminating their sombre habits. Appropriately (or ironically) placed between the friars and the Abbot, the Duke enters '*in mourning manner*' (35.3)—the phrase dictates the actor's clothing, and perhaps his bearing (see note)—and he is followed on to the stage by a large silent gathering. By my reckoning, the scene requires sixteen or seventeen actors, possibly the entire company of Queen Henrietta's Men (see p. 18, above). The mourners are directed to '*kneel*' before Bianca's tomb, '*making show of ceremony*' (35.7), before the Duke rises and '*goes to the tomb*' (35.7). There is no indication that the others rise before he begins to speak, or even before Fernando's sudden entrance after line 56, so it may be that they remain on their knees during Caraffa's address to Bianca's 'disturbèd ghost' (41). If so, their kneeling position would emphasise their role in what is ostensibly a religious ceremony, and perhaps underscore Caraffa's arrogation of the Abbot's role in delivering the funeral address.

The Duke's speech (36–56) is an impressive piece of writing. Strong emotion is conveyed by means of poetic devices that retard the pace of the lines: the consecutive spondees and internal rhyming of 'sweet rest sleep here' (36), the mid-line caesura after 'fairest purity' (38), the trochaic 'Roaring' (44), its ictus swollen with grief. At other points the regular iambic rhythm is harnessed to render the falling cadences of the Duke's weariness and misery: 'in the bloom and pride / Of all her years, untimely took her life' (53–4). Yet the predominance of masculine line-endings contributes to an overall effect of ceremonial composure which has its counterpart in the '*sad sound of soft music*' required for the funeral procession. Speech here, as so often in *The Broken Heart*, is a channel for highly ritualised emotion.

Fernando's entrance from the tomb

A few moments later, these orderly verbal patterns are violently disrupted. At the conclusion of his speech, Caraffa orders that the tomb be opened, 'that I may take / My last farewell, and bury griefs with her' (55–6), the last phrase perhaps hinting at his suicidal intentions. But he finds himself forestalled by his rival:

One goes to open the tomb, out of which ariseth FERNANDO *in his winding-sheet, only his face discovered. As* CARAFFA *is going in he puts him back.*

FERNANDO. Forbear! What art thou that dost rudely press
Into the confines of forsaken graves?

(56.1–58)

Suddenly the syntactical units are attenuated, the speech-rhythms more urgent; language both reflects and aggravates the shocking disturbance. If the mourners have not risen by this time, Fernando's entrance, with its faint echo of Hamlet's confrontation of Laertes at Ophelia's grave ('What is he whose grief / Bears such an emphasis', 5.1.250–1), would surely bring them to their feet. Earlier, Fernando had claimed that his passion for Bianca had 'changed' him to 'a lean anatomy' (2.1.131). An 'anatomy' is a withered creature, but also a skeleton and therefore 'the bony figure of Death himself'.[207] Ford could hardly have thought of a better final appearance for his handsome, morbid courtier.

Again I am reminded of Giovanni's last entrance (*'Tis Pity* 5.6.9.1). Fernando manages his own final appearance with the same macabre, singularly theatrical flair, and both entries depend for their effect on the power of a carefully contrived, emblematic image. Fernando seems a walking corpse, a man risen from the dead—such may be the audience's first impressions in that instant before they realise it is a living man in his winding-sheet. These powerful resonances never entirely seep away, even as the dialogue returns to the love-conflict between Caraffa and his courtier; for, with his assumption of his winding-sheet, Fernando takes on a new guise. Fernando, seen as Cupid or Amor in the discovery scene of 2.4, is now unmasked as Death, who comes amongst the mourners to remind them that 'all is death's' (*R&J* 4.4.67). He is Death the guardian of Bianca's tomb ('Forbear!', 57). He is Death the leveller, the parodist of social distinction, mocking Caraffa's 'power' and scorning his 'low-fawning parasites' (78, 69). He is Death the 'threatening Other', a 'morbid anti-self', an 'uncanny companion', a 'hidden double' for Caraffa, who had once spoken of Fernando as 'my but divided self' (1.1.196). He is Death the wrecker of burial customs, 'traditional society's last line of defence against mortality'.[208] His entrance from the tomb is an instance of what Michael Neill calls the 'envisaging' of death in late medieval and Renaissance art: Death, observes Neill, is credited in this period with a 'startling physical presence', a personality, a face (3–5), and Fernando, as he emerges from the tomb, has '*only his face discovered*'.

But Fernando's last entrance is an act of character as well as an emblem of mortality. In a play in which 'form' so often 'prevail[s] above affection' (1.1.160–1), his entrance is a moment of alarming personal disclosure, a kind of dramatised impresa portrait. Self-consciously dressed in 'robes that fit the grave' (82), Fernando uses the trappings of death to reveal his true 'face', to enact his own death-obsessed, passionate identity as 'man of darkness' (70) and lover of the dead Duchess. In such ways, his final entrance reflects the growing tension which Robert N. Watson identifies between declining confidence in personal salvation and growing 'attachment to both the external properties and the internal subjectivities of the human individual'.[209] Fernando's voluntary act of self-discovery might also remind the audience of Ferentes' forced exposure in 3.4. Both of the play's principal set-pieces, the murderous 'antic masque' and Bianca's funeral, culminate in a kind of unmasking—as if 'form', even at its very height (perhaps especially at its height), is unable to contain underlying passions.

Lorenzo de' Medici (perhaps glanced at in 4.1.4) observes that 'the beginning of the *vita amorosa* proceeds from death, because whoever lives for love, first dies to everything else'.[210] Quite early in the play, Fernando registers this dying 'to everything else' by picturing himself as 'a coffin to my cares' (1.2.276). But it is his final appearance that most vividly suggests the propinquity of death and desire. Throughout the play, Fernando's irresistible physical presence (2.4.40–3) has been a focus of obsessive interest. Fiormonda and her proxy, D'Avolos, hover around him, tempting him with words, promises of honour, kisses, a picture, a ring (1.1.201ff, 1.2.94ff, 2.2.32ff). Bianca ministers to his enticing lip (3.2.43–8), and watches him sleeping (2.4.1–4). The mere clasp of his hand—thrice repeated (2.3.90–2, 4.1.175.1, 5.1.4.2–3)—attains enormous significance for spectators on- and off-stage. Now this pre-eminently desirable courtier enters as a seeming cadaver.

'Had eager lust intrunked my conquered soul', Fernando insists, 'I had not buried living joys in death' (65–6). This, as Peter Ure observes,[211] is the rationale for his suicide. He is affirming that, if his love for Bianca had not become pure, it would have been unworthy of self-sacrifice. Like Petrarch after the death of Laura, he believes that it was 'for the best' that his beloved withstood his desire and tempered his 'burning youthful lusts'; for through her chaste resistance she has 'turned my course toward a better shore' (*Rime* 289, ll. 5–8; 290, ll. 12–14). But to what extent will an audience participate in Fernando's vision of redemptive love? H. J. Oliver, Herbert W. Hoskins and Mark Stavig argue that the final scene of *Love's Sacrifice* should in fact be interpreted as an ironic commentary on the love of Bianca and Fernando. For Oliver, the lovers' deaths betray Ford's own disapproval of their adulterous attachment; for Hoskins and Stavig, their tragedy is the unavoidable outcome of 'irrational emotion' and 'the folly of love'.[212] Yet these 'ironic' readings do scant justice to the play's profound equivocality. Certainly, Bianca and Fernando, like most members of Pavia's court, have been shown to be susceptible to 'irrational emotion'. Here in the final scene, though, there are changes in mood and verbal texture that seem to call for a corresponding shift in the audience's judgement of their relationship. Indeed, Eugene M. Waith argues that this scene's masque-like revelatory spectacle seems designed to achieve a genuine affirmation of Bianca and Fernando's love. Waith remarks that Ford appears to have been struck fairly early in his career both by 'the note of admiration on which the masque traditionally ended' and by 'the contribution that staging made to this effect'.[213] Ford had collaborated with Thomas Dekker on *The Sun's Darling* (1623/4), a 'moral masque' with just the kind of revelatory final spectacle witnessed in, say, Thomas Nabbes's *Microcosmos* or the court masques of Ben Jonson, and similar effects can be seen at work in his independent plays, especially *'Tis Pity* (Waith, 'Exaltation', 52). Ford's elaborate staging in the last scene of *Love's Sacrifice*—the music, the large funeral procession, the disclosure of the tomb, Fernando's sudden emergence in his winding-sheet—creates a masque-like quality which can have a powerful, mitigating effect on an audience's perception of the love between Bianca and Fernando:

> While our knowledge of Bianca's barely suppressed sensuality and our memory of her brazen assertion to the Duke of her preference of Fernando undoubtedly color the effect of the Duke's extravagant praise of his friend and his wife, the mixture of feelings differs radically from that in *'Tis Pity* or *Perkin Warbeck*, where irony cuts more deeply into the final exaltation. Even though the fact of Bianca's physical chastity may weigh less with us than with Ford's audience, we are bound to recognize that she is neither a sinner like Giovanni nor an imposter like Perkin. What operates most powerfully to make the principal impression a positive one is, I believe, the visual impact of the altar-like tomb and the ceremony enacted in front of it. They constitute the theatrical *tour de force* by which the audience is to be surprised into admiration. (Waith, 'Exaltation', 59)

Thus, Waith argues, the climactic spectacle of *Love's Sacrifice* carries 'major overtones of romance', and imparts a sense of 'something miraculous and wonderful' (54).

On the face of it, the entrance of Fernando in his winding-sheet seems at odds with this interpretation, and yet, in its echo of the raising of Lazarus, it too may contribute to the affirmatory tone observed by Waith. The gospel of St John relates that, when Jesus came to the grave of Lazarus, he found a cave, with a stone laid upon it. Jesus said 'Take ye away the stone', and 'they took away the stone from the place where the dead was laid'. Jesus lifted his eyes and spoke to his heavenly father. 'And when he thus had spoken, he cried with a loud voice, Lazarus, come forth. And he that was dead came forth, bound hand and foot with graveclothes' (John 11:38–44). The miracle was evidently witnessed by a sizeable company, since the following verse refers to the 'many' Jews who had 'seen the things which Jesus did' (11:45). Fernando's emergence from the tomb, in his own graveclothes, is also witnessed by a large assembly, and Caraffa's direction to 'set ope the tomb' (55) seems like a distant echo of Christ's 'Take ye away the stone'. For an audience familiar with the gospels, this audacious parallel would add considerably to the drama of Ford's scene, lending Fernando the aspect of one risen from the grave.

Such impressions may be bolstered by recollections of sixteenth- and seventeenth-century English resurrection monuments and funerary brasses in which the deceased is shown raised from the dead, and emerging, in some cases, from a coffin or vault. Whereas the earlier forms of transi tombs dwelt obsessively on the physical realities of death, English resurrection monuments expressed hope for life beyond the grave at the Last Judgement.[214] The most famous example of this type of monument is the shroud figure of John Donne in St Paul's Cathedral. Izaak Walton relates that, shortly before his death in March 1631, Donne posed for a full-length portrait of himself standing upon a funerary urn in his shroud, 'with so much of the sheet turned aside as might shew his lean, pale, and death-like face'.[215] This provided the sculptor Nicholas Stone with a design for the monument in St Paul's. Ford happened to be a friend of Donne's younger son George,[216] and, if he wrote *Love's Sacrifice* after March 1631, he may well have had Donne's dramatic gesture in mind as he devised Fernando's entry. But there are other examples of this form of monument from which he may have drawn inspiration.[217]

Fernando's appearance from the tomb is thus a powerfully ambiguous stage image. In performance, it could be genuinely unsettling: a dramatised *memento mori*, a sudden reminder, not only of the vanities of the image-conscious Pavian court but of the transitory nature of theatre itself—this death-figure may, after all, be emerging from the tiring house. But a perceived allusion to Lazarus, or to the reanimated figures in English resurrection monuments, may also lend Fernando an aura of triumph over mortality, as he scorns the fears of 'life-hugging slaves' (79) and, like Cleopatra, anticipates the reunion with his beloved: 'I come, Bianca' (95; cf. *A&C* 5.2.282). If, as Alan C. Dessen suggests, he arises from a 'single coffin'[218]—a coffin which the audience believes to contain only the dead Bianca—it might seem for a fleeting instant that the Duchess herself has been resurrected in the body of her lover, and that these two passionate beings have at last been 'incorporated' (2.2.93–4). At any rate, in the midst of a ceremony which emphasizes the finality of death (36), Fernando's entrance speaks, awkwardly and controversially, of renewal.

It is also funny. As Martin White notes, funerals have long been popular subjects for plays seeking the effects of the Grotesque: touches of absurdity in the midst of tragedy, distortion, sudden switches in mood.[219] All of these are present in Ford's scene, which merges its 'overtones of romance' in a contradictory range of effects comparable to the 'roughness of texture and conscious mingling of opposites' that Peter Brook finds in Shakespeare.[220] Even at his death, Fernando remains faintly ludicrous, a predicament not helped by the 'pattern of self-conscious reversals' evident in this scene, nor by the echoes of mock-resurrections in comic and tragicomic plays such as Marston's *Antonio and Mellida* (5.2.246), Middleton's *A Chaste Maid in Cheapside* (5.4.29.1) and Fletcher's *The Mad Lover* (5.4).[221] Despite his Romeo-like intention to set up his 'everlasting rest' with his beloved (*R&J* 5.3.110; cf. *LS*, 91n), Fernando seems a little too earnest in his desire for a final agony: 'It works, it works already, bravely, bravely!' (89). Such hints of farce ensure that his death is not quite the 'fiery apotheosis' of a Bussy D'Ambois or a Cleopatra.[222] His exaltation of a renegade love is thus simultaneously mooted and mocked by the dramaturgy: enhanced in some respects by the final scene's masque-like spectacle, as Waith shows, it is also undermined by more worldly touches of scepticism and irreverent laughter.

Caraffa receives similar treatment. His realisation that he has been upstaged by his rival's *coup de théâtre* smacks of petulance: 'Thou hast robbed / My resolution of a glorious name' (72–3). Fernando's suicide is evidently enough to restore his faith in his 'unequalled friend' (104),[223] but one cannot help observing that he resumes his praise of Fernando only after the courtier has been silenced by death. Caraffa's suicide speech (99–116) looks strained and melodramatic in comparison with that of his exemplar, Othello (*Oth.* 5.2.349–65). Both men, for example, anticipate the tales future generations will tell of them (*LS*, 106–16, *Oth.*, 349–65), but while Othello concerns himself with the substance of his story, and with its accurate relation—'Nothing extenuate' (351)—Caraffa seems bothered only with the *effect* of his tale: 'let each letter in that tragic sound / Beget a sigh' (108–9). Here he reminds me of nothing so much as T. S. Eliot's remark about Othello 'adopting an aesthetic rather than a moral attitude, dramatizing himself against his environment'. Indeed, to a large extent, Ford's vain, deluded Duke is the man Eliot (and Leavis) took Othello to be.[224] In his last moments, he appears to 'creep' towards (perhaps even into) Bianca's tomb (127), his final action perfectly expressive of the weakness and ineptitude he has shown throughout the play.

From an orthodox point of view, at least, Caraffa's wishes regarding his tomb are unlikely to amend such impressions: 'Sister, when I have finished my last days, / Lodge me, my wife, and this unequalled friend / All in one monument' (103–5). Yet the tomb he envisages, and which his successor considers it a duty to build, will be a stone replica of the play itself: a controversial monument to the 'fatal loves' of all three 'unhappy lovers' (154–5). The closing moments, with their conventional tidying-up of loose ends (128ff), do nothing to allay any qualms provoked in the audience by Caraffa's unusual 'testament' (153).

RESPONSES[225]

From the late seventeenth century until the early nineteenth century, *Love's Sacrifice* seems to have been all but forgotten. Detailed critical discussion of the play began only with Henry Weber's introductory remarks in his edition of *The Dramatic Works of John Ford* (1811), the first collected edition of Ford's drama. Weber found *Love's Sacrifice* an uneven work, containing a number of 'truly pathetic scenes and passages', but disfigured by the Ferentes subplot and the conduct of Bianca, 'which, though it does not absolutely realize the suspicions of the Duke, yet is sufficient to awaken them' (I, xxxv). William Gifford, who edited *Love's Sacrifice* in his own collected edition of Ford's drama in 1827, agreed:

> the duchess dying in odour of chastity, after confessing and triumphing in her lascivious passion; the poor duke, in defiance of it, affirming that 'no man was ever blest with so good and loving a wife,' and falling upon his sword, that he may the sooner share her tomb, together with 'his unequalled friend,' who so zealously had laboured to dishonour him; with other anomalies of a similar kind, render this one of the least attractive of Ford's pieces. (Gifford, I, 494–5)

Writers from Hartley Coleridge to Charles Algernon Swinburne were equally outraged. Swinburne (1871) found *Love's Sacrifice* 'intolerable': 'The conception is essentially foul because it is essentially false', and there is 'a coarseness of moral fibre in the whole work which is almost without parallel among our old poets'. The main cause of his distaste is obvious: 'nowhere else, as far as I know, shall we find within the large limits of our early drama such a figure as Ford's Bianca set up for admiration as a pure and noble type of woman' (48–9). While Swinburne finds 'the incestuous indulgence' of Giovanni and Annabella 'not improper for tragic treatment', the 'abstinence' of Fernando and Bianca is judged to be 'obscene' (48). He grants that the play's language is 'in the main elaborate, pure, and forcible', but insists there is nothing beyond this 'to plead in extenuation of uncleanness and absurdity' (49). Critics also followed Weber in objecting to the Ferentes sub-plot. In a bowdlerised version of Gifford's text printed in 1831, this strand of the action is entirely removed.[226]

There had been little change in critical attitudes to *Love's Sacrifice* when Havelock Ellis prepared his selection of Ford's drama in 1888. Yet Ellis included *Love's Sacrifice* with *The Lover's Melancholy*, *'Tis Pity*, *The Broken Heart* and *Perkin Warbeck*, claiming that 'these five plays embody whatever is best in Ford's work' (Ellis, xiii). In his introduction, Ellis stresses Ford's modernity (xvi) and the skill with which the playwright explores 'the mysteries of the heart' (xiv). His praise for *Love's Sacrifice* is enthusiastic but qualified: it contains Ford's 'subtlest work', he writes, but is marred 'by the feeble and foolish sentiment of the conclusion' (xii). Not surprisingly, the author of *The New Spirit* is especially taken with the character of Bianca, 'who had thrown such scorn on her lover that he vowed never to speak to her again of unlawful love, and who comes to him in his sleep the night after, unclad and alone, in the last abandonment of passion' (xv). While in other instances Ellis deems Ford to be 'reckless of consistency in action or time' (xiv), Bianca's about-face is seen as a mark of his skill as an 'analyst', as a Renaissance Flaubert (xvii) who 'meditated deeply on the springs of human action, especially in women' (xvi).[227] Here he aligns himself with those critics who have found Bianca's sudden changes a sign of shrewd characterisation rather than inconsistency. The general debate about the consistency of Ford's characterisation can be traced back at least as far as Weber, who argued that variations in the characters' behaviour are 'always fully accounted for by the exact delineation of the progress of the mind from innocence to guilt, or the reverse' (I, xlv). Francis Jeffrey (1811) thought just the opposite, arguing (in one of several hostile reviews of Weber's edition[228]) that the startling transformations of Ford's characters were no 'master-stroke of art' but a result of 'the writer's carelessness, or change of purpose' (288–9).

New understanding of Ford's theatrical background and a relaxation in attitudes to morality brought about more sympathetic appraisals of *Love's Sacrifice* in the twentieth century. But the play was still widely regarded as a failure. The nineteenth century's condemnation of its 'immorality' was replaced, in the main, by rejection on aesthetic grounds. Thus, in 1906, Herbert J. C. Grierson insisted that Ford cannot be condemned for his morals, as he handles his themes with 'the detached seriousness of the artist'. In *Love's Sacrifice*, however, 'the intention is noble and tragic, but the execution very imperfect' (131). Indeed, the overwhelming verdict on *Love's Sacrifice* in the twentieth century was that it is 'imperfect', 'inconsistent', or 'misjudged' in some fundamental respect. Una Ellis-Fermor (1936), for example, describes it as an 'inconsistent' play with only 'flashes' of Ford's true power (232). The relations of the principal characters, she writes, are fatally 'touched with . . . uncertainty'. The final, seemingly irresolvable ambiguities are indications of a 'hastily written fifth act', though it may still be possible to discern 'the design from which Ford meant to build' (244, n. 1).

Many twentieth-century critics mount similar attacks on the play's lack of consistency, or on its blurring of moral issues. A number of critics find the causes of the apparent confusion in Ford's own outlook. In W. A. Neilson's view (1910), it is a product of a 'lawless idealism' which, when 'given form with all the skill in characterisation, dialogue and action' that Ford inherited from 'the masters of realism', becomes 'a fountain of anarchy' (196). For G. F. Sensabaugh (1939), it is a result of Ford's being 'beguiled' by the 'ethical casuistry' of the Platonic love cult (211). To L. G. Salingar (1955), it illustrates Ford's immersion in 'the pathos of frustration' (438). Felix E. Schelling (1959) attributes the play's confusions to Ford's 'poetical casuistry, which stretches art and ethics beyond their legitimate spheres, and which, clothed, as all is, in consummate poetic art, has the quality of a strange and unnatural originality like a gorgeous and scented but poisonous exotic of the jungle' (330–1). T. B. Tomlinson (1964) is more matter-of-fact: 'It is all too easy; the conventionalizing of motives and character glances too contemptuously at the real difficulties of the situation' (269). Bianca's defiance of her husband is confusing: 'Ford leaves us in doubt as to what relation all this bears to Bianca's earlier puritanical restraint'. If she is chaste, then 'her boldly amoral praise of her lover was not quite what it seemed to be, but in fact was really concealing some other, less obvious emotion in order to delude the Duke into thinking she alone was at fault and so sparing Fernando. Or was it?' Tomlinson thinks 'heroic self-sacrifice of this kind is almost always suspect; particularly when it tempts an author to confuse issues of tone, significance and morality in this way' (270).

Perhaps the most formidable attack on the play's 'confusions' is mounted by R. J. Kaufmann (1960), who writes of the 'disastrously wrong point of view from which Ford chooses to "narrate" or project his play'. The 'uselessly novel obliquity of Ford's vision is what subtracts from tragic concentration and spoils his dramatic scheme' (363):

> The Duke's presence as a lens for conventionally evaluating [the lovers'] acts . . . is a technical embarrassment not to be overcome. Either the Duke is right, in which case the lovers are morally swamped; or he is as irrelevant as Soranzo in *'Tis Pity*, a person whose claims are negligible and whose sufferings have no dramatic assertion whatsoever. Ford, by borrowing the half-remembered authority of Othello's compelling figure, has deepened his artistic predicament. It makes it harder to ignore the Duke, a thing we must do if we are to feel the effect of what is viable in the play. What he has yet to learn is that the noble lover and the jealous lover must be one and the same. Ford, the student of misalliance, has misallied themes in this play. As a result, the whole play has a dreamlike quality, and an uninvited irony of tone playing over its surface. (365)

Yet must 'the noble lover' and 'the jealous lover' be 'one and the same'? Is it not possible that Ford's divergence from his Shakespearean model was deliberate? And is there not a risk of underestimating the difficulty and delicacy of the play's central conundrum in insisting that the Duke is either 'right' *or* 'irrelevant'?

In fact, *Love's Sacrifice* is often said to fail because it does not fit a putative pattern or mould. According to M. Joan Sargeaunt (1935), for example, the play's contradictions are 'inartistic' (139). In Robert Ornstein's view (1965), Ford set out to write 'a more ironic and richly plotted version of *Othello*' (217), but Bianca's transition from dalliance to rebellion against marital restriction meant that 'the tragedy of martyred innocence' was no longer possible (218–19). Since Ford's characterisation of the Duchess 'overstepped the bounds of his original intention, he had either to alter his dramatic design or juggle his moral values. He chose to do the latter.' Hence the climax of the play is 'the silliest final scene in Jacobean tragedy' (219). Evidently Ornstein would prefer Ford to have shown only 'the tragic fall of a woman who attempted an impossible compromise between fidelity and passion' (219). Lois E. Bueler (1980) similarly argues that *Love's Sacrifice* blends two confusingly different narrative structures, a 'tested woman' plot and a 'courtly love drama' (338–9).

Other critics have turned the play's apparent inconsistencies to advantage by arguing that the most obvious reading—that Bianca is to some extent idealised at the conclusion—is in fact wrong, and that Ford intended both lovers to be viewed unsympathetically. For these critics, Bianca and Fernando meet their deserved fate, and the eulogies of the final scene are shrouded in dramatic irony (Oliver, 79; Hoskins, 19–21, 78, 83–4; Stavig, 122–4, 127, 143). By such means the play is made to seem consistent after all. (Indeed, Stavig considers the possibility of making *Love's Sacrifice* 'coherent as well as more consistent with Ford's other plays and his thought as a whole', surmising that 'serious glorification' of the lovers might be possible by carefully excising 'the more glaring revelations of confused weakness in the characters', and by 'playing down the symbolic significance of the ending' (143). Samuel A. Eliot, Jr, chose a similar homogenising approach in his 1917 adaptation of the play; see p. 85, below.) A number of critics seek to demonstrate the play's structural unity through analysis of themes or motifs. Herbert W. Hoskins (1963) presents the play as a discourse on the dangers of broken vows (cf. Huebert, *Baroque*, 91–5). Theodore Tucker Orbison (1963) finds that 'frustrated love' is the 'radical situation' of the main and subordinate plots (108). For other commentators *Love's Sacrifice* becomes explicable only when it is related to the theories of Burtonian psychology (Boas, Ewing) or the fashionable ideas of the court Platonists (Ure, Sensabaugh).

Peter Ure (1950) presents the most detailed of the 'Platonic' interpretations, arguing that Fernando and Bianca agree upon a platonic relationship after they have confessed their love for each other, but that Bianca is too infatuated with Fernando to maintain her platonic vows (97–8). However, there are reasons for caution in pursuing Platonic readings of *Love's Sacrifice.* Firstly, although Bianca welcomes Fernando's virtuous resolution (2.4.82–4), the text gives no indication that she initially hoped for such an outcome. On the contrary, Bianca's lines reveal that she is racked by the 'tyranny' of passion (21), and has 'resolved' to 'ruin' herself in his arms (1, 48). The seemingly 'platonic' arrangement agreed on by the end of this scene (79–96) thus looks more like a makeshift attempt to deal with the insurmountable difficulties of their situation than a conscious acceptance of the Neoplatonic love ethics then in vogue at Henrietta Maria's court. Secondly, in trying to connect *Love's Sacrifice* with Henrietta's Platonic love cult, there is a risk of missing the precise tenor of the Neoplatonic idealism promoted by the Queen. According to Erica Weevers, the form of *préciosité* favoured by Henrietta was a blend of Devout Humanism and Neoplatonic idealism which emphasised the concept of *honnêteté* and invested women with Neoplatonic qualities of Beauty, Virtue, and Love; 'but instead of the extreme "woman-worship" of Honoré d'Urfé's pastoral romance *L'Astrée* . . . it recommended a conservative feminism'.[229] There were, then, two distinct versions of *préciosité*, and the form treated by Jonson in *The New Inn* and by Davenant in *The Platonic Lovers* 'may not reflect (even as criticism) the version favoured by the Queen' (Weevers, 3, 53). Henrietta's fashion, with its blend of Neo-platonic idealism and Christian love, led to an idealising of love and a promotion of the paradigm of 'mutual love and marriage' (47; Chapter 6). The Queen was therefore 'not . . . a typically sophisticated *précieuse* of the Parisian *salons*': she was 'devout, but without being severe' (35). As Weevers observes, Henrietta's 'happy marriage (after 1630) brought in a fashion for married love' (36). One might add that arguments relating the 'Platonic' features of *Love's Sacrifice* to Henrietta's cult tend to rely on an outmoded conception of the professional drama as a mere appendage of the Caroline court—a view which Martin Butler has done much to discount.[230] None of this, of course, rules out the possible influence of the court Platonists on a drama staged by the Queen's own company. But the 'Platonic' elements in *Love's Sacrifice* should not be too readily pigeonholed, and can be evaluated in the light of a centuries-old interest in courtly and chaste love extending far beyond the sphere of Queen Henrietta's coterie.[231]

Ronald Huebert broke new critical ground in 1977 by treating Ford as the 'English baroque dramatist *par excellence*' (*Baroque*, 34). Founding his discussion on Heinrich Wölfflin's and Erwin Panofsky's distinctions between the Renaissance and baroque styles, Huebert draws attention to numerous baroque qualities in Ford's plays: the self-conscious celebration of virtuosic style, the indulgence in uninhibited emotion, the interest in subjective vision, the movement towards 'a glimpse of the higher reality beyond reason' (69), the fusion of the erotic and the mystical, and the depiction of death as 'a moment of consummate emotional rapture' (8). *Love's Sacrifice*, in Huebert's view, is a clear example of Ford's baroque dramaturgy. Each of the major characters may be seen as a baroque martyr, 'willing to sacrifice life for the sake of love' (48), and in the deaths of the three principals, 'the sweet exhilaration of dying bears a curious resemblance to the warm excitement of erotic passion' (51). In *Love's Sacrifice*, Huebert writes, Ford reveals an essentially baroque spirit in his 'consistent attempt to combine the intensity of erotic passion and the ecstasy of religious pathos' (41). Words like 'martyrdom', 'shrine' and 'altar' tend to 'cluster around the moment of death' (47–8), stressing, not the theological implication of the action, but the 'sheer emotionalism' of the tragic moment (48). The exaltation of Bianca after her death exemplifies a fundamental archetype of baroque art, the apotheosis (213): 'The altars, flames, and incense of the last act are ways of intensifying, sustaining, and even celebrating the consummation of death' (213–14). The lovers, initially seen as part of the sensual world, are 'glorified with the supernatural incense of martyrdom' (75) in a final unifying vision. As baroque lovers, they become part of 'the world of mysterious illusion' (75), free from the laws of ordinary reality. Their love is perfected in death, for death is 'the ultimate negation of reason and all its works' (76).

Other recent critics have been concerned with the play's 'theatricality'. R. J. Kaufmann (1960), who, as we have seen, deplores the play's 'misallied themes', concludes that it is 'centerless', 'stagey and false' (363). Arthur C. Kirsch (1972) notes that 'Bianca's alternating purity and coyness . . . resembles the behavior of a host of Fletcherian heroines' (114), and argues that Ford's plays, like Fletcher's, are 'concerned with acute, ostensibly moral dilemmas, designed to produce alternating or varying states of emotion in the characters and to allow them opportunity for debate and displays of passion' (115). Hence in *Love's Sacrifice* 'no dialectical or emotional turn is neglected' (115). All of Ford's plays, Kirsch declares, are 'theatrical to their core, and there seems no reason to make more pretentious claims for them than most critics are prepared to make for the plays of Fletcher' (121).

Similarly, Kathleen McLuskie (1988, 1989) interprets *Love's Sacrifice* as an exhibition of Ford's 'deft and varied combination of a limited repertoire of dramatic sequences' ('Language', 103). The play's 'scenes of sexual encounter circle around the poles of seduction and rejection and their outcome has more to do with the dramatic pleasures of expectations fulfilled and reversed than engagement with consistent character, narrative or motivation' ('Language', 104). Ford is depicted as exploiting the audience's familiarity with 'traditional dramatic structures', while Bianca 'goes through the whole gamut of possible roles for a tragic heroine' (*Ren. D.*, 153). Such an approach may not do full justice to the experience of an audience in the theatre, however. Spectators are likely to see the plot of *Love's Sacrifice* as more than a sequence of reworked scenes and topoi, and the characters as more than two-dimensional slaves to the dramatist's instinct for the 'piling up of dramatic ironies' ('Language', 109). Moreover, the text of the play suggests that they would not be mistaken in doing so. Take the scene in which Fiormonda woos Fernando (1.2.94–167). For McLuskie, this scene is a 'set piece' which has nothing to do with the overall narrative action but much to do with 'local dramatic effect'—the re-enactment and inversion of familiar dramatic structures ('Language', 104). The 'narrative question' of whether Fiormonda's seduction will succeed or fail 'does not lead anywhere,' writes McLuskie, 'the scene is simply broken off by the entrance of other characters and closed by Fernando's aside: "Blessed deliverance"' (104). On a formal level, this is an accurate description of Ford's eclectic dramaturgy (allusions to the wooing scene from *The Duchess of Malfi* are particularly prominent here; see p. 44, above). But in fictional terms it neglects the fact that Fiormonda maintains her suit throughout the play—a crucial point, since it is Fernando's rejection of her in 4.1 which provides the final spur to her murderous intentions: 'Then 'tis too late / To hope; change peevish passion to contempt' (265–6). For an audience involved in a performance of the play, as for the player of Fiormonda herself, the 'narrative question' of the widow's suit would by no means end with Ford's wooing scene.

Martin Butler (1988) presents the most comprehensive and convincing of the 'theatrical' interpretations of the play. Butler argues that much of what has been termed 'decadent' in Ford's work—the self-consciousness and sophistication, the radical shifts in style and tone, the 'verbal fireworks'—can be seen as a response to his theatrical milieu, in particular to the demands of a sophisticated audience dominated by 'my wity young masters o' the *Innes o' Court*'.[232] Such influences may be discernible in the fact that 'Neither Biancha nor Fernando can be pinned down comfortably either as brazen adulterers or as heroic lovers', while 'the Duke's role veers wildly between betrayed husband and penitent murderer' (Butler, 207). Butler remarks that 'it is as though the play sets out to tantalize the spectators with their incapacity to judge the participants' (207–8). Ford's fashioning of the characters 'after pre-existing theatrical types' (219) makes it especially difficult to judge them in the final act, for the allusions produce the impression that their identities are in some way 'no more than performances'. The 'authenticity of their feelings . . . is rendered deeply suspect; nor will it be clear whether they are freely playing their parts or, so to speak, being played by them' (219). In particular, it is the tendency in *Love's Sacrifice* 'to foreground our consciousness of the characters as players in a play . . . that makes Biancha's actions in V.i. so difficult to assess' (220). Butler argues that the final scene 'contrives to rewrite the roles of all the participants into a startling finale in which revenge tragedy is displaced by heroic transcendence' (224). But he thinks the scene is 'frankly indecipherable unless it is read with allowance for the element of self-conscious playfulness, the delight in witty exploitation of theatrical artifice and self-reference which is patently crucial here' (226).

TWENTIETH-CENTURY PRODUCTIONS

In the autumn of 1917, the Washington Square Players rehearsed an adaptation of *Love's Sacrifice* by Samuel A. Eliot, Jr, at the Cincinnati Art Theatre. However, the production was never staged. Eliot's adaptation, *The Duchess of Pavy*, is a single-act play for five speaking characters and extras. It was published in 1921.[233] In his introduction, Eliot writes of his admiration for the character of Bianca, and of his intention to reduce the 'chaos' surrounding her 'to a compass manageable by modern actors and producers, and create from it a unified play of definite artistic quality' (184). Thus events are condensed and rearranged, speeches are cut, re-positioned and given to other characters, and new lines are invented to smooth over the joins. The Ferentes and Mauruccio plots are entirely removed. Eliot's version begins with Caraffa's first entrance (1.1.126.1–2), and moves in what can be no more than half an hour's playing time to the tragic climax. Caraffa, a far more unstable character than Ford's Duke, is jealous from the outset; and despite Eliot's admiration for the character of Bianca, his Duchess has none of the ambiguity of the original, revealing many signs of her barely controlled passion for Fernando.

Eliot does, however, show a keen awareness of the overtly theatrical features of *Love's Sacrifice*. He urges that 'an aesthetic atmosphere' be maintained in performance: 'an illusion of unreality, of art existing for itself, unconscious of an audience, unaware of the world outside, innocent of any relation to life'. If this is attained, 'the play will be accepted and by artistic souls profoundly enjoyed' (185). Eliot stipulates that the setting of the play should be 'a stage. Not "a room in the palace," but a stage draped with the black velvet of tragedy' (187). Stage furniture should be 'flamboyantly ornamental'

(188), the period costumes in luminous colours, reminding the spectator 'that what he sees enacted is not a reflection or a criticism of life, but a play, a melodrama if he will, living only in, by, through, and for the theatre' (189).

Love's Sacrifice was revived at the Bristol Old Vic Theatre School on 20–1 June 1980, in a production directed by Brian Carter. It was also performed at the Workshop Theatre in the University of Leeds in the 1992–3 session. This was a studio production, staged in an intimate setting with the audience on three sides of the performance space. It was directed by Christian Billing and performed by students from the School of English. Martin Butler recalls that the staging 'emphasized the play's metatheatrical and intertextual dimensions', and that its ritual aspects, especially in the final scene, 'came across very powerfully'. Much of the action was 'accompanied by images of the 1633 text, projected on screens at the back of the stage. This was done not so insistently that one read them in preference to watching the action, but they were sufficiently visible to draw attention to the play as performed text' (private correspondence). *Love's Sacrifice* was also staged at the Bristol Old Vic Theatre School in the autumn of 1995. This production, directed by Elwyn Johnson, was set in 1950s Italy and drew its inspiration from film noir of the late 1940s and early 1950s.

The play was most recently staged in March 1997 in the reproduction of the Inigo Jones playhouse at the Wickham Theatre of the University of Bristol. This production, directed by Martin White and performed by students, was presented in period costume. Aspects of its staging are referred to in my discussion of 'The play' (see pp. 47, 53) and in the commentary (2.4.0.2).

CONCLUSION

The 'indecipherable' features of *Love's Sacrifice* have often been taken as marks of artistic failure. They might instead be signs of a problematic richness: the hallmarks of an uncertain but nevertheless highly distinctive aesthetic response to cultural changes that were themselves 'indecipherable' to Ford and his contemporaries. In its representation of women, and of love, *Love's Sacrifice* may be seen as enacting 'a contest between and a negotiation among competing ideological positions' in 'a gender struggle whose outcome could not have been known in advance'.[234] The very uncertainty of that struggle colours the play's language, action, and even its dramatic form, adding much to the interest—and the difficulty—of this sceptical, idealistic, farcical, and intensely moody romantic tragedy.

The play often expresses its intimations about women and love through the rhetoric of scandal: 'The selfsame appetite which led you on / To marry me', Bianca tells Caraffa, 'led me to love your friend' (5.1.96–7). Some in Ford's audience may have been inclined to class Bianca's 'appetite' with the 'carnall libertie, enormitie, syn and babilonicall confusion' which the Church saw as a threat to 'right ordre'.[235] *Love's Sacrifice* registers, and indeed courts, this conservative view in various ways: in its portrayal of the destruction attendant on illicit passion, for example, and in Bianca's own brazen declaration of her 'appetite'. But the play also shows Bianca enjoying a degree of autonomy in seeing and judging for herself. Like the increasing numbers of women in the Phoenix audience, she is—or rather, is shown to be—a 'subject who looks',[236] with her own 'affections, / Desires for sport, and frailty' (*Oth.* 4.3.99–100; cf. *LS* 2.4, 3.2.43ff, 5.1). This may be more apparent in performance, since, for a number of reasons, performance is likely to encourage perceptions of a presence within which Bianca's conflicting poses are accommodated. Most obviously, enactment provides, in the body of the performer, a place from which the character 'Bianca' may speak. At the same time, the play's dialogue and action repeatedly emphasise Bianca's physical presence in the imagined scenes. I have already noted this effect in the discovery scene, 2.4. The later image of her 'open breast', as she prepares herself for Caraffa's sword (5.1.160), similarly brings home the reality of her impassioned being. Caraffa's words here, as he hesitates to kill her, seem to reflect a momentary, heightened awareness of her human reality: 'She may live and change' (167). In her own speeches, too, Bianca seizes, as it were, new meaning and presence for herself.[237] Her declarations of passion, though perhaps melodramatic, convey a real sense of 'shame', 'fear' and the 'violence' of love (2.4.17–22). Her single brief soliloquy, as she contemplates the sleeping Fernando, seems to offer a glimpse of unfeigned suffering: 'O happy man, / How sweetly sleep hath sealed up sorrows here' (2.4.3–4). Such perceptions of Bianca as a unified though contradictory presence, 'living and changing', may not endure, but they are nevertheless a part of the experience of the play on the stage; and they have a lasting effect in complicating Caraffa's and Fernando's simplistic veneration of her as a 'shrine / Of fairest purity' (5.3.37–8). The men's limited perceptions of Bianca—and of 'women' in general (cf. 2.4.61–3, 5.1.110–12)—should not be confused with those offered by the play as a whole.

To be sure, what happens after Bianca's death looks like an attempt to restore the status quo. As the competing mourners strive to possess her eternally,[238] the rebellious woman is translated into a 'monument' (5.3.64) for male veneration, her passionate defiance of the 'iron laws of ceremony' (5.1.6) laughably restyled as 'the life of innocence and beauty' (5.3.48). As in *The Duchess of Malfi*, the 'radical act' seems to have culminated in 'sacrifice and extinction'.[239] But when the object of Bianca's scandalous love springs so inconveniently to life in the midst of Caraffa's funeral rites, he renews Bianca's transgression. Fernando's emergence from the tomb is a precise reversal of Bianca's entry into it; and the notion of a 'spiritualized marriage' transcending the letter of the law[240] which he revives, here at the end of the play, gains no little credibility through being opposed to the 'lawful' claims of a wife-murderer.

But it is only in such indirect ways that *Love's Sacrifice* could be said to move beyond entrenched male anxieties about women's assertiveness, independence and sexuality.[241] The play's acknowledgement of the equivalence of 'appetites'—male and female, lawful and adulterous—is never a simple matter. It creates, in fact, 'a conflict of total commitments'.[242] It also sparks a war of styles within the play: tragedy, romance and satire are constantly undercutting each other as opposing views of passion (especially Bianca's passion) collide. The result is a cloven tragedy in which the idealistic baroque elements identified by Ronald Huebert—Bianca's near-apotheosis, Fernando's self-sacrifice in 'loue's delicious Fire',[243] the fervid imagery of their marriage-in-death—mingle uneasily with mannerist[244] features expressive of a far more sceptical attitude to love: the Ferentes and Mauruccio sub-plots, the fortunes of Roseilli, the scheming of D'Avolos and Fiormonda, the bitter ironies and discords of D'Avolos's and Ferentes' prose. Indeed, the play's obsession with the contradictory nature of love, its scepticism about the possibility of achieving harmony between the spiritual and the physical, and its preoccupation with the fatal division between appearance and reality all reflect its origins in what Cyrus Hoy calls the 'essentially mannerist' world of Jacobean tragedy (53).[245] Bianca and Fernando, the would-be baroque martyrs, cannot entirely elude the pessimism that holds sway in that world. Both invite dark laughter with their rapid alternations between 'platonic' restraint and passionate abandon. If part of the challenge for the audience is to resist the Puritan equation of sexual pleasure with sin and death and to see Bianca and Fernando's adulterous passion in a different light from the false Ferentes' lust,[246] the play's own anxious confusion of styles constantly insists on the difficulty of sustaining such a view.

Long dismissed as a poor mish-mash of Jacobean tragic conventions, *Love's Sacrifice* is a challenging, ingenious drama which touches on—but does not wholly articulate—perceptions of women as the bearers of authentic and defensible thoughts and feelings. The uncertainty raised by these perceptions haunts the play, contributing much to its uneasy mixture of baroque lyricism, mannerist doubt and even absurdity. That mixture is never more evident than in the final scene, and yet this scene is also distinguished by a splendid audacity. Ford has dared to put on stage what he imagined, however awkward or provocative that may prove to be. Of course, the baroque flourish, the gesture of sheer indulgence, does not quite come off—not least because the play itself has already shown too much of the ambiguous nature of love's sacrifices. It is bitter discretion, not romantic fantasy, which has the final say, as Roseilli, perhaps the only significant character to remain 'an innocent in the business' (3.4.60), leaves the stage already estranged from his wife: 'Please you to walk, lord Abbot?' (5.3.166). A play about marital problems ends, not with resolution, but with the virtual dissolution of another marriage. Yet in such ways *Love's Sacrifice* manages to be both ethereal and worldly about romantic passion, and to express, in the contradictory fabric of its language, action and dramatic form, a capacious vision of love.

NOTES

1 Adapting Jonathan Bate's comment on Shakespeare, *The Genius of Shakespeare* (London: Picador, 1997), 323.

2 E.g. Gurr, 'A Select List of Plays and their Playhouses', *Sh. Stage*, 232–43, *passim*, 'Singing', 90–3; Neill, *Critical Re-Visions*, Intro., 2; Waith, 'Exaltation', 50; Barker, 3–4; Lomax, ed., *Plays*, xii, xvi, xxi; Wymer, 86.

3 The following biographical sketch is based on the fuller account in Sargeaunt, 1–16.

4 The date is universally cited as 17 April, but see my note on 'The Date of John Ford's Baptism', *N&Q*, n.s., 41, 1 (March 1994), 70–1.

5 A commendatory poem in the 1638 edition of *The Fancies* refers to him as '*Master Iohn* FORD, *of the middle Temple*'.

6 *'Tis Pity*, xix.

7 Sargeaunt, 8.

8 Quotation from the Minute Book of the Temple, Sargeaunt, 14.

9 Hopkins, *Political Theatre*, 14. Hopkins goes so far as to claim that Ford was 'the dramatist' of this coterie (179).

10 For further details see Telford Moore, 76, 87; Sargeaunt, 25–6; *JCS* III, 437; Hopkins, *Political Theatre*, 4–5.

11 G. C. Moore Smith, ed. (Oxford, 1923), ll. 81–2.

12 *'Tis Pity*, xx. There is a picture of a melancholy lover ('*Inamorato*') with wide-brimmed hat and folded arms on the title-page of Burton's *The Anatomy of Melancholy*, 3rd edn, 1628 (reproduced as frontispiece in *LM*).

13 *Edmonton* (with Dekker and Rowley), *SR* 27 April, 1621, published that year; *Darling* (with Dekker), licensed 3 March 1623/4; *The Fairy Knight* (lost; with Dekker), 11 June 1624; *A Late Murther of the Sonn upon the Mother, or Keep the Widow Waking* (lost; with Dekker, Webster and Rowley), Sept. 1624; *The Bristow Merchant* (lost, with Dekker), 22 October, 1624; *The Fair Maid of the Inn* (Fletcher, possibly with Ford and/or Massinger; see *JCS* III, 337–9), 22 Jan. 1625/6.

14 Orbison (1974), 17.

15 *Histriomastix* bears the date 1633, but was issued 'late in 1632' (*JCS* III, 451). Prynne claimed that his book was 'finished at the press above x. weeks, and . . . published in the country above four weekes before her Majesty's pastorall' (Gardiner, 51–2). But the references to the 'whorish impudence' of female players which he added to the index—if not the similar abuses in the text—are unlikely to have been written without some knowledge of the Queen's preparations for the play. (See Gardiner, xxxviii; and William M. Lamont, *Marginal Prynne, 1600–1669*, London: Routledge & Kegan Paul, 1963, 29.)

16 Gardiner, 20.

17 From the Salvetti Correspondence, *Historical Manuscripts Commission*, XVI, 47, quoted by Harbage, 12.

18 'I heare not much honor of the Quene's maske', wrote Henry Manners, 'for, if they were not all, soome were in men's apparell' (quoted by Harbage, 12). A correspondent of the Reverend Joseph Mead commented that the masque 'is said to have been preparing and performing from three in the afternoon to four next morning . . . Doubtless it cost abundance' (letter dated 19 Jan. 1626/7, quoted in Thomas Birch, ed., *The Court and Times of Charles the First*, 2 vols (London, 1848), I, 185). A foreign observer, in an account preserved in the Venetian state papers, noted that Henrietta's masque 'did not give complete satisfaction, because the English objected to the first part . . . being declaimed by the Queen' (Harbage, 12). Charles, too, may have been displeased with these manifestations of 'Gallic buoyancy', for a few months later many of Henrietta's French attendants were dismissed (Harbage, 12). Most of them did eventually return, however, and there are numerous

further references to Henrietta's 'pastorals and comedies and other pleasant diversions' (*Calendar of Venetian State Papers*, 1632–6; Harbage, 13) in the years before Prynne published *Histriomastix*.

19 See 4.1.199–200 Longer Note (LN) for further possible dating evidence involving Prynne.

20 Oliver, 48.

21 Martin, ed., *Poems* of Crashaw, 181. The couplet is also found in Bodleian MSS Tanner 465 and 466: manuscripts of 'a collection of poems by various seventeenth-century writers, but mainly by Crashaw, in the handwriting and formerly in the possession of Archbishop Sancroft' (Martin, lviii). The poems in this collection probably belong 'to the period of Crashaw's residence both at Pembroke and Peterhouse, though chiefly at the former' (lviii). Crashaw seems to have been elected to his Fellowship at Peterhouse in 1635 (Martin, xxii). The couplet also appears on p. 41v of British Museum Add. MS 33219, which is 'likely to contain only poems written before 1635' (lxxiv). It is attributed to Crashaw on p. 298 of Tanner 465 (Martin, lxi, lxxvi).

22 *BH*, 25. Oliver suggests that these lines point to the fact that both plays deal with a woman 'widowed' by marriage to the wrong man (76). But there is nothing to prove that Crashaw read or witnessed either tragedy. Sargeaunt (139) argues, instead, that Crashaw uses the two title phrases 'in their religious significance'. Perhaps she is referring to the words of the Psalmist: 'The sacrifices of God are a broken spirit: a broken and a contrite heart' (Psalms 51:16–17). This teaching informs Crashaw's own poem 'The Weeper' and, perhaps, *BH* (32).

23 *JCS* IV, 754–5; Edwards and Gibson I, xxi.

24 *JCS* IV, 862. Daalder states that it was written in 1622 (xiii).

25 See *JCS* IV, 907; *WBW*, xxxii–xxxviii. The similarities between *WBW* and *LS* are noted by Hoskins, 58; Butler, 215–16; McLuskie, 'Language', 105.

26 Frederick Gard Fleay, *A Biographical Chronicle of the English Drama, 1559–1642*, 2 vols (London: Reeves & Turner, 1891), I, 233–4.

27 Adams, 59; Bawcutt, 169.

28 Lawrence, 129.

29 Adams, 59.

30 *Histriomastix*, 414, marginal note.

31 For a more detailed discussion of evidence relating to the play's date, see Telford Moore, 39–52.

32 This short account of the history of the Phoenix draws on information provided in *JCS* VI, 47–76. See also Telford Moore, 141–3. The theatre was probably opened by the start of the law term in 1616 (Gurr, *Playgoing*, 176).

33 Gurr, *Playgoing*, 183.

34 If the original cockpit resembled other structures built for the same purpose, it would have been a round or polygonal building, perhaps about 40 feet across, with a pointed or conical roof and small windows (Orrell, 'Inigo Jones', 165). Incorporation of part of the old cockpit shell would have saved Beeston considerable effort and expense, and would have enabled him to abide by regulations restricting new construction work to additions of no more than a third of the size of

the original structure (Orrell, 166). Beeston may have felt a special obligation to heed these regulations, since his property was close to the road to Royston which King James used on his frequent hunting trips; James took a strong interest in the enforcement of the building restrictions (Orrell, 162). The phrasing of a protest by lawyers at the nearby Inns of Court about the new building work 'att and adjoyninge to the Cocke-pitt' (from a record of the Middlesex Judicial Sessions of 5 and 6 Sept. 1616; quoted by Orrell, 162) supports the theory that the work involved reconstruction and extension of the original cockpit. For information about Beeston's career as actor and theatre manager, see *JCS* VI, 48.

35 Glynne Wickham, *Early English Stages 1300 to 1660*, 4 vols (London: Routledge & Kegan Paul, 1959–72), II, Part 2, 79–81.

36 As Gurr argues, it is likely that the apprentices attacked the Phoenix rather than any other theatre because they resented the removal of their favourite plays from the Red Bull to the more expensive private playhouse ('Singing', 83; see also Gurr, *Companies*, 123–5). But it does not seem to have been remarked that two of the traditional activities of Shrove Tuesday were cockfighting and 'throwing at the cock' (Brand, 35–41). Perhaps the loss of the cockpit for these noble pursuits also fuelled the apprentices' resentment.

37 See Rowan[1], Rowan[2]; Iain Macintosh, 'Inigo Jones—Theatre Architect', *TABS* 31 (1973), 101–4; Orrell, 'Inigo Jones', *Theatres*, 39–77, *Rebuilding*, 125–47. For the recent views of two authorities, see R. A. Foakes's chapter on 'Playhouses and players' in *Camb. Comp.*, 36, and Gurr, *Sh. Stage*, 160–4. Also see App. 2.

38 Richard Leacroft, *The Development of the English Playhouse* (London and New York: Methuen, 1973, rev. 1988), 73.

39 Sturgess, 31. Indeed, according to Sturgess, Jones's design was used as the model for a synagogue at Newport in the United States in 1759.

40 These details of the theatre's dimensions are taken from Orrell's chapter on 'The Inigo Jones Designs' in *Rebuilding*, and from his article, 'Inigo Jones'.

41 Rowan[2] (70) and Sturgess (41) suggest a capacity of about 500; Orrell estimates 700 (*Rebuilding*, 130); White (158) suggests 700–750.

42 Rowan[2], 70.

43 Orrell, *Rebuilding*, 130.

44 Orrell, *Theatres*, 54–5.

45 Sturgess, 45. The *Wits* picture is reproduced in Foakes, *Illustrations*, 160.

46 Sturgess, 46. Thomas Killigrew, who wrote *Claracilla* and *The Prisoners* for the Phoenix, remarked to Pepys on the gloom of the Elizabethan indoor theatres (Pepys, *Diary*, 12 Feb. 1667).

47 Sturgess, 54.

48 Gurr, *Sh. Stage*, 164; Orrell, 'Inigo Jones', 168. See also Rowan[2], 72.

49 Examples from Nabbes's *Covent Garden* (1638, C2r–4v), Davenport's *The City-Night-Cap* (1661, C1v), and Heywood's *The English Traveller* (1633, F1v) are discussed by Markward, 329–32. Huebert believes that Markward's argument for three doors 'exploits the possibly contaminated evidence offered by Nabbes's *Covent Garden* and . . . *The English Traveller*. King's analysis of thirty pure Cockpit plays yields only two

necessary doors' (*Lady of Pleasure*, 194–5). But I am unaware of any reason for doubting that these two plays were performed at the Phoenix, or that the extant texts relate to performance there.

50 Markward, 329, 264–6, 276–7, 287–8, 291.

51 See Markward, 250–329, for references to these scenes.

52 One obvious advantage of this arrangement would be that, in preparing for discovery scenes, stage-hands could move hefty props such as Fernando's bed directly from the tiring house area into position behind the curtains or hangings of the central entrance.

53 King, 'Staging', 165.

54 King, 'Staging', 165.

55 Cf. the stage direction in Massinger's Phoenix play *The Bondman*: '*Enter aboue,* Pisander, Poliphron, Cimbrio, Graculo, *& the rest*' (1624, H1v). For further discussion of Ford's permissive stage direction here, see 'Printing', 304.

56 See King, 'Staging', 157.

57 In a number of Phoenix plays music is described as coming from a window (e.g., *The Bondman*, 1624, 3.3, F4v; *The Opportunity*, 1640, 2.1, E1r). This could easily have been staged in the Jones playhouse if the musicians were positioned in a room behind the balcony. There is a reference to an arras on the upper stage, possibly at the rear of the balcony, in *The Cunning Lovers* (1654, 3.1. F1v).

58 Between 1613 and 1615, Jones was in Italy in the train of the Earl of Arundel. During his visit he spent some time in Vicenza, where he saw and was much influenced by Palladio's Teatro Olimpico (see Foakes, *Illustrations*, 66).

59 Rowan[2], 67; Foakes, *Illustrations*, 66.

60 *Rebuilding*, 134–5.

61 Orrell, *Theatres*, 52, 56; *Rebuilding*, 134.

62 Butler, *Crisis*, 109. Also see Neill, 'Wits'.

63 Jean E. Howard, 'Women as Spectators, Spectacles, and Paying Customers', in *Staging the Renaissance: Reinterpretations of Elizabethan and Jacobean Drama*, ed. David Scott Kastan and Peter Stallybrass (New York and London: Routledge, 1991), 68–74; 73. For further discussion of female theatre-goers in this period, see Howard's revised version of the above essay in her book *The Stage and Social Struggle in Early Modern England* (London: Routledge, 1994), Ch. 4; Gurr, *Sh. Stage*, 222; Neill, 'Wits', 343; McLuskie, *Ren. D.*

64 Among the predominant features of such cases identified by Laura Gowing are: the crucial role of servants or social inferiors as witnesses to adulterous behaviour (cf. *LS* 2.3.53.1, 4.2.1–19), the husband's expression of concern about the risk of bastardy (5.1.61–4), the wife's humiliation of her husband, often in sexual terms (5.1.52ff) and the husband's use of violence against his wife (5.1.173.1). (See Gowing, 69, 88–9, 189, 197, 206–29.) Discoveries of adulterous liaisons were the crux of many defamatory stories, and the focus of numerous adultery cases (Gowing, 69, 189); cf. *LS* 5.1.

65 *JCS* III, 232–3, 569–71; IV, 811–15, 935; V, 1164.

66 *JCS* I, 221–2. The *Renegado* cast includes three actors (John Blaney, Edward Shakerley and William Reignolds) who do not appear in any of

the later lists. The *Renegado* list also omits Richard Perkins, William Sherlock, Hugh Clark and Anthony Perkins.

67 John Blaney, William Reignolds and Edward Shakerley probably left Queen Henrietta's Men some time before May 1626, after performing in *The Renegado* (*JCS* I, 221). George Stutville and Ezekiel Fenn do not seem to have been associated with the company before their performances in Nabbes's *Hannibal and Scipio* in 1635 (*JCS* I, 433, 580–2); and Andrew Pennycuicke is unlikely to have been a member of the company before 1634 (*JCS* II, 525).

68 Though only fourteen members were ever granted livery, the same number as the King's Men (*JCS* I, 229, 247).

69 The play has fifteen speaking parts. But the stage direction at 5.3.35.1–8 requires at least sixteen or seventeen players on stage: Caraffa, the Abbot, Fiormonda, Colona, Julia, Roseilli, Petruccio, Nibrassa and D'Avolos, as well as '*four with torches*', '*two Friars*', and '*a Guard*' (usually two or more armed men). Even if we assume that the actors who had played Ferentes, Mauruccio, Giacopo and Bianca took parts as torch-bearers, friars and guards, at least three or four other players would have been required as supernumeraries. The masque scene (3.4) has fourteen actors with speaking parts on stage at the same time, as well as two or more attendants carrying lights (6.1).

70 The cast list for Davenport's *King John and Matilda* declares that his performance in the part 'gave Grace to the Play'.

71 See *JCS* II, 528.

72 Huebert, 'Staging', 23, 50.

73 John Russell Brown suggests that Perkins played Flamineo in *W. Devil*, staged by Queen Anne's Men at the Red Bull, probably early in 1612 (xxii–xxiii, 187; *JCS* II, 525).

74 I am grateful to Kate Bignold at the Dulwich Picture Gallery for information on the dating of this portrait.

75 Edward Rogers played the parts of Donusa and Millicent in the company's productions of *The Renegado* and *The Wedding*; John Page played Jane in *The Wedding* (though by 1635 he was old enough to take on male roles); and Timothy Reade played Cardona, a minor female part in *The Wedding*, before turning to comic male roles in later years (*JCS* II, 406).

76 There are signs that Bird may have been a close friend of Ford's. His name appears at the end of the prologues to *Trial* (1639) and *Edmonton* (1658), and he was the co-author of a dedication to the Earl of Southampton for *Darling* (1656). See *JCS* II, 378–9.

77 *Historia Histrionica*, quoted in *JCS* II, 583.

78 King, *Casting*, 18.

79 If Robbins did play the part in *LS*, then the Roseilli seen at the Phoenix may have been extremely thin. Robbins's casting as '*Rawbone*, a thin Citizen' in the cast list for *The Wedding* suggests that unusual thinness was an important part of his comic persona. In 1.3, Rawbone and Chameleon engage in badinage on the theme of their spindle-shanked physiques.

80 John Dobson played the minor comic part of Chameleon, Rawbone's servant, in *The Wedding*. Perhaps he also played Giacopo. Since three of

Anthony Turner's known roles were old men (Justice Landby in *The Wedding*, Old Lord Bruce in *King John and Matilda*, and Piston in *Hannibal and Scipio*: see *JCS* II, 607–8), he may have been thought suitable for the part of Petruccio, Nibrassa or the Abbot.

81 T. J. King's analysis of the few surviving performance MSS from the period shows that principal actors played 'a wide variety of parts'. King argues that 'the most important consideration in casting a given part was not the type of role to be acted but the *length* of that role' (*Staging*, 18). However, Gurr comments that 'Consistent type-casting of the major roles is the easiest way to cope with the demands of any repertory system', though 'it could not have been an invariable practice' (*Sh. Stage*, 105). Cf. Sturgess, 60.

82 This copy is held at the Folger Shakespeare Library; see *L. Stage*, Part 1: 1660–1700, plate between pp. 64 and 65. The *LS* cast lists are noticed by Sutfin, 16, and reproduced in Telford Moore, 181.

83 Howe, 1.

84 *L. Stage*, 1, 22.

85 Pepys, *Diary*, vol. 5, 232, n. 5.

86 Wilson, 170. Van Lennep, *L. Stage*, Part 1, 15, lists Beck Marshall as a member of the King's Company for the season 1660–1, but does not cite the documents which connect her with the company for this season. I am therefore unaware of any record of her involvement in a King's Company (or any other) production for the 1660–1 season. The first (indirect) mention of her possible involvement in the King's Company seems to be Pepys's diary reference to 'the elder Marshall' (i.e. her sister Anne) on 1 February 1664. Other evidence concerning the date of the lists is conflicting. A patent dated 25 April 1662 stipulated that only women should play female parts (quoted in Howe, 25–6). If Thomas Loveday played (or was at least chosen to play) Morona, as the right-hand list suggests, this might put the list before that date. Loveday was associated with the Duke's Company in the 1660–1 season, but he seems to have joined the King's Company in the season of 1661–2 (*L. Stage*, Part 1, 16, 36, 54, 69, 81). On the other hand, the inclusion of the name 'Blagdun' in the right-hand list may suggest that this list (if not the other) dates from the 1662–3 season. Nicholas Blagden was linked to the Duke's Company in the 1660–1 and 1661–2 seasons (*L. Stage*, Part 1, 16, 36), and Allardyce Nicoll supposes that he may have joined the King's Company 'at a late date' (I, 295). But the matter is complicated by the appearance of Blagden's name in connection with the King's Company in documents of an earlier date (Nicoll, 297, 363–4). If Blagden did not join Killigrew's company until the 1662–3 season, his omission from the left-hand list could suggest that it was prepared before then—the only possible evidence I have come across to suggest that the two lists may have been prepared at different times.

87 *W. Devil*, 4.

88 New Arden Shakespeare edn (Walton-on-Thames: Nelson, 1997), 1, 344–50.

89 Sargeaunt, 2.

90 Account Book of Edmund Tilney, Master of the Revels; see Norman Sanders's New Cambridge edn of *Othello* (Cambridge: Cambridge

University Press, 1984), 1. The other performances mentioned are documented by Chambers, *WS* II, 336, 343, 348.

91 Sanders ed., *Othello*, 17.

92 T. S. Eliot, 'Shakespeare and the Stoicism of Seneca', in *Selected Essays* (London: Faber, 1932), 130–1; F. R. Leavis, 'Diabolic Intellect and the Noble Hero: or the Sentimentalist's *Othello*', in *The Common Pursuit* (Harmondsworth: Penguin, 1952), 146.

93 Perhaps the earliest-known praise of the two scenes is found in Abraham Wright's commonplace book (c. 1637; quoted in *Shakspere Allusion-Book: A Collection of Allusions to Shakspere from 1591 to 1700*, compiled by C. M. Ingleby, L. Toulmin Smith and F. J. Furnivall; re-edited by J. Munro, 2 vols, London: Chatto & Windus, 1909, I, 411).

94 McLuskie 'shows how Ford constructed his plays out of combinations and variations upon familiar scenes which enabled the dramatist to put together creditable versions of the work of his contemporaries' ('Language', 120). McLuskie is well aware, however, that this approach can give an impression of 'a lack of consistent and original "vision" in Ford's work'—a view to which she does not fully subscribe (120–1).

95 Unlike *Oth.*, *LS* does have subsidiary plots. Yet the Ferentes and Mauruccio stories sharpen the audience's attention to the main plot by restating its prominent themes. Also, the narrative is gradually pruned to a single strand, Ferentes and Mauruccio having spoken their last lines by early in Act 4.

96 Alvin Kernan's description of *Oth.* in *Revels History* III, 407–8.

97 Opie, 251.

98 Intro. to Sanders's edn, 29.

99 For discussion of how D'Avolos may interpret what he hears, see p. 51, below.

100 Fletcher, and perhaps Webster, were also involved in this play. See Cyrus Hoy, 'Massinger as Collaborator: The Plays with Fletcher and Others', in *Philip Massinger; A Critical Reassessment*, ed. Douglas Howard (Cambridge: Cambridge University Press, 1985), 66. For the date of *The Fair Maid*, see *JCS* III, 338–9.

101 It is possible that Massinger's Phoenix plays of 1621–5 represent a short severance of his attachment to the King's company at Blackfriars; see *JCS* IV, 754–5, Edwards and Gibson I, xxi. *Edmonton* (performed 1621), *Darling* (licensed 1623/4) & *Gypsy* (licensed 1623) all belong to what Roper calls Ford's 'early Phoenix period' (*'Tis Pity*, xxv). See Telford Moore, 47.

102 Edwards and Gibson I, 200.

103 Farr, 62.

104 Butler, 212.

105 Butler, 212. The borrowing is also noted by Hoskins, 60, and Oliver, 80.

106 Cf. Paris's words to Romeo as he attempts to break into the monument—'Stop thy unhallowed toil, vile Montague! / Can vengeance be pursued further than death?' (*R&J* 54–5)—with Fernando's warning to Caraffa at 57–9.

107 Smallwood, 66.

108 Butler, 212.

109 Gray and Heseltine, 66–7.
110 Both thesis and article were written under Hopkins's maiden name, Cronin.
111 Biographical details are taken from Gray and Heseltine, 7; Watkins, 3–7; Zarrella, 27–37.
112 Watkins, 7.
113 Quotations from the Corona MS are taken from the translation in Watkins, 7–13 (reproduced in App. 3, with adjusted line numbers).
114 The Corona MS gives the date as 16 October 1590 (ll. 228–9), but this is incorrect. It is clear from the *Informatione presa dalla Gran Corte della Vicaria. Die 27 Octobris, 1590, in quo habitat Don Carolus Gesualdus* (a report of the proceedings of the Grand Court of the Vicaria) that the murders occurred on the night of 26 October. See Watkins, 18, 21.
115 Chapter on 'Ford and Shirley' in *CHEL* VI, 192. Also noted by Sargeaunt, 112, Skretkowicz, xlix.
116 Hopkins, 'Coterie Values', 179.
117 Skretkowicz, liii–lxxix; Robertson, ed., the *Old Arcadia*, xlii–lxvi.
118 All quotations and page references for the *New Arcadia* are taken from Skretkowicz.
119 E.g. Gifford and Dyce, 73; Sargeaunt, 112.
120 Parrott and Ball, *A Short View of Elizabethan Drama* (New York: Scribner, 1943; 1958), 244–5. Stuart P. Sherman suggests that the story of Penthea in *BH* was influenced by the circumstances of Penelope Devereux's life; see Neilson's chapter on 'Ford and Shirley' in *CHEL* VI, 191.
121 Quotations from *Astrophel and Stella* are taken from Ringler.
122 Biographical details here are taken from Ringler's commentary, 435–47.
123 Ringler, 438, 441; Duncan-Jones, 230. For a very different account of Sidney writing *Astrophel and Stella* as 'a kind of game' rather than as an expression of real love for Penelope, see Duncan-Jones, 246–7.
124 See Stavig, 4–5; Ringler, 445–6.
125 Oliver, 11, Stavig, 5.
126 Russell Brown, *W. Devil*, xxii; *Malfi*, xviii–xxv; *JCS* I, 27–8.
127 The two men collaborated on the lost play *A Late Murther of the Sonn upon the Mother* (licensed 1624), and perhaps on *The Fair Maid of the Inn* (c. 1624–5; *JCS* III, 338–9; Sargeaunt, 18–19; Hoy, 'Massinger as Collaborator' (note 100), 66). Ford wrote a commendatory poem for the 1623 edition of *Malfi*. Webster may have been a member of the Middle Temple when Ford was admitted in 1602 (*JCS* V, 1240).
128 Leech, 80; Farr, 64.
129 *Woman Killed*, xvi.
130 See Butler, 209, 222; Farr, 72–3; Arthur C. Kirsch, *Jacobean Dramatic Perspective* (Charlottesville: University Press of Virginia, 1972), 114; Hoskins, 58; Telford Moore, 92–4. For the date of *Maid's Tragedy*, see *Maid's Trag.*, 2–3.
131 E.g. 'gamesters', *WBW*, 269, 'gamester', *LS*, 5; 'I shall be too hard for thee', *WBW*, 294, 'you are grown too hard for me', *LS*, 3; and perhaps *WBW*, 295, *LS*, 5–6.
132 See Merchant's Intro. to *Eng. Trav.*, 13–14; *JCS* IV, 565–7.

133 Like Massinger, Marston may have been a personal associate of Ford's: he was probably at the Middle Temple when Ford was admitted in November 1602 (Jackson and Neill, ix).

134 Hoskins, 60–1; see below, p. 47; 4.1.143 LN.

135 Butler, 206; Wymer, 91.

136 Stuart P. Sherman suggests that the plot of *LS* was based in part on George Gascoigne's *The Adventures of Master F.J.*, a prose romance first published in *A Hundreth Sundrie Flowres Bounde vp in One Small Poesie*, 1573, and again, in a revised form and with the new title of *The Pleasant Fable of Ferdinando Ieronomi and Leonara de Valasco*, in *The Posies of George Gascoigne*, 1575 ('Ford's Debt to His Predecessors and Contemporaries, and His Contribution to the Decadence of the Drama', Ph.D. dissertation, Harvard University, 1906; *CHEL* VI, 192). Gascoigne's romance tells the story of the promiscuous Leonora, the wife of a noble lord, who engages in an affair with the young courtier Ferdinando. After many romantic trials and tribulations, Ferdinando learns of Leonora's true nature. Apart from Ferdinando's name, and the fact that he is a favourite of Leonora's husband, I can find no specific similarities with *LS*, although Dame Frances's tale of another husband-wife-lover triangle is perhaps a little closer to the plot of Ford's play than Gascoigne's principal story (see *A Hundreth Sundrie Flowres*, 278–84).

137 'All writers of tragedy must engage with and surpass their predecessors in order to achieve the desired emotional effects' (Wymer, 93, who nevertheless finds *LS* 'Ford's least satisfactory tragedy', 101).

138 Neill, *Issues*, 282. Neill states that the practice of using black hangings and curtains for tragedies was 'standard in both public and private playhouses, as well as in the court theatres' (282, n. 34), though the available evidence is not very strong or plentiful in regard to the hall playhouses; see *ES* III, 79.

139 The parallel is noticed by Oliver, 80; Leech, 79; Farr, 62–3; Hoskins, 58–9; and Butler, 212–13. Quotations from *W. Devil* and *Malfi* are taken from the Revels editions.

140 Butler, 213, who also notices the *Malfi* parallel.

141 Cf. *Milan* 1.1.102–5, 1.3.11–18. Both Sforza and Caraffa use 'rapt' in a similar context (*Milan* 1.3.133, *LS* 1.1.127–9), a minor verbal correspondence which points up each duke's inclination to irrationality and childish euphoria. Caraffa and Sforza also share a contempt for lesser amatory beings (*LS* 1.1.184–90, *Milan* 1.3.76–8), and their obsessive stress on the happiness and security of their matches creates similar expectations of marital strife (*Milan* 1.3.11–78, 201–8, 3.1.267–9; *LS* 1.1.132–4).

142 Huebert, *Baroque*, 208.

143 McMaster, 158–9.

144 Cf. Huebert, *Baroque*, 96; Farr, 64–7; Neill, 'Neo-stoicism', 75.

145 Webster's tragedy was revived by the King's Men c. 1619 and again in 1630 (*Malfi*, xviii–xxv; *JCS* I, 27–8).

146 Butler, 214; also see Neill, 'Neo-stoicism', 31.

147 In 1694 Charles Gildon claimed that the original actor of Iago 'was in much esteem for a Comoedian' (Chambers, *WS* II, 261).

148 *Anatomy*, I.3.1.2, p. 384.
149 *Private Life*, 164.
150 According to Heywood, *An Apology for Actors* (1612), an actor needs 'a comely and elegant gesture, a gratious and a bewitching kinde of action, a naturall and a familiar motion of the head, the hand, the body, and a moderate and fit countenance sutable to all the rest' (C4r).
151 *Private Life*, 165.
152 Joseph Hall associates Tamburlaine with 'stalking steps' in *Vergidemiarvm* (1602, B3v–4r); Middleton pictures spiders stalking 'as if they had been conning of *Tamburlaine*' in *The Black Book* (1604; Bullen, ed., *Works* VIII, 25); and in *The Wonderfull Yeare* (1603?), Dekker refers to Death as being 'like a Spanish Leagar, or rather like stalking Tamberlaine' (D1r). Dekker and Middleton may well have been referring to Alleyn, who was described as 'stalking and roaring' by Everard Guilpin in *Skialetheia* (1598, B2v); see Gurr, 'Strutted'; *Poetaster* 3.4.165n.
153 See Leggatt in *Revels History* III, 98, 103. Ford may have had the opportunity to see Alleyn on stage, for the actor was probably still performing with the Lord Admiral's Men when Ford was admitted to the Middle Temple in November 1602 (Sargeaunt, 2; Chambers, *WS* II, 298). In the Preface to his play *Tamerlane the Great* (1681), Charles Saunders refers to Marlowe's work as '*a Cock-Pit Play*', but there is no earlier record to support this.
154 Mauruccio's 'Helicon' at l. 38 (cf. 3.2.110) recalls Pistol in *2H4* 5.3.105. His comment at 4.1.143 echoes Pistol in *2H4* 5.3.108–9. See 4.1.143 LN for further comment. The reminiscence of Malvolio is noted by Hoskins, 60–1.
155 King, 'Staging', 165. See also Markward, 432.
156 Butler, 220. Neill argues that the 'oddly archaic stichomythia' of this speech betrays 'Fernando's effort to project a conflict which he does not really feel' ('Neo-stoicism', 78).
157 Noted by Butler, 220. Fernando is also reading, like Hamlet earlier in the same scene.
158 *OED passion* sb. 3, 6a, d; Butler, 220; cf. *MND* 5.1.310.
159 Markward (530–84) notes that the Phoenix repertory made use of many small properties: letters, books, jewels, gloves, flowers, looking-glasses, and even a chamber pot. In such an intimate setting small items could be incorporated into the action without risk of incomprehension.
160 Foakes, *Illustrations*, 96–7.
161 *The Wits or, Sport upon Sport*, ed. John James Elson (Ithaca, New York: Cornell University Press, 1932), 427.
162 Una Ellis-Fermor, *The Jacobean Drama: An Interpretation* (London: Methuen, 1936), 232, n. 3; Butler, 215.
163 Jan Kelch, in the *Catalogue* of the Gemäldegalerie, Berlin, compiled by Henning Bock, Rainald Grosshans, Jan Kelch, Wilhelm H. Köhler and Erich Schleier, translated by John Gabriel (London: Weidenfeld and Nicolson, 1986), 170.
164 Q gives no stage direction to indicate a response to Bianca's request for 'Lights for our sister, sirs' (20); possibly some attendants with lights would have entered at this point. But perhaps Bianca addresses Julia and D'Avolos ('sirs' occasionally being used to address both men and

women, as in *LLL* 4.3.210), who then take some of the candles or tapers brought in at the beginning of the scene and depart with Fiormonda. The removal of some of this illumination would have left Bianca and Fernando with more intimate lighting—perhaps a single candelabrum—on a *comparatively* darker stage. Martin White reports that the pair were 'isolated in light' in the Bristol production (private correspondence).

165 McLuskie, *Ren. D.*, 153. There is also an echo of Marcelia's rejection of Francisco in *Milan* (see *LS* 2.3.68–70n).

166 Mendelson and Crawford, 116–17. Evidently the 'art of scorning' was 'practised by women of every social rank' (117).

167 Commenting on the moment in which Giovanni '*Offers his dagger*' to Annabella and invites her to 'Rip up my bosom, there thou shalt behold / A heart in which is writ the truth I speak' (*'Tis Pity* 1.2.209–11), Styan remarks that Ford 'insinuates a strange wedge of ritualism into the realism' (234). David Cecil notes the 'ritualistic strain' in Ford's imagination ('The Tragedies of John Ford', *The Fine Art of Reading and Other Literary Studies*, London: Constable, 1957, 90).

168 Neill observes that the idea of discovery was integral to the new Vesalian anatomy: 'Where medieval dissections had been essentially static and iconic, Vesalius' is presented as dynamic and dramatic; and carefully staged though it may be, what is being mimed here is not the familiar ritual of confirming authority, but a scene of revelation and discovery' (*Issues*, 125).

169 Dessen, *Conventions*, 36.

170 In the story of Cupid and Psyche, as told by Lucius Apuleius in *The Golden Ass* (VII, VIII, IX), the beautiful princess Psyche is loved by Cupid, who allows her to live in his gorgeous palace. Psyche does not know her lover's identity, and is not permitted to see him; he visits her only at night, always departing before daybreak. However, Psyche's malicious sisters, jealous of her happy circumstances, persuade her that her unseen lover is a monstrous serpent who must be killed. Psyche provides herself with a knife and a lamp, and one night, as her lover sleeps beside her, she uncovers the lamp to look at him. As she gazes at his beauty, a drop of hot oil falls from the lamp on to his right shoulder. Cupid awakes and flees in anger. Left in solitude, Psyche wanders far in search of him, becoming the slave of Venus before eventually being reunited with her lover. The story was well known in the early seventeenth century. Thomas Heywood staged Psyche's discovery of her lover in his masque *Love's Mistress* (1634). There, Psyche enters '*in night-attire, with a Lamp and a Raizor*' (3.1, D3r), and Cupid is '*discovered, sleeping on a bed*' (D3v). Like *LS*, *Love's Mistress* was performed at the Phoenix, where the King and Queen apparently saw it in 1634 (*JCS* IV, 582). Ford may also have read the treatment of the story in Book III of William Browne's *Britannia's Pastorals*. Although not printed until 1852, this last book of Browne's poem may have been written before 1628 (Frederic W. Moorman, *William Browne, His Britannia's Pastorals and the Pastoral Poetry of the Elizabethan Age*, Strassburg: Tröbner, 1897, 15).

171 Opie, 249.

172 White (170) makes a similar observation about Giovanni and Annabella's dual confession of love in *'Tis Pity* 2.2.

173 *Oth.* is known to have been performed by the King's Men, probably at Blackfriars, in late 1629. Sir Humphrey Mildmay saw the play at Blackfriars in 1635 (Chambers, *WS* II, 348, 352).
174 Quotation from Martin Elliott, *Shakespeare's Invention of 'Othello': A Study in Early Modern English* (New York: St Martin's Press, 1988), 135.
175 See 3.3.57–9n and 5.1.136n for further evidence that Ford was familiar with a version of *Oth.* that was closer to the F text.
176 Markward, 488–528.
177 Dessen, *Conventions*, 31.
178 Prologue to *Hannibal and Scipio* (1637), A3v. (A Phoenix play, performed by Queen Henrietta's Men.)
179 *Private Life*, 195.
180 Neill, *Issues*, 73.
181 The Basel *Totentanz*, writes Neill, imparts 'a notion of death as not merely imminent (as in the *memento mori* tradition) but *immanent*, as an ending implicit in every beginning, and constantly present in every middle' (*Issues*, 73).
182 For comparison of Mercutio and Bergetto in *'Tis Pity*, see Smallwood, 49–70; also Telford Moore, 99–100.
183 *Anatomy*, I.2.3.2, p. 254.
184 Leavis, 'Diabolic Intellect', 143.
185 Edgar Wind, *Pagan Mysteries in the Renaissance* (Harmondsworth: Penguin, rev. edn, 1967), 162; see also Madelaine, 45.
186 Markward (258) points out a reference to 'Lynes to drawe curtens with' in the Revels Account for 1578–9; see also A. Feuillerat, ed., *Documents Relating to the Office of the Revels in the Time of Queen Elizabeth* (*Materialien zur Kunde des älteren Englischen Dramas*, 21, Louvain, 1908), 296.
187 Ure, 102.
188 Madelaine, 45.
189 Butler, 223, makes a similar point.
190 Markward, 258.
191 Also cf. Domitia's demand that Paris consent to 'that yet which a brother may / Grant to his sister' and *LS* 5.2.57–61.
192 Butler, 223, observes that the play hovers here between tragedy and tragicomedy. Caesar similarly hesitates in *Rom. Actor* 4.2.141–52.
193 Butler, 223.
194 Brockbank's comment on Othello in the murder scene, 'The Theatre of *Othello*', 198.
195 The biblical episode was itself the subject of a tragedy, *Abraham's Sacrifice* (printed 1577), translated by Arthur Golding from the French original of Theodore Beza (*ES* III, 322). Cf. *Woman Killed* 13.68–9.
196 These comments on Hebrew sacrifice are based on articles in *The Interpreter's Dictionary of the Bible*, 4 vols, ed. G. A. Buttrick *et al.* (New York: Abingdon, 1962).
197 Rajiva Verma, *Myth, Ritual and Shakespeare* (New Delhi: Spantech, 1990), 79.
198 Amyclas speaks of the sacrifices due to the Spartan gods in *BH* 1.2.1–3, and Bassanes' words at 4.2.34–7 reflect the ancient belief that sacrifice could be used to obtain benefits or to avert the gods' anger. Perhaps more significantly, there are at least two references in *BH* to the sacri-

ficial flames on the altar of Vesta, the Roman divinity of the hearth and household who was served by the Vestal Virgins; see 1.1.98n, 2.3.27–31. Vesta was regarded in Renaissance mythology as the goddess of chastity. Ford may have learned about heathen sacrifice from the Bible and from the writings of the Roman historians (Verma (note 197), 92). There are discussions of human sacrifice in sources as diverse as Pliny, Plutarch and Montaigne (Brockbank, 'Upon Such Sacrifices', 227). William Harrison gives an account of the human sacrifices offered by the ancient religions of Britain in his *Description of Britain*, printed in Holinshed's *Chronicle*, 1587, i, p. 39 (quoted in Brockbank, 227).

199 As Michael Cameron Andrews comments, 'Since Fernando's chaste forbearance has been motivated by his respect for Biancha's marriage vows, not his fidelity to the Duke, this account of his conduct seems calculated to save his life' (*The Action of Our Death: The Performance of Death in English Renaissance Drama*, Newark, DE: University of Delaware Press, 1989, 110).

200 Kaufmann (1961, 364–5) makes a similar point about Caraffa's function in the play.

201 Gowing discusses the case of Susanna Wilson, accused of adultery at the Chichester court in 1602: 'The range of threats that Susanna Wilson's behaviour posed to her marriage, her household, and her husband were articulated most clearly in the words attributed to her: about her domestic power, her sexual desires, and her antipathy for her husband. In stories like these the speech of adulterous women defines their characters, in line with the cultural association of women's sexuality with their words' (198).

202 Gowing, 230.

203 Markward, 561.

204 Markward, 306. The papers of the theatre manager Philip Henslowe refer to '1 tomb' (*Henslowe's Diary*, ed. R. A. Foakes and R. T. Rickert, Cambridge: Cambridge University Press, 1961, 319). Dessen comments that this 'apparent all-purpose tomb . . . suggests the availability of a theatrical property that may have corresponded to our sense of "tomb"' (*Recovering*, 179).

205 Dessen, *Recovering*, 179.

206 Markward, 561.

207 Neill, *Issues*, 133; see also 2.1.131n.

208 Neill, *Issues*, 3, 8, 9–13, 18.

209 Robert N. Watson, *The Rest Is Silence: Death as Annihilation in the English Renaissance* (Berkeley: University of California Press, 1994), 2.

210 From de' Medici's commentary on his sonnets, quoted in Wind (note 185), 157.

211 Ure, 102.

212 Oliver, 79–84; Hoskins, 19, 78, 83–4; Stavig, 122–3, 142–3.

213 Waith, 'Exaltation', 58.

214 Kathleen Cohen, *Metamorphosis of a Death Symbol: The Transi Tomb in the Late Middle Ages and the Renaissance* (Berkeley: University of California Press, 1973), 128–32. On transi tombs, 'the traditional idealized portrayal of the deceased was replaced by a gruesome depiction of the physical ravages of death' (Cohen, 1–2). Enshrouded corpses and ema-

ciated cadavers were the dominant forms of transi tombs in England (Cohen, 2).

215 Izaak Walton, *The Lives of John Donne, Sir Henry Wotton, Richard Hooker, George Herbert & Robert Sanderson* (first published separately, 1640–78), ed. George Saintsbury (Oxford: Oxford University Press, 1912), 78. Also see R. C. Bald, *John Donne, A Life* (Oxford: Clarendon Press, 1970), 528–9.

216 George Donne wrote commendatory verses to *LM* and *PW*, referring to Ford as a 'friend' in both poems.

217 Cohen (note 214) gives details of English examples dating from the sixteenth and seventeenth centuries (130–2). See also Houlbrooke, 350.

218 Dessen, *Recovering*, 179.

219 White, 180–4.

220 Peter Brook, *The Empty Space* (Harmondsworth: Penguin, 1990, first published 1968), 98.

221 Quotation from Neill, *Issues*, 357; see 5.3.56.2n for further examples of mock-resurrections. Neill ('Feasts', 55) comments that 'mock funerals and comic resurrections seem to have been a widespread convention of folk drama. They occur as a standard *burla* in the *commedia del l'arte* with its strong carnival links, as well as playing a significant part in the jig convention'. See K. M. Lea, *Italian Popular Comedy* (New York: Russell, 1962), I, 190–1; Charles Read Baskervill, *The Elizabethan Jig and Related Song Drama* (Chicago: University of Chicago Press, 1929), 223.

222 Neill, *Issues*, 313.

223 Neill, 'Neo-stoicism', 37.

224 Eliot, 'Shakespeare and the Stoicism of Seneca' (note 92), 130–1; Leavis, 'Diabolic Intellect', 146.

225 See the Select Bibliography for details of critical studies referred to in this section.

226 *The Dramatic Works of John Ford: with an Introduction, and Notes Critical and Explanatory*, 2 vols (London: John Murray, 1831).

227 S. P. Sherman's 1908 essay on 'Forde's Contribution to the Decadence of the Drama' (in Bang) similarly argues that Ford 'probes the mystery of passion, and presents a study in sex-psychology unequalled and unapproached in the drama of his predecessors and contemporaries' (xi).

228 Francis Jeffrey, 'Article I', review of Weber's edition of Ford, *The Edinburgh Review* XVIII (August 1811), 275–304; 288–9. See also George Downing Whittington, *A Letter to J. P. Kemble, Esq., Involving Strictures on a Recent Edition of John Ford's Dramatic Works* (Cambridge, 1811); John Mitford (?), *A Letter to Richard Heber, Esq., Containing Some Observations on the Merits of Mr Weber's Late Edition of Ford's Dramatic Works* (London, 1812); Octavius Gilchrist, *A Letter to William Gifford, Esq. on the Late Edition of Ford's Plays; Chiefly as Relating to Ben Jonson* (London, 1811). The Whittington piece may have been written by Mitford; see Sargeaunt, 221, n. 35.

229 Erica Weevers, *Images of Love and Religion: Queen Henrietta Maria and Court Entertainments* (Cambridge: Cambridge University Press, 1989), 2–3.

230 Butler argues that there were three distinct and largely independent 'tra-

ditions' of Caroline theatrical activity: the private court theatre, the elite professional theatre and the 'popular tradition' at the open-air playhouses; see *Crisis*, Ch. 8, 'The survival of the popular tradition'.

231 See Hoskins, 28–9, on the possible influence of various courtly love traditions. Attempts to blend Platonic idealism with courtly and Christian love were also familiar from the writings of Marsilio Ficino, whose commentary to the *Symposium* may have influenced Mauruccio's mirror caprice (see 2.1.62LN), and from the work of Pico, Bruno, Bembo and Castiglione (see *Courtier* IV, 303–7, 314). D'Urfé's *L'Astrée*, with its Ficinian principles and chaste heroines, had been available in English (though only in part) since 1620. Notions of courtly love are also prominent in the poetry of Sidney (*Astrophel and Stella* V, LXXI) and Spenser (the *Fowre Hymnes*), and in plays such as *The New Inn*, *The Parliament of Love*, *The Queen's Arcadia*, *The Lover's Progress*, *The Elder Brother*, *Valentinian*, *Monsieur Thomas* and *The Mad Lover*, the last three of which show the influence of *L'Astrée* (Mincoff, 3; Hoskins, 31–2, 34–6, 55).

232 Ben Jonson, Induction to *B. Fair*, quoted by Butler, 201.

233 In *Little Theater Classics*, vol. 3 (Boston: Little, Brown, and Co., 1921).

234 Howard, *The Stage and Social Struggle* (note 63), 83, 92.

235 'Exhortacion concernyng Good Ordre and Obedience to Rulers and Magistrates', in *Certain Sermons or Homilies (1547) and A Homily against Disobedience and Wilful Rebellion (1570): A Critical Edition*, ed. Ronald B. Bond (Toronto: University of Toronto Press, 1987), 161.

236 Howard, 79.

237 'To speak is to possess meaning, to have access to the language which defines, delimits and locates power. To speak is to become a subject' (Belsey, 191).

238 Belsey writes of the 'eternity of possession' which is 'implicit' in the spectacle of Giovanni holding Annabella's heart before him on his dagger (208).

239 Mary Beth Rose, *The Expense of Spirit: Love and Sexuality in English Renaissance Drama* (Ithaca and London: Cornell University Press, 1988), 174.

240 Belsey, 210.

241 Anthony Fletcher, *Gender, Sex and Subordination in England 1500–1800* (New Haven and London: Yale University Press, 1995), 401.

242 G. K. Hunter, *English Drama 1586–1642: The Age of Shakespeare* (Oxford: Clarendon, 1997), 445, in reference to *'Tis Pity*.

243 'I dy in loue's delicious Fire. / O loue, I am thy SACRIFICE' (Crashaw, 'A Song', 1–5).

244 John Greenwood argues that the mannerist practices of Jacobean dramatists include: 'cultivation of illusory awareness'; attempts to 'disrupt or reorient' the audience's perspective (e.g., through 'abrupt juxtapositions'); 'exploitation of picaresque plotting to startle or amaze'; and 'wilful proliferation of the play metaphor . . . to keep the audience continually aware of artifice' (*Shifting Perspectives and the Stylish Style: Mannerism in Shakespeare and His Jacobean Contemporaries*, Toronto: University of Toronto Press, 1988, 22). Neill finds in Ford's plays both 'the distinctive characteristics of mannerist formalism—the demonstrations of artifice and *maniera*, the witty games with convention, the frag-

menting concentration on individual marvels' and 'the more serious aspects of the style—its paradoxical vision of reality, its obsession with relativity and flux, its disintegrated psychology' ('Neo-stoicism', 11). Also see Cyrus Hoy, 'Jacobean Tragedy and the Mannerist Style', *SS* 26 (1973); Mincoff; Jean-Pierre Maquerlot, *Shakespeare and the Mannerist Tradition* (Cambridge: Cambridge University Press, 1995), 24–7.

245 Hoy, 'Jacobean Tragedy'; see also 50, 56.

246 Cf. Robson, 132–3; Rose (note 239), 135.

SELECT BIBLIOGRAPHY

The following is a selection of works presenting critical commentary on *Love's Sacrifice*. Works discussed in 'Responses' in the Introduction are marked with an asterisk. Works referred to in the Abbreviations and References are given only in abbreviated form.

Ali, Florence, *Opposing Absolutes: Conviction and Convention in John Ford's Plays*, Salzburg Studies in English Literature; Jacobean Drama Studies (Institut für Englische Sprache und Literatur, Universität Salzburg, 1974).

Anderson, Donald K., ed., *Concord in Discord*.

——, *John Ford* (New York: Twayne, 1972).

Andrews, Michael Cameron, *The Action of Our Death: The Performance of Death in English Renaissance Drama* (Newark: University of Delaware Press, 1989).

[Anonymous], 'The Early English Dramatists; John Ford', *The Southern Literary Messenger* 15 (1849), 656–64.

Boas, Frederick S., *An Introduction to Stuart Drama* (Oxford: Oxford University Press, 1946).

Bueler, Lois E., 'Role-splitting and Reintegration: The Tested Woman Plot in Ford', *SEL* 20 (1940), 325–44.

Bullen, A. H., 'John Ford', *DNB*, VII.

*Butler (1988).

Clark, Ira, *Professional Playwrights; Massinger, Ford, Shirley, & Brome* (Lexington: University Press of Kentucky, 1992).

Davril (1954).

Dessen, *Recovering* (1995).

Eliot, T. S., 'John Ford', *Elizabethan Dramatists* (London: Faber, 1963).

*Ellis-Fermor, Una, *The Jacobean Drama, An Interpretation* (London: Methuen, 1936).

Ewing, S. Blaine, Jr, *Burtonian Melancholy in the Plays of John Ford*, Princeton Studies in English, 19 (Princeton: Princeton University Press, 1940).

Farr (1979).

Gifford, William, 'Article IX' (Review of Weber's edition of Ford's dramatic works), *The Quarterly Review* 6 (1811), 462–87.

*Grierson, Herbert J. C., *The First Half of the Seventeenth Century* (Edinburgh and London: Blackwood, 1906).

Hillman, Richard, *Self-speaking in Medieval and Early Modern English Drama: Subjectivity, Discourse and the Stage* (Basingstoke: Macmillan, 1997).

Hopkins, 'Coterie Values'.

——, *Political Theatre*.
*Huebert, *Baroque*.
*Jeffrey, Francis, 'Article I' (review of Weber's edition), *The Edinburgh Review* XVIII (August 1811), 275–304.
*Kaufmann (1960).
*Kirsch, Arthur C., *Jacobean Dramatic Perspectives* (Charlottesville: University Press of Virginia, 1972).
Leech (1957).
Levin, Richard, *The Multiple Plot in English Renaissance Drama* (Chicago and London: University of Chicago Press, 1971).
Lomax, *Stage Images* (1987).
Lowell, James Russell, *Conversations on some of the Old Poets* (Cambridge: Owen, 1846).
*McLuskie, 'Language and Matter' (1988).
*——, *Renaissance Dramatists* (1989).
McMaster (1969).
Madelaine (1988).
Merrivale, J. H., 'Article IV' (review of Gifford's edition of Ford), *The Monthly Review*, 3rd series, 5 (1829).
Neill, ed., *Critical Re-Visions*.
*——, *Issues of Death* (1997).
——, 'Neo-stoicism' (1974).
*Neilson, W. A., 'Ford and Shirley', in *CHEL*, ed. A. W. Ward and A. R. Waller (Cambridge: Cambridge University Press, 1910; repr. 1969), VI.
*Oliver (1955).
Opie (1988).
*Orbison (1963).
*Ornstein, Robert, *The Moral Vision of Jacobean Tragedy* (Madison and Milwaukee: University of Wisconsin Press, 1965).
Parrott, Thomas Marc, and Robert Hamilton Ball, *A Short View of Elizabethan Drama* (New York: Scribner, 1958).
Robson (1983).
Salingar, Leo, 'The Decline of Tragedy', in *The Age of Shakespeare*, ed. Boris Ford, Pelican Guide to English Literature (Harmondsworth: Penguin, 1955).
*Sargeaunt (1935).
Schelling, Felix E., *Elizabethan Drama 1558–1642*, 2 vols (New York: Russell, 1959).
*Sensabaugh, G. F., 'John Ford and Platonic Love in the Court', *SP* 36 (1939), 206–26.
*——, *The Tragic Muse of John Ford* (New York and London: Blom, 1944).
*Sherman, S. P., 'Forde's Contribution to the Decadence of the Drama', in Bang, vol. 23, 1908.
Sorge, Thomas, 'Baroque Theatricality and Anxiety in the Drama of John Ford', in *Jacobean Drama as Social Criticism*, ed. James Hogg (Lewiston, New York and Salzburg: Edwin Meller Press, 1995), 125–45.
*Stavig (1968).
*Swinburne, Charles Algernon, 'John Ford', *The Fortnightly Review*, n.s., 10 (1871), 42–63.

Telford Moore (1993).
*Tomlinson, T. B., *A Study of Elizabethan and Jacobean Tragedy* (Cambridge: Cambridge University Press, 1964).
*Ure (1974).
Waith (1986).
Ward, Adolphus William, *A History of English Dramatic Literature to the Death of Queen Anne*, 3 vols (London: Macmillan, 1899).
Wymer (1995).

LOVE'S SACRIFICE

The Epistle Dedicatory

To my truest friend, my worthiest kinsman,
John Ford of Gray's Inn, Esquire

The title of this little work, my good cousin, is in sense but the argument of a dedication, which being in most writers a custom, in many a compliment, I question not but your clear knowledge of my intents will in me read as the earnest of affection. My ambition herein aims at a fair flight, borne upon the double wings of gratitude for a received, and acknowledgement for a continued love. It is not so frequent to number many kinsmen, and amongst them some friends, as to presume on some friends, and amongst them little friendship. But in every fullness of these particulars, I do not more partake through you, my

3. this little work] *italic in Q.* my] *all eds;* may *Q.* 5. a custom] *italic in Q.* compliment] *italic in Q.* 7. earnest of affection] *italic in Q.* 8. upon] vp on *Q.* 13. through you] *italic in Q.*

Neill notes a 'remarkable proliferation of occasional material' in the early seventeenth century. The numerous dedications, prefaces and encomiastic verses attached to editions of plays, especially after 1616, constitute 'a claim to serious regard' and reflect 'a growing esteem for the drama in educated circles' ('Wits', 350–1).

2. *John Ford*] The playwright's older cousin; a member of Gray's Inn since 1614. Also a dedicatee of *LM* (1629), he contributed commendatory verses to *PW* (1634).

3–4. *The . . . dedication*] i.e. the theme (*argument*) of this dedication is a sacrifice of my love to you. Cf. *Elegy by WS*, 205–7, 'And I here to thy memorable worth, / In this last act of friendship, sacrifice / My love to thee'.

4–7. *which . . . affection*] i.e. while for other writers such dedications are a mere custom or complimentary show, I am confident that your *clear knowledge* of my intentions will enable you to interpret this dedication as a genuine token (*earnest*) of my affection. *Intents* = 'purposes, wishes, meaning', or 'mind, spirit' (*OED* 1, 4, 5). For *earnest*, see 2.2.236n.

11–12. *some . . . friendship*] Cf. *GM*, 1128–30; *Trial*, Epistle, 16–20, *CBS*, 905–6 (*Nondram. Wks*, 415, n.1128–30).

12–13. *in . . . particulars*] i.e. in every aspect of kinship and friendship (Hoskins).

cousin, the delight, than enjoy the benefit of them. This inscription to your name is only a faithful deliverance to memory of the truth of my respects to virtue, and to the equal in honour with virtue, desert. The contempt thrown on studies of this kind by such as dote on their own singularity hath almost so outfaced invention and prescribed judgement, that it is more safe, more wise, to be suspectedly silent than modestly confident of opinion herein. Let me be bold to tell the severity of censurers how willingly I neglect their practice, so long as I digress from no becoming thankfulness. Accept then, my cousin, this

15. inscription . . . name] *italic in Q.* 16. memory] *italic in Q.* 17. desert] *italic in Q.* 18. studies . . . kind] *italic in Q.* 19. invention] *italic in Q.* prescribed] *Q;* proscribed *GD.* 20. judgement] *italic in Q.* 20–21. suspectedly silent] *italic in Q.* 21. modestly confident] *italic in Q.*

---

16. *memory*] posterity, remembrance.

17–21. *The . . . herein*] A reference to 'hypercritical' audiences, or to William Prynne, who had attacked the drama in *Histriomastix* (1632). See LN and headnote to Shirley's poem.

18–19. *singularity*] probably 'the fact or quality of differing or dissenting from others or from what is generally accepted, especially in thought or religion; personal, individual, or independent action, judgement, etc., especially in order to render one's self conspicuous' (*OED* 7). The sense 'eccentricity' is not recorded before 1768 (*OED* 8b; cf. *singular* 9b). Perhaps refers to the kind of opinionated theatre-goer satirised by Jonson in the figure of Mr Damplay in *The Magnetic Lady* (see Neill, 'Wits', 349).

19. *outfaced*] put out of countenance, silenced by impudence or arrogance (*OED* v. 1).

invention] creativity, imagination.

prescribed] 'dictated' or 'limited, restricted' (*OED* 2, 4). Gifford's 'proscribed' is plausible, since 'prescribe' was 'formerly frequent for proscribe' (*OED*).

20–1. *more safe . . . herein*] 'Generall collections [i.e. remarks] meet (not seldome) with particular applications, and those so dangerous, that it is more safe, more wise, to professe a free silence, then a necessarie industrie' (*LOL*, Preface, 9–12).

21. *opinion*] probably 'favourable estimate; esteem' (*OED* 5b).

herein] i.e. in regard to *invention* and *judgement.*

22. *severity of censurers*] A frequent concern in Ford's prefaces; cf. those for *Trial*, 23–6; *LM*, 7–8; *BH*, 19–20.

23. *neglect*] disregard, slight (*OED* 1).

practice] Has a range of senses, from 'dealings, intercourse' to 'collusion, machinations, schemes' (*OED* 6a, b).

24. *becoming*] befitting.

witness to posterity of my constancy to your merits; for no ties of blood, no engagements of friendship, shall more justly live a precedent than the sincerity of both in the heart of

JOHN FORD

25. witness to posterity] *italic in Q.* 26. ties] *italic in Q.* friendship] *italic in Q.* 27. precedent] *GD;* President *Q;* president *W.* both] *italic in Q.*

---

27. *justly*] truly, accurately.

precedent] sign, token, example. Perhaps picturing his heartfelt feelings as the 'original document' (another sense of *precedent*) of his *ties* to his cousin (*OED* 1d, e).

To my Friend Mr John Ford

Unto this altar, rich with thy own spice,
I bring one grain to thy *Love's Sacrifice*;
And boast to see thy flames ascending, while
Perfumes enrich our air from thy sweet pile.

Look here, thou that hast malice to the stage,
And impudence enough for the whole age:
Voluminously ignorant! Be vexed
To read this tragedy, and thy own be next.

JAMES SHIRLEY

1–8.] *Poem set in italic.* 5. thou] *capitals in Q.* 6. impudence] *roman in Q.* 7. Voluminously ignorant!] *roman in Q.*

See LN for comment on (a) Shirley's association with Ford; (b) the poem's apparent references to William Prynne.

1. *spice*] incense, often used in Hebrew sacrifice (Leviticus 16:12–13), and usually seen as representing the worshipper's prayer (Psalms 141:2). Thus Shirley is adding his own 'prayer' to Ford's sacrifice to love. The *altar* (1) may = the play itself or possibly the printed book in which it is presented.

3. *flames ascending*] perhaps with the complimentary implication that Ford's stature as a dramatist is continuing to grow.

4. *thy sweet pile*] i.e. the play itself. Sacrifical offerings are 'of a sweet savour unto the Lord' (Leviticus 1:9).

5. *thou*] addressing William Prynne (see LN); Q's 'THOV' highlights the change of addressee. 'Thov towards strangers who were not inferiors was an insult' (Abbott 233).

8. *thy own*] Gilchrist (33–4) suspects that this is a reference to Prynne's anticipated downfall, prompted by the full title of his work: *Histriomastix, the Players Scourge, or Actor's Tragedie*. In his epistle to *The Bird in a Cage* (1633) Shirley mockingly remarks that he had heard that Prynne had 'lately written a TRAGEDIE'. Shirley's prophecy was all too accurate. Prynne had his ears cropped and was heavily fined, deprived of his academic degrees, and sentenced to life imprisonment. He was released by the Long Parliament in 1640. (See LN for this poem.)

The Speakers in this Tragedy

Philippo Caraffa	DUKE of Pavy
Paolo Baglione	Uncle to the Duchess [and ABBOT of Monaco]
FERNANDO	Favourite to the Duke
FERENTES	A wanton courtier
ROSEILLI	A young nobleman
PETRUCCIO, NIBRASSA	Two counsellors of state
Roderico D'AVOLOS	Secretary to the Duke
MAURUCCIO	An old antic
GIACOPO	Servant to Mauruccio
Attendants	
Guards	
Two Friars	
	Women
BIANCA	The Duchess
FIORMONDA	The Duke's sister

'The Speakers in this Tragedy'] *Arranged as in Q.* Paolo] *Q (Paulo);* Paul *H (as in 1.1.115, 2.2.76).* and ABBOT of Monaco] *this ed.; E lists 'Abbot of Monaco' as separate character.* PETRUCCIO] *Petruchio Q (spelt thus throughout).* D'AVOLOS] *GD; D'auolos Q.* MAURUCCIO] *Maurucio Q (spelt thus throughout).* Guards] *this ed.* Two Friars] *this ed.*
BIANCA] *Biancha Q (spelt thus throughout).*

---

1. *Caraffa*] Carafa (*sic*) was the name of Donna Maria D'Avalos's lover, Fabrizio, of her first husband, Federico, and of the husband of Donna Maria's daughter by her first marriage, Marcantonio. See Intro., p. 30, App. 3.

2. *ABBOT*] He is said to have become a cardinal at 3.2.10–11, but dialogue and SDs continue to refer to him as an Abbot.

9. *Roderico D'AVOLOS*] The Habsburg army which defeated Francis I of France at Pavia in 1525 was commanded by Fernando Francisco de Avalos, Marchese di Pescara. The name also features in the Corona MS; see Intro., p. 30, App. 3. Iago's sidekick is named *Roderigo*.

10. *antic*] clown; player of a grotesque or ludicrous part (*OED* B 4).

16. *BIANCA*] Italian, 'white'. There are several plays on her name; see 2.3.84n.

COLONA Daughter to Petruccio
JULIA Daughter to Nibrassa
MORONA An old lady

The Scene: PAVY

PAVY] *PAVYE Q.*

---

21. *PAVY*] Pavia, the province and its capital in the Lombardy region of northern Italy, 20 miles south of Milan. The seat of government under the Lombards and the Carolingian kings, and a rival of Milan from as early as the eleventh century, Pavia was subdued by the Visconti in 1360 and later became part of the Duchy of Milan. In 1525, Francis I of France was defeated there by the Habsburg emperor Charles V. Spanish forces played a decisive role in the battle, and the Spanish hegemony in Italy (perhaps alluded to in 1.2.248–59) dates from that time. The Duchy of Milan was annexed to the Spanish crown in 1540. See 2.2.115n for possible references to Pavian landmarks.

With its petty-minded, egotistical ruler and its air of intrigue and ruthless individualism, the Italy of *LS* is essentially that of the Italianate plays of Marston, Webster and Massinger, a product of a deliberately selective approach to Italian history: 'The world of competing princelings, bearing names like Sforza, Gonzaga, d'Este, and Medici, belongs to the period portrayed in Guicciardini's *Storia d'Italia* (1492–1534)' (G. K. Hunter, 'English Folly and Italian Vice: The Moral Landscape of John Marston', *Jacobean Theatre*, Stratford-upon-Avon Studies I, 1960, 95).

Act I

ACT I SCENE I

Enter ROSEILLI *and* RODERICO D'AVOLOS.

Roseilli. Depart the court?
D'Avolos. Such was the Duke's command.
Roseilli. You're secretary to the state and him,
Great in his counsels, wise, and, I think, honest:
Have you, in turning over old records,
Read but one name descended of the house
Of Lesui in his loyalty remiss?
D'Avolos. Never, my lord.
Roseilli. Why then should I now, now, when glorious peace
Triumphs in change of pleasures, be wiped off,

Act I, etc.] *Actus Primus*, etc. *Q*. 1.1.1. court?] court. *Q*; court *W*. 3. You're] You'ar *Q*. 7. Lesui] *Q*; Lesim *H*.

1.1.1–25.] *W. Devil* also begins with a banishment. Ford's debts to *W. Devil* and *Malfi* (for which he wrote commendatory verses) are discussed on pp. 35–6, 40–1, 44.

3. *secretary . . . him*] i.e. a minister as well as private secretary to the Duke. The title 'Secretary of State/Estate' was used throughout the seventeenth century for either of the two officials jointly holding the position. Cf. 'Speakers' Names' and 2.2.60n. *Secretary* also = one who is privy to personal or secret matters. (*OED* sb.[1] 1, 2, 3).

4. *Great . . . counsels*] fully in his confidence; eminent in his private discussions. Hoskins compares Jeremiah 32:19, 'Great in his counsel, and mighty in work' (1611).

7. *Lesui*] apparently Ford's invention. Hoskins conjectures that Ford may have written 'Lesim', thinking of Lesima, a mountain 30 miles south of Pavia.

10. *change*] 'Variety, advent', or 'mutual interchange', as in *'Tis Pity* 1.2.201. A favourite word of Ford's; cf. 41, 152.

pleasures] May refer to entertainments (triumphs) celebrating the 'peace' (9). Perhaps an early sign that 'the society of the court is completely given over to self-gratification' (Robson, 113).

Like to a useless moth, from courtly ease;
And whither must I go?

D'Avolos. You have the open world before you.

Roseilli. Why then, 'tis like I'm banished.

D'Avolos. Not so: my warrant is only to command you from the court, within five hours to depart after notice taken, and not to live within thirty miles of it, until it be thought meet by his Excellence to call you back. Now I have warned you, my lord, at your peril be it if you disobey. I shall inform the Duke of your discontent. *Exit.*

Roseilli. Do, politician, do. I scent the plot
Of this disgrace. 'Tis Fiormonda, she,
That glorious widow, whose commanding check
Ruins my love. Like foolish beasts, thus they
Find danger that prey too near the lion's den.

Enter FERNANDO *and* PETRUCCIO.

Fernando. My noble lord Roseilli.
Roseilli. Sir, the joy

11. ease;] ease? *W;* ease: *Q.* 15–20.] *As verse in Q.* 21–2.] *W;* Doe . . . doe: / I . . . shee, *Q.* 23. check] *Q;* cheek *W.* 25. lion's] *W;* lions *Q;* lions' *GD.*

---

11. *moth*] 'idler' (?), as in *Oth.* 1.3.256; but also a type of insignificance and fragility (*OED* 1c). The simile may be influenced by the proverbial image of moth burnt by flame (Tilley F 394), the flame here being the court, or perhaps Fiormonda.

courtly ease] leisurely life at court; cf. 'court-ease', *BH* 2.2.118.

15. *from*] to go from (with the common ellipsis of the verb of motion; cf. 90).

17–18. *until . . . back*] Apparently misrepresenting Caraffa's order; cf. 1.2.246–7.

18. *meet*] proper.

21. *politician*] crafty plotter.

21–2. *plot Of*] scheme behind.

23. *glorious*] haughty.

widow] Popular culture characterised the widow 'as rampantly sexual, calculating, disorderly, and knowing . . . Medical theorists constructed the widow's sexuality as voracious: unlike the maid, she knew what sexual pleasure was, and sought it'. 'Attitudes to the remarriage of widows were increasingly negative during the early modern period' (Mendelson and Crawford, 68–9).

check] curb, rebuff, reproof (*OED* sb.[1] 4).

25. *lion's den*] archetypal place of great danger (cf. Psalms 22:21; 2 Tim. 4:17; Whitney, 210).

I should have welcomed you with is wrapped up
In clouds of my disgrace. Yet, honoured sir,
Howsoever frowns of great ones cast me down,
My service shall pay tribute in my lowness
To your uprising virtues.

Fernando. Sir, I know
You are so well acquainted with your own,
You need not flatter mine. Trust me, my lord,
I'll be a suitor for you.

Petruccio. And I'll second
My nephew's suit with importunity.

Roseilli. You are, my lord Fernando, late returned
From travels. Pray instruct me. Since the voice
Of most supreme authority commands
My absence, I determine to bestow
Some time in learning languages abroad.
Perhaps the change of air may change in me
Remembrance of my wrongs at home. Good sir,
Inform me: say I meant to live in Spain,
What benefit of knowledge might I treasure?

29. Howsoever] *Q;* Howso'er *GD.*

---

27. *wrapped up*] hidden.

30. *service*] respect, duty.

lowness] (a) reduced circumstances; (b) humility.

31. *uprising virtues*] i.e. admirable qualities that are winning Fernando greater favour at court. Roseilli contrasts these with his own 'low' circumstances, perhaps aware that he and Fernando are at opposite points on the Wheel of Fortune (Hoskins).

32. *acquainted*] familiar (because Roseilli, too, has virtues).

33. *flatter*] praise too fully, exaggerate.

34. *suitor*] petitioner.

36–83.] Such discussions of national characteristics were something of a set piece in the drama; cf. *Malcontent* 3.1.91–6; Massinger, *The Guardian* 2.1.1–6; Shirley, *The Humorous Courtier* 4.2, *Gypsy* 1.1.3–7. *Malfi* opens with an account of developments at the French court.

36. *late*] recently.

37. *travels*] According to Peacham's *The Compleat Gentleman* (1622), 'a necessary prerequisite for anyone who sought to be a true gentleman'. The book's great popularity 'testifed to what had become by then a fixed habit among the gentry and aristocracy' (Howarth, 32).

instruct] inform, advise.

39. *determine to bestow*] have decided to spend.

44. *treasure*] 'lay up (in the mind)' or 'cherish' (*OED* 2, 4).

Fernando. Troth, sir, I'll freely speak as I have found.
In Spain you lose experience. 'Tis a climate
Too hot to nourish arts; the nation proud,
And in their pride unsociable; the court
More pliable to glorify itself
Than do a stranger grace. If you intend
To traffic like a merchant, 'twere a place
Might better much your trade, but as for me,
I soon took surfeit on it.
Roseilli. What for France?
Fernando. France I more praise and love. You are, my lord,
Yourself for horsemanship much famed, and there
You shall have many proofs to show your skill.
The French are passing courtly, ripe of wit,
Kind, but extreme dissemblers. You shall have
A Frenchman ducking lower than your knee,
At th'instant mocking even your very shoe-ties.
To give the country due, it is on earth
A paradise; and if you can neglect
Your own appropriaments, but praising that

47. Too] *W*; To *Q*, *H*.

---

45. *Troth*] in truth, indeed.

46–53.] Contemporary references to Spanish affluence and pride—'the disease of the Spaniard' (Nashe, *Pierce Penilesse*, 176)—are legion; see Sugden.

46. *lose*] fail to profit from, waste (*OED* v.[1] 6).

47. *arts*] 'learning,' or perhaps 'the arts'. The plural form was applied in the Middle Ages to the liberal arts, the seven subjects of the *trivium* and *quadrivium*; but the second sense was current in Ford's time.

49. *pliable*] inclined (*OED* 2).

glorify] exult triumphantly in, vaunt (*OED* v.[1] 1).

50. *grace*] kindness, favour.

53–65.] More conventional observations about a country's character. Cf. *BH* 2.3.124; Webster, *Cure for a Cuckold* 5.1.328–30.

56. *many . . . skill*] Perhaps referring to 'the numerous tournaments and chivalrous games at the French court' (Weber). French expertise in horsemanship was much admired; cf. *Haml.* 4.7.82. *Proofs* = trials.

57. *passing*] exceedingly.

59. *ducking*] bowing. The French practice of bowing very low was much commented upon; e.g. Jonson, *The Case Is Altered* 2.3.7; Brome, *Antipodes* 1.3.65.

62–3. *neglect . . . appropriaments*] ignore or dispraise your own parts or accomplishments. *Appropriament* = 'what is proper or peculiar to one; a characteristic' (*OED*).

In others wherein you excel yourself,
You shall be much beloved there.
Roseilli. Yet methought
I heard you and the duchess, two nights since,
Discoursing of an island thereabouts
Called—let me think—'twas—
Fernando. England?
Roseilli. That. Pray, sir,
You have been there; methought I heard you praise it.
Fernando. I'll tell you what I found there. Men as neat,
As courtly as the French, but in condition
Quite opposite. Put case that you, my lord,
Could be more rare on horseback than you are:
If there—as there are many—one excelled
You in your art as much as you do others,
Yet will the English think their own is nothing
Compared with you, a stranger. In their habits
They are not more fantastic than uncertain.
In short, their fair abundance, manhood, beauty,
No nation can disparage but itself.
Roseilli. My lord, you have much eased me. I resolve.
Fernando. And whither are you bent?
Roseilli. My lord, for travel
To speed for England.
Fernando. No, my lord, you must not.

68. England?] *GD;* England. *Q.* That.] *this ed.;* That, *Q;* That: *W.* 78. fantastic than] *all eds.;* fantasticket han *Q.* 79. fair abundance] *GD;* fare abundance; *Q;* fare, abundance *W.*

---

70. *neat*] spruce.

71. *condition*] temper, character.

72. *Put case*] suppose. To 'put case' = 'to propound a hypothetical instance or illustration' (*OED case* sb.[1] 12).

73. *rare*] outstanding.

75. *art*] 'skill' or 'skilled occupation'.

77. *stranger*] foreigner.

78. *fantastic*] capricious, extravagant, odd, irrational (*OED* 4b); 'whimsical' (Coles).

uncertain] irresolute, unassured.

79. *abundance*] plentiful supply of the good things in life, affluence.

manhood] manliness; 'qualities becoming a man, bravery, fortitude, honour' (Schmidt; cf. *A&C* 3.10.22–3).

83. *speed*] make haste. Fernando replies that Roseilli must not leave hastily; he does not necessarily oppose his going altogether.

I have yet some private conference
To impart unto you for your good. At night
I'll meet you at my lord Petruccio's house.
Till then, be secret.
Roseilli. Dares my cousin trust me?
Petruccio. Dare I, my lord? Yes, 'less your fact were greater
Than a bold woman's spleen.
Roseilli. The Duke's at hand,
And I must hence. My service to your lordships. *Exit.*
Petruccio. Now, nephew, as I told you, since the Duke
Hath held the reins of state in his own hand,
Much altered from the man he was before
(As if he were transformèd in his mind),

* * *

To soothe him in his pleasures, amongst whom
Is fond Ferentes; one whose pride takes pride
In nothing more than to delight his lust.
And he—with grief I speak it—hath, I fear,
Too much besotted my unhappy daughter,
My poor Colona, whom, for kindred's sake,
As you are noble, as you honour virtue,
Persuade to love herself. A word from you

85. To impart] *Q;* T'impart *GD.* good. At night] *W;* good: at night *Q.*
95. *As S; lacuna not indicated in Q; GD place lacuna at 94.*

---

84. *conference*] Usually = 'discourse, conversation', but here = 'information, news' or 'plan, scheme'—senses not recorded by *OED*. Gifford claims that Fernando's plan never comes to light, but the *conference* may have to do with the disguise plot of Act 3.

87. *secret*] discreet.

88. *'less*] unless.

fact] misdeed, wrongdoing. Cf. the phrase 'accessary before the fact'.

89. *spleen*] malice, ill humour, proud temper. He evidently knows that Fiormonda is behind Roseilli's fall from grace. 'Spleen' is specifically associated with women in *'Tis Pity* 2.2.127; see Barker, 118–19.

90. *hence*] go from here (see 15n).

service] see 30n.

93–5.] Editors agree that a line or so has been lost at this point. The subject of Petruccio's speech, corruption at court, raises the possibility that the lacuna is a result of censorship; see App. 1a.

96. *soothe*] humour, flatter.

97. *fond*] foolish.

103. *love*] show regard for.

May win her more than my entreats or frowns.
Fernando. Uncle, I'll do my best. Meantime, pray tell me
Whose mediation wrought the marriage
Betwixt the Duke and Duchess? Who was agent?
Petruccio. His roving eye and her enchanting face,
The only dower nature had ordained
T'advance her to her bride-bed. She was daughter
Unto a gentleman of Milan, no better;
Preferred to serve in the Duke of Milan's court,
Where for her beauty she was greatly famed.
And passing late from thence to Monaco,
To visit there her uncle, Paul Baglione,
The Abbot, Fortune—queen to such blind matches—
Presents her to the Duke's eye on the way
As he pursues the deer. In short, my lord,
He saw her, loved her, wooed her, won her, matched her;

104. entreats] *GD*; entreaties *Q*; intreats *W.* 107. Duchess?] *Q*; duchess, *GD.* agent?] *Q*; agent. *GD.* 111. of] *Q*; at *W.* 112. in the] *Q*; i' th' *W.* 115. Baglione] *W*; *Bagloone Q.*

---

104. *entreats*] entreaties.
106. *marriage*] (trisyllabic).
107. *agent*] intermediary or initiator.
110. *advance*] raise to a higher social position.
bride-bed] marriage bed.
112. *Preferred*] promoted, favoured; cf. *BH* 1.1.104–5.
the Duke of Milan] Recalling *The Duke of Milan* (published 1623), by Ford's friend Philip Massinger; an important influence on *LS* (see notes to 127–34, 128, 132–4, etc.; Intro., p. 28). For historical details see note to 'Pavy' in 'The Speakers of this Tragedy'.
114. *late*] recently.
115. *Paul*] Thus named here and at 2.2.76, but called '*Paulo*' in Q's list of characters.
116. *Fortune*] The goddess Fortune—proverbially blind (Tilley F 604).
119.] A common expression (Tilley W 731; cf. *Shrew* 1.1.142; *FM*, 168; *PW* 1.2.60). Gifford cites Ovid, *Fasti*, III.21: 'Mars videt hanc, visamque cupit, potiturque cupita' ('Mars sees her, seeing he desires, desiring he enjoys her', transl. Henry T. Riley, London: George Bell, 1879)—a passage quoted in part in *Anatomy* III.2.2.2, p. 76. 'Levinus Lemnius reckons up three things which generally disturb the peace of marriage: the first is when they marry intempestive or unseasonably, "as many mortal men marry precipitately and inconsiderately when they are effete and old; the second, when they marry unequally for fortunes and birth; the third, when a sick impotent person weds one that is sound"' (*Anatomy*, III.3.4.2, p. 302). Cf. 4.1.224–7, 5.1.73–7.

No counsel could divert him.
Fernando. She is fair.
Petruccio. She is. And to speak truth, I think right noble
In her conditions.
Fernando. If, when I should choose,
Beauty and virtue were the fee proposed,
I should not pass for parentage.
Petruccio. The Duke
Doth come.
Fernando. Let's break off talk. [*Aside*] If ever, now,
Good angel of my soul, protect my truth.

Enter DUKE, BIANCA, FIORMONDA, NIBRASSA, FERENTES, JULIA *and* D'AVOLOS.

Duke. Come, my Bianca, revel in mine arms,
Whiles I, rapt in my admiration, view

122. conditions] *Q;* condition *G.* 125. *Aside*] *GD; no aside Q.* 128. Whiles] *Q;* Whilst *W.*

---

121. *right*] truly.
122. *conditions*] character, quality.
123. *fee*] payment; dowry.
124. *pass for*] care about. Cf. *1 Tamb.* 1.1.109, 'I pass not for his threats'. *parentage*] 'extraction, birth' or 'noble descent' (*OED* 4).
125. Aside] Q does not indicate asides. These words are marked thus because: (a) Petruccio gives no indication that he knows of Fernando's love for Bianca; (b) Fernando has just asked his uncle to 'break off talk'. The difficulty of knowing *how* asides were indicated in the theatre is discussed by Dessen, *Recovering*, 53–5.
126. *Good angel . . . soul*] genius, tutelary spirit, daemon, 'that thy spirit which keeps thee' (*A&C* 2.3.17). Cf. 5.1.110. Guardian angels were said to be appointed by the 'higher Powers' to 'protect or punish [human beings], as they see cause; and are called *boni* and *mali Genii* by the Romans' (*Anatomy*, I.2.1.2, p. 181; quoted in *'Tis Pity* 2.2.159n).
truth] genuineness, honesty, righteousness or fidelity. Cf. *BH* 2.3.79.
127–34.] Perhaps modelled on the first speech of Sforza in *Milan* 1.3.11–27. Also cf. the Duke's speech in *WBW* 3.3.22–8 (which ends with the line 'Glory of Florence, light into mine arms!'). See Intro., p. 28.
127. *revel*] indulge in pleasures. The whole phrase could = 'enjoy my embraces'.
128. *rapt in*] (a) enraptured, transported with (cf. *Mac.* 1.5.5–6); (b) enwrapped, as she is enveloped in his arms. Q's spelling, 'wrapt', points up the double sense. Sforza uses 'rap't' in *Milan* 1.3.133.
admiration] wonder mingled with reverence (*OED* 2).

Lilies and roses growing in thy cheeks.
Fernando! O thou half my self! No joy
Could make my pleasures full without thy presence.
I am a monarch of felicity,
Proud in a pair of jewels rich and beautiful:
A perfect friend, a wife above compare.
Fernando. Sir, if a man so low in rank may hope,
By loyal duty and devoted zeal,
To hold a correspondence in friendship
With one so mighty as the Duke of Pavy,
My uttermost ambition is to climb
To those deserts may give the style of servant.
Duke. —Of partner in my dukedom, in my heart,
As freely as the privilege of blood

132. of] *Q;* in *W.* 134. above] *Q;* without *W.* 137. correspondence] *Q, this ed.;* correspondency *all other eds.* 140. give] *Q;* grace *W.*

---

129. *Lilies and roses*] Symbolising 'Chastitie' and 'Shamfastness' in Henry Hawkins's *Parthenia sacra* (1633, quoted in *Private Life*, 212). A conventional image; cf. *'Tis Pity* 1.2.200–1; *Queen*, 2407–13; *Historie of Orlando Furioso*, 1062–4; Campion's 'There is a Garden in her Face', l. 2.

130. *thou . . . self*] 'Well said one of his friend, Thou half of my soul: for I still thought my soul and his soul to have been but one soul in two bodies' (St Augustine, *Confessions* IV, vi, in William Watts's 1631 translation; Loeb, 1912). Friends were often seen as 'Like to a double cherry: seeming parted, / But yet an union in partition' (*MND* 3.2.210–11). Like lovers, they were thought to desire union in one body, for 'human nature was originally one . . . and the desire and pursuit of the whole is called love' (Plato, *Symposium* 192–3; cf. Aristotle, *Ethics* 4.4; Horace, *Odes* 3, l. 8; Tilley F 696; *Son.* 42, l.13; *LS*, 196).

131. *pleasures*] 'enjoyment' or 'wishes'.

132–4. *I am . . . compare*] Cf. Sforza in *Milan* 3.1.267–9: 'I am stor'd with / Two blessings most desir'd in humaine life, / A constant friend, an vnsuspected wife'.

132.] perhaps with implication that even happiness is at his command.

137. *correspondence*] relation (*OED* 4). Weber's popular emendation to 'correspondency' regularises the metre but is not strictly necessary.

139–40. *My . . . servant*] Rather formulaic; cf. Philomusus, 63–4: 'An humble addresse to a great Lord', where the courtier is advised to protest to the lord that he is bound 'to desire that you would always reckon me in the number of your most obliged servants'.

140. *deserts*] dues, merits (which).

style] title.

142. *freely*] with the rights of free birth; with absolute possession (*OED* 5, quoting *TwN* 1.4.39–40: 'thou shalt live as freely as thy lord, / To call his fortunes thine').

Hath made them mine. Philippo and Fernando
Shall be without distinction. Look, Bianca,
On this good man. In all respects to him
Be as to me. Only the name of husband
And reverent observance of our bed
Shall differ us in persons; else in soul
We are all one.

Bianca. I shall, in best of love,
Regard the bosom-partner of my lord.

Fiormonda. [*Aside*] Ferentes.

Ferentes. [*Aside*] Madam?

Fiormonda. [*Aside*] You are one loves courtship:
He had some change of words; 'twere no lost labour
To stuff your table-books. The man speaks wisely.

143. mine.] *this ed.; mine, Q;* mine; *W.* 151. *Fiormonda. Aside*] *aside to Feren. G; no aside Q. Ferentes. (Aside)*] *aside to Fior. GD; no aside Q.* courtship:] *W;* courtship, *Q;* courtship; *S.* 152. had] *Q;* hath *GD.* 153. table-books.] *this ed.;* table-books, *Q;* table-books; *W;* table-books: *H.*

---

143. *them*] i.e. *my dukedom* and *my heart.*

144. *without distinction*] 'Equal, without discrimination' (cf. *PW* 3.2.105); but perhaps also 'indistinguishable', since Caraffa thinks of Fernando, in Platonic terms, as 'thou half my self' (130) and 'my but divided self' (196). Sforza tells his friend Francisco that he has 'in my Dukedome made you next my selfe', and calls Francisco 'My second selfe' (*Milan* 1.3.279, 4.3.71).

148. *differ*] distinguish.

in persons] 'as individuals'—in a physical sense, as distinct from *in soul.* 'Person' often refers to the identity of royalty (e.g., *LLL* 1.1.179), a distinction Caraffa wishes to overlook.

151. *one loves*] one who loves (common omission of relative pronoun—Abbott 244).

courtship] courtliness, elegance of speech and manners (*OED* 5; cf. *Trial* 2.1.624–6; 'Contract', 22).

152. *change of words*] skilful, or deceitful, modulations of speech (*OED change* 8c). For *change,* see 10n. The common emendation of *had* to 'hath' (see Coll.) is unnecessary if Fiormonda is referring to what Fernando has just said rather than to his general verbal facility.

153. *table-books*] Notebooks (called table-books because they were made up of 'tables' or 'tablets' of cardboard, slate etc.) used by gallants 'to put down sentences of plays, witticisms uttered in company, and new-coined phrases' (Weber). A. R. Humphreys (Arden edition of *2H4,* 1966, 2.4.264n) observes that table-books were also used to record assignations—another reason why Ferentes might be expected to have one. See *Haml.* 1.5.107–9, *Antonio's Rev.* 1.3.21.1–2, and Nashe's *Have with You to Saffron-Walden,* 46, for further allusions.

Ferentes. [*Aside*] I'm glad your highness is so pleasant.
Duke. Sister.
Fiormonda. My lord and brother?
Duke. You are too silent.
Quicken your sad remembrance. Though the loss
Of your dead husband be of more account
Than slight neglect, yet 'tis a sin against
The state of princes to exceed a mean
In mourning for the dead.
Fiormonda. Should form, my lord,
Prevail above affection? No, it cannot.
You have yourself here a right noble Duchess—
Virtuous at least—and should your grace now pay,
Which heaven forbid, the debt you owe to nature,
I dare presume she'd not so soon forget
A prince that thus advanced her.—Madam, could you?
D'Avolos. [*Aside*] Bitter and shrewd.

154. *Aside*] *aside to Fior. GD; no aside Q.* I'm] *Q;* I am *W.* 155. brother?] *W;* brother. *Q.* 167. *Aside*] *W; no aside Q, H.*

154. *pleasant*] good-humoured, facetious.

155. *too silent*] '[W]hatever was removed from the public eye, whether deliberately or not, tended to be seen as uncivil' (*Private Life*, 184).

156. *Quicken*] cheer, refresh.

158. *slight*] careless.

159. *state*] dignity, majesty.

a mean] moderation. The literature of civility (e.g. Erasmus, *De civilitate*, 1530) urged forbearance from excess of any sort.

160. *form*] formality, etiquette, outward ceremony (cf. *W. Devil* 4.3.144, *Conspiracy of Byron* 1.2.116–18, *Son.* 125, l. 5). '[T]he development of a new language of manners, and the expansion of the courtly and urban milieu in which such a language was appropriate, created what was often an acute and pervasive sense of the gap between moral and social imperatives' (Bryson, 207; *Private Life*, 199–205). Fiormonda's antithesis between 'form' and 'affection', with its echo of 'the corrupt libertine dialectic of Giovanni' (see *'Tis Pity* 1.1.24–7), shows that she 'understands her brother's principles only too well' (Neill, 'Neo-stoicism', 74).

163. *Virtuous at least*] Fiormonda's second thoughts about *noble* (162) emphasise Bianca's low rank.

163–4. *pay . . . nature*] Ford was fond of this proverbial expression (Tilley D 168): see *Queen*, 323–4, *BH* 5.2.91. Cf. *Elegy by WS*: 'Which paid to heaven the debt that it did owe' (182).

166. *advanced*] see 110n.

167. *shrewd*] piercing, maliciously acute. Applied to Fiormonda again at 4.1.81. She uses 'shrewdly' herself at 4.1.224.

Bianca. Sister, I should too much bewray my weakness
To give a resolution on a passion
I never felt nor feared.
Nibrassa. A modest answer.
Fernando. If credit may be given to a face,
My lord, I'll undertake on her behalf
Her words are trusty heralds to her mind.
Fiormonda. [*Aside to D'Avolos*] Exceeding good, the man will 'undertake'.
Observe it, D'Avolos.
D'Avolos. [*Aside*] I do, lady, 'tis a smooth praise.
Duke. Friend, in thy judgement I approve thy love,
And love thee better for thy judging mine,
Though my grey-headed senate in the laws
Of strict opinion and severe dispute

174. *Aside to D'Avolos*] *GD; no aside Q.* 176. *Aside*] *aside to Fior. GD; no aside Q.* I . . . praise] *Q;* I . . . lady; / 'Tis . . . praise *W.* I do, lady] *Q;* Lady I do *G, GD.*

---

168. *bewray*] betray, reveal.

169. *resolution*] opinion (*OED* 11).

passion] sorrow for Caraffa's imagined death—or perhaps ingratitude (Gifford).

170. *modest*] (a) appropriate to feminine decorum, becomingly diffident, etc.; (b) moderate (*OED* 2, 3, 4).

171.] Hoskins (41) compares *'Tis Pity* 2.5.15–19.

172. *undertake*] 'warrant', as in *Tit.* 1.1.433–4. Partridge notes the innuendo 'take under', i.e. under the garments, or 'underneath'. Williams glosses as 'copulate', and cites numerous examples, including *TwN* 1.3.55, 'I would not undertake her in this company'. Also cf. *Antipodes* 1.1.166. Fiormonda continues to mock Fernando's 'change of words' (152).

176. *smooth*] suave, ingratiating (cf. 'smooth-tongued').

177. *approve*] confirm (*OED* v.[1] 2).

178. *thy judging mine*] i.e., your judgement of mine.

179. *senate*] administrative or legislative body governing a free city of Europe (*OED* 1b, c). This scornful comment may be directed at Petruccio and Nibrassa (described as 'counsellors of state' in Q's dramatis personae).

180. *opinion*] The three most likely senses: (a) 'the Thought of him who gives his Advice upon any thing that is debated or consulted upon' (Phillips); (b) legal opinion; (c) 'the judgements or sentiments formed about persons and their qualities' (Schmidt; cf. *'Tis Pity* 5.3.1–3).

dispute] disputation, formal discussion.

Would tie the limits of our free affects,
Like superstitious Jews, to match with none
But in a tribe of princes like ourselves.
Gross-nurtured slaves, who force their wretched souls
To crouch to profit, nay, for trash and wealth,
Dote on some crooked or misshapen form,
Hugging wise nature's lame deformity,
Begetting creatures ugly as themselves.
But why should princes do so, that command
The store-house of the earth's hid minerals?
No, my Bianca, thou art to me as dear
As if thy portion had been Europe's riches,
Since in thine eyes lies more than these are worth.
Set on. They shall be strangers to my heart
That envy thee thy fortunes. Come, Fernando,
My but divided self, what we have done
We are only debtor to heaven for.—On.

Fiormonda. [*Aside to D'Avolos*] Now take your time, or never, D'Avolos.
Prevail, and I will raise thee high in grace.

181. affects] *G, GD;* effects *Q.* 186. or] *Q;* and *W.* 191. thou art] *Q;* thou'rt *W* 195–6. That . . . done] *W;* That . . . Fortunes: / Come, . . . done *Q.* 197. debtor] *Q;* debitor *GD.* 198. *Aside to D'Avolos*] *W; no aside Q.*

181. *tie*] restrict, circumscribe.

affects] desires, inclinations. Hoskins retains Q's 'effects', but none of its known senses seems very appropriate. Cf. 1.2.123n.

184–8. *Gross-nurtured . . . themselves*] Burton observes that the practice of marrying for financial benefit 'is not amongst your dust-worms alone, poor snakes that will prostitute their souls for money, but with this bait you may catch our most potent, puissant, and illustrious princes' (*Anatomy* III.2.2.3, p. 101).

184. *slaves*] abject fellows completely dominated by a specified influence: here, the desire for 'trash and wealth,' 185 (*OED* 2b).

185. *crouch*] (a) stoop; (b) fawn, cringe, bow humbly.

187. *Hugging*] Cf. *Lerma* 1.3.22, 'Hugging her sin'.

wise nature] This sounds proverbial, but Tilley and Dent give no obvious sources. Also occurs in *Rom. Actor* 2.1.32.

191–3.] 'Who can find a virtuous woman? for her price is far above rubies' (Proverbs 31:10).

192. *portion*] dowry (*OED* 3).

194. *Set on*] go on.

196. *My . . . self*] See 130n.

198. *take your time*] i.e. seize your opportunity.

D'Avolos. [*Aside*] Madam, I will omit no art.
[*Exeunt*; D'AVOLOS *stays* FERNANDO]
My honoured lord Fernando.

Fernando. To me, sir?

D'Avolos. Let me beseech your lordship to excuse me, in the nobleness of your wisdom, if I exceed good manners. I am one, my lord, who in the admiration of your perfect virtues do so truly honour and reverence your deserts, that there is not a creature bears life shall more faithfully study to do you service in all offices of duty and vows of due respect.

Fernando. Good sir, you bind me to you. Is this all?

D'Avolos. I beseech your ear a little, good my lord. What I have to speak concerns your reputation and best fortune.

Fernando. How's that? My reputation? Lay aside
Superfluous ceremony. Speak, what is't?

D'Avolos. I do repute myself the blessed'st man alive that I shall be the first gives your lordship news of your perpetual comfort.

Fernando. As how?

200. *Aside*] *aside to Fior. GD; no aside Q.* 200. SD.] *this ed.; Q, H give Exeunt after 199, and 'Da'uolos stayes Fernando' after 200; Exeunt all excepting* D'AV. *who detains* FERN. *W; Exeunt all but* D'AV., *who recalls* FERN. *GD; Exeunt* [*all but*] *D'avolos* [*who*] *stayes Fernando. S.* 203–9.] *As verse in Q.* 211. I beseech] *Q;* I do beseech *W.* 211–12.] *As verse-cum-prose in Q.* 215–17.] *As verse in Q.*

---

200. *art*] cunning, craftiness.

203–4. *the nobleness . . . wisdom*] The same phrase occurs in *GM*, 167.

205. *perfect*] fully realised, accomplished, faultless.

206. *deserts*] dues, merits (as at 140).

207. *creature*] (a) human being; (b) servant, dependant, puppet. 'When they [kings, etc.] giue any man a qualitie which he had not afore they terme him their Creature, as hauing made somewhat of nothing, in respect of the qualitie wherewith he was indued' (Golding and Sidney, transl., P. de Mornay's *Woorke Concerning the Trewnesse of the Christian Religion* (1587) x.139; quoted in *OED* sb. 5).

212. *best fortune*] prosperity.

214. *ceremony*] Didactic authors of the sixteenth and seventeenth centuries expressed doubts about the value and legitimacy of 'ceremonies', 'a term used . . . to designate many stereotyped gestures of deference and respect: head-baring, bowing, kneeling, titles of respect, and compliments' (Bryson, 208).

217. *comfort*] happiness.

D'Avolos. If singular beauty, unimitable virtues, honour, youth, and absolute goodness be a fortune, all those are at once offered to your particular choice.

Fernando. Without delays, which way?

D'Avolos. The great and gracious lady Fiormonda loves you, infinitely loves you. But, my lord, as ever you tendered a servant to your pleasures, let me not be revealed that I gave you notice on't.

Fernando. Sure you are strangely out of tune, sir.

D'Avolos. Please but to speak to her, be but courtly ceremonious with her; use once but the language of affection. If I misreport aught besides my knowledge, let me never have place in your good opinion. O these women, my lord, are as brittle mettle as your glasses: as smooth, as slippery. Their very first substance was quicksands. Let

219–21.] *As verse-cum-prose in Q.* 223–6.] *As verse-cum-prose in Q.* 223. loves] *W;* loue *Q.* 224. you.] you.—*Q.* 228–37.] *As verse and verse-cum-prose in Q.* 229. once but] *all eds.* 233. very first substance] *Q;* very substance *W.* 233–4. Let 'em] *Q;* let them *W.*

220. *absolute*] perfect, complete.

222. *which way*] how, in what respect.

224–5. *tendered . . . pleasures*] permitted a servant to minister to your wishes. *Tendered* probably = 'received favourably'; *pleasures* = 'wishes' or 'enjoyment'. Seventeenth-century Royal Proclamations ended with 'as they [you, etc.] tender our pleasure [or displeasure]' (*OED tender* v.[2] 3b, f).

227. *out of tune*] out of harmony, speaking incoherently or with impropriety.

229. *once but*] In this, the Q reading, D'Avolos urges Fernando to use, just once, the *mere language* of affection. But the phrase may be an error for 'but once'.

229. *affection*] 'emotion, passion' or 'affectation, artificiality' (*OED affection* 13, quoting *LLL* 5.2.406–7 (QF), 'Taffata phrases, silken tearmes, precise, / Three-pil'd Hyperboles, spruce affection').

231–3. *these women . . . slippery*] The brittleness of glass and the glass-like fickleness of women are proverbial notions (Tilley G 134, W 673, W 698). 'There be some women so brytell, that as a glasse, with a fylloppe wyll breke' (Lord Berners transl., Antonio de Guevara, *The Golden Boke of Marcvs Avrelius* (1535), 241; quoted in Tilley, 'A woman and a glass are ever in danger', W 646). Unbroken glass was also associated with a woman's virginity; cf. *Meas.* 2.4.124–6, and *Per.*, 1609 Q, H1r (4.6.150–1).

232. *mettle*] metal; substance; disposition. *Mettle* was a variant spelling of 'metal', 'used indiscriminately in all senses' (*OED mettle* sb.).

233. *slippery*] (a) 'inconstant, changeable'; (b) 'licentious,' as in *WT* 1.2.275 (Williams).

Their . . . quicksands] See LN.

'em look never so demurely, one fillip chokes them. My lord, she loves you, I know it. But I beseech your lordship not to discover me. I would not for the world she should know that you know it by me.

Fernando. I understand you, and to thank your care
Will study to requite it; and I vow
She never shall have notice of your news
By me or by my means. And, worthy sir,
Let me alike enjoin you not to speak
A word of that I understand her love.
And as for me, my word shall be your surety
I'll not as much as give her cause to think
I ever heard it.

D'Avolos. Nay, my lord, whatsoever I infer, you may break with her in it if you please; for rather than silence should hinder you one step to such a fortune, I will expose myself to any rebuke for your sake, my good lord.

Fernando. You shall not indeed, sir. I am still your friend, and will prove so. For the present, I am forced to attend the Duke. Good hours befall ye, I must leave you. *Exit.*

D'Avolos. Gone already? 'Sfoot, I ha' marred all. This is worse

235. it.] *this ed.;* it.—*Q.* 237. should know that] *Q;* should that *E.* 247–50.] *As verse in Q.* 251–3.] *as G; as verse in Q.* 251. sir.] *this ed.;* sir, *Q;* sir; *G.* 253. leave you] leave ye *W.*

---

234. *demurely*] meekly; with an affected or unnatural modesty.

fillip] (a) flick or smart stroke; (b) trifle. The verb could = 'enjoy sexually' (Williams; cf. 230–2n).

chokes] 'disconcerts', but since the verb can refer to any action which temporarily deprives one of 'breath, power of speech, or command of one's faculties' (*OED* v. 3), there may be a sexual allusion.

236. *discover*] expose.

240. *notice*] report.

243. *that*] the fact that (*OED conj.* 1c).

understand] know of.

247. *infer*] tell, relate (*OED* 2).

247–8. *break . . . in it*] broach the subject with her (cf. *JC* 2.1.149).

251. *still*] 'ever, constantly' or 'now as much as before'. Both senses were current.

254. *'Sfoot*] corruption of 'God's foot', an oath. D'Avolos slips back into the vernacular.

and worse. He's as cold as hemlock. If her highness knows how I have gone to work, she'll thank me scurvily. A pox of all dull brains! I took the clean contrary course. There is a mystery in this slight carelessness of his: I must sift it, and I will find it. 'Ud's me, fool myself out of my wit? Well, I'll choose some fitter opportunity to inveigle him, and, till then, smooth her up that he is a man overjoyed with the report. *Exit.*

ACT I SCENE 2

Enter FERENTES *and* COLONA.

Ferentes. Madam, by this light, I vow myself your servant: only yours, inespecially yours. Time, like a turn-coat, may order and disorder the outward fashions of our bodies,

259. and I will] *Q;* and will *W.* 'Ud's me, fool] vd's me, foole *Q (corr.), all later eds;* We's me foole, *Q (uncorr.).*

1.2.2. inespecially] *Q;* in especially *W.* 3. fashions] *Q;* fashion *W.*

255. *cold as hemlock*] In the physiology of the time, 'cold', 'hot', 'moist' and 'dry' were applied to the 'complexion' of things—the humours, elements, seasons, planets—and to the properties of herbs and drugs (*OED cold a.* 6). 'Classical writers on pharmacology had defined the qualities of both narcotics and poisons as very cold'; hemlock was cold in the fourth and highest degree (Hoeniger, 252).

256–7. *A pox of*] a mild curse: 'a pox on . . .'.

257. *clean*] wholly.

258. *mystery*] (a) mysterious quality; (b) secret.

slight] perhaps 'slighting, contemptuous' (*OED a.* 6).

sift] scrutinise, examine, pry into (*OED* 3); cf. 4.1.257–8; *BH* 3.1.63.

259. *find*] almost = 'get to the bottom of, resolve'. *OED* does not record this precise sense, though cf. v. 13. Or perhaps *mystery* (257) = 'personal secret' (*OED mystery*[1] 5b).

'Ud's me] 'God save me'. The minced forms *'Ud and 'Od* avoided 'overt profanation' (*OED od*[1]).

1.2.1. *by this light*] A common oath; he need not indicate a particular light-source.

servant] (a) one who is devoted to the service of a lady (frequent in the language of courtly romance); (b) lover. *Serve* can = 'render sexual service' (Williams).

2. *inespecially*] especially (derived from the phrase 'in especial', in particular; *OED*, quoting this example).

turn-coat] one who changes principles, party etc., with a literal play on *outward fashions* (3). Cf. Tilley T 343.

but shall never enforce a change on the constancy of my mind. Sweet Colona, fair Colona, young and sprightful lady, do not let me, in the best of my youth, languish in my earnest affections.

Colona. Why should you seek, my lord, to purchase glory by the disgrace of a silly maid?

Ferentes. That I confess, too. I am every way so unworthy of the first fruits of thy embraces, so far beneath the riches of thy merit, that it can be no honour to thy fame to rank me in the number of thy servants. Yet prove me how true, how firm I will stand to thy pleasures, to thy command, and as time shall serve, be ever thine. Now prithee, dear Colona.

Colona. Well, well, my lord, I have no heart of flint;
Or if I had, you know by cunning words
How to outwear it.—But—

Ferentes. But what? Do not pity thy own gentleness, lovely Colona. Shall I speak? Shall I? Say but ay, and our wishes are made up.

Colona. How shall I say ay when my fears say no?

Ferentes. You will not fail to meet two hours hence, sweet?

Colona. No—yes, yes, I would have said. How my tongue trips!

7. my earnest] *Q;* my most earnest *W.* 9. disgrace] *Q;* disgraces *G.* 14. pleasures] *Q;* pleasure *W.* 15. prithee] *G;* prethe *Q.* 20–2.] *As verse in Q.* 21. Shall . . . I?] *Q;* Shall I? Speak, shall I? *G.* 24. meet two] *Q;* meet me two *G.*

---

5. *sprightful*] full of spirit, lively—perh. with an implication that Colona is sexually over-active (cf. Williams, 'spirit' and 5.3.120n).

9. *silly*] 'lowly, humble' or 'defenceless, pitiful' (*OED* 1a, b, 3b).

13. *prove*] (a) put to the test; (b) try sexually (Williams).

14. *how firm . . . pleasures*] (with a bawdy quibble).

15. *serve*] be favourable. 'Take time while time serves' (Tilley T 312).

15. *prithee*] corruption of '(I) pray thee'.

17. *heart of flint*] proverbial (Tilley H 311).

20. *Do not . . . gentleness*] Do not pity or regret your susceptibility to my advances.

21. *Shall I speak? Shall I?*] Gifford remarks that Ferentes' thoughts 'run on something very different from speaking', and emends accordingly (see Coll.). In Q's reading (retained here), Ferentes is asking for consent to 'speak' of their anticipated liaisons (which is what he proceeds to do), but the request merges into a direct sexual proposition.

22. *made up*] fulfilled.

Ferentes. I take that promise and that double yes as an assurance of thy faith. In the grove—good sweet, remember—in any case alone—d'ee mark, love?—not as much as your duchess's little dog—you'll not forget?—two hours hence—think on't and miss not. Till then—

Colona. O, if you should prove false and love another!

Ferentes. Defy me then. I'll be all thine, and a servant only to thee, only to thee. *Exit* COLONA.

Very passing good, three honest women in our courts here of Italy are enough to discredit a whole nation of that sex. He that is not a cuckold or a bastard is a strangely happy man, for a chaste wife or a mother that never slept awry are wonders, wonders in Italy. 'Slife, I have got the feat on't, and am every day more active in my trade. 'Tis a sweet sin, this slip of mortality, and I have tasted enough for one passion of my senses. Here comes more work for me.

Enter JULIA.

And how does my own Julia? Mew upon this sadness. What's the matter, you are melancholy? Whither away, wench?

27–31.] *As verse in Q.* 33–43.] *As verse in Q.* 41–2. I have tasted] *all eds except W* (I tasted). 44. my] *Q;* mine *W.* Julia?] *W;* Julia, *Q.*

---

29. *d'ee mark*] do ye hear.

31. *miss not*] do not fail to keep (the rendezvous).

33. *Defy*] reject, despise (*OED* v.[1] 5).

35. *passing*] surpassingly.

honest] chaste.

38. *strangely*] extraordinarily, unusually.

39. *slept awry*] acted promiscuously. To 'tread the shoe awry' = to fall from virtue (*OED awry* 2c).

'Slife] abbreviation of 'God's life', a mild oath.

40. *have . . . feat on't*] have the knack or art of it (*OED feat* 6, quoting this example). 'On' was often used where we would use 'of' (Abbott 181).

41. *slip of mortality*] mortal foible or transgression. Emendation to 'morality' is tempting, since *slip* is more readily associated with a moral lapse (*OED* sb.[3] 10; cf. *Fancies*, 1883, *W. Devil* 5.1.184, *Meas.* 1.2.126). But Ford may have been thinking of the frailty of mortal flesh.

42. *passion of my senses*] erotic rapture, abandonment to sensual pleasures (*OED passion* 6a, c).

44. *Mew upon*] a derisive exclamation. *Mew* = an echoic name for the cry of the cat (*OED mew* int. and sb.[3] 2).

Julia. 'Tis well, the time has been when your smooth tongue
Would not have mocked my griefs, and had I been
More chary of mine honour, you had still
Been lowly as you were.

Ferentes. Lowly? Why, I am sure I cannot be much more lowly than I am to thee. Thou bring'st me on my bare knees, wench, twice in every four-and-twenty hours, besides half-turns instead of bevers. What must we next do, sweetheart?

Julia. Break vows on your side, I expect no other,
But every day look when some newer choice
May violate your honour and my trust.

Ferentes. Indeed forsooth, how shay by that, la? I hope I neglect no opportunity to your *nunquam satis* to be called in question for. Go, thou art as fretting as an old grogram:

47–50.] *W;* 'Tis . . . tongue / Would . . . more / Chary . . . were. *Q.* 49. mine honour] *Q;* mine own honour *G.* 51–5.] *As verse in Q.* 59–65.] *As verse in Q.* 59. shay by] *Q* (shey), *S;* shy be *W;* say you by *G;* say ye by *GD.*

---

50. *lowly*] humble in demeanour. Ferentes picks up a coarser sense in his reply.

54. *half-turns . . . bevers*] brief sexual liaisons instead of my usual meals or snacks (?). See LN.

do] with probable sexual implications (*'Tis Pity* 4.3.20n). '[*Bufo*] I would desire, intreat, and beseech you. [*Herophil*] What to do? *Buf.* There you have it, and thank you too. *Her.* I understand you not. *Buf.* Why, to do with you, forsooth, to do with you' (*Queen*, 995–1002). Cf. *T&C* 4.2.29, 'You bring me to do'. Williams gives many other examples.

59. *forsooth*] in truth.

how shay by that] 'what do you mean by saying that?' or 'do you say so?'. *Shay* is apparently an idiomatic form; see LN.

la] exclamation expressing surprise, irony etc. Dekker observes that anyone committing their work to print must suffer the 'Indeed, la!' of the 'puritanical citizen' (*Wonderful Year*, 'To the Reader').

60. *opportunity* . . . nunquam satis] i.e. opportunity to gratify your insatiate desires. *Nunquam satis* = Lat., 'never enough'.

60–1. *called . . . for*] doubted, challenged about.

61. *Go*] (a rebuke).

fretting] (a) impatient, chafing, irritating; (b) worn.

grogram] garment made of grogram, a coarse, often stiff, fabric of silk (or mohair and wool sometimes mixed with silk), from French, *gros grain* (*OED* 1, 2). After some use the material was liable to *fret* (i.e. become worn) and lose its gloss (Gifford).

by this hand, I love thee for't. It becomes thee so prettily to be angry. Well, if thou shouldst die, farewell all love with me forever. Go, I'll meet thee soon in thy lady's back lobby. I will, wench, look for me.

Julia. But shall I be resolved you will be mine?

Ferentes. All thine. I will reserve my best ability, my heart, my honour, only to thee, only to thee.—Pity of my blood, away, I hear company coming on. Remember, soon I am all thine. I will live perpetually only to thee.—Away!

Exit JULIA.

'Sfoot, I wonder about what time of the year I was begot. Sure it was when the moon was in conjunction and all the other planets drunk at a morris-dance. I am haunted above patience. My mind is not as infinite to do as my occasions are proffered of doing. Chastity? I am an eunuch if I think there be any such thing; or if there be, 'tis amongst us men, for I never found it in a woman, throughly tempted, yet. I have a shrewd hard task coming on, but let it pass. Who comes now?

Enter FERNANDO.

My lord the Duke's friend. I will strive to be inward with him.—My noble lord Fernando.

62. love thee] *Q;* love you *G.* 67–81.] *As verse in Q.* 77. I never] *Q;* I have never *W.* 79. SD] *Thus placed in Q; before* 'My noble lord' *(81) in GD.* 81. noble] *omitted G.*

---

66. *resolved*] satisfied, assured (*OED ppl.a.* 2, 3a).

68. *only to thee*] echoing 31–2.

Pity . . . blood] 'Pity on my life', 'Mercy on me'.

70. *to thee*] i.e. for thee.

72. *in conjunction*] See LN.

73. *planets . . . morris-dance*] Probably alluding to the 'dance' of the stars; cf. *Queen*, 1584–6: 'Wee'll tickle it till the welkin blussle [bustle?] again, and all the fixt Stars dance the old measures' (a passage which may have been influenced by *TwN* 2.3.56; cf. *MAdo* 2.1.314).

haunted] importuned, pursued, bothered (by his lovers). Cf. *Changeling* 1.1.236, *Edw. II* 2.2.153.

74. *to do*] See 50n.

78. *throughly*] thoroughly.

shrewd hard task] With another innuendo. *Shrewd* intensifies *hard*, and was often used thus with words expressing something bad or undesirable.

80. *inward*] familiar, intimate.

Fernando. My lord Ferentes, I should change some words
Of consequence with you, but since I am
For this time busied in more serious thoughts,
I'll pick some fitter opportunity.
Ferentes. I will wait your pleasure, my lord. Good day to your
lordship. *Exit.*
Fernando. Traitor to friendship, whither shall I run,
That, lost to reason, cannot sway the float
Of the unruly faction in my blood?
The Duchess, O the Duchess! In her smiles
Are all my joys abstracted.—Death to my thoughts,
My other plague comes to me.

Enter FIORMONDA *and* JULIA.

Fiormonda. My lord Fernando, what, so hard at study?
You are a kind companion to yourself,
That love to be alone so.
Fernando. Madam, no;
I rather chose this leisure to admire
The glories of this little world, the court,
Where, like so many stars on several thrones,
Beauty and greatness shine in proper orbs:

82. should] *Q;* would *W.* 86–7.] *As verse in Q.*

---

82. *change*] exchange.

82–3. *some words Of consequence*] Perhaps referring to his promise (1.1.99–105) to help resolve the problem of the affair between Colona and Ferentes (Stavig, 125–6), although he was asked only to speak to Colona.

86. *wait*] attend, await.

89. *sway the float*] 'control the high tide or flood' (*OED float* 2), as the moon holds sway over ocean tides. Probably influenced by the ancient notion of tidal movements in the blood; see Hoeniger, 148–9. William Harvey published his discovery of the circulation of the blood in 1628. For *float* see 2.3.88, *Gypsy* 1.5.28–9, *'Tis Pity* 1.1.64–5. *FM*, 561, *GM*, 48.

92. *abstracted*] presented in abstract; concentrated, epitomised (*OED* ppl.a. 4, quoting only *The Guardian* 3.6.33).

94. *study*] meditation.

98–100. *this . . . orbs*] Faret describes the ladies accompanying the Queen at court as 'lesse lights, shining in a spheare inferiour to the first' (344).

99. *several*] separate.

100. *proper*] (a) their own; (b) becoming. In Ptolemaic astronomy, the sun, moon, planets and stars were thought to revolve around the earth in

Sweet matter for my meditation.

Fiormonda. So, so, sir—leave us, Julia—your own proof,

Exit JULIA.

By travel and prompt observation,
Instructs you how to place the use of speech.
But since you are at leisure, pray let's sit.
We'll pass the time a little in discourse.
What have you seen abroad?

Fernando. No wonders, lady,
Like these I see at home.

Fiormonda. At home? As how?

Fernando. Your pardon if my tongue, the voice of truth,
Report but what is warranted by sight.

Fiormonda. What sight?

Fernando. Look in your glass and you shall see
A miracle.

Fiormonda. What miracle?

Fernando. Your beauty,
So far above all beauties else abroad,
As you are in your own, superlative.

Fiormonda. Fie, fie, your wit hath too much edge.

Fernando. Would that,

104. Instructs] *W;* Instruct *Q.*

---

separate, concentric spheres (*orbs*). Thus Fernando pictures the beautiful and great revolving like stars around *this little world, the court.* For 'orb' meaning 'sphere of action' (with the same astronomical allusion), see *1H4* 5.1.17–18.

102. *proof*] experience

103. *prompt*] ready, quick.

104. *place the use*] dispose, present. Again she expresses distrust of his verbal facility (cf. 1.1.151–3). The gentleman's 'mastery of social discourse' was founded on rhetoric (Bryson, 175). Yet for Castiglione and his followers the courtier's pleasing conversation should exclude 'all signs of the inner man' (*Private Life*, 192).

109. *voice of truth*] means by which truth is expressed (*OED voice* 12; cf. *Son.* 69, 3).

111. *glass*] mirror. 'If you would see a beauty more exact / Than art can counterfeit or nature frame, / Look in your glass, and there behold your own' (Giovanni to Annabella, *'Tis Pity* 1.2.205–7).

114. *your own*] 'your own country' or 'your own beauty' (cf. 111n).

115. *hath too much edge*] is too 'sharp', too keen.

that] i.e., my wit.

Or anything that I could challenge mine,
Were but of value to express how much
I serve in love the sister of my prince.
Fiormonda. 'Tis for your prince's sake, then, not for mine.
Fernando. For you in him, and much for him in you.
I must acknowledge, madam, I observe
In your affects a thing to me most strange,
Which makes me so much honour you the more.
Fiormonda. Pray tell it.
Fernando. Gladly, lady.
I see how, opposite to youth and custom,
You set before you in the tablature
Of your remembrance the becoming griefs
Of a most loyal lady, for the loss
Of so renowned a prince as was your lord.
Fiormonda. Now good my lord, no more of him.
Fernando. Of him!
I know it is a needless task in me
To set him forth in his deservèd praise.
You better can record it, for you find
How much more he exceeded other men
In most heroic virtues of account,
So much more was your loss in losing him.
Of him! His praise should be a field too large,
Too spacious, for so mean an orator
As I to range in.
Fiormonda. Sir, enough. 'Tis true,

119. mine.] *Q;* mine? *GD.* 126. the] *W;* your *Q, H.*

---

116. *challenge*] claim as.

120. *For you . . . in you*] i.e. for the part of you in him, and especially for the part of him in you.

121. *acknowledge*] confess, admit.

122. *affects*] kind feelings, affections (*OED* 3, quoting this instance).

126. *tablature*] tablet bearing some design or inscription (*OED* 2; cf. *HT*, 556). Q's 'your Tableture' looks like a compositorial error.

127. *becoming*] 'proper, fit' and perhaps 'lending grace'.

135. *of account*] of worth or importance in the eyes of others (*OED account* sb. 11).

139. *range*] roam.

He well deserved your labour. On his deathbed
This ring he gave me, bade me never part
With this but to the man I loved as dearly
As I loved him. Yet, since you know which way
To blaze his worth so rightly, in return
To your deserts, wear this for him and me.
[*Offers him the ring.*]

Fernando. Madam!

Fiormonda. 'Tis yours.

Fernando. Methought you said he charged you
Not to impart it but to him you loved
As dearly as you loved him.

Fiormonda. True, I said so.

Fernando. O then far be it my unhallowed hand
With any rude intrusion should annul
A testament enacted by the dead.

Fiormonda. Why, man, that testament is disannulled,
And cancelled quite by us that live; look here,
My blood is not yet freezed. For better instance,
Be judge yourself, experience is no danger.

145. SD.] *GD; not in Q.* 147. impart] *W;* imparr *Q.* 150. annul] *GD;* vnuaile *Q;* unveil *W, G.*

140ff.] Very similar to *Malfi* 1.1.403ff, in which the Duchess, a widow like Fiormonda, gives Antonio her wedding ring: 'I did vow never to part with it, / But to my second husband' (406–7; Leech, 80). In *LS* there is no sign that Fernando accepts the ring. See Intro., p. 43, for further comment.

143–4. *which . . . rightly*] how to proclaim his worth so justly.

145. *deserts*] meritorious actions or qualities (*OED desert* sb. 1, 2).

146. *charged*] enjoined.

150. *annul*] Dyce's emendation of Q's 'vnuaile' allows Fiormonda to pick up the word two lines below with *disannulled* (= 'annulled'), and is in keeping with the legal tone of *testament* (= 'posthumous wish') and *enacted* (= 'ordained').

152–6. *Why . . . warm*] Malfi to Antonio: 'This is flesh, and blood, sir; / 'Tis not the figure cut in alabaster / Kneels at my husband's tomb. Awake, awake, man! / I do here put off all vain ceremony' (1.1.453–6). A few moments later she kisses him.

155. *experience . . . danger*] Contradicting the proverb, 'Experience is sometimes dangerous' (Tilley E 218). *Experience* = 'proof or trial upon sight or observation' (Coles).

Cold are my sighs, but feel, my lips are warm.

Kisses him.

Fernando. What means the virtuous Marquess?

Fiormonda. To new-kiss
The oath to thee which whiles he lived was his.
Hast thou yet power to love?

Fernando. To love?

Fiormonda. To meet
Sweetness of language in discourse as sweet.

Fernando. Madam, 'twere dullness past the ignorance
Of common blockheads not to understand
Whereto this favour tends; and 'tis a fortune
So much above my fate that I could wish
No greater happiness on earth. But know,
Long since I vowed to live a single life.

Fiormonda. What was't you said?

Fernando. I said I made a vow.—

Enter BIANCA, PETRUCCIO, COLONA *and* D'AVOLOS.

[*Aside*] Blessèd deliverance!

Fiormonda. [*Aside*] Prevented? Mischief on this interruption!

Bianca. My lord Fernando, you encounter fitly,
I have a suit t'ee.

Fernando. 'Tis my duty, madam,
To be commanded.

Bianca. Since my lord the Duke

158. whiles] *Q;* whilst *W.* 159. power] *Q;* pow'r *W.* To love?] *Q;* To love! *G.* 168. *Aside*] *GD; no aside Q.* 169. *Aside*] *GD; no aside Q.*

156. *Cold*] (a) literally cold; (b) gloomy, dispirited.

157. *Marquess*] A common form in the sixteenth and seventeenth centuries, equivalent to the later 'marchioness' (*OED marquis* 3).

new-kiss] renew by kisses.

160. *discourse*] Three possible senses: (a) the language of love; (b) familiarity (cf. *Haml.* 3.1.109–10); (c) course of arms, combat (*OED* 1b). If the latter sense is applicable, *meet* (155) may = 'oppose, fight' (cf. Fiormonda's 'lists of love', 4.1.227).

161–3. *'twere dullness . . . tends*] Antonio to Malfi: 'Conceive not I am so stupid but I aim / Whereto your favours tend' (1.1.425–6).

166. *single*] celibate.

169. *Prevented*] hindered, frustrated.

170. *encounter fitly*] i.e., meet us at an opportune time. But *fitly* can also = 'becomingly' (*OED* 1), and *suit* (171) readily suggests romantic interest.

Is now disposed to mirth, the time serves well
For mediation that he would be pleased
To take the lord Roseilli to his grace.
He is a noble gentleman, I dare
Engage my credit; loyal to the state,
And, sister, one that ever strove, methought,
By special service and obsequious care,
To win respect from you. It were a part
Of gracious favour if you pleased to join
With us in being suitors to the Duke
For his return to court.

Fiormonda. To court! Indeed,
You have some cause to speak. He undertook
Most champion-like to win the prize at tilt
In honour of your picture—marry, did he.
There's not a groom o'th' querry could have matched
The jolly riding man. Pray get him back,
I do not need his service, madam, I.

Bianca. Not need it, sister? Why, I hope you think
'Tis no necessity in me to move it,

---

173. *disposed to mirth*] perhaps referring to his moodiness.

174. *mediation*] 'intercession in favour of another' (Schmidt). Oliver notes that this episode is 'a variation on the Desdemona-Cassio story' (80).

177. *Engage my credit*] pledge my reputation. An ordinary enough remark, but characters in this play often vow by something that is significant to their role: deceptive Ferentes by 'all my fidelity' (2.2.126); foolish, amorous Mauruccio by 'my wisdom' (2.1.90) and 'the pith of generation' (2.2.142); scheming D'Avolos 'in the name of policy' (2.2.33–4); and the dishonest Fiormonda 'on my conscience' (4.1.233).

180. *part*] 'act' or 'share in an undertaking' (*OED* 8, 11).

185. *at tilt*] i.e. in a tilt, a competition in which riders jousted with each other or rode with lances at a target or ring. *Tilt* was susceptible to bawdy quibbles (e.g. *W. Devil* 3.1.66, *Malfi* 1.1.120, *Meas.* 4.3.15). *Prize* = 'a reward or trophy' or 'contest, match' (cf. *Tit.* 1.1.396). In *Malfi* we hear that Antonio 'took the ring oftenest' (1.1.88–9).

186. *In honour of*] for the sake of honouring (*OED honour* 9c).
picture] portrait.

187. *th' querry*] the equerry: the stables of a royal household or the body of officers in charge of them (*OED* 1).

188. *jolly*] (a) gallant, sprightly; (b) fine (ironic); (c) overweeningly self-confident (?) (*OED* 2, 5, 6, 12b).

191. *move*] propose.

More than respect of honour.
Fiormonda. Honour? Puh!
Honour is talked of more than known by some.
Bianca. Sister, these words I understand not.
Fernando. [*Aside*] Swell not, unruly thoughts.—
Madam, the motion you propose proceeds
From the true touch of goodness. 'Tis a plea
Wherein my tongue and knee shall jointly strive
To beg his highness for Roseilli's cause.
Your judgement rightly speaks him: there is not
In any court of Christendom a man
For quality or trust more absolute.
Fiormonda. [*Aside*] How, is't even so?
Petruccio. I shall forever bless
Your highness for your gracious kind esteem
Of my disheartened kinsman; and to add
Encouragement to what you undertake,
I dare affirm 'tis no important fault
Hath caused the Duke's distaste.
Bianca. I hope so, too.
D'Avolos. Let your highness and you all, my lords, take advice how you motion his excellency on Roseilli's behalf. There is more danger in that man than is fit to be publicly reported. I could wish things were otherwise for his own sake; but I'll assure ye, you will exceedingly alter his excellency's disposition he now is in, if you but mention the name of Roseilli to his ear. I am so much acquainted in the process of his actions.
Bianca. If it be so, I am the sorrier, sir.
I'm loath to move my lord unto offence,
Yet I'll adventure chiding.

195. *Aside*] *W; no aside Q.* 204. *Aside*] *W; no aside Q.* 209–16.] *As verse in Q.* 215. so] *Q;* too *W.* 218. I'm] *Q;* I am *W.*

196. *motion*] suit, suggestion.
197. *the . . . goodness*] genuine goodness. *Touch* probably = 'sense, feeling' (cf. *R3* 1.2.71).
202. *absolute*] perfect, faultless.
208. *hope*] trust.
210. *motion*] appeal to, petition.
216. *the . . . actions*] his 'ways', the way he acts.
219. *adventure*] risk.

Fernando. [*Aside*] O had I India's gold, I'd give it all
T'exchange one private word, one minute's breath,
With this heart-wounding beauty.

Enter DUKE, FERENTES and NIBRASSA.

Duke. Prithee no more, Ferentes, by the faith
I owe to honour, thou hast made me laugh
Beside my spleen. Fernando, hadst thou heard
The pleasant humour of Mauruccio's dotage
Discoursed, how in the winter of his age
He is become a lover, thou wouldst swear
A morris-dance were but a tragedy
Compared to that. Well, we will see the youth.
What counsel hold you now, sirs?
Bianca. We, my lord,
Were talking of the horsemanship in France,
Which, as your friend reports, he thinks exceeds
All other nations.
Duke. How? Why, have not we
As gallant riders here?
Fernando. None that I know.

225. hadst thou] *Q;* thou hast *W.* 231. counsel] *Q* (Councell)*;* counsels *W;* Council *G.* 231–2. We . . . France] *W; one line Q.*

220. *India*] the Indian peninsula *or* the West Indies *or* Spanish South America. Each was associated with great wealth in gold and gems (Sugden). Cf. *1 Tamb.* 1.2.85, *1H4* 3.1.164–5.

221. *breath*] speech—perhaps whispered, and therefore intimate (*OED* 9).

224–5. *laugh . . . spleen*] i.e. beside myself with laughter. Although 'nourished by melancholy', the spleen is often connected with 'merriness and laughter' in Shakespeare (Hoeniger, 177). Melancholy people are humorous 'beyond all measure', writes Burton, 'sometimes profusely laughing, extraordinarily merry, and then again weeping without a cause' (*Anatomy* I.3.1.2, p. 393). Caraffa displays similar changeability in this scene.

226. *pleasant*] amusing, ridiculous (*OED* 4).

humour] caprice, odd or fantastical behaviour (cf. *OED*, *humour* 6c).

227–8. *in the winter . . . lover*] Caraffa himself is not young; see 5.1.69. Richard Perkins, who may have played Caraffa in the earliest performances, was in his forties during the period 1626–33, when *LS* was probably first staged. See Intro., p. 19.

231. *counsel*] consultation (*OED* 1). Q's form, 'Councell', was used for both 'counsel' and 'council' (*OED*).

235. *None that I know*] Fernando is well aware that Roseilli is 'famed' for his horsemanship (I.1.54–5).

Duke. Pish, your affection leads you. I dare wage
A thousand ducats not a man in France
Out-rides Roseilli.
Fiormonda. [*Aside*] I shall quit this wrong.
Bianca. I said as much, my lord.
Fernando. I have not seen
His practice since my coming back.
Duke. Where is he?
How is't we see him not?
Petruccio. What's this, what's this?
Fernando. I hear he was commanded from the court.
D'Avolos. [*Aside*] O confusion on this villainous occasion.
Duke. True, but we meant a day or two at most
Should be his furthest term. Not yet returned?
Where's D'Avolos?
D'Avolos. My lord.
Duke. You know our mind:
How comes it thus to pass we miss Roseilli?
D'Avolos. My lord, in a sudden discontent I hear he departed towards Benevento, determining, as I am given to understand, to pass to Seville, minding to visit his cousin Don Pedro de Toledo in the Spanish court.

236–7.] *W;* Pish . . . dare / Wage . . . *France. Q.* 239. *Aside*] *W; no aside Q.* 242. What's . . . this?] *aside GD.* 244. *Aside*] *W; no aside Q.* 247. mind] *G;* minds *Q.*

---

236. *affection leads*] inclination or partiality misleads (*OED affection* 5, 8; cf. *LM* 2.1.90–1).

wage] wager, bet.

237. *A thousand ducats*] The ducat or ducato was originally an Italian coin, though the name was used of gold (and formerly silver) coins in many European countries. Often associated with large sums (e.g., *Shrew* 2.1.365).

239. *quit*] requite.

244. *confusion*] a curse; cf. *Cor.* 4.6.31, *History of King Lear* 7.260.

246. *furthest term*] longest period (of absence). The time-scheme seems loose. Caraffa apparently believes that Roseilli has been absent from the court for more than 'a day or two', but Petruccio's question to Fernando at 271–2, 'please you to see your friend tonight?', seems to refer to the meeting arranged between Fernando and Roseilli in 1.1.85–6 ('At night / I'll meet you'). If so, the present scene takes place on the day Roseilli learned of his banishment.

250. *Benevento*] Italian city about 95 miles south-east of Rome (hardly the most direct route to Seville, but see p. 289).

Duke. The Spanish court? Now by the blessèd bones
Of good Saint Francis, let there posts be sent
To call him back, or I will post thy head
Beneath my foot. Ha, you! You know my mind,
Look that you get him back. The Spanish court,
And without our commission—say!

Petruccio. [*Aside*] Here's fine juggling.

Bianca. Good sir, be not so moved.

Duke. Fie, fie, Bianca,
'Tis such a gross indignity. I'd rather
Have lost seven years' revenue. The Spanish court!
How now, what ails our sister?

Fiormonda. On the sudden
I fall a-bleeding. 'Tis an ominous sign.
Pray heaven it turn to good—your highness' leave.
Exit

Duke. Look to her. Come, Fernando, come, Bianca,

258. say!] *omitted G, GD.* 264. a-bleeding] *GD;* a bleeding *Q, W.*

254–5. *posts, post*] (1) express messengers on horseback; (2) 'to dispatch post-haste' or 'to place' (though the latter sense is not recorded before 1683; *OED* v.[3] 1, v.[1] 4, sb.[2] 1, 2).

258. *commission*] authorisation.

259. *juggling*] trickery, legerdemain. The remark is not necessarily an aside, since an openly critical remark about the disgraced secretary might not seem inappropriate here; but the comment does suggest that Petruccio suspects (or knows) more about D'Avolos's doings than Caraffa. The Duke, in his anger, speaks only of 'smooth officious agents' (270), while Petruccio seems to sense outright villainy, an awareness which he *may* not wish to convey to Caraffa at this point. Also see 1.1.125n.

262. *revenue*] (accent on second syllable).

264. *a-bleeding*] Perhaps a nose-bleed, considered an omen of good *or* ill fortune (thus her wish that it 'turn to good', 265). Cf. *Malfi* 2.3.41–3. Halliwell relates that when Charles II was concealed at Boscobel House, 'his majesty, coming down into the parlour, his nose fell a bleeding, which put his poor faithful servants in a fright' (quoted in New Variorum edition, *MerVen.* 2.5.27n). Brand, 676–7, gives many examples of this superstition.

265. *Pray heaven*] probably equivalent to 'I pray to heaven'; cf. *Maid's Trag.* 5.2.30n

266. *Look to her*] Since Julia is not present, this could be addressed to Petruccio, Nibrassa or to no one in particular. A director may wish to provide an attendant to follow Fiormonda from the stage.

Let's strive to overpass this choleric heat.
[*To D'Avolos*] Sirrah, see that you trifle not. How we
Who sway the manage of authority
May be abused by smooth officious agents!—
But look well to our sister.

Exeunt all but PETRUCCIO *and* FERNANDO.

Petruccio. Nephew, please you
To see your friend tonight?

Fernando. Yes, uncle, yes.
[*Aside*] Thus bodies walk unsouled. Mine eyes but follows
My heart entombed in yonder goodly shrine.
Life without her is but death's subtle snares,
And I am but a coffin to my cares. *Exeunt.*

268. *To D'Avolos*] *W; not in Q.* 271. SD.] *W; Exeunt Q.* 272.] *Exit* Pet. *W.* 273. *Aside*] *this ed.* follows] *Q;* follow *W.* 276. *Exeunt*] *Q; Exit W.*

---

267. *overpass . . . heat*] i.e. 'get over' this anger. One of the four 'humours' of early physiology, choler was supposed to cause irascibility. Each humour was related to one of the four elements, choler being considered hot and dry like fire.

268. *Sirrah*] address used to social inferiors or, as here, to indicate contempt or annoyance.

trifle not] do not dally (in recalling Roseilli; *OED* v.[1] 4).

269. *sway the manage*] control the administration. Cf. *Rom. Actor* 1.1.92, 'swayes the power of things'.

270. *agents*] ministers, intermediaries.

273–4. *Thus . . . shrine*] Fernando will dramatise these words in his death (5.3.56.1ff). The *shrine* = Bianca. English adaptations of the Petrarchan notion of the lover's soul (or heart) imprisoned in the beloved's body (*Rime* 23, ll. 68ff) include Sidney, 'My true love hath my hart, and I have his' (*Old Arcadia* 45, Ringler, p. 75); Donne, 'The Legacie'; *R&J* 2.1.1. Laurie A. Finke argues that tragedy in this period reveals and exploits 'male fears that link the feminine with death' ('Painting Women: Images of Femininity in Jacobean Tragedy', *Theatre Journal* 36, 3, Oct. 1984, 359).

273. *follows*] The very common third-person plural in -s (Abbott, 333).

Act 2

ACT 2 SCENE I

Enter MAURUCCIO *looking in a glass, trimming his beard,* GIACOPO *brushing him.*

Mauruccio. Beard, be confined to neatness, that no hair
May stover up to prick my mistress' lip,
More rude than bristles of a porcupine.
Giacopo.

Giacopo. My lord?

Mauruccio. Am I all sweet behind?

Giacopo. I have no poulterer's nose, but your apparel sits about you most debonairely.

Mauruccio. But Giacopo, with what grace do my words proceed out of my mouth? Have I a moving countenance?

2.1.7–8.] *As verse in Q.*

2.1.0.1–2 Enter . . . him] Inspired, like *Fancies* 1.2, by *A&M* 3.2.123.1–8; see Intro., p. 46, LN.

1–2. *Beard . . . lip*] Faret urges the courtier to 'keep his beard carefully in order' (358)

2. *stover up*] bristle up, stiffen (*OED*, quoting only this instance). *Stover* is used substantively of stubble, winter fodder or litter for cattle, etc. *EDD* records the verb as a West Country usage.

3. *More rude . . . porcupine*] refers to *hair* (1).

6. *sweet*] pleasing to the sight, neat (cf. *OED* 5b). Giacopo plays on another sense, 'sweet-smelling' (*OED* 2), in his reply.

7. *poulterer*] dealer or seller of poultry, and sometimes hare and other game. Would presumably be able to tell the freshness of the goods by their smell.

9–13.] 'Manner of speech was regarded . . . as a clear indication of a man's inner civil qualities'; and the 'conception of the gentleman as orator' was associated with 'the overall concept of "civil society"' (Bryson, 160, 173; see Puttenham, 129–30).

10. *moving*] expressive or capable of stirring emotion (such as romantic passion). 'The chiefest force of the head is in the countenance, and of the countenance, in the eyes, which expres liuelilie euen anie conceit or passion of the mind: as therfore the face & countenance must bee comelilie and

Is there harmony in my voice? Canst thou perceive, as it were, a handsomeness of shape in my very breath as it is formed into syllable, Giacopo?

Enter DUKE, [FIORMONDA, BIANCA, FERNANDO,] *Lords and Ladies above.*

Giacopo. Yes indeed, sir, I do feel a savour as pleasant as— [*Aside*] a glister-pipe—calamus or civet.

Duke. Observe him and be silent.

Mauruccio. Hold thou the glass, Giacopo, and mark me with what exceeding comeliness I could court the lady Marquess, if it come to the push.

Duke. Sister, you are his aim.

Fiormonda. A subject fit
To be the stale of laughter.

Bianca. That's your music.

13. syllable] *Q;* syllables *W.* 13. SD.] *subst. G; Enter Duke, Lords and Ladies aboue. Q.* 21. stale] *W;* stall *Q.*

---

orderlie composed, so the eyes verie diligentlie are to be regarded' (Fraunce, II, 4; also Puttenham, 250–1).

11. *harmony*] Fraunce likens the 'pleasant and delicate tuning of the voyce' to the 'consent and harmonie of some well ordred song' (II, 1).

13. *syllable*] Often emended to 'syllables' (see Coll.), but the singular form may be used here for 'speech', or perhaps 'each syllable'. *OED* does not record a substantive sense to support this reading, but consider the verbal sense of *syllable*: 'to utter or express in . . . syllables or articulate speech' (*OED* 2; quotations from 1633 and 1634). Cf. 2.3.96.

13.1–2. Enter . . . above] See Intro., pp. 46–8.

14. *savour*] odour. Faret advises the courtier on this point (358).

15. *glister-pipe*] a tube or pipe for administering enemas. Iago uses the more common form, 'clyster-pipe', in *Oth.* 2.1.179. '[*Balurdo.*] How lik'st thou my suit? *Dildo.* All, beyond all . . . you are wondered at [*Aside*] for an ass' (*A&M* 3.2.144–6). Cf. *Sea Voyage* 1.3.22.

calamus] Sweet Calamus, a name applied to various eastern or native aromatic plants (*OED* 2).

civet] perfume derived from the musky-smelling secretions of glands in the anal pouch of the civet cat (*OED* sb.[1] 2).

17. *mark*] observe.

19. *push*] actual trial. Could also = 'attack, vigorous onset', with bawdy suggestion (*OED push sb.*[1] 3, 6).

21. *stale of laughter*] laughing-stock. A *stale* = (a) a person or thing made use of as a means for inducing some result; or (b) a lover 'whose devotion is turned into ridicule for the amusement of a rival or rivals' (*OED sb.*[3] 5, 6).

your music] i.e. laughter.

Mauruccio. Thus I reverse my pace, and thus stalkingly in courtly gait I advance, one, two, and three.—Good, I kiss my hand, make my congee, settle my countenance, and thus begin. Hold up the glass higher, Giacopo.

Giacopo. Thus high, sir?

Mauruccio. 'Tis well. Now mark me:

Most excellent Marquess, most fair la-dy,
Let not old age or hairs that are sil-ver
Disparage my desire; for it may be
I am than other green youth nimb-ler.
Since I am your grace's servant so true,
Great lady, then love me for my vir-tue.
O Giacopo! Petrarch was a dunce, Dante a jig-maker,

22. stalkingly] *Q;* stalking *GD.* 23. two, and three] *Q;* two, three *W.* 28–33. *All eds except W break final words of lines:* 'la-dy', *etc.* 31. nimb-ler] *Q;* nimblelèr *W;* nimblé-er *G;* nimbeler *GD;* nimbe-ler *H.* 34–8.] *As W; verse in Q.* 34. Dante] *W; Dantes Q;* Dante's *S.*

---

22. *stalkingly*] 'with long, measured strides', probably suggesting haughtiness or indifference to one's surroundings (*OED stalking* ppl.a. 2d; *stalk* v.[1] 4; the one recorded instance of the adverb dates from 1891). Cf. *Poetaster* 3.4.165n. Perhaps the word (and Mauruccio's behaviour) are intended to recall the actor Edward Alleyn; see p. 47.

23–4. *kiss my hand*] a courtly, and probably affected, token of respect (cf. *TwN* 3.4.30–1; cf. *LLL* 4.1.145).

24. *congee*] bow. 'They are most commonly in [ladies'] greatest fauour, which know best how to bend, and submit themselues before them' (Faret, 365).

countenance] facial expression. Mauruccio may settle his features in a look of calmness and composure (another sense of the word, as in the phrase 'to lose countenance', *OED* 4, 6); or he may adopt a 'moving' expression (8).

28–33. *Most . . . vir-tue*] Gasparo, the master of the 'Complement School' in Shirley's *Love's Tricks* (a Phoenix play), teaches Bubulcus a rather more absurd poem to recite to his mistress (3.5). 'The aesthetic principles of courtly poetry—an elegant rhetoric of personal display—were justified as arising from and enhancing the principles of courtly behaviour' (Bryson, 125).

30. *Disparage*] discredit (*OED* v. 2).

31. *green*] raw, inexperienced (*OED* 8c).

nimb-ler] prob. pronounced 'nimble-er' for the sake of the pedantic metre.

34. *Petrarch*] Francesco Petrarca (1304–74), Italian poet and humanist; *dunce* (34) perhaps scorns his achievements as classical scholar.

Dante] Dante Alighieri (1265–1321), Florentine poet and prose-writer.

jig-maker] *Jig* = the jocular, often scurrilous, ballads of the time, or the farcical entertainments devised as afterpieces to plays. The theatrical

Sannazar a goose, and Ariosto a puckfist, to me. I tell thee, Giacopo, I am rapt with fury, and have been, for these six nights together, drunk with the pure liquor of Helicon.

Giacopo. I think no less, sir.—[*Aside*] For you look as wild and talk as idly as if you had not slept these nine years.

Duke. What think you of this language, sister?

Fiormonda. Sir,
I think in princes' courts no age nor greatness
But must admit the fool. In me 'twere folly
To scorn what greater states than I have been.

Bianca. O, but you are too general.

Fiormonda. —A fool?
I thank your highness. Many a woman's wit

35. Sannazar] *W (subst.); S'anazar Q.* 36. rapt] *G;* wrap'd *Q.* 39–41.] *As verse in Q.* 40. idly] *W;* idlely *Q.* 41–2. Sir . . . greatness] *One line in Q.* 42. princes'] *GD;* prince's *W;* princes *Q.*

---

jig-maker was usually the company's leading clown (Hibbard, ed., *Haml.* 3.2.116n).

35. *Sannazar*] The Neapolitan poet Jacopo Sannazaro (1456–1530), author of the popular *Arcadia* (1502–4), a pastoral work in prose and verse. He is also mentioned in *'Tis Pity* 2.2.1–18. Q's '*S'anazar*' and '*Galzazzo*' (for 'Galeazzo', 2.2.115) suggest that the compositor had difficulty with foreign names.

goose] simpleton.

Ariosto] Lodovico Ariosto (1474–1533), Ferrarese poet and dramatist.

puckfist] empty braggart. 'Puck' = the name of the mischievous goblin or sprite; 'fist' = 'a breaking wind, a foul smell' (*OED puckfist* 2; *puck* sb.[1]; *fist* sb.[2] 1). He scoffs at Ariosto's achievement in writing *Orlando Furioso*, a famous romantic epic, or derides the 'fury' of the poem's hero (see 36 LN and cf. 94n). Cf. *Poetaster* 5.3.34.

to] compared to.

36. *rapt with fury*] transported with poetic inspiration. See LN.

38. *Helicon*] (a) the mountain in Boeotia considered sacred to the Muses, or (as often in the sixteenth and seventeenth centuries) the fountains of Aganippe and Hippocrene that arose there; (b) poetic inspiration (*OED* 1; cf. *Staple* 2.4.135). Pistol, possibly one of Mauruccio's theatrical forebears (see Intro., p. 37), uses 'Helicons' in *2H4* 5.3.105.

41. *language*] speech, talk.

42–3. *no age . . . fool*] i.e. there is no person, whatever their age or eminence, who will not tolerate (*admit*) a fool.

44. *greater states*] more eminent persons.

45. *A fool?*] (interpreting *general* as = 'thorough'; *OED* adj. 1).

Have thought themselves much better, was much worse.

Bianca. You still mistake me.

Duke. Silence, note the rest.

Mauruccio. God-a-mercy brains! Giacopo, I have it.

Giacopo. What, my lord?

Mauruccio. A conceit, Giacopo, and a fine one. Down on thy knees, Giacopo, and worship my wit. Give me both thy ears; thus it is: I will have my picture drawn most compposituously in a square table of some two foot long, from the crown of the head to the waist downward, no further.

Giacopo. Then you'll look like a dwarf, sir, being cut off by the middle.

Mauruccio. Speak not thou, but wonder at the conceit that follows. In my bosom on my left side I will have a leaf of blood-red crimson velvet, as it were part of my doublet, open, which being opened, Giacopo—now mark—I will have a clear and most transparent crystal in the form of a heart. Singular admirable! When I have framed this, I will, as some rare, outlandish piece of workmanship, bestow it on the most fair and illustrious lady Fiormonda.

Giacopo. But now, sir, for the conceit.

50. What,] *W;* What? *Q.* 54. two] *W;* too *Q.* 55. no] *Q;* not *W.* 62–3. form of a] *omitted W.* 65. lady] *omitted W.*

---

47. *much worse*] 'It is better to be a fool than a knave' (Tilley F 446; cf. *Tragedy of King Lear* 2.2.251–8).

48. *still*] constantly.

49. *God-a-mercy*] literally, 'God have mercy'; an exclamation of applause or thanks (*OED* 1).

51. *conceit*] idea or ingenious notion.

53. *drawn*] depicted—in this case, painted (*OED draw* 60b).

53–4. *compposituously*] '[incorrect form for compositiously.] With good composition' (*OED*, quoting only this example).

54. *table*] board or other flat surface on which a picture was presented (*OED* 3).

58. *thou*] The choice of pronoun expresses his annoyance (Abbott 231).

59. *leaf*] petal or flap (*OED* 2).

62. *crystal*] mirror of 'crystal-glass', a very clear (*transparent*) quality of glass. Cf. *VA* 962–3; see LN.

63. *framed*] fashioned, constructed. *OED* records no instance of 'frame' in the sense 'to set in a frame' before 1705 (*OED* 7, 9). Cf. *Queen*, 2445–6.

64. *rare*] (a) uncommon, extraordinary; (b) excellent.

Mauruccio. Simplicity and ignorance, prate no more! Blockhead, dost not understand yet? Why, this being to her instead of a looking-glass, she shall no oftener powder her hair, surfle her cheeks, cleanse her teeth, or conform the hairs of her eyebrows, but having occasion to use this glass—which for the rareness and richness of it she will hourly do—but she shall as often gaze on my picture, remember me, and behold the excellence of her excellency's beauty in the prospective and mirror, as it were, in my heart.

Giacopo. Ay, marry sir, this is something.

All above. Ha, ha, ha. *Exit* FIORMONDA.

Bianca. My sister's gone in anger.

Mauruccio. Who's that laughs? Search with thine eyes, Giacopo.

Giacopo. O my lord, my lord, you have gotten an everlasting fame. The Duke's grace, and the Duchess' grace, and my lord Fernando's grace, with all the rabble of courtiers, have heard every word. Look where they stand. Now you shall be made a count for your wit, and I, lord for my counsel.

Duke. Beshrew the chance, we are discovered.

Mauruccio. Pity o' my wisdom! I must speak to them:
O Duke most great, and most renownèd Duchess,

68. Simplicity and ignorance] *nouns italicised in Q.* 90. Pity . . . wisdom] *this ed.;* Pitty,—oh my wisdome *Q, eds.* 91. renownèd] *GD;* renowned *W;* renowed *Q.*

---

68. *Simplicity*] 'stupidity, simple-mindedness', or 'simpleton'. Q's italicisation of *Simplicity* and *ignorance* may indicate personification (cf. *'Tis Pity* 2.6.100).

71. *surfle*] paint or wash with a cosmetic (*OED* 2; Brome, *The City Wit* (1653), E3v; *Malcontent* 2.4.32).

76. *prospective*] Probably a prospective glass, a magic crystal in which it was supposed one could view distant events. In Day, Rowley and Wilkins's *The Travels of the Three English Brothers*, Fame gives to each of the parted brothers '*a prospective glass*' in which '*they seem to see one another and offer to embrace*' (13.13.5–7). See Parr, *Travel Plays*, 19, for an illustration of such a device. From at least 1630 a *prospective* also = an ordinary telescope (*OED sb.* 2); *prospective glass* was used in this sense as early as 1626 (*OED* 2).

85. *rabble*] disorderly assemblage.

89. *Beshrew the chance*] curse the happening or mischance.

91. *renownèd*] Q's spelling, 'renowed', is not recorded by *OED*, and may

Excuse my apprehension, which not much is.
'Tis love, my lord, that's all the hurt you see:
Angelica herself shall plead for me.

Duke. We pardon you, most wise and learned lord,
And, that we may all glorify your wit,
Entreat your wisdom's company today,
To grace our table with your grave discourse.
What says your mighty eloquence?

Mauruccio. Giacopo, help me, his Grace has put me out my own bias, and I know not what to answer in form.

Giacopo. 'Uds me, tell him you'll come.

Mauruccio. Yes, I will come, my lord the Duke, I will.

Duke. We take your word, and wish your honour health.
Away, then. Come, Bianca, we have found
A salve for melancholy: mirth and ease.

Bianca. I'll see the jolly lover and his glass

94. herself shall plead] *this ed.;* her selfe plead *Q;* herself must plead *W;* herself doth plead *GD.* 98. our table with your grave] *G;* our talke with your graue *Q;* our talk with your most grave *W.* 100. out my] *Q;* out of my *W.*

---

be a compositor's error; or perhaps Ford wrote 'renomed' (= renowned), a form which by the seventeenth century was just the kind of old-fashioned term Mauruccio favours (see *OED*).

92. *apprehension*] perhaps 'the action of feeling anything emotionally' (i.e. his love for Fiormonda; *OED apprehension* 6).

94. *Angelica . . . me*] A deliberate echo of Orlando's words in Greene's *The Historie of Orlando Furioso* (c. 1591) 1.1.134–5; see LN.

97. *Entreat*] a vogue-word in the early seventeenth century. 'Philomusus' suggests the following formula for a dinner invitation: 'Pray let me prevaile . . . to entreate your company to dinner' (105).

100–1. *put . . . bias*] thrown me 'off track', confused me. *Bias* = the oblique line in which the bowl runs owing to its shape or weighting (*OED* sb. 2, 4). *Out* = 'out of' or 'out from' (Abbott 183). Mauruccio's predicament is anticipated in *GM*: 'As it oftentimes is seene the onely way to put some notorious foole that esteemes the perfection of a brave spirit to consist in the fopperie of unseemely behaviour (fitly and yet more grossely tearmed swaggering) out of his vaine bias is by once daring him in his owne qualitie' (187–91).

101. *in form*] according to established practice. Cf. 1.1.160; *Candy* 4.1, p. 280.

106. *salve*] remedy (*OED* sb.[1] 2a). Burton cites mirth and merry company as remedies for melancholy (II.2.6.4).

107. *jolly*] fine, handsome, youthful, sprightly (all more or less ironic); showy (*OED* 2, 6, 7, 8, 12; cf. 1.2.188).

Take leave of one another.

[*Exeunt above all but* FERNANDO *and* BIANCA.]

Mauruccio. Are they gone?

Giacopo. O my lord, I do now smell news.

Mauruccio. What news, Giacopo?

Giacopo. The Duke has a smackering towards you, and you shall clap up with his sister the widow suddenly.

Mauruccio. She is mine, Giacopo, she is mine! Advance the glass, Giacopo, that I may practise as I pass to walk a portly grace like a Marquess, to which degree I am now a-climbing.

Thus do we march to honour's haven of bliss,
To ride in triumph through Persepolis.

Exit GIACOPO *going backward with the glass,*
[*followed by*] MAURUCCIO *complimenting.*

Bianca. Now, as I live, here's laughter worthy our presence. I will not lose him so. *She is going out.*

Fernando. Madam.

Bianca. To me, my lord?

Fernando. Please but to hear
The story of a castaway in love;
And O, let not the passage of a jest

108. SD.] *W (subst., but after 101); 'Exit Duke cum suis. / Manent Biancha & Fernando' after 101 Q.* 119.2 *followed by*] *G; not in Q.* 120–1.] *As verse in Q.* 120. worthy] *Q;* worth *W.* 121. SD. *She . . . out*] *Q; Going W.*

112. *smackering*] inclination (*OED* vbl. sb.[1] 2).

113. *clap up*] make a hasty match (*OED* v.[1] 13b; cf. *'Tis Pity* 3.1.14–15).

114. *Advance*] raise or bring forward.

115. *pass*] pass along.

115–16. *walk . . . grace*] i.e. walk with a stately, graceful deportment.

118–19.] A send-up of a passage in *1 Tamb.* 2.5.48–54: '*Menaphon.* Your majesty shall shortly have your wish, / And ride in triumph through Persepolis . . . *Tamburlaine.* And ride in triumph through Persepolis! / Is it not brave to be a king, Techelles? / Usumcasane and Theridamas, / Is it not passing brave to be a king, / And ride in triumph through Persepolis?' *Tamb.* continued to be performed throughout the first half of the seventeenth century (see Gayton, 271), though from the late 1590s it is often parodied in the drama; see *2H4* 2.4.161–4; *A&M*, Ind.103–5, 3.1.0.1–2.

119.1–2.] A final visual quotation from *A&M* 3.2. *Complimenting* = bowing or practising acts of formal courtesy (*OED compliment* v.1).

123. *castaway*] He is 'cast away' by his beloved as well as cast adrift on the seas of woe (Hoskins, 124).

124. *passage*] 'occurrence' (cf. *Trial* 2591).

Make slight a sadder subject, who hath placed
All happiness in your diviner eyes.

Bianca. My lord, the time—

Fernando. The time! Yet hear me speak,
For I must speak, or burst. I have a soul
So anchored down with cares in seas of woe,
That passion, and the vows I owe to you,
Have changed me to a lean anatomy.
Sweet princess of my life—

Bianca. Forbear, or I shall—

Fernando. Yet as you honour virtue, do not freeze
My hopes to more discomfort than as yet
My fears suggest. No beauty so adorns
The composition of a well-built mind
As pity. Hear me out.

Bianca. No more. I spare

---

125. *slight*] insignificant.

sadder] (a) graver; (b) more sorrowful.

subject] Various senses seem applicable: (a) inferior owing allegiance; (b) person under dominion of another—here, in emotional sense; (c) thing having real existence; (d) person or thing which is the recipient of some treatment; (e) topic or theme—perhaps of a literary composition or artistic representation, etc. (*OED* 1–3, 6b, 12–15). See Intro., p. 48.

126. *diviner*] of surpassing, divine beauty. *OED* gives no instance of this use, but cf. *R&J* 3.2.77.

128–9. *a soul . . . woe*] merging the proverbial 'sea of troubles [or sorrows]' (Dent[1] S 177.1; cf. *Haml.* 3.1.61) with the ancient metaphor of a person (or their soul) as a ship upon the voyage of life (e.g. Ovid, *Amores*, II, iv, 8; Petrarch, *Rime* 80, 132). The many examples in English include Wyatt's 'My galley charged with forgetfulness' (transl. of *Rime* 189). Cf. Alciati, 50, Whitney, 137.

130. *vows*] (of love and fidelity).

131. *anatomy*] withered or emaciated creature, 'skin and bone'. Cf. Petrarch's *Rime* 37 (translated by Wyatt as 'So feeble is the thread that doth the burden stay'). *Anatomy* also = 'skeleton' (*OED* 4, 6; cf. Donne, 'A Valediction: of My Name in the Window', l. 24), and hence 'the bony figure of Death himself, the "fell anatomy" hailed by Constance in *King John* [3.4.40]; for what the science of dissection ultimately seemed to disclose was nothing less than the "original of Death"—the death that is . . . already inside us' (Neill, *Issues*, 133). See Intro., pp. 71–3.

132. *Sweet . . . life*] Pyrocles addresses Philoclea thus in the *New Arcadia*, II, 234.

134. *discomfort*] sorrow.

136. *well-built*] noble, refined. *OED*'s earliest figurative use is from 1681.

137. *spare*] refrain (*OED* v.[1] 6).

To tell you what you are, and must confess
Do almost hate my judgement, that it once
Thought goodness dwelt in you. Remember now
It is the third time since your treacherous tongue
Hath pleaded treason to my ear and fame;
Yet for the friendship 'twixt my lord and you,
I have not voiced your follies. If you dare
To speak a fourth time, you shall rue your lust.
'Tis all no better: learn, and love yourself. *Exit.*

Fernando. Gone? O my sorrows, how am I undone!
Not speak again? No, no, in her chaste breast
Virtue and resolution have discharged
All female weakness. I have sued and sued,
Kneeled, wept and begged; but tears, and vows, and words
Move her no more than summer winds a rock.
I must resolve to check this rage of blood;
And will. She is all icy to my fires,
Yet even that ice inflames in me desires. *Exit.*

ACT 2 SCENE 2

Enter PETRUCCIO *and* ROSEILLI

Roseilli. Is't possible the Duke should be so moved?
Petruccio. 'Tis true. You have no enemy at court

149. Virtue and resolution] *nouns italicised in Q.* 151. Kneeled] *Q (*Kneel'd*); Knelt W.*

---

142. *pleaded*] urged, sued for.
fame] reputation.
146. *'Tis . . . better*] i.e. it is no use, it is quite hopeless.
love] show regard for (as at 1.1.103).
150. *All female weakness*] 'A woman is the weaker vessel' (Tilley W 655; cf. 1 Peter 3:7). Women were considered 'unequal in moral as well as intellectual capacity' (Mendelson & Crawford, 36).
150–1. *sued . . . words*] A lover's language—perhaps predictably so. Cf. Sidney, 'Vertue, beawtie, and speach, did strike, wound, charme', *Old Arcadia* 60; and *A&C* 3.2.16–18 (see Wilders's note to this, Arden[3] edition).
153. *rage*] violent passion (of which the blood was the supposed seat).
154. *icy . . . fires*] a proverbial, and Petrarchan, antithesis. Cf. Tilley F 284; *Rime* 134, 182. Fire and ice = emblems of sexual passion and chastity (e.g., *SMT* 2.2.58).

2.2.1. *moved*] 'influenced, incited' or 'stirred to anger' (*OED move* 9b, 10, 12).

But her, for whom you pine so much in love.
Then master your affections. I am sorry
You hug your ruin so.
What say you to the project I proposed?

Roseilli. I entertain it with a greater joy
Than shame can check.

Enter FERNANDO.

Petruccio. You are come as I could wish.
My cousin is resolved.

Fernando. Without delay
Prepare yourself, and meet at court anon
Some half-hour hence: and Cupid bless your joy.

Roseilli. If ever man was bounden to a friend—

Fernando. No more, away. Love's rage is yet unknown.

[*Exeunt* PETRUCCIO *and* ROSEILLI.]

In his, ay me, too well I feel my own.
So, now I am alone, now let me think.
She is the Duchess: say she be; a creature
Sewed up in painted cloth might so be styled;
That's but a name. She's married, too, she is:
And therefore better might distinguish love.
She's young and fair: why madam, that's the bait
Invites me more to hope. She's the Duke's wife:
Who knows not this? She's bosomed to my friend:
There, there, I am quite lost. Will not be won:
Still worse and worse. Abhors to hear me speak:

2.2.4–5.] *W; one line in Q.* 8–9. You . . . resolved] *W; one line in Q.* 8. You are] *Q;* You're *W.* 13. SD.] *This ed.; Exeut Q; Exeunt H; 'Exeunt' after* 'away' *(13) W; 'Exeunt Pet. and Rose.' after* 'away' *G.* 14. ay me] *Q;* ah me *G.* 23. There, there] *italic in Q.*

---

5. *hug*] (a) court; (b) cherish, cling to (*OED* 1 b–d).
ruin] i.e. the cause of your downfall (*OED* 8).
12. *bounden*] indebted.
13. *Love's rage*] probably 'the height of love's violent passion' (*OED rage* 6).
14. *his*] i.e. his 'Love's rage' (13).
ay me] alas! ah me!
15. *So . . . alone*] Echoing *Haml.* 2.2.551; see Intro, p. 49.
17. *styled*] titled.
22. *bosomed*] joined in intimate companionship (*OED bosom* v. 3).
23. *There, there*] Italicised in Q, perhaps to convey rhetorical emphasis.

Eternal mischief! I must urge no more;
For were I not belepered in my soul,
Here were enough to quench the flames of hell.
What then? Pish, if I must not speak, I'll write.
Come then, sad secretary to my plaints,
Plead thou my faith, for words are turned to sighs.
What says this paper?
[*He draws a letter and reads to himself.*]

Enter D'AVOLOS *with two pictures.*

D'Avolos. [*Aside*] Now is the time. Alone, reading a letter: good. How now, striking his breast? What, in the name of policy, should this mean? Tearing his hair? Passion, by all the hopes of my life, plain passion. Now I perceive it. If this be not a fit of some violent affection, I am an ass in understanding. Why, 'tis plain, plainer and plainer: love

28. if I must] *G;* I must *Q.* 31. SD.] *G (subst.);'he reads to himselfe' on 31, 'he draws / a letter' in margin of 30–1 Q.*

26. *belepered*] Leprosy was an 'emblem of sexual depravity'; and 'occurs as punishment for moral offences' in the Bible (Williams). Cf. *Candy* 5.1, p. 288; *'Tis Pity* 1.1.74, 4.3.61; *Lerma* 4.1.105.

27. *Here . . . hell*] with an implicit comparison of hell's flames and the 'fires' (2.1.154) of his passion.

28. *if . . . write*] As in Petrarch, *Rime* 23, ll. 98–100.

if] Gifford's emendation (see Coll.) repairs sense and metre.

29. *sad . . . plaints*] i.e. the letter, regarded as a confidant (cf. 1.1.3n). *Plaints* = lamentations.

31. *What . . . paper?*] Perhaps he has already written part, or all, of a letter to Bianca. Letters were important hand-props; see Kiefer. In Dutch genre painting, the image of a young man reading a letter 'signified love' (*Private Life*, 246).

31.2. pictures] i.e. portraits or, more likely, miniatures. See LN and Intro., p. 49, for comment on this episode.

32–8. *Alone . . . extremest*] Fernando's behaviour is a conventional representation of the melancholy lover; see LN.

33. *striking his breast*] In the theatre, 'the Breast stricken with the Hand is an action of Grief, sorrow, repentance and indignation' (Bulwer, quoted by White, 168, who discusses the similar episode in *'Tis Pity* 1.2.136–9).

34. *policy*] 'political sagacity', with the same overtones of cunning as 'politician' at 1.1.21. See 1.2.177n on Ford's use of vows and asseverations as a means of characterisation.

in the extremest. O for the party, who now? The greatness of his spirits is too high-cherished to be caught with some ordinary stuff, and if it be my lady Fiormonda I am strangely mistook. Well, that I have fit occasion soon to understand. I have here two pictures, newly drawn, to be sent for a present to the Abbot of Monaco, the Duchess's uncle: her own and my lady's. I'll observe which of these may, perhaps, bewray him. 'A turns about. [*To Fernando*] My noble lord?

Fernando. Y'are welcome, sir, I thank you.

D'Avolos. Me, my lord? For what, my lord?

Fernando. Who's there? I cry you mercy, D'Avolos,
I took you for another; pray, excuse me.
What is't you bear there?

D'Avolos. No secret, my lord, but may be imparted to you. A couple of pictures, my good lord, please you see them?

Fernando. I care not much for pictures; but whose are they?

D'Avolos. Th'one is for my lord's sister, the other is the Duchess.

Fernando. Ha, D'Avolos, the Duchess's?

D'Avolos. Yes, my lord.—[*Aside*] Sure the word startled him: observe that.

Fernando. You told me, master secretary, once,
You owed me love.

D'Avolos. Service, my honoured lord, howsoever you please to term it.

39. too] *W;* to *Q.* 45–6. A . . . lord?] *W (subst.);*—a turnes about, my noble Lord. *Q.* 45. 'A] *Q (a); He W.* 47. Y'are] *Q;* You're *W.* 52–3.] *Verse in Q.* 58. *Aside*] *G; no aside Q.*

38–9. *The greatness . . . high-cherished*] i.e. he entertains too lofty a disposition, or too conceited a self-regard.

41. *strangely*] oddly, surprisingly.

45. *bewray*] expose (cf. *CBS*, 1173).

'A] he.

49. *I . . . mercy*] a stock phrase: 'I beg your pardon'.

52. *No . . . you*] Perhaps spoken ironically if Fernando has hidden the letter.

55. *for*] of. As 42–4 and 75–8 make clear, the pictures are to be sent to Baglione.

60. *master secretary*] possibly equivalent to the modern 'Mr Secretary'; cf. 1.1.3n.

Fernando. 'Twere rudeness to be suitor for a sight,
Yet trust me, sir, I'll be all secret.

D'Avolos. I beseech your lordship: they are, as I am, constant to your pleasure. [*Showing the first picture*] This, my lord, is the widow Marquess's, as it now newly came from the picture-drawer's, the oil yet green. A sweet picture; and in my judgement, art hath not been a niggard in striving to equal the life. Michelangelo himself needed not blush to own the workmanship.

Fernando. A very pretty picture; but, kind signor,
To whose use is it?

D'Avolos. For the Duke's, my lord, who determines to send it with all speed as a present to Paul Baglione, uncle to the Duchess, that he may see the riches of two such lustres as shine in the court of Pavy.

Fernando. Pray, sir, the other?

D'Avolos. This, my lord, is for the Duchess Bianca; a wondrous sweet picture, if you well observe with what singularity the arts-man hath strove to set forth each limb in exquisitest proportion, not missing a hair.

66–72.] *Verse, verse-cum-prose in Q.* 67. *Showing . . . picture*] *W; no SD Q.* 73–4.] *W;* A . . . Picture; / But . . . it? *Q.* 76. Paul] *Q;* Paulo *G.*

64.] Emphasising the sexual and voyeuristic tone of this scene, D'Avolos is almost cast in the role of pander.

66. *constant*] steadfast in attachment to a person or cause (*OED* 2). He means that both he and the pictures are at Fernando's service.

69. *picture-drawer*] painter.

the oil yet green] the oil-colour still fresh.

71. *Michelangelo*] Vasari's view of Michelangelo's work as the high-point of artistic achievement predominated for more than two centuries, and influenced the first English account of Italian painting, in Henry Peacham's *The Compleat Gentleman* (1622, 117–37; see J. Hale, *England and the Italian Renaissance*, London, 1954, 60–3).

72. *own*] acknowledge as his.

73. *signor*] Perhaps a dab of local colour.

75. *determines*] intends.

78. *lustres*] radiant beauties. *OED* does not record this personified usage before 1814 (*lustre sb.*[1] 2b).

81–2. *singularity*] distinction (*OED* 6). 'In the theory and practice of Italian Renaissance painting . . . the portrayal of a beautiful woman . . . came to function as a synecdoche for the beauty of painting itself' (Cropper, 176).

82. *arts-man*] artist (*OED* 3, quoting only this example; but see the possibly earlier *LM* 5.2.95, and *FM*, 30).

Fernando. A hair!

D'Avolos. She cannot more formally, or—if it may be lawful to use the word—more really behold her own symmetry in her glass than in taking a sensible view of this counterfeit. When I first saw it, I verily almost was of a mind that this was her very lip.

Fernando. Lip!

D'Avolos. [*Aside*] How constantly he dwells upon this portraiture!—Nay, I'll assure your lordship there is no defect of cunning. [*Aside*] His eye is fixed as if it were incorporated there.—Were not the party herself alive to witness that there is a creature composed of flesh and blood as naturally enriched with such harmony of admiral beauty as is here artificially counterfeited, a very curious eye

91, 93. *Asides*] *W; not in Q.*

---

85. *formally*] 'as regards outward appearance, seemingly' or 'accurately, with exact correspondence'. The latter sense would predate *OED*'s earliest instance (*OED* 1c, 4c). 'Formal' is used in the first sense in *Darling* 963; see next note.

85–6. *if . . . really*] Painting was admired for its capacity to 'equal the life' (71), but it was also regarded as a deception. Hilliard observes that perspective and shadowing enable the painter 'by falshood to expresse truth' and 'deceave the eye' (20). Cf. Meleander's praise of a miniature in *LM* 5.2.95–8, and Jonson's lines on the Droeshout portrait of Shakespeare in the First Folio. D'Avolos's insistence that the portrait succeeds in capturing Bianca's beauty should also be seen in the context of the ancient debate about the difficulties (or impossibility) of representing physical beauty (see Cropper, 181).

86. *symmetry*] well-proportioned figure or form (*OED* 2a (b), quoting this example).

87. *sensible*] 'pertaining to the senses' or 'close, acute' (*OED* 1d, 8).

87–8. *counterfeit*] likeness, portrait.

90. *Lip!*] Cf. 3.2.43: '*Bianca.* [*To Fernando*] Your lip, my lord!'

93. *cunning*] skill.

93–4. *incorporated*] combined, embodied (*OED incorporate* v. 2). The verb could = copulate (*Fawn* 2.226; *Oth.* 2.1.262; Williams), but also had connotations of romantic or mystical union (cf. *R&J* 2.5.37). In Donne's 'The Message', the speaker asks his lover to 'Send home my long strayd eyes to mee, / Which (Oh) too long have dwelt on thee' (ll. 1–2; cf. 'Aire and Angels', l. 14).

96. *admiral*] obsolete by-form of 'admirable'.

97. *curious*] careful, particular, sceptical. *Pace* Donald W. Foster (*PMLA* 11, 5, Oct. 1996, p. 1085), the phrase 'curious eye' is not uncommon; see *CBS*, 1513, *Mariam* 4.1.22, *Elegy by WS*, 29; MacDonald P. Jackson, *RORD* 37 (1998), 8.

might repute it as an imaginary rapture of some transported conceit, to aim at an impossibility, whose very first gaze is of force almost to persuade a substantial love in a settled heart.

Fernando. Love! Heart!

D'Avolos. My honoured lord.

Fernando. O heavens!

D'Avolos. [*Aside*] I am confirmed.—What ails your lordship?

Fernando. You need not praise it, sir, itself is praise.
[*Aside*] How near had I forgot myself!—I thank you.
'Tis such a picture as might well become
The shrine of some feigned Venus. [*Aside*] I am dazzled
With looking on't.—Pray, sir, convey it hence.

D'Avolos. I am all your servant. [*Aside*] Blessed, blessed discovery!—Please you to command me?

Fernando. No, gentle sir. [*Aside*] I'm lost beyond my senses.
D'ee hear, sir, good, where dwells the picture-maker?

D'Avolos. By the castle's farther drawbridge, near Galeazzo's

105, 107. *Asides*] *W; not in Q.* 109. feigned] *Q* (fain'd), *H;* fan'd *W;* famed *G.* *Aside*] *this ed.; not in Q.* 111. *Aside*] *G; not in Q.* 113. *Aside*] *GD; not in Q.* I'm] *Q* (I'me)*;* I am *G.* 115. Galeazzo's] *W;* Galzazzo's *Q.*

---

98. *imaginary rapture*] rapturous fantasy; 'visual rhapsody' (*OED rapture* 5, 6). Gazing on the picture of Philoclea, Palladius 'could not choose but ask who she was that, bearing show of one being indeed, could with natural gifts go beyond the reach of invention' (*New Arcadia*, 15).

99. *conceit*] imagination, fancy.

99–100. *whose . . . force*] the first sight of which has the power. He encourages *and* comments on Fernando's responses to the portrait.

100. *substantial*] 'firm' or 'true' (*OED* 10, 15).

101. *settled*] steadfast (and thus able to resist lesser attractions).

109. *feigned*] fabled, imaginary (*OED* 3). See LN for comment on this crux.

Venus] Roman goddess of beauty and sensual love, a frequent subject of paintings. In the ancient world, her principal *shrine* was at Paphos, on the west coast of Cyprus (see *Golden Ass* VII, 114). Her adulterous love for Mars was discovered by her husband Vulcan (*Metamorphoses* IV, 173ff).

114. *good*] good man.

115. *castle*] Perhaps the Visconti Castle, north of Pavia.

Galeazzo] Either: (a) Galeazzo II Visconti (c. 1321–78), who shared the rule of Milan and its environs with his brothers, Bernabò and Matteo, and who governed from Pavia (where he built the castle and founded the uni versity); or (b) Galeazzo's son, Gian Galeazzo (1351?–1402), the 'Conte di Virtù', whose shrewd political and military exploits enabled him to become ruler of all the Visconti territories in northern Italy. He was made Count of statue. His name is Alphonso Trinultio. [*Aside*] Happy above all fate!

Fernando. You say enough, my thanks t'ee. *Exit* D'AVOLOS.
Were that picture
But rated at my lordship, 'twere too cheap.
I fear I spoke or did I know not what;
All sense of providence was in mine eye.

Enter FERENTES, MAURUCCIO *and* GIACOPO.

Ferentes. Youth in three-score years and ten! Trust me, my lord Mauruccio, you are now younger, in the judgement of those that compare your former age with your latter, by seven and twenty years than you were three years ago. By all my fidelity, 'tis a miracle. The ladies wonder at you.

Mauruccio. Let them wonder. I am wise as I am courtly.

Giacopo. The ladies, my lord, call him the green broom of the court—he sweeps all before him—and swear he has a stabbing wit: it is a very glister to laughter.

116. Trinultio] *Q;* Frinulzio *W.* 116. *Aside*] *W; not in Q.* 118–19.] *W;* You . . . t'ee. / Were . . . picture / But . . . cheape. *Q.* 122. Youth . . . ten!] *aside in G.* in] *Q;* is *W.*

Pavia in 1396, founded Pavia's famous Carthusian monastery, the Certosa, and made many contributions to the city's university.

116. *Alphonso Trinultio*] Evidently Ford's invention. In *Malfi*, the Cardinal suggests that Bosola might be able to trace Antonio by going to 'th' picture-makers' and finding out 'Who bought [the Duchess's] picture lately' (5.2.141–2).

119. *rated*] valued.

121. *providence*] prudence, foresight (cf. *Fancies* 2060–3). Neill suggests a quibble on 'fate', and argues that Fernando, Caraffa and Bianca all attempt to 'justify their subjection to passionate impulse' by appealing to destiny ('Neo-stoicism', 76–7). He also notes the play's persistent references to 'the deceits of the eye' (75).

126. *By . . . fidelity*] Another characterising—and this time ironic—asseveration; see 1.2.177n.

128–9. *green . . . court*] playing on the proverb 'A new broom sweeps clean' (Tilley B 682). *Green* = new, youthful.

130. *stabbing*] 'incisive' (cf. *Fancies* 1387). But 'stab' also = 'phallic lunge' (Williams). The obscene quibble is carried on in *glister* (31): a glister- or clyster-pipe, used for administering enemas (*OED clyster* 2; cf. 2.1.15n). Giacopo thus pictures Mauruccio's *stabbing wit* as a phallic instrument, injecting or releasing laughter, as a clyster-pipe injects or releases matter from the bowels. Q's hyphen after 'laughter' (130) may indicate that Giacopo's comment is an aside, or that he is interrupted by Mauruccio.

Mauruccio. Nay, I know I can tickle 'em at my pleasure. I am stiff and strong, Ferentes.

Giacopo. [*Aside*] A radish-root is a spear of steel in comparison of I know what.

Ferentes. The Marquess doth love you.

Mauruccio. She doth love me.

Ferentes. And begins to do you infinite grace.

Mauruccio. Infinite grace.

Fernando. I'll take this time. [*Comes forward*] Good hour, my lords, to both.

Mauruccio. Right princely Fernando, the best of the Fernandos! By the pith of generation, the man I look for. His highness hath sent to find you out. He is determined to weather his own proper individual person, for two days' space, in my lord Narbassa's forest, to hunt the deer, the buck, the roe, and eke the barren doe.

Fernando. Is his highness preparing to hunt?

131–2.] *W; verse Q.* 133. *Aside*] *W; not in Q.* 136. me.] *Q;* me? *S.* 138. *Mauruccio*. Infinite grace.] *this ed., S* (grace?)*; Q & other eds give as part of speech at 137.* 139–40.] *W; verse Q.* 139. SD.] *W; no SD Q.* 143. He is] *Q* (hee 'is)*;* he's *W.* 145. Narbassa's] *Q, this ed.;* Nibrassa's *all other eds.*

---

138. Mauruccio. *Infinite grace*] Given as part of preceding speech in Q. But Q's full-stop after the first 'grace' supports the impression that the last three words are actually the SH for Mauruccio, together with his inane repetition of Ferentes' remark (cf. 136, 'She doth love me'). An easy mistake for the compositor to make if Mauruccio's speech was run on from Ferentes' in the MS (part-lines of verse are printed thus in the quarto of *BH*).

139–40. *I'll take . . . both*] Possibly a verse line, though Fernando usually speaks in prose in this encounter.

142. *By . . . generation*] By the essence (or vigour, or spirit) of procreation (perhaps literally semen, as in *BH* 4.3.108–9). He swears by something he presumably lacks; see 1.2.177n on similar uses of vows.

144. *weather*] probably 'subject to the beneficial action of the wind and sun; air', a term used in hawking (*OED* 1).

proper] comically pleonastic, like the whole of this speech: equivalent to *own, individual*.

145. *Narbassa*] probably Mauruccio's mistake rather than the compositor's.

to hunt] Carlo Gesualdo was said to have feigned a hunting trip; see Corona MS (App. 3), ll. 183–4, also p. 288.

146. *eke*] also. A deliberate archaism; cf *Dream* 3.1.89. Weber and Hoskins suspect a reference to some old ballad here, but no definite source has been found.

Ferentes. Yes, my lord, and resolved to lie forth for the breviating the prolixity of some superfluous transmigration of the sun's double cadence to the western horizon, my most perspicuous good lord.

Fernando. O sir, let me beseech you to speak in your own mother tongue. [*Aside*] Two days' absence; well.—My lord Mauruccio, I have a suit t'ee.

Mauruccio. My lord Fernando, I have a suit to you.

Fernando. That you will accept from me a very choice token of my love. Will you grant it?

Mauruccio. Will you grant mine?

Fernando. What is't?

Mauruccio. Only to know what the suit is you please to prefer to me.

Fernando. Why, 'tis, my lord, a fool.

Mauruccio. A fool?

Fernando. As very a fool as your lordship is—hopeful to see in any time of your life.

Giacopo. Now good my lord, part not with the fool on any terms.

Mauruccio. I beseech you, my lord, has the fool qualities?

Fernando. Very rare ones: you shall not hear him speak one wise word in a month's converse; passing temperate of diet, for keep him from meat four-and-twenty hours, and he will fast a whole day and a night together. Unless you urge him to swear, there seldom comes an oath from his mouth. And of a fool, my lord, to tell ye the plain truth, had 'a but half as much wit as you, my lord, he would

148. *Ferentes*] *Q*; *Mauruccio W.* 154. t'ee] *Q*; t'ye *W.* 164–5.] *Verse-cum-prose Q.* 175. had 'a] *Q* (had 'a); had he *W.*

148–51.] *Lie forth* = lodge away from home; *breviating* = shortening (of); *cadence* = falling. (thus *double cadence* = two days). *Perspicuous* may = (a) a mistake for 'perspicacious' (an erroneous usage which *OED* notes in Reginald Scot's *Discoverie of Witchcraft*, 1584, but see also Webster's Dedication to *Malfi*, 28); (b) 'eminent, distinguished'; or (c) lucid in expression (i.e. what he himself is failing to be) (*OED perspicuous* 2b, 3b, 4). See LN on speech attribution.

168. *qualities*] skills, accomplishments.

171. *meat*] food.

174. *of a fool*] 'as regards a fool' or 'in the matter of folly'. Cf. *WT* 3.2.185–6 (Abbott 173).

be in short time three-quarters as arrant-wise as your lordship.

Mauruccio. Giacopo, these are very rare elements in a creature of little understanding. O that I long to see him!

Enter PETRUCCIO *and* ROSEILLI, *like a fool.*

Fernando. A very harmless idiot.—And as you could wish, look where he comes.

Petruccio. Nephew, here is the thing you sent for. Come hither, fool, come, 'tis a good fool.

Fernando. Here, my lord, I freely give you the fool. Pray use him well for my sake.

Mauruccio. I take the fool most thankfully at your hands, my lord. Hast any qualities, my pretty fool? Wilt dwell with me?

Roseilli. A, a, a, a, ay.

Ferentes. I never beheld a more natural creature in my life.

Fernando. Uncle, the Duke, I hear, prepares to hunt.
Let's in and wait. Farewell, Mauruccio.

Exeunt FERNANDO *and* PETRUCCIO.

Mauruccio. Beast that I am, not to ask the fool's name. 'Tis no matter, 'fool' is a sufficient title to call the greatest lord

178. rare] *Q; omitted W.* 179. SD. *like a fool*] *Q; disguised as a Fool W; dressed like a fool G.* 180–5.] *Verse in Q.* 192. SD *and*] *W;* et *Q.* 193–5.] *Verse in Q.*

176. *arrant-wise*] Taken as pure compliment by Mauruccio, since *arrant* could be used without opprobrious force (as at 196); but the word's more common use in phrases such as 'arrant knave' (*Haml.* 1.5.128) would probably have inverted the praise in spectators' ears.

178. *elements*] parts, features.

179.1. like a fool] He is probably dressed in the long coat of the 'natural fool' (i.e. one who is by nature deficient in intelligence; *OED natural* a. 14a), and may refer to such a coat at 3.2.87. See Intro., p. 50, for further comment on his garb. Like his exemplar Antonio in *The Changeling* (see p. 22), Roseilli disguises himself as a fool in order to be with his beloved, immediately becoming 'the incarnation of foolishness in love' (Diehl, 118).

184. *give you the fool*] with the secondary meaning, 'call you a fool'. Thus Mauruccio's reply (186) would be construed by his on-stage and off-stage audiences as = 'I am obliged to you for calling me a fool'.

use] treat.

190. *natural creature*] The joke (unintentional on Ferentes' part) is that Roseilli is not a 'natural fool' at all; see 179.1n. *Creature* = a term of affection, perhaps with a shade of patronage (*OED* 3b).

in the court by, if he be no wiser than he.

Giacopo. O my lord, what an arrant-excellent pretty creature 'tis! Come, honey, honey, honey, come.

Ferentes. You are beholding to my lord Fernando for this gift.

Mauruccio. True. O that he could but speak methodically! Canst speak, fool?

Roseilli. Can speak, de e e e e—

Ferentes. 'Tis a present for an emperor. What an excellent instrument were this to purchase a suit or a monopoly from the Duke's ear.

Mauruccio. I have it, I am wise and fortunate. Giacopo, I will leave all conceits, and instead of my picture, offer the lady Marquess this mortal man of weak brain.

Giacopo. My lord, you have most rarely bethought you; for so shall she no oftener see the fool, but she shall remember you better than by a thousand looking-glasses.

Ferentes. She will most graciously entertain it.

Mauruccio. I may tell you, Ferentes, there's not a great woman amongst forty but knows how to make sport with a fool. Dost know how old thou art, sirrah?

Roseilli. Dud—a clap cheek for nown sake, gaffer, heeeeee!

204. ear.] *W;* ear? *Q;* ear! *GD.* 208–10.] *Verse in Q.*

---

199. *methodically*] 'with order and regularity', perhaps with connotations (absurd in this context) of scholarly rigour (see *OED methodical* 2, *methodically*).

203. *monopoly*] (a) favour, special privilege; (b) exclusive trading rights (*OED* 2). Monopolies (in the latter sense) granted to members of the aristocracy were a controversial topic. Elizabeth and James prohibited the practice in 1601 and 1603 respectively.

212–13. *there's not . . . fool*] 'Fools and little dogs [or 'fool's baubles'] are ladies' playfellows' (Tilley F 528, quoting *Queen*, 824–9, *'Tis Pity* 1.2.128–9). *Sport* was frequently bawdy; see Williams.

215. *Dud . . . gaffer*] Roseilli's fool-speak is a hotch-potch of 'matter and impertinency': *Dud* probably = a nonsense word; to *clap* or pat someone's *cheek* was a sign of affection; *nown* = a variant of 'own' (through wrong division of 'mine own', 'thine own'). *Gaffer* = a title of address equivalent to 'my good fellow' or (more respectfully) 'master'. Originally a rural term for 'an elderly man or one whose position entitled him to respect' (*OED* 1), it may be used here with some affectation of rusticity; perhaps Roseilli puts on a country accent. Grilla, who enters wearing a countrywoman's farthingale and a fool's coxcomb, uses the word in *LM* 3.3.50 (see 3.3.48.1–2n). Mauruccio later remarks that the fool is 'slow of speech' (3.2.84).

Ferentes. Alas, you must ask him no questions, but clap him on the cheek. I understand his language; your fool is the tender-hearted'st creature that is.

Enter FIORMONDA *and* D'AVOLOS.

Fiormonda. No more; thou hast in this discovery
Exceeded all my favours, D'Avolos.
Is't mistress madam Duchess? Brave revenge.
D'Avolos. But had your grace seen the infinite appetite of lust in the piercing adultery of his eye, you would—
Fiormonda. Or change him or confound him, prompt dissembler!
Is here the bond of his religious vow?
And that now, when the Duke is rid abroad,
My gentleman will stay behind, is sick—or so.
D'Avolos. Not altogether in health, it was the excuse he made.
Mauruccio. Most fit opportunity; her grace comes just i'th' nick. Let me study.
Ferentes. Lose no time, my lord.
Giacopo. To her, sir.
Mauruccio. [*Coming forward*] Vouchsafe to stay thy foot, most Cynthian hue,
And from a creature ever vowed thy servant,

218. SD.] *Enter Fiormonda and D'Avolos, in close conversation G; Enter Fiormonda, D'auolos, Iulia Q.* 226. that] that, *Q.* 229–30.] *Verse in Q.* 231. *Ferentes*] *Q; Giacopo W.* 232. *Giacopo*] *Q; Ferentes W.*

218.1. Q includes Julia's name here. I omit her because: (1) she is given no lines in this episode; (2) Q—usually quite accurate in its SDs—does not mention her in the exeunt at 260.1, and it is very unlikely that she would remain on stage then; (3) upon entrance, Fiormonda and D'Avolos are '*in close conversation*', as Gifford's SD has it.

221. *Brave*] fine, excellent (ironic).

224. *Or . . . or*] either . . . or.

confound] destroy.

225. *his religious vow*] see 1.2.166.

230. *study*] think, concentrate.

233. *Cynthian hue*] Likening Fiormonda's form or appearance (*hue, OED* 1) to that of the moon, conventionally personified as the goddess Cynthia or Diana. The comparison is (unintentionally) ironic, since Diana was the goddess of chastity. Another possible echo of Greene's *Historie of Orlando Furioso*: 'thrice hath . . . Cynthia chang'd her hiew' (4.2, l.1324). Cf. 2.1.94n, LN.

234. *creature*] see 1.1.207n.

Accept this gift, most rare, most fine, most new,
The earnest-penny of a love so fervent.

Fiormonda. What means the jolly youth?

Mauruccio. Nothing, sweet princess, but only to present your grace with this sweet-faced fool. Please you to accept him to make you merry. I'll assure your grace, he is a very wholesome fool.

Fiormonda. A fool? You might as well ha' given yourself.
Whence is he?

Mauruccio. Now, just very now, given me out of special favour by the lord Fernando, madam.

Fiormonda. By him? Well, I accept him; thank you for't.
And in requital, take that toothpicker.
'Tis yours.

Mauruccio. A toothpicker! I kiss your bounty.—No quibble now?—And madam,
If I grow sick, to make my spirits quicker,
I will revive them with this sweet toothpicker.

Fiormonda. Make use on't as you list. Here, D'Avolos,
Take in the fool.

D'Avolos. Come, sweetheart, wilt along with me?

Roseilli. U u umh—u u umh—won not, won not—u u umh.

Fiormonda. Wilt go with me, chick?

238–41.] *Verse and prose Q.* 242. ha'] *Q* (ha); have *W.*

236. *earnest-penny*] (a) a small sum of money (perhaps originally a penny) paid as earnest to secure a bargain; (b) a pledge or foretaste (*OED earnest-penny*, *earnest* sb.[2] 1). Sutfin argues that 'the strain on the figurative use' puzzles Fiormonda. But the expression probably sounded quaint or affected rather than unfamiliar. It was frequent in religious use in the sixteenth and seventeenth centuries (*OED*). Ford uses it himself in *HT*, 235 (cf. *LS*, Epistle, 7). Fiormonda's responds with scorn or embarrassment, not incomprehension (cf. 2.3.43).

237. *jolly*] see 2.1.107n.

247. *toothpicker*] an emblem of affectation and a worthless trifle. Already out of fashion by the time of *AWW* (see 1.1.152–5; Massinger, *Great Duke of Florence* 3.1.383–7).

249. *quibble*] play upon words. 'Philomusus' provides the aspiring courtier with verses 'Vpon a scarfe presented', and 'Upon a paire of Sissers presented', to be recited to the giver of these gifts (157–8).

251. *quicker*] more vigorous, lively.

253. *list*] wish.

Roseilli. Will go, teee—go will go—
Fiormonda. Come, D'Avolos, observe tonight, 'tis late.
Or I will win my choice or curse my fate.
Exeunt FIORMONDA, ROSEILLI *and* D'AVOLOS.

Ferentes. This was wisely done now. 'Sfoot, you purchase a favour from a creature, my lord, the greatest king of the earth would be proud of.

Mauruccio. Giacopo!

Giacopo. My lord?

Mauruccio. Come behind me, Giacopo, I am big with conceit, and must be delivered of poetry, in the eternal commendation of this gracious toothpicker.—But first I hold it a most healthy policy to make a slight supper:
For meat's the food that must preserve our lives,
And now's the time when mortals whet their knives—
on thresholds, shoe-soles, cart-wheels, et cetera. Away, Giacopo. *Exeunt.*

ACT 2 SCENE 3

Enter COLONA *with lights,* BIANCA, FIORMONDA, JULIA, FERNANDO *and* D'AVOLOS. COLONA *placeth the lights on a table, and sets down a chess-board.*

Bianca. 'Tis yet but early night, too soon to sleep.
Sister, shall's have a mate at chess?

2.3.0.2. *placeth*] *Q; places G*

259. *observe*] pay heed to (?; *OED* 6a).
266. *big*] pregnant.

2.3.0.3. table] presumably with chairs for Bianca and Fernando. Tables and chairs were common properties in Phoenix plays (King, 'Staging', 155, 158).

2. *shall's*] shall us, shall we.

a mate] i.e. a game (a sense not recorded by *OED*). Fiormonda picks up the bawdy sense in her reply. Chess was especially popular with the Spaniards and Italians; two other plays featuring chess-games, Fletcher's *The Spanish Curate* (3.4), and Middleton's *WBW* (2.2), are set respectively in Spain and Italy (J. W. Harper, ed., *A Game at Chess*, New Mermaids, 1966, xvi). The game was frequently treated as a metaphor for love-play; see Intro., p. 51. Parallels with the *WBW* scene are discussed on p. 36.

Fiormonda. A mate?
No, madam, you are grown too hard for me.
My lord Fernando is a fitter match.
Bianca. He's a well-practised gamester; well, I care not
How cunning soe'er he be. To pass an hour,
I'll try your skill, my lord. Reach here the chess-board.
D'Avolos. [*Aside*] Are you so apt to try his skill, madam Duchess? Very good.
Fernando. I shall bewray too much my ignorance
In striving with your highness. 'Tis a game
I lose at still, by oversight.
Bianca. Well, well,
I fear you not. Let's to't.
Fiormonda. You need not, madam.
D'Avolos. [*Aside*] Marry, needs she not: how gladly will she to't! 'Tis a rook to a queen she heaves a pawn to a knight's place—by'r Lady, if all be truly noted, to a duke's place; and that's beside the play, I can tell ye.
FERNANDO *and* DUCHESS *play.*

5–7.] *W;* He's . . . gamester: / Well . . . be, / To . . . Lord; / Reach . . . Chesse-board. *Q.* 6. be. To] *this ed.;* be, To *Q;* be, to *W.* 8. *Aside*] *W; not in Q.* 13. *Fiormonda*] *Q; Fernando W.* 14. *Aside*] *H; Aside to Fior. W; not in Q.*

5–7.] The relineation adopted by other eds (see Coll.) produces a speech of three extrametrical lines.

5. *gamester*] (a) game-player; (b) one addicted to amorous sport, a lewd person (*OED* 1a, 5). Shirley's comedy *The Gamester*, a Phoenix play much admired by Charles I, was licensed in the year *LS* was printed (*JCS* V, 1110–11).

7. *Reach*] pass.

12. *still*] constantly.

13. *You need not*] i.e. you need not fear him (ironic).

14–17. *Marry . . . tell ye*] (a general aside or an aside to Fiormonda).

14. *Marry*] exclamation derived from the name of the Virgin Mary: 'indeed, to be sure'.

15. *'Tis . . . queen*] 'I wager a rook against a queen' (though the queen is more valuable).

heaves] (a) moves the chess-piece; (b) raises Fernando (= *pawn*) in social station; exalts (cf. *Sejanus* 4.193); (c) draws him into sexual intercourse. The word-play perhaps continues with *knight's place* (17). *WBW* 2.2.262ff has a similar series of quibbles on chess terms.

16. *by'r Lady*] by our Lady (the Virgin Mary).

17. *beside the play*] i.e. aside from the chess-game (?).

Fiormonda. Madam, I must entreat excuse. I feel
The temper of my body not in case
To judge the strife.
Bianca. Lights for our sister, sirs.
Good rest t'ee. I'll but end my game and follow.

FIORMONDA *takes her leave, attended by* D'AVOLOS *and* JULIA; *as she goes out, she speaks to D'Avolos*:

Fiormonda. Let 'em have time enough, and as thou canst,
Be near to hear their courtship, D'Avolos.
D'Avolos. Madam, I shall observe 'em with all cunning secrecy.
Bianca. Colona, attend our sister to her chamber.
Colona. I shall, madam.

Exeunt FIORMONDA, COLONA, JULIA *and* D'AVOLOS.

Bianca. Play.
Fernando. I must not lose th'advantage of the game.
Madam, your queen is lost.
Bianca. My clergy help me.
My queen, and nothing for it but a pawn?
Why, then, the game's lost, too; but play.
Fernando. What, madam?

FERNANDO *often looks about.*

Bianca. You must needs play well, you are so studious.
Fie upon't! You study past patience.
What d'ee dream on? Here's demurring
Would weary out a statue. Good now, play.

22–3.] *Aside to D'Av. G.* 24. 'em] *Q;* them *W.* 26.] *omitted by S.* 29. th'] *Q;* the *W.* 35. d'ee] *Q;* do ye *W;* do you *G.* Here's] *Q;* here is *GD.*

19. *temper*] state.
case] (suitable) condition.
20. *strife*] (a) contest; (b) love-battle (cf. 4.1.227n).
Lights . . . sirs] See Intro., p. 51, for comment on staging here.
21.1. takes her leave] perhaps with some formal show of leave-taking (see *OED leave* sb. 2).
30. *clergy*] i.e. the chess-pieces called bishops.
35. *demurring*] hesitation, deliberation (*OED demur* v. 3). Cf. *Candy* 5.1, p. 293.
36. *Good now*] Expression of entreaty; *good* = a vocative (Jenkins, Arden edition, *Haml.* 1.1.73n.; Abbott 13).

Fernando. Forgive me, let my knees forever stick
He kneels.
Nailed to the ground, as earthy as my fears,
Ere I arise to part away so cursed
In my unbounded anguish, as the rage
Of flames, beyond all utterance of words,
Devour me, lightened by your sacred eyes.
Bianca. What means the man?
Fernando. To lay before your feet,
In lowest vassalage, the bleeding heart
That sighs the tender of a suit disdained.
Great lady, pity me, my youth, my wounds,
And do not think that I have culled this time
From motion's swiftest measure to unclasp
The book of lust. If purity of love
Have residence in virtue's quest, lo here,
Bent lower in my heart than on my knee,
I beg compassion to a love as chaste

50. quest] *Q;* breast *G.*

38. *earthy*] (a) earth-bound; (b) lowly; (c) heavy (a property of the element earth); and thus, in regard to his fears, 'grave, oppressive'.

39–42. *Ere . . . eyes*] 'Before I arise and leave, so wretched in my boundless (or unchecked) anguish, consumed by the raging, indescribably painful flames (that have been) kindled by your blessed eyes.' *Rage* = 'desire' or 'violent emotion' (*OED* 6). Cf. Petrarch, *Rime* 75, ll. 12–14.

45. *tender*] offer.

47. *culled*] chosen.

48. *motion's . . . measure*] time's brief duration (*swiftest* may simply intensify the radical sense; cf. 'severer', 56). If this reading is correct, these instances of *motion* and *measure* predate *OED*'s earliest comparable examples (*motion* 1b, *measure* 2f). Alternatively, the phrase could = 'brief impulse', 'sudden desire or inclination'. For this sense of *motion* cf. *GM*, 129–30, *PW* 3.4.42–4, *Queen*, 12–13 (*OED motion* 9).

49. *book of lust*] perhaps a variation on 'book of love', a common phrase (cf. *R&J* 1.3.89; *'Tis Pity* 1.1.13; Daniel, *Sonnets to Delia* 1, ll.5–6). Ford's characters demonstrate the 'logocentric nature of Renaissance culture' (Kiefer, 12) by frequently imagining their thoughts or secrets as internalised texts. Books, especially bibles, were often fastened with clasps.

49–50. *If . . . quest*] if pure love (untainted by lust) has a place in the quest for virtue. But cf. 'belepered', 2.2.26n.

As softness of desire can intimate.

Enter D'AVOLOS [*secretly*], *jeering and listening.*

D'Avolos. At it already? Admirable haste!
Bianca. Am I again betrayed? Bad man—
Fernando. Keep in,
Bright angel, that severer breath, to cool
That heat of cruelty which sways the temple
Of your too-stony breast. You cannot urge
One reason to rebuke my trembling plea
Which I have not, with many nights' expense,
Examined; but, O madam, still I find
No physic strong to cure a tortured mind
But freedom from the torture it sustains.

D'Avolos. Not kissing yet? Still on your knees? O for a plump bed and clean sheets to comfort the aching of his shins! We shall have 'em clip anon, and lisp kisses. Here's ceremony with a vengeance.

53. SD.] *this ed.; Enter D'auolos, ieering and listening Q; Enter* D'AVOLOS, *standing apart, jeering and listening W; Re-enter* D'AVOLOS *behind G.* 54.] *aside GD.*

---

53. *softness*] gentleness.

53.1. listening] Robson argues that D'Avolos is unlikely to make the comments he does 'if he can hear what is actually spoken' (140, n. 6), and nothing he says here (or at 117ff) proves that he does really listen. But *OED* gives scant support to the notion that *listen* = 'spy on' or 'observe'. It notes the extended sense, 'give heed to' (v. 2b), but all of the cited examples involve giving heed to speech or writing. See Intro., p. 51.

57. *sways*] rules.

58. *urge*] advance.

62. *physic*] (spiritual) remedy.

65. *aching . . . shins*] A 'broken shin' is Elizabethan slang for 'a sexual disappointment' (see *LLL* 3.1.68n, Arden edition, 1951; cf. Dent[1] S 342.1). Painful nodes on the shin-bones are a symptom of syphilis (John Charles Bucknill, *The Medical Knowledge of Shakespeare*, London, 1860, 251, commenting on *Tim.* 4.3.151–66).

66. *clip*] embrace.

lisp] associated with affectation and lasciviousness (cf. *Haml.* 3.1.147; Middleton, *Father Hubbard's Tales* VIII, 80).

66–7. *ceremony*] courtliness.

67. *with a vengeance*] intensive phrase signalling sarcasm (*OED vengeance* 4b).

Bianca. Rise up, we charge you, rise. Look on our face.

He riseth.

What see you there that may persuade a hope
Of lawless love? Know, most unworthy man,
So much we hate the baseness of thy lust,
As, were none living of thy sex but thee,
We had much rather prostitute our blood
To some envenomed serpent than admit
Thy bestial dalliance. Couldst thou dare to speak
Again, when we forbade? No, wretched thing,
Take this for answer: if thou henceforth ope
Thy leprous mouth to tempt our ear again,
We shall not only certify our lord
Of thy disease in friendship, but revenge
Thy boldness with the forfeit of thy life.
Think on't.

D'Avolos. Now, now, now, the game is afoot! Your grey jennet with the white face is curried, forsooth. Please your lordship leap up into the saddle, forsooth. Poor Duke, how does thy head ache now?

83–6.] *aside GD.* 83. game is] *Q;* game's *W.* 86. does] *Q;* must *G.*

68–70. *Rise . . . love*] '[*Marcelia.*] Reade my life, / And finde one act of mine so loosely carried, / That could inuite a most selfe-louing Foole, / Set of, with all that fortune could throw on him, / To the least hope to find way to my fauour' (*Milan* 2.1.307–11).

68. *we charge*] 'I command' (using the formal royal pronoun).

74. *admit*] allow (*OED* 2a).

75. *dalliance*] wanton toying (*OED* 2).

79. *certify*] inform, assure (*OED* v. 3).

80. *disease in friendship*] italicized in Q.

83. *afoot*] started, in action.

jennet] literally, a small Spanish horse known for its sexual vigour.

84. *white face*] perhaps playing on the meaning of her name in Italian: 'white' (cf. *Shrew* 5.2.191); but she may also have the fair complexion then regarded as an ideal of female beauty. She is also called a 'sallow-coloured brat' (4.1.18) and possibly a 'pale widgeon' (4.2.2n). At 5.1.139 she becomes a 'black angel'.

curried] (a) rubbed down or dressed with a comb (one of the duties of the *manège*); (b) won over by flattery; cf. 'to curry favour' (*OED curry* v.[1] 1, 4).

forsooth] in truth, certainly.

85–6. *how . . . ache*] alluding to the fanciful notion that cuckolds grew horns from their foreheads.

Fernando. Stay, go not hence in choler, blessèd woman!
Y'have schooled me; lend me hearing. Though the float
Of infinite desires swell to a tide
Too high so soon to ebb, yet by this hand,
Kisses her hand.
This glorious, gracious hand of yours—
D'Avolos. Ay, marry, the match is made, clap hands and to't, ho!
Fernando. —I swear
Henceforth I never will as much in word,
In letter, or in syllable, presume
To make a repetition of my griefs.
Good night t'ee. If, when I am dead, you rip
This coffin of my heart, there shall you read,
With constant eyes, what now my tongue defines:
Bianca's name carved out in bloody lines.
For ever, lady, now good night.
Bianca. Good night.
Rest in your goodness. Lights there!

Enter [Attendants] with lights

Sir, good night.
Exeunt [BIANCA *and* FERNANDO] *sundry ways* [*with Attendants*].

D'Avolos. So, via! To be cuckold—mercy and providence!—is

88. Y'have] *Q;* You have *W;* You've *GD.* 103. SD.] *G; 'Enter with lights' after 101 Q.* 103. SD.] *GD; Exeunt sundry wayes. Q.* 104. via!] *this ed.;* via—*Q.*

---

87. *choler*] anger (see 1.2.267n).
88. *schooled*] (a) enlightened; (b) chastened, reproved.
float] flood (*OED* 2; cf. 1.2.89n).
92. *match*] (a) agreement, bargain; (b) pairing, romantic or sexual covenant.
clap] join.
98. *rip*] cut or tear open.
99–101. *there . . . lines*] Echoed by Bianca at 2.4.93–5. See LN.
100. *constant*] probably 'confident, certain' (of his constancy, of finding her name in his heart). (*OED* 3; cf. *Rom. Actor* 5.2.38; *'Tis Pity* 5.5.75–6.)
defines] expresses.
103.3. sundry ways] Emphasising that Bianca and Fernando have not made a 'match'.
104. *via*] 'an aduerbe of encouraging . . . go on, away, go to, on, forward' (Florio).

as natural to a married man as to eat, sleep or wear a nightcap. Friends? I will rather trust mine arm in the throat of a lion, my purse with a courtesan, my neck with the chance on a die, or my religion in a synagogue of Jews, than my wife with a friend. Wherein do princes exceed the poorest peasant that ever was yoked to a sixpenny strumpet but that the horns of the one are mounted some two inches higher by a chopine than the other? O Actaeon! the goodliest-headed beast of the forest amongst wild cattle is a stag, and the goodliest beast amongst tame fools in a corporation is a cuckold.

Enter FIORMONDA.

Fiormonda. Speak, D'Avolos, how thrives intelligence?

D'Avolos. Above the prevention of fate, madam. I saw him kneel, make pitiful faces, kiss hands and forefingers, rise, and by this time he is up, up, madam. Doubtless the youth aims to be Duke, for he is gotten into the Duke's seat an hour ago.

106. Friends?] *this ed.;* Friends! *Q.*

106–9. *I will . . . friend*] T. W. Craik (private correspondence) compares *MWW* 2.2.291–4: 'I will rather trust a Fleming with my butter, Parson Hugh the Welshman with my cheese, an Irishman with my aqua-vitae bottle, or a thief to walk my ambling gelding, than my wife with herself'.

108. *die*] dice.

110. *sixpenny*] that may be hired for sixpence, or worth only sixpence (*OED* 2).

112. *chopine*] type of shoe raised high above the ground by a cork sole or the like, popular in Italy and Spain about 1600 (*OED*), and not only a stage property in early seventeenth-century England (Linthicum, 250). Cf. *Haml.* 2.2.428–30; Moryson, *Itinerary* III, iv, 172.

113. *Actaeon*] Mythological hunter turned into a stag by Diana because he had seen her bathing. His horns became 'a prototype of cuckoldom' (Schmidt). The myth, found in *Metamorphoses* III, ll. 160–304, was a popular theme of literature and the visual arts.

114. *cattle*] animals.

goodliest] i.e. 'goodliest-headed', possessing the largest pair of horns. Cf. *'Tis Pity* 5.2.7.

115. *corporation*] (a) group; (b) (jocular) trade-guild holding a monopoly in a particular area (*OED* 2, 4; cf. *Queen* 1755–60).

116. *intelligence*] spying (cf. *1H4* 4.3.100).

120–1. *Duke's seat*] with similar bawdy quibble as 'duke's place', 2.3.16. *Seat* may = 'vulva' (Williams) or 'saddle', with sexual allusion to 'riding'

Fiormonda. Is't true?

D'Avolos. Oracle, oracle: siege was laid, parley admitted, composition offered, and the fort entered. There's no interruption; the Duke will be at home tomorrow—gentle animal! What d'ee resolve?

Fiormonda. To stir up tragedies as black as brave,
And send the lecher panting to his grave. *Exeunt.*

ACT 2 SCENE 4

Enter BIANCA, *her hair about her ears, in her night-mantle [and bearing a candle]. She draws a curtain, where* FERNANDO *is discovered in bed, sleeping. She sets down the candle before the bed and goes to the bedside.*

Bianca. Resolve and do: 'tis done. What, are those eyes,
Which lately were so overdrowned in tears,

124–5. interruption;] *this ed.;* interruption, *Q;* interruption. *W.* 125–6. —gentle animal!] *this ed.;* (gentle animal) *Q.* 128. send] *G;* sending *Q, W.*

(2.4.1–91 Selected by L) 0. SD.] *Q, W, G, GD, C, E (subst.); Biancha. Fernando, sleeping L.* 0.2. *and bearing a candle*] *this ed.; not in Q.*

(see Blakemore Evans, New Cambridge edition *Son.* 41, 9n). Cf. *Oth.* 2.1.295.

123. *Oracle, oracle*] either a mocking invocation of an oracle, or an affirmation that what he says is 'oracle', i.e. undeniable truth (*OED* 8; cf. *Milan* 4.1.37, *Fancies* 2218–20).

siege] Partridge notes bawdy uses in Shakespeare. The military theme is continued in *parley*, an informal conference with the enemy, under a truce (*OED* sb.[1] 2), and *composition* (123–4): (a) an agreement for submission on particular terms; terms for surrender (*OED* 23b; cf. 3.1.36); (b) physical union.

125–6. *gentle animal*] cf. 'goodliest-headed beast' (113).

128. *send*] Gifford's emendation of Q's 'sending' rectifies both sense and metre. The compositor's eye may have skipped to *panting* in the same line.

panting] Cf. *Tragedy of King Lear* 5.3.218, 'I pant for life'.

2.4.] In the 1997 Bristol production, D'Avolos watched from above. See Intro., p. 53, for discussion of the staging. The episode is somewhat reminiscent of a scene in Fletcher's *Monsieur Thomas*, a Phoenix play composed c. 1610–16 (*ES* III, 228). See LN.

0.1–4] An authorial-looking SD; cf. 3.3.89.1–7, 3.4.17.1–12, 5.3.35.1–8; see p. 274.

0.1. her hair about her ears] Common theatrical signal of sorrow or distraction (e.g. *BH* 4.2.57.1; see Dessen and Thomson).

0.1–2. night-mantle] Possibly a nightgown, a garment which often

So easy to take rest? O happy man,
How sweetly sleep hath sealed up sorrows here.
But I will call him.—What, my lord, my lord,
My lord Fernando.
Fernando. Who calls me?
Bianca. My lord,
Sleeping or waking?
Fernando. Ha! who is't?
Bianca. 'Tis I.
Have you forgot my voice? Or is your ear
But useful to your eye?
Fernando. Madam the Duchess!
Bianca. She, 'tis she. Sit up,
Sit up and wonder, while my sorrows swell.
The nights are short and I have much to say.
Fernando. Is't possible 'tis you?
Bianca. 'Tis possible.

3. man,] *this ed.;* man! *Q.* 4. here.] here? *Q;* here! *G.* 5. What,] *W;* What? *Q* 5–6. my lord . . . Fernando] *italic in Q.* 6. me] *omitted L.* 10. Duchess!] *G;* Duchess? *Q.*

appears in sexual or romantic contexts or as an indication of interrupted sleep (Dessen, *Conventions*, 41–3, cf. *Woman Killed* 13.77.1); but more likely a a loose sleeveless outer covering of some sort. Antecedes *OED*'s earliest example (*night* 13b, *mantle* 1).

0.2. candle] White (171) observes that it would have taken time to extinguish and relight candles, and points out that in *LS*, *'Tis Pity* and other indoor plays, scenes 'in which candlelight plays a key role in establishing place and mood are grouped together in a specific sequence' (cf. 2.3.0.3, 20, 103.1).

curtain] The central stage-entrance of the Jones theatre is about 4 feet 6 inches wide (Orrell, *Theatres*, 50)—perhaps large enough to be used as a discovery space for a bed. But White (private correspondence) doubts that entire scenes were ever played within this opening. In the Bristol production the bed was pushed out on to the stage. 'A bed is usually discovered by drawing open a curtain' (Dessen and Thomson, s.v. *discover*).

2. *overdrowned*] flooded (*OED*).

3. *easy*] 'free' and perhaps 'at ease' (*OED* 1, 2).

4. *How . . . sorrows*] 'When sorrow is asleep wake it not' (Tilley S 662; cf. *Mac.* 2.2.35, *MND* 3.3.23).

5–6. *my lord . . . Fernando*] Italicised in Q, possibly to emphasise the drama and significance of Bianca's first address to Fernando. Or could the italic indicate that she whispers?

8–9. *is . . . eye*] i.e. is your hearing only useful when it is supported by your sight? Perhaps she reveals herself at this point.

11. *swell*] 'grow' or 'well up' (in tears).

Why do you think I come?
Fernando. Why! To crown joys
And make me master of my best desires.
Bianca. 'Tis true, you guess aright. Sit up and listen.
With shame and passion now I must confess,
Since first mine eyes beheld you, in my heart
You have been only king. If there can be
A violence in love, then I have felt
That tyranny. Be record to my soul,
The justice which I for this folly fear.
Fernando, in short words, how e'er my tongue
Did often chide thy love, each word thou spak'st
Was music to my ear. Was never poor,
Poor, wretched woman lived, that loved like me—
So truly, so unfeignedly.
Fernando. O madam—
Bianca. To witness that I speak is truth, look here.
Thus singly I adventure to thy bed,
And do confess my weakness. If thou tempt'st
My bosom to thy pleasures, I will yield.
Fernando. Perpetual happiness!
Bianca. Now hear me out.
When first Caraffa, Pavy's duke, my lord,
Saw me, he loved me; and, without respect
Of dower, took me to his bed and bosom,
Advanced me to the titles I possess,

23. how e'er] *Q, S;* howe'er *W.* 28. speak] *Q;* spake *W.*

---

14. *crown*] consummate, perfect (*OED* v.[1] 9, 10).
17. *passion*] sorrow.
19. *only*] sole.
21. *Be record*] be witness (*OED* 3d; cf. *R2* 1.1.30).
24. *thou*] She begins the speech addressing him as 'you' (16) but adopts the more familiar pronoun as her tone becomes more intimate.
28. *that*] that what.
29. *singly*] 'alone'—rather than 'thus lightly clad', as Gifford suggests (cf. *LOL*, 820).
31. *bosom*] (considered the seat of thought and feelings).
34. *respect*] consideration (cf. *Haml.* 3.1.70–1).
35. *dower*] dowry.
36. *Advanced*] see 1.1.110n.

Not moved by counsel or removed by greatness;
Which to requite, betwixt my soul and heaven,
I vowed a vow to live a constant wife.
I have done so; nor was there in the world
A man created could have broke that truth,
For all the glories of the earth, but thou,
But thou, Fernando. Do I love thee now?
Fernando. Beyond imagination.
Bianca. True, I do,
Beyond imagination. If no pledge
Of love can instance what I speak is true
But loss of my best joys, here, here, Fernando,
Be satisfied and ruin me.
Fernando. What d'ee mean?
Bianca. To give my body up to thy embraces,
A pleasure that I never wished to thrive in
Before this fatal minute. Mark me now:
If thou dost spoil me of this robe of shame,
By my best comforts, here I vow again,
To thee, to heaven, to the world, to time,
Ere yet the morning shall new-christen day,
I'll kill myself.
Fernando. How, madam, how!
Bianca. I will.

37. counsel] *italic in Q.* greatness] *italic in Q.* 48. d'ee] *Q;* d'ye *W;* do you *G.* 52. robe of shame] *italic in Q.*

---

37. *removed by greatness*] made remote or aloof by his high rank (*OED remove* 1b). The parallel structure—*moved*: *removed, counsel*: *greatness*—is emphasised by Q's italicisation of the two nouns. Cf. *Shrew* 1.2.71, 2.1.195–6.

39. *I vowed a vow*] See Huebert, *Baroque*, 91, on the significance of vows in *LS*.

41. *truth*] solemn engagement or promise (*OED* 2).

45. *pledge*] token, sign.

46. *instance*] prove.

47. *my best joys*] perhaps a conscious echo of Fernando's 'my best desires' (15).

52. *spoil . . . shame*] 'despoil, strip me of my shamefastness or decency'; perhaps with reference to her 'night-mantle' (*OED shame* 2; cf. *'Tis Pity* 2.2.89–90; *MND* 3.2.286–7). *Spoil* connotes ruin and plunder (*OED* 6, 8).

55. *new-christen*] christen anew.

56. *How*] expression of alarm.

Do what thou wilt, 'tis in thy choice. What say ye?
Fernando. Pish, do you come to try me? Tell me first,
Will you but grant a kiss?
Bianca. Yes, take it; that,
Or what thy heart can wish. I am all thine. *Kisses her.*
Fernando. O me.—Come, come, how many women, pray,
Were ever heard or read of, granted love,
And did as you protest you will?
Bianca. Fernando,
Jest not at my calamity. I kneel: *She kneels.*
By these dishevelled hairs, these wretched tears,
By all that's good, if what I speak my heart
Vows not eternally, then think, my lord,
Was never man sued to me I denied;
Think me a common and most cunning whore,
And let my sins be written on my grave,
My name rest in reproof.—Do as you list.
Fernando. I must believe ye; yet I hope anon,
When you are parted from me, you will say
I was a good cold easy-spirited man;
Nay, laugh at my simplicity—say, will ye?
Bianca. No, by the faith I owe my bridal vows,

60. SD.] *Q; omitted L.*

---

58. *Pish*] exclamation of impatience or annoyance.
try] put to trial.
63. *protest*] 'declare, vow' (cf. *Haml.* 3.2.219, 'The lady protests too much').
64. *calamity*] 'misery' (Cockeram), 'distress' (*OED* 1). Cf. *Haml.* 3.1.70–1; *Candy* 5.1, p. 298; *Queen*, 469–70.
71. *My . . . reproof*] i.e. 'let my posthumous reputation remain in disgrace'; perhaps echoing 'May he/she rest in peace' (*OED reproof* 1; cf. *PW* 3.4.82).
72. *hope anon*] expect that presently.
74. *good cold easy-spirited*] passionless, careless. *Good* has a mildly depreciatory sense, implying weakness (*OED* 7c, quoting *H8* 3.2.357, 'good easy man').
75. *simplicity*] 'artlessness' or 'folly'.
76. *by . . . vows*] another significant asseveration, contributing to the characterisation of Bianca and drawing the audience's attention to the unusual complications of this scene (see 1.2.177n).

But ever hold thee much, much dearer far
Than all my joys on earth, by this chaste kiss.
[*Kisses him.*]

Fernando. You have prevailed; and heaven forbid that I
Should by a wanton appetite profane
This sacred temple. 'Tis enough for me
You'll please to call me servant.

Bianca. Nay, be thine.
Command my power, my bosom, and I'll write
This love within the tables of my heart.

Fernando. Enough; I'll master passion, and triumph
In being conquered, adding to it this:
In you my love, as it begun, shall end.

Bianca. The latter I new-vow—but day comes on.
What now we leave unfinished of content,
Each hour shall perfect up. Sweet, let's part.

Fernando. This kiss—best life, good rest. *Kiss.*

Bianca. All mine to thee.
Remember this, and think I speak thy words:
When I am dead, rip up my heart and read
With constant eyes what now my tongue defines:

78. SD.] *W; not in Q, L.* 90. let's] *Q;* let us *W.* 91. This kiss] *Q; L omits, ending selection with* 'good rest'. life,] *W;* life *Q.* 91. SD.] *Q; Kisses her W; omitted L.* 93–5. When . . . lines] *italic in Q.*

---

77. *hold*] regard.

82. *servant*] one who is devoted to the service of a lady; a professed—but in this case not actual—lover (*OED* 4b).

be thine] 'I'll be *your* servant' or 'I'll be yours'.

83. *power*] ability, capacity.

84. *tables*] writing tablets (perhaps those comprising a 'table-book' or notebook; see 1.1.153n).

89. *of content*] as regards our satisfaction or pleasure. This idiom is preserved in phrases such as 'swift of foot' and 'ready of wit' (Abbott 173); cf. 'of a fool', 2.2.174. The plural 'contents' = 'pleasures' in *'Tis Pity* 2.1.6, and 'satisfaction' in *BH* 1.1.109.

90. *perfect up*] bring to completion.

91. *best life*] perhaps a vocative: 'my best life'; cf. *MND* 3.2.247.

All mine] i.e. all my *good rest* (?).

92. *think*] know, bear in mind.

93–5. *When . . . lines*] echoing Fernando's words at 2.3.98–101.

Fernando's name carved out in bloody lines.
Once more, good rest, sweet.

Fernando. Your most faithful servant.

Exeunt.

---

96. SD.] *Q; Exit Bianca W; The scene closes G; Exit Bia.—Scene closes GD.*

Act 3

ACT 3 SCENE I

Enter NIBRASSA *chafing; after him* JULIA *weeping.*

Nibrassa. Get from me, strumpet, infamous whore, leprosy of my blood. Make thy moan to ballad singers and rhymers; they'll jig out thy wretchedness and abominations to new tunes. As for me, I renounce thee, th'art no daughter of mine. I disclaim the legitimation of thy birth, and curse the hour of thy nativity.

Julia. Pray, sir, vouchsafe me hearing.

Nibrassa. With child! Shame to my grave. O whore, wretched beyond utterance or reformation! What wouldst say?

Julia. Sir, by the honour of my mother's hearse,
He has protested marriage, pledged his faith.
If vows have any force, I am his wife.

Nibrassa. His faith? Why, thou fool, thou wickedly credulous

3.1.0. SD *after him*] *Q; followed by GD.* 4. th'art] *Q;* thou'rt *W.* 5. disclaim] diclayne *Q.* 8–9.] *Verse Q.* 13–18.] *Verse and prose Q.*

3.1.] The Ferentes plot is borrowed from the *Arcadia*; see Intro., p. 32.

0.1. chafing] incensed, raging.

1. *whore*] Ali points out the ironic juxtaposition of Nibrassa's accusations and the closing lines of the preceding scene, 'in which the apparently unfaithful wife of the Duke has been idealised by her lover' (39).

leprosy] foul infection, specifically referring to sexual depravity (see 2.2.26n).

2. *moan*] complaint.

ballad singers] See LN.

rhymers] inferior poets (*OED rhymer*).

3. *jig out*] (a) sing to the tune of a *jig*, a 'song or ballad of lively, jocular, or mocking (often scurrilous) character' (*OED jig* 3); (b) act out as a *jig*, 'a dramatic ballad or a ballad drama written to dance music, and capable of presentation by dance action on the stage' (C. H. Firth, *SE* II, 515).

5. *legitimation*] legitimacy.

6. *nativity*] birth.

11. *protested*] vowed.

fool, canst thou imagine luxury is observant of religion? No, no, it is with a frequent lecher as usual to forswear as to swear; their piety is in making idolatry a worship; their hearts and their tongues are as different as thou, thou whore, and a virgin.

Julia. You are too violent. His truth will prove
His constancy, and so excuse my fault.

Nibrassa. Shameless woman! This belief will damn thee. How will thy lady Marquess justly reprove me for preferring to her service a monster of so lewd and impudent a life. Look to't: if thy smooth devil leave thee to thy infamy I will never pity thy mortal pangs, never lodge thee under my roof, never own thee for my child. Mercy be my witness—

Enter PETRUCCIO, *leading* COLONA.

Petruccio. Hide not thy folly by unwise excuse,
Thou art undone, Colona. No entreaties,
No warning, no persuasion, could put off
The habit of thy dotage on that man
Of much deceit, Ferentes. Would thine eyes
Had seen me in my grave ere I had known
The stain of this thine honour.

Colona. Good my lord,
Reclaim your incredulity. My fault
Proceeds from lawful composition
Of wedlock. He hath sealed his oath to mine,
To be my husband.

23. life.] *this ed.;* life? *Q;* life! *G.* 24. thy infamy] *Q;* thine infamy *G.*

---

14. *luxury*] lechery.

16. *making . . . worship*] 'Works of the flesh are idolatry' (Galatians 5:20).

19. *truth*] probably 'fidelity to his vow'.

22. *preferring*] recommending.

25. *mortal pangs*] 'extreme pain' (in bringing forth a *mortal* life)?; 'fatal pain'?

26–7. *Mercy . . . witness*] An interjectional use of *mercy*, originating from the phrase 'may God have mercy'; cf. 'mercy on me' etc. (*OED mercy* 4).

31. *habit*] (a) proclivity; (b) clothing (fig.).

35. *Reclaim your incredulity*] i.e. have more faith in me or in what I tell you. *Reclaim* = 'subdue, moderate' or 'call back from a mistaken course' (*OED* 2, 3; cf. *1 Tamb.* 3.1.39, *W. Devil* 4.2.82).

36. *composition*] agreement, contract (*OED* 22; cf. 2.3.123–4).

Nibrassa. Husband? Heyday, is't even so? Nay then, we have partners in affliction. If my jolly gallant's long clapper have struck on both sides, all is well. Petruccio, thou art not wise enough to be a paritor; come hither, man, come hither. Speak softly, is thy daughter with child?

Petruccio. With child, Nibrassa?

Nibrassa. Foh! do not trick me off, I overheard your gabbling. Hark in thine ear: so is mine too

Petruccio. Alas, my lord, by whom?

Nibrassa. Innocent! By whom—what an idle question is that! One cock hath trod both our hens: Ferentes, Ferentes, who else? How dost take it? Methinks thou art wondrous patient. Why, I am mad, stark mad.

Petruccio. How like you this, Colona? 'Tis too true?
Did not this man protest to be your husband?

Colona. Ay me, to me he did.

Nibrassa. What else, what else, Petruccio? And madam, my *quondam* daughter, I hope h'ave passed some huge words of matrimony to you too?

Julia. Alas, to me he did.

Nibrassa. And how many more the great incubus of hell

39. Heyday,] *W*;heyda! *Q*. 44. Nibrassa?] *Q*;Nibrassa! *GD*. 45–6.] *Verse and prose Q*. 48. Innocent!] *W*; Innocent *Q*. 50. art] att *Q*. 56. h'ave] *Q*;he has *W*; hath *H*. 57. too?] *this ed.*;too. *Q*. 59. incubus] *italic in Q*.

---

39. *Heyday*] exclamation of surprise; a compound of the interjection 'hey'. Q's 'heyda' was a common spelling (*OED*).

40. *clapper*] the tongue of a bell (with bawdy quibble not recorded by Williams).

42. *paritor*] aphetic form of 'apparitor', a summoning officer of a civil or ecclesiastical court. Nibrassa pictures Petruccio as an officer dealing with a prostitute (*OED apparitor* 1b, c).

48. *Innocent*] a naive, silly fellow.

idle] foolish.

49. *trod*] copulated with (Williams, *tread*).

56. quondam] former, one-time (Lat.).

hope h'ave] believe he has.

59. *incubus*] 'A feigned evil spirit or demon (originating in personified representations of the nightmare) supposed to descend upon persons in their sleep, and especially to seek carnal intercourse with women' (*OED* 1). James I describes one form of incubus in *Daemonologie* (Edinburgh, 1597): 'the Deuill onelie as a spirite, and stealing out the sperme of a dead bodie, abuses [women] that way, they not graithlie seeing anie shape or feeling anie thing, but that which he so conuayes in that part' (67). Nibrassa refers to Ferentes.

knows best. Petruccio, give me your hand; mine own daughter in this arm, and yours, Colona, in this. There, there, sit ye down together. Never rise, as you hope to inherit our blessings, till you have plotted some brave revenge. Think upon it to purpose, and you shall want no seconds to further it. Be secret, one to another. Come, Petruccio, let 'em alone, the wenches will demur on't, and for the process, we'll give 'em courage.

Petruccio. You counsel wisely. I approve your plot.
Think on your shames, and who it was that wrought 'em.

Nibrassa. Ay, ay, ay, leave them alone. To work, wenches, to work! *Exeunt* NIBRASSA *and* PETRUCCIO.

Colona. We are quite ruined.

Julia. True, Colona:
Betrayed to infamy, deceived and mocked
By an unconstant villain. What shall's do?
I am with child.

Colona. Heigh-ho, and so am I;
But what shall's do now?

Julia. This: with cunning words
First prove his love. He knows I am with child.

Colona. And so he knows I am. I told him on't
Last meeting in the lobby, and in troth
The false deceiver laughed.

Julia. Now by the stars,
He did the like to me, and said 'twas well
I was so haply sped.

Colona. Those very words

62.] *'Jul. and Col. sit down' after* 'together' *G.* 71. SD.] *G; Exeunt Q.* 78. love.] *this ed.;* love; *Q.* 81–3. The . . . sped] *W;* The . . . laugh'd. / *Iul.* Now . . . me, / And . . . sped. *Q.*

64. *to purpose*] i.e. with this purpose in mind (*OED purpose* 12c).

66. *demur*] dwell, think. The word often connotes legal deliberation; cf. *process* (67): (a) action of revenge; (b) (commencement of) legal action or suit (*OED demur* v. 1, 5; *process* 7a; Weber).

75. *shall's*] shall us, shall we.

76. *Heigh-ho*] exclamation of despondency, disappointment, etc. Cf. *M Ado* 2.1.299–300.

78. *prove*] test, try.

83. *haply*] fortunately.

sped] dispatched, dealt with (*OED speed* v. 7b; cf. *Shrew* 5.2.190).

He used to me. It fretted me to'th' heart.
I'll be revenged.

Enter FERENTES *and* MORONA, *an old lady.*

Julia. Peace, here's a noise, methinks.
Let's rise. We'll take a time to talk of this.

[*They rise and withdraw.*]

Ferentes. Will ye? Hold: death of my delights, have ye lost all sense of shame? Y'are best roar about the court that I have been your woman's barber and trimmed ye, kind Morona.

Morona. Defiance to thy kindness! Th'ast robbed me of my good name; didst promise to love none but me, me, only me; swor'st, like an unconscionable villain, to marry me the twelfth day of the month, two months since; didst make my bed thine own, mine house thine own, mine all and everything thine own. I will exclaim to the world on thee, and beg justice of the Duke himself. Villain, I will.

Ferentes. Yet again? Nay, and if you be in that mood, shut up your fore-shop, I'll be your journeyman no longer. Why,

84. to'th'] *Q* (to'th)*;* to th' *W.* 85. SD.] *Q; Enter Ferentes and Morona G (after 85).* 86. this.] *W;* this? *Q.* 86. SD.] *GD (subst.); not in Q; They walk apart W.* 87. Will ye? Hold:] *Q;* Will ye hold? *GD.* 88. Y'are] *Q;* You're *W;* You were *G.* 89. woman's barber] womans-barber *Q.* 91. kindness!] *W;* kindness, *Q.* 95. mine all] *W;* mine, all *Q.* 98. again?] *GD;* again; *Q;* again: *W.* and] *Q;* an *W.*

---

84. *fretted*] vexed, grieved.

85.1. an old lady] Yet she is only 'six-and-forty' (101–2). Average life expectancy in this period probably varied between thirty and forty years (Houlbrooke, 7).

87. *Hold*] forbear. See Coll. for differing treatment of the punctuation.

88. *shame*] shamefastness, modesty (cf. 2.4.52n).

roar] shout or cry.

89. *trimmed*] Williams (s.v. *trim*) cites *Fancies*, 2384–6, and numerous other bawdy usages.

96. *exclaim*] accuse loudly (*OED* 2b).

98. *and if*] if.

99. *fore-shop*] stall at front of shop (see *SE* II, 63; *OED fore-*, prefix 3). Perhaps referring to shopkeepers' practice of using women to draw custom (see Francis Lenton, *Characterismi; or Lentons Leasures*, 1631, sigs E3v–4r); but more likely analogous to *fore-room*, where *room* = vagina (Williams, s.v. *shop*).

journeyman] (a) employee, servant or hireling; (b) lover, where *journey* and *journey-work* = sex (Williams, s.v. *journey*).

wise Madam Dry-fist, could your mouldy brain be so addle to imagine I would marry a stale widow at six-and-forty? Marry gip, are there not varieties enough of thirteen? Come, stop your clap-dish, or I'll purchase a carting for you. By this light, I have toiled more with this tough carrion hen than with ten quails scarce grown into their first feathers.

100. Madam Dry-fist] *italic in Q.* 102. varieties] varieries *Q.* 103. clap-dish] *italic in Q.* 105. tough . . . hen] *italic in Q.* quails] *italic in Q.* 106. first feathers] *italic in Q.*

---

100. *Dry-fist*] *OED*, quoting this example, glosses as 'a niggardly or stingy person'; but a dry hand was considered a sign of age and sterility (cf. *2H4* 1.2.179–82, *Bussy* 3.2.229–31), and *dry* = 'lacking semen' (Williams). A *moist* hand was a proverbial sign of an amorous nature (Tilley H 86, *Oth.* 3.4.36–44).

101. *addle*] muddled, like an addle egg which, being infertile, has begun to rot (*OED addle* B1, 2).

stale] jaded (especially in sexual sense); past the age for marriage (*OED* a.[1] 4, Williams).

102. *Marry gip*] expression of surprise, indignation etc. The combination of two independent interjections was apparently suggested by the oath 'by Mary Gypcy' (*sic*), referring to Saint Mary of Egypt, 'an actress and courtesan who fled into the desert beyond Jordan to expiate her sins; she was found dead . . . c. 500'. The legend which developed around this narrative was popular in the Middle Ages (Attwater; *OED gip* int., *marry* int.).

varieties] (of females).

103. *clap-dish*] wooden dish with lid carried by lepers, beggars and mendicants to give warning of their approach, and to receive alms; here referring disparagingly to Morona's talkative mouth (*OED*). Gifford quotes *Greene's Tu Quoque* by John Cook (1614), ed. Dodsley, VII, 85.

104. *carting*] Common punishment for prostitutes and bawds. Elizabeth Hollande, a brothel-keeper, was sentenced thus on 23 November 1639: 'she shalbe put into a carte at Newgate, and be carted with a paper on her hed shewinge her offence, from thence to Smythfeilde, from thence to her howse, from thence to Cornehill, from thence to the Standerd in Chepe, from thence to Bridewell, and all the way basons to be runge before her, at Bridewell to be punished, and from thence to be broughte to Newgate' (*Middlesex County Records*, I, p. 234, quoted by Herford and Simpson, *Epicoene*, 3.5.87–8n; cf. *2 Honest Whore* 5.2.366.1–4).

105. *tough carrion hen*] old hen with tough, inedible (or rotten) flesh (*OED carrion*).

quails] slang for prostitutes or loose women (cf. *Troilus* 5.1.49, *B. Fair* 4.5.16).

Morona. O treason to all honesty or religion! Speak, thou perjured, damnable, ungracious defiler of women, who shall father my child which thou hast begotten?

Ferentes. Why thee, countrywoman. Th'ast a larger purse to pay for the nursing. Nay, if you'll needs have the world know how you, reputed a grave, matron-like, motherly madam, kicked up your heels like a jennet whose mark is new come into her mouth, e'en do, do. The worst can be said of me is that I was ill-advised to dig for gold in a coal-pit. Are you answered?

Morona. Answered?

Julia. Let's fall amongst 'em. [*Coming forward with* COLONA]
—Love, how is't, chick, ha?

Colona. My dear Ferentes, my betrothèd lord.

Ferentes. [*Aside*] Excellent! O for three Barbary stone-horses

108. perjured . . . defiler] periur'd-damnable-vngracious-defiler *Q.* 110. countrywoman] Country woman *Q.* Th'ast] *Q;* Thou'st *W;* thou'st *GD.* 112–13. a grave . . . madam] *a graue-Matron-like Motherly-Madam Q.* 115–16. dig . . . coal-pit] *italic in Q.* 118. SD.] *G (subst.); no SD Q; Coming forward W.* 118. chick, ha?] *this ed.;* chick? ha. *Q.* 120. *Aside*] *G; no aside Q.*

110. *countrywoman*] 'a woman from rural parts' (*OED*), probably with implication of foolishness or lack of sophistication. There may be an indecent pun on the first syllable, as, perhaps, in *Haml.* 3.2.111 (see 3.2.115n, Arden edition, 1982, and Williams, s.v. *country*, on the pun's popularity). Cf. next note.

purse] punning on 'vagina'. Williams sees 'an insensitive quibble on the stretching involved in child-bearing'. *Purse* could also = scrotum (Williams); thus, perhaps, *larger purse.*

113. *jennet*] see 2.3.83n.

mark] depression in the enamel of a horse's incisor tooth which appears in youth and disappears by the age of seven or eight years; used as an indication of the animal's age. *OED* has seventeenth-century quotations referring to the mark being 'out' of the horse's mouth (sb.[1] 10c).

115–16. *dig . . . coal-pit*] Cf. 'Look not for musk in a dog's kennel' (Tilley M 1329). *Coal* was 'used variously in allusion to the heat of passion', and also referred to sexually exhausted females (Williams). *Pit* and various combinations such as *pit-hole* = vagina (Webb).

120. *Barbary stone-horses*] stallions of a breed originally imported from North Africa; *Barbary* = the Saracen countries along the north coast. *Stone* = testicle; combinations such as 'stone-priest' and 'stone-puritan' indicate lustfulness (*OED stone-horse, stone* 11, 17f; cf. 'Barbary horse,' *Oth.* 1.1.113–14).

to top three Flanders mares.—Why, how now wenches, what means this?

Morona. Out upon me, here's more of his trulls.

Julia. Love, you must go with me.

Colona. Good love, let's walk.

Ferentes. [*Aside*] I must rid my hands of 'em, or they'll ride on my shoulders.—By your leave, ladies, here's none but is of common counsel, one with another. In short, there are three of ye with child, you tell me by me. All of you I cannot satisfy, nor indeed handsomely any of ye. You all hope I should marry you, which for that it is impossible to be done, I am content to have neither of ye. For your looking big on the matter, keep your own counsels, I'll not bewray ye; but for marriage, heaven bless ye, and me from ye. This is my resolution.

Colona. How, not me?

Julia. Not me?

Morona. Not me?

Ferentes. Nor you, nor you, nor you. And to give you some satisfaction, I'll yield you reasons. You, Colona, had a pretty art in your dalliance, but your fault was you were too suddenly won. You, madam Morona, could have pleased well enough some three- or four-and-thirty years ago, but you are too old. You, Julia, were young enough,

121. mares.] *this ed.;* mares? *Q;* mares! *W.* 125. *Aside*] *GD; no aside Q.* 127. common counsel] *italic in Q.* 128. by me] *italic in Q.* 134. from] fró *Q.* 138. Nor you . . . nor you] *separate line in Q.* 141. too suddenly won] *italic in Q.* 143. too old] *italic in Q.*

---

121. *Flanders mares*] (a) the beasts valued as carriage-horses in England, though apparently difficult to control (*OED*, *Flanders* 2); (b) lascivious women (*J. Malta*, 3.4.111–12n; *Edmonton* 4.1.113;.Williams).

123. *Out upon me*] exclamation of abhorrence or reproach.

trulls] drabs, strumpets.

125. *ride*] a sexual quibble, prob. with word-play on *rid*.

130. *for that*] because.

131. *neither*] could be used with more than two subjects (antedates *OED*'s earliest instance; B2c).

132. *looking big*] (a) being pregnant; (b) swelling with anger, looking threatening (cf. *Shrew* 3.3.100).

133–4. *me from ye*] i.e. 'bless' (protect, keep) me from you.

138–44.] A direct borrowing from the *Arcadia*; see Intro., p. 33.

140. *art*] skill.

but your fault is, you have a scurvy face. Now every one knowing her proper defect, thank me that I ever vouchsafed you the honour of my bed once in your lives. If you want clouts, all I'll promise is to rip up an old shirt or two. So wishing a speedy deliverance to all your burdens, I commend you to your patience. [*Exit.*]

Morona. Excellent.

Julia. Notable.

Colona. Unmatched villain.

Julia. Madam, though strangers, yet we understand
Your wrongs do equal ours, which to revenge,
Please but to join with us, and we'll redeem
Our loss of honour by a brave exploit.

Morona. I embrace your motion, ladies, with gladness, and will strive by any action to rank with you in any danger.

Colona. Come, gentlewomen, let's together, then;
Thrice-happy maids that never trusted men. *Exeunt.*

ACT 3 SCENE 2

Enter DUKE, BIANCA, *supported by* FERNANDO, FIORMONDA, PETRUCCIO, NIBRASSA, FERENTES, *and* D'AVOLOS.

Duke. Roseilli will not come, then? Will not? Well,
His pride shall ruin him.—Our letters speak

144. scurvy face] *italic in Q.* 148. deliverance] deliuerace *Q.* burdens] burdes *Q.* 149. SD *Exit*] *W; not in Q.*

---

144. *scurvy*] vile.
145. *proper*] peculiar, individual.
147. *clouts*] cloths for swaddling clothes (*OED* sb.[1] 5).
148. *burdens*] 'Burden' often = the child borne in the womb.
149. *commend . . . patience*] i.e. recommend that you be patient.
154. *brave*] (a) fine; (b) intrepid.
155. *motion*] proposal, scheme. See Mark Thornton Burnett, *Masters and Servants in English Renaissance Drama and Culture* (Houndmills, Basingstoke: Macmillan, 1997), 121–5, on the 'voiceless' plight of maid-servants in similar situations; also *Edmonton* 1.1.
156. *rank with you*] be reckoned among (*OED rank* v.[1] 6b).

3.2.0.1. supported] escorted by the arm (*OED support* 7c).
1. *will not*] as distinct from 'cannot'.
2. *speak*] report, say.

The Duchess' uncle will be here tomorrow.
Tomorrow, D'Avolos?

D'Avolos. Tomorrow night, my lord, but not to make more than one day's abode here, for his Holiness has commanded him to be at Rome the tenth of this month, the conclave of cardinals not being resolved to sit till his coming.

Duke. Your uncle, sweetheart, at his next return
Must be saluted cardinal. Ferentes,
Be it your charge to think on some device
To entertain the present with delight.

Fernando. My lord, in honour to the court of Pavy,
I'll join with you. Ferentes, not long since,
I saw in Brussels, at my being there,
The Duke of Brabant welcome the Archbishop
Of Mainz with rare conceit, even on a sudden
Performed by knights and ladies of his court,

3.2.4. D'Avolos?] *W;* D'Avolos. *Q.* 13. present] *Q;* presence *W.* 18. Mainz] *Mentz Q.*

---

6. *abode*] stay.

his Holiness] i.e. the Pope.

8. *conclave of cardinals*] body of cardinals who are to convene for the purpose of appointing the Abbot as a cardinal. A *conclave* originally = the assembly of cardinals who gathered in a private chamber, or 'conclave', to elect a new Pope.

11. *saluted*] addressed in homage (as). In fact the Abbot is so addressed throughout the play.

12. *device*] fanciful dramatic invention; sometimes (as here) a masque played by private persons (*OED* 6, 11; cf. *MND* 5.1.50, *PW* 2.3.155, *LM* 1.2.155). What eventuates is also a *device* in another sense: a stratagem or trick (cf. *BH* 3.5.86).

13. *present*] occasion in hand (*OED* sb.[1] 2).

17. *Brabant*] ancient duchy in the Netherlands. Sugden suggests an allusion to Archduke Albert, Duke of Brabant, 1598–1621, but no specific reference has been proved. The title had existed since 1190.

18. *Mainz*] German city in Hesse-Darmstadt, seat of an archbishop who was one of the seven Electors (Sugden).

with rare conceit] i.e. in a strikingly imaginative fashion. *Conceit* = 'fancy, imagination', or 'a fanciful, ingenious notion' (*OED* 8). 'Masques were major political events . . . where the court displayed itself not only to itself, but also to foreign ambassadors and diplomats' (David Lindley, ed., *Court Masques: Jacobean and Caroline Entertainments 1605–1640*, Oxford: Oxford University Press, 1995, ix).

In nature of an antic; which, methought,
For that I ne'er before saw women antics,
Was for the newness strange, and much commended.

Bianca. Now good my lord Fernando, further this
In any wise. It cannot but content.

Fiormonda. [*Aside to D'Avolos*] If she entreat, 'tis ten to one the man
Is won beforehand.

Duke. Friend, thou honour'st me.
But can it be so speedily performed?

Fernando. I'll undertake it, if the ladies please
To exercise in person only that;
And we must have a fool, or such an one
As can with art well act him.

Fiormonda. I shall fit ye,
I have a natural.

Fernando. Best of all, madam,
Then nothing wants. You must make one, Ferentes.

Ferentes. With my best service and dexterity, my lord.

Petruccio. [*Aside to Nibrassa*] This falls out happily, Nibrassa.

25. *Aside to D'Avolos*] *Aside W; no aside Q.* 30. an] *Q;* a *W* 32–3.] *GD;* I . . . naturall. / *Fer.* Best . . . wants: / You . . . *Ferentes. Q.* 35. *Aside to Nibrassa*] *G; no aside Q.*

---

20. *antic*] grotesque theatrical representation. *Antics* (21) = 'performers playing grotesque or ludicrous parts'. They often danced; cf. the phrase 'to dance antics' (*OED antic* B3, 4, 4c).

21. *I . . . antics*] Perhaps alluding to Queen Henrietta's participation in court theatricals, or to the appearance of certain French actresses on the London stage in 1629. See Intro., pp. 5–8, for a discussion of this possible evidence of the play's date.

24. *wise*] way.

content] please.

29. *exercise . . . that*] i.e. perform as themselves—as ladies. *MND* 3.1.55–6 also uses *person* in a theatrical sense.

31. *with art*] by skill.

fit ye] provide what you need. A darker sense, '"fix" you, punish you', is suggested by the apparent reminiscence of *Span. Trag.* 4.1.70; see LN.

32. *natural*] natural fool; see 2.2.179.1n. Hoskins notes the dramatic irony in her claim.

33. *wants*] is lacking.

make one] 'be included', as in *LM* 1.2.158 and *Euphues and his England*, pp. 103, 25–7.

Nibrassa. [*Aside to Petruccio*] We could not wish it better: heaven is an unbribed justice.

Duke. We'll meet our uncle in a solemn grace
Of zealous presence, as becomes the church.
See all the choir be ready, D'Avolos.

D'Avolos. I have already made your highness' pleasure known to them.

Bianca. [*To Fernando*] Your lip, my lord!

Fernando. Madam?

Bianca. Perhaps your teeth have bled, wipe't with my handkercher. Give me, I'll do't myself. [*Aside to Fernando*] Speak, shall I steal a kiss? Believe me, my lord, I long.

Fernando. [*Aside to Bianca*] Not for the world.

Fiormonda. [*Aside*] Apparent impudence.

D'Avolos. Beshrew my heart, but that's not so good.

Duke. Ha! What's that thou mislik'st, D'Avolos?

D'Avolos. Nothing, my lord—but I was hammering a conceit of mine own, which cannot, I find, in so short a time thrive as a day's practice.

Fiormonda. [*Aside to D'Avolos*] Well put off, secretary.

36. *Aside to Petruccio*] *GD; no aside Q.* 36–7.] *W; verse Q.* 43. *To Fernando*] *this ed.* 44. Madam?] *GD;* Madam. *Q.* 45. Wipe't] *Q* (wip't); wipe it *W.* 45–6. handkercher] *Q;* handkerchief *W.* 46. *Aside to Fernando*] *G; no aside Q.* 48. *Aside to Bianca*] *H; no aside Q.* 49. *Aside*] *GD; no aside Q.* 50.] *Half aloud) W; no aside Q.* 55. *Aside to D'Avolos*] *this ed.; aside GD; no aside Q.*

---

37. *justice*] judge (?).

38–9. *in . . . presence*] with graceful solemnity in a pious assembly.

39. *becomes*] is fitting for.

45–6. *handkercher*] perhaps recalling *Oth.* 3.3.291ff; see Intro., p. 55.

49. *Apparent*] manifest, plain.

50–4.] Modelled on *Oth.* 3.1.33–5 (after Cassio's exit): '*Iago.* Ha! I like not that. *Othello.* What dost thou say? *Iago.* Nothing, my lord. Or if, I know not what'. Also cf. *Oth.* 4.1.23, 'That's not so good now'. For discussion of Ford's adaptation of *Oth.*, see Intro., pp. 25–8, and notes to 68, 3.3.6–7, 57–9, 71–4, 77.

52. *hammering*] devising (*OED hammer* v. 2a).

conceit] idea.

54. *thrive*] come to fruition.

55. *put off*] evaded.

Duke. We are too sad; methinks the life of mirth
Should still be fed where we are. Where's Mauruccio?

Ferentes. An't please your highness, he's of late grown so affectionately inward with my lady Marquess's fool, that I presume he is confident there are few wise men worthy of his society who are not as innocently harmless as that creature. It is almost impossible to separate them, and 'tis a question which of the two is the wiser man.

Duke. Would 'a were here. I have a kind of dullness
Hangs on me since my hunting, that I feel
As 'twere a disposition to be sick.
My head is ever aching.

D'Avolos. A shrewd ominous token; I like not that neither.

Duke. Again! What is't you like not?

D'Avolos. I beseech your highness excuse me. I am so busy with this frivolous project, and can bring it to no shape, that it almost confounds my capacity.

Bianca. My lord, you were best to try a set at maw.
I and your friend, to pass away the time,

57.] *W;* Should . . . are; / Where's *Maurucio*? *Q.* 58. An't] *W;* And't *Q.* 64. Would 'a] *Q (subst.); '*Would he *W.* 66–7.] *W; one line Q.* 69. not?] *W;* no ? *Q.* 71. with this] *W;* with his *Q.* 73. a set] *Q;* to set *W.*

56–7. *the life . . . are*] i.e. mirthful spirits should always be indulged in our (the royal plural) presence. *Fed* has connotations of satisfying an appetite or passion (see quotation from Northbrooke, *OED, feed* 2b). Cf. 2.1.105–6.

58. *An't*] if it.

59. *inward*] familiar.

61. *innocently*] with implication of foolishness; cf. 3.1.48.

64. *'a*] he.

dullness] gloominess or lethargy (*OED* 2, 3)—recognised symptoms of melancholy (*Anatomy* I, 3, 1, 1, p. 384).

68. *shrewd*] used intensively, as at 1.2.78; cf. *Oth.* 3.3.434. He implies that Caraffa's aching head portends the growth of cuckold's horns.

71. *shape*] definite or proper form, orderly arrangement (the first recorded example in this sense; *OED* sb.[1] 11).

73. *set at maw*] a game of maw, 'an old game at cards. It was played with a piquet pack of thirty-six cards, and any number of persons from two to six' (Halliwell). Harington shared Caraffa's dim view of 'heauing of the Maw': 'A game without Ciuility or Law, / An odious play, and yet in Court oft seene, / A sawcy knaue to trump both King and Queene' (*The Most Elegant and Witty Epigrams of Sir Iohn Harrington*, 1618, IV, 12; quoted by Gifford).

74–5. *I . . . sister*] cf. *Woman Killed* 8.126–8.

Will undertake your highness and your sister.

Duke. The game's too tedious.

Fiormonda. 'Tis a peevish play;
Your knave will heave the queen out, or your king.
Besides, 'tis all on fortune.

Enter MAURUCCIO, ROSEILLI *like a fool, and* GIACOPO.

Mauruccio. Bless thee, most excellent Duke! I here present thee as worthy and learned a gentleman as ever I—and yet I have lived three-score years—conversed with. Take it from me, I have tried him, and he is worthy to be privy counsellor to the greatest Turk in Christendom; of a most apparent and deep understanding, slow of speech, but speaks to the purpose. [*To Roseilli*] Come forward, sir, and appear before his highness in your own proper elements.

Roseilli. Will—tye—to da new toate sure la now.

Giacopo. A very senseless gentleman, an please your highness, one that has a great deal of little wit, as they say.

Mauruccio. O sir, had you heard him, as I did, deliver whole histories in the Tangay tongue, you would swear there

77. knave, queen, king] *italic in Q.* 78. SD *like a fool*] *Q; as a Fool W; disguised as before GD.* 82. and he is] *G;* and is *Q.* 83. Turk in Christendom] *italic in Q.* 85. *To Roseilli*] *this ed.* 88. an] and *Q.* 91. Tangay tongue] *italic in Q.*

---

75. *undertake*] 'take on', challenge (cf. *OED* 5b, 1.1.172n).

76. *peevish play*] childish, silly game. (Cf. quotation in 73n).

82. *tried*] tested.

83. *greatest . . . Christendom*] to 'turn Turk' was proverbial for an utter change, 'as from a Christian to an infidel' (*ODEP*). Q's italicisation perhaps highlights the absurdity.

86. *in . . . elements*] i.e. as your true self (unintentionally ironic). *Elements* = (a) the 'raw material' of which he is composed; (b) the constituent parts of his character (*OED element* 1, 2, 5a; viz. the four elements).

87. *da new toate*] 'the new coat', i.e. his fool's coat? (Perhaps responding to the request for him to appear in his *own proper elements*, 86.)

88. *an*] if it.

91. *histories*] historical accounts or stories.

Tangay tongue] Perhaps 'the language of Tangier, the Moorish name of which is Tanja' (Sugden, quoting only this instance of *Tangay*). 'Tanga' = various coins in India, Persia and Turkestan; *OED* quotes instances in English from 1598 and 1615–16.

were not such a linguist breathed again; and did I but perfectly understand his language, I would be confident, in less than two hours, to distinguish the meaning of 'bird', 'beast' or 'fish' naturally as I myself speak Italian, my lord.—Well, he has rare qualities.

Duke. Now prithee question him, Mauruccio.

Mauruccio. I will, my lord:
Tell me, rare scholar, which in thy opinion,
Doth cause the strongest breath—garlic or onion?

Giacopo. Answer him, brother fool, do, do. Speak thy mind, chuck, do.

Roseilli. Have bid seen all da fine knack, and d'ee naughty tat-tle of da kna-ve, dad la have so.

Duke. We understand him not.

Mauruccio. Admirable, I protest, Duke. Mark, O Duke, mark!—What did I ask him, Giacopo?

Giacopo. Which caused the strongest breath, garlic or onions, I take it, sir.

Mauruccio. Right, right, by Helicon, and his answer is that a knave has a stronger breath than any of 'em. Wisdom—or I am an ass—in the highest! A direct figure: put it down, Giacopo.

100. garlic, onion] *italic in Q.* 103–4.] *Verse Q.* 103. d'ee] *Q;* dee *W;* de, e, *G.* 104. tat-tle] *Q;* tattle *W.* kna-ve] *Q;* knave *W.*

---

92. *breathed*] (a) lived; (b) spoke.

95. *naturally . . . Italian*] probably a metatheatrical joke (cf. Portia's claim to have only 'a poor pennyworth in the English', *MerVen* 1.2.68–9).

96. *qualities*] skills, accomplishments (as at 2.2.168).

102. *chuck*] term of affection.

103–4. *Have . . . so*] 'I have seen all the fine knacks (tricks, crafty devices: *OED* sb.[2] 1) and the naughty tattle (wicked gossip) of the knave (D'Avolos?), indeed, I have so'. (*Dad la* may = a simpleton's version of 'indeed la', cf. 1.2.59.) He is perhaps trying to warn Fernando about the machinations of D'Avolos and Fiormonda—as he does more openly at 134ff, when alone with Fernando. Like Lear's Fool, this seeming idiot speaks cryptic sense.

106. *protest*] declare (an asseveration; *OED* 1c).

110. *Helicon*] See 2.1.38n.

111. *stronger*] (a) more effectual; (b) more dangerous.

breath] (a) expiration; (b) speech. Cf. 'naughty tat-tle', 103–4.

112. *direct figure*] a veritable (or unambiguous) aphorism or figure of speech (*OED direct* adj. 5a 5c; *figure* 21; cf. *AYL* 5.1.40–2).

Duke. How happy is that idiot whose ambition
Is but to eat and sleep and shun the rod.
Men that have more of wit and use it ill
Are fools in proof.

Bianca. True, my lord. There's many
Who think themselves most wise that are most fools.

D'Avolos. Bitter girds, if all were known—but—

Duke. But what? Speak out, plague on your muttering grumbling! I hear you, sir, what is't?

D'Avolos. Nothing, I protest, to your highness pertinent to any moment.

Duke. Well, sir, remember.—[*To Fernando*] Friend, you promised study.
I am not well in temper. Come, Bianca.
Attend our friend, Ferentes.

Exeunt; FERNANDO, ROSEILLI, FERENTES, MAURUCCIO [*and* GIACOPO *remain*].

Fernando. Ferentes, take Mauruccio in with you.
He must be one in action.

Ferentes. [*To Mauruccio*] Come, my lord, I shall entreat your help.

Fernando. I'll stay the fool and follow instantly.

120–1.] *this ed.; verse Q.* 124. *To Fernando*] *this ed.* 126. friend,] *W;* friend *Q.* 126. SD *and* GIACOPO] *not in Q.* 129. *To Mauruccio*] *this ed.* 130.] *this ed.;* I'le . . . Foole: / And . . . instantly. *Q.*

114–15. *How . . . rod*] 'Some think fools and dizzards [blockheads] live the merriest lives, as Ajax in Sophocles, *Nihil scire vita jucundissima,* 'tis the pleasantest life to know nothing' (*Anatomy* II.3.1.1, p. 206). The *rod* (a single straight stick or a bundle of twigs) was a common instrument of punishment and control for fools and mad people (Robert Rentoul Reed, Jr, *Bedlam on the Jacobean Stage,* Cambridge, Mass.: Harvard University Press, 1952, 35–6).

117. *in proof*] 'truly, certain; proven so' (by their actions).

119. *girds*] gibes (*OED* sb.[2] 4).

120. *muttering*] (participial adjective).

122. *protest*] swear, promise.

122–3. *to . . . moment*] of any consequence to your highness (*OED moment* 4).

124. *study*] i.e. studied endeavour (*OED* 4) in arranging the masque.

125. *temper*] physical condition and/or mental state; cf. 2.3.19.

128. *action*] performance (*OED* 12; cf. *'Tis Pity,* Ep., 11–12).

130. *stay*] wait for (*OED* v.[1] 19).

Mauruccio. Yes, pray, my lord.
Exeunt FERENTES, MAURUCCIO [*and* GIACOPO].
Fernando. How thrive your hopes now, cousin?
Roseilli. Are we safe?
Then let me cast myself beneath thy foot,
True, virtuous lord. Know then, sir, her proud heart
Is only fixed on you in such extremes
Of violence and passion that I fear
Or she'll enjoy you or she'll ruin you.
Fernando. Me, coz? By all the joys I wish to taste,
She is as far beneath thy thought as I
In soul above her malice.
Roseilli. I observed
Even now a kind of dangerous pretence
In an unjointed phrase from D'Avolos.
I know not her intent, but this I know:
He has a working brain, is minister
To all my lady's counsels; and, my lord,
Pray heaven there have not anything befall'n
Within the knowledge of his subtle art
To do you mischief.
Fernando. Pish! should he or hell
Affront me in the passage of my fate,
I'd crush them into atomies.
Roseilli. I do admit you could; meantime, my lord,

131. SD *and* GIACOPO] *not in Q.* 139. thy] *Q;* my *G.* 143. her] *W;* hir *Q;* his *GD.* 146. befall'n] *Q* (befalne), *GD;* befallen *W.* 151. I do admit] *W;* I, doe; admit *Q.*

---

136. *violence*] vehemence, intensity (*OED* 5; cf. *Oth.* 2.1.223).
137. *Or . . . or*] either . . . or.
138. *coz*] contraction of 'cousin', used in fond or familiar address to relatives and friends (*OED*).
141. *pretence*] a feigned or hypocritical profession; a design (*OED* 3a, b).
142. *unjointed*] incoherent (cf. *1H4* 1.3.64).
144. *working*] active, scheming.
minister] attendant, agent (*OED* 1, 2).
145. *counsels*] private thoughts, secret designs (*OED counsel* 5; cf. 1.1.4).
147. *art*] cunning.
149. *Affront*] confront.
passage] course (*OED* 2).
150. *atomies*] atoms, smithereens (*OED atomy*[2] 1).

Be nearest to yourself. What I can learn
You shall be soon informed of. Here is all
We fools can catch the wise in: to unknot,
By privilege of coxcombs, what they plot. *Exeunt.*

ACT 3 SCENE 3

Enter DUKE *and* D'AVOLOS.

Duke. Thou art a traitor. Do not think the gloss
Of smooth evasion, by your cunning jests
And coinage of your politician's brain,
Shall jig me off. I'll know't, I vow I will.
Did not I note your dark abrupted ends
Of words half-spoke? Your 'wells, if all were known'?
Your short 'I like not that'? Your girds and 'buts'?
Yes, sir, I did. Such broken language argues
More matter than your subtlety shall hide.
Tell me, what is't? By honour's self, I'll know.

3.3.6. wells . . . known] *italic in Q.* 7. I . . . that] *italic in Q.*

152. *Be . . . yourself*] 'keep your own counsel' or 'consider your own welfare' (cf. *PW* 2.2.51).

153–5. *Here . . . plot*] 'Fools set stools for wise men to stunble at' (Dent[2], Tilley F 543).

155. *privilege of coxcombs*] See LN.

3.3.1–77.] Modelled on *Oth.* 3.3.91–261; see following notes, Intro., p. 56.

1. *gloss*] deceptive lustre.

2. *smooth*] shifty, sly.

3. *coinage*] invention (*OED* 6).

4. *jig me off*] put me off by using a *jig*: 'a sportive trick or cheat' (*OED* sb. 5; v. 4).

5. *dark . . . ends*] obscure, broken-off fragments (*OED dark* 6; *abrupted*; *end* 5b).

6–7. *Your . . . 'buts'*] 'I heard thee say even now thou liked'st not that, / When Cassio left my wife. What didst not like? / And when I told thee he was of my counsel / In my whole course of wooing, thou cried'st "Indeed?"' (Othello to Iago, 3.3.113–16). *Girds* = gibes (*OED* sb.[2] 4).

9. *matter*] meaning, purport (*OED* sb.[2] 11). D'Avolos picks up the word in his reply (14), where it = 'material, things to say' (*OED* sb.[1] 9). 'these stops of thine fright me the more . . . in a man that's just, / They're close dilations, working from the heart' (*Oth.* 3.3.125–8).

10. *By honour's self*] by honour itself (*OED self* C1b). 'By heaven, I'll know thy thoughts' (*Oth.* 3.3.166).

D'Avolos. What would you know, my lord? I confess I owe my life and service to you, as to my prince. The one you have, the other you may take from me at your pleasure. Should I devise matter to feed your distrust, or suggest likelihoods without appearance? What would you have me say? I know nothing.

Duke. Thou liest, dissembler. On thy brow I read
Distracted horrors figured in thy looks.
On thy allegiance, D'Avolos, as e'er
Thou hop'st to live in grace with us, unfold
What, by the parti-halting of thy speech,
Thy knowledge can discover. By the faith
We bear to sacred justice, we protest,
Be it or good or evil, thy reward
Shall be our special thanks and love untermed.
Speak, on thy duty; we thy prince command.

D'Avolos. O my disaster! My lord, I am so charmed by those powerful repetitions of love and duty, that I cannot conceal what I know of your dishonour.

Duke. Dishonour? Then my soul is cleft with fear.
I half presage my misery. Say on,
Speak it at once, for I am great with grief.

21. by the] *G;* by thy *Q.*

---

11. *confess*] acknowledge, avow (*OED* 4); but playing on the 'confession' of his thoughts which Caraffa is seeking from him.

11–12. *I owe . . . prince*] Iago also refers to his duty, *Oth.* 3.3.139.

15. *appearance*] clear manifestation (*OED* 7). Nares quotes *Tragedy of Byron* 1.3.14–15.

18. *Distracted*] crazed (*OED* 5).

figured] (a) expressed in 'figures': written characters, images, etc., perhaps with reference to the lines in D'Avolos's *brow* (= his forehead or countenance); (b) prefigured (*OED* v. 5). For the latter sense, cf. *Tragedy of Byron* 2.1.128–9, *3H6* 2.1.32. Othello says Iago 'didst contract and purse thy brow together / As if thou then hadst shut up in thy brain / Some horrible conceit' (3.3.117–19).

21. *by*] i.e. according to, judging by (Abbott 145).

parti-halting] faltering, 'stops and starts'.

22. *discover*] reveal.

23. *protest*] vow, swear.

25. *untermed*] unbounded (*OED*).

27. *disaster*] misfortune (*OED* 2).

charmed] influenced, enthralled, as if by a magic charm; cf. *powerful repetitions*, 28 (*OED charm* v.[1] 5).

32. *great*] (a) full; (b) pregnant (probably with a sense of the heart or breast swelling with feeling). Cf. *Per.* 21.95.

D'Avolos. I trust your highness will pardon me, yet I will not deliver a syllable which shall be less innocent than truth itself.

Duke. By all our wish of joys, we pardon thee.

D'Avolos. Get from me cowardly servility; my service is noble and my loyalty an armour of brass. In short, my lord, and plain discovery, you are a cuckold.

Duke. Keep in the word—a cuckold?

D'Avolos. Fernando is your rival, has stolen your Duchess' heart, murdered friendship, horns your head, and laughs at your horns.

Duke. My heart is split.

D'Avolos. Take courage, be a prince in resolution. I knew it would nettle you in the fire of your composition, and was loath to have given the first report of this more than ridiculous blemish to all patience or moderation. But O my lord, what would not a subject do to approve his loyalty to his sovereign? Yet, good sir, take it as quietly as you can. I must needs say 'tis a foul fault, but what man is he under the sun that is free from the career of his destiny? Maybe she will in time reclaim the errors of her youth; or 'twere a great happiness in you if you could not believe it. That's the surest way, my lord, in my poor counsel.

36. joys] *Q;* loves *W.* 39–40. cuckold] *italic in Q.* 54. 'twere] *Q;* t'were *W.*

---

39. *discovery*] disclosure.

42. *horns your head*] (with cuckold's horns).

45. *resolution*] resoluteness, determination.

46. *nettle . . . composition*] vex you and stir the fiery spirit in your nature. Referring to the belief that 'life's composition' (*Son.* 45, l. 9) comprised the four elements, earth, fire, air and water. Caraffa seems grief-stricken rather than angry (44), and D'Avolos seeks to incite him by implying that he is a courageous, fiery-spirited (i.e. 'choleric') man. (*OED nettle* 2, 3; *fire* 13b; *composition* 16b).

48. *ridiculous*] perhaps 'causing ridicule or derision' (*OED* 1a).
blemish] moral 'stain', slur (*OED* 3).

49. *approve*] prove.

52. *career*] course (*OED* 3, 4).

53. *reclaim*] amend (*OED* 2d).

Duke. The icy current of my frozen blood
Is kindled up in agonies as hot
As flames of burning sulphur. O my fate!
A cuckold? Had my dukedom's whole inheritance
Been rent, mine honours levelled in the dust,
So she, that wicked woman, might have slept
Chaste in my bosom, 't had been all a sport.
And he, that villain, viper to my heart,
That he should be the man!
That he should be the man. Death above utterance!
Take heed you prove this true.
D'Avolos. My lord.
Duke. If not,
I'll tear thee joint by joint.—Pew, methinks
It should not be. Bianca? Why, I took her
From lower than a bondage. Hell of hells!
See that you make it good.

65. That . . . man!] *Q; omitted G.* 68. Pew] *Q;* Phew *H.*

57–9. *The icy . . . sulphur*] 'Like to the Pontic Sea, / Whose icy current and compulsive course / Ne'er knows retiring ebb' (*Oth.* 3.3.456ff—a passage only in F; cf. *LS* 5.1.136n).

59. *sulphur*] or brimstone, popularly associated with the fires of hell. Iago observes that 'Dangerous conceits are in their natures poisons' which at first 'are scarce found to distaste', but soon 'act upon the blood, / Burn like the mines of sulphur' (*Oth.* 3.3.330–3).

60–3. *A cuckold? . . . sport*] 'Had it pleased God / To try me with affliction' (Othello to Desdemona, 4.2.49–57).

61. *rent*] torn apart, ruined.

62. *So*] if only, so long as (*OED* 26).

63. *bosom*] 'the place of tender affections and favour' (Schmidt).

sport] jest, amusement.

64. *viper . . . heart*] Pliny relates that the serpent's offspring 'eat through the sides of their dam' at birth, killing her (*Natural History*, Bk 10, LXII; translated by Philemon Holland, 1601, 302). Frequently cited in reproof of persons who were false to those who supported or advanced them (*OED* 3; cf. *BH* 2.2.1–2, *PW* 3.4.33).

65–6. *That . . . man*] Gifford removed the first line, judging it to be an error. But the repetition makes good theatrical sense, allowing the actor to stress what is both a vital concern for his character and a predominant theme of the play. Significantly, Q gives italic emphasis to *he* in both lines.

70. *bondage*] position of servitude.

71. *make it good*] prove it. D'Avolos picks up the phrase in his reply. Othello warns Iago: 'Villain, be sure thou prove my love a whore. / Be sure of it. Give me the ocular proof' (3.3.364–5).

D'Avolos. As for that, would it were as good as I would make it, I can, if you will temper your distractions, but bring you where you shall see it; no more.

Duke. See it?

D'Avolos. Ay, see it, if that be proof sufficient. I, for my part, will slack no service that may testify my simplicity.

Enter FERNANDO.

Duke. Enough.—What news, Fernando?

Fernando. Sir, the Abbot
Is now upon arrival. All your servants
Attend your presence.

Duke. We will give him welcome
As shall befit our love and his respect.
Come, mine own best Fernando, my dear friend.

Exeunt DUKE *and* FERNANDO.

D'Avolos. Excellent! now for a hornèd moon.

Sound of music

But I hear the preparation for the entertainment of this great Abbot. Let him come and go, that matters nothing to this. Whiles he rides abroad in hope to purchase a purple hat, our Duke shall as earnestly heat the peri-

72. would it] *Q*; 'would it *W.* 78–80.] *W;* Enough . . . *Fernando*? / *Fer*, Sir . . . seruants / Attend . . . presence. / *Duke.* We . . . welcome *Q.* 82. SD.] *G (subst.); Exeunt Q.* 83. SD.] *Q; Music within G.* 85. great Abbot] *italic in Q.* 86. Whiles] *Q;* whilst *W.* 87–8. pericranion] *Q;* pericranium *W.*

72–4.] Cf. *Oth.* 3.3.399–401: '[*Iago.*] But how, how satisfied, my lord? / Would you, the supervisor, grossly gape on, / Behold her topped? *Othello.* Death and damnation! O!'

73. *distractions*] (outbursts of) disturbed emotion.

77. *simplicity*] sincerity, freedom from deceit. Cf. *Oth.* 3.3.414–18.

79. *upon*] at the point of (*OED* prep. 6d).

80. *Attend*] await.

81. *respect*] eminence.

83. *now . . . moon*] i.e. all we need now is for the moon to grow cuckold's horns (referring to the horns of the crescent moon). Cf. *MND* 5.1.235–8.

84. *entertainment*] 'reception', and perh. 'amusement'.

85. *great Abbot*] Q's italicisation of the phrase perhaps signals sarcasm.

86. *rides*] Particularly associated with riding in triumphs and processions: perhaps implying ostentatious display (*OED ride* v. 2b). Cf. *LLL* 4.3.33, *LM* 3.3.29.

purchase] 'acquire', perhaps hinting at payment (*OED* 4, 6a).

87. *purple hat*] i.e. the rank of cardinal, whose hat and garments are actually scarlet; *purple* formerly = various shades of red (*OED purple* sb. 1).

cranion of his noddle with a yellow hood at home. I hear 'em coming.

Loud music. Enter three or four with torches; after, the DUKE, FERNANDO, BIANCA, FIORMONDA, PETRUCCIO, NIBRASSA *at one door. Enter at another door two Friars,* ABBOT *and Attendants. The* DUKE *and* ABBOT *meet and salute.* BIANCA *and the rest salute and are saluted. They rank themselves, and go out, the choir singing.* D'AVOLOS *only stays.*

D'Avolos. On to your vittailes; some of ye, I know, feed upon wormwood. *Exit.*

ACT 3 SCENE 4

Enter PETRUCCIO *and* NIBRASSA *with napkins, as from supper.*

Petruccio. The Duke's on rising. Are you ready, ho?

89.1. *four*] *Q; four servants W.* 89.3–4. *Enter . . . door*] *Q; At the other, W.* 89.7. D'AVOLOS . . . *stays*] *Q; omitted W.* 90.] *(going out.) W.*

87–8. *heat . . . noddle*] i.e. 'keep his head warm' or perhaps 'become agitated'. *Pericranion* (Q's Greek form was common in the sixteenth and seventeenth centuries) = (a) the membrane enveloping the skull; (b) humorous term for the skull or brain. *Noddle* = a contrastingly idiomatic term for the same thing, usually implying foolishness (*OED pericranium* 1, 2; *noddle* sb.[1] 3).

88. *yellow hood*] a hood was a proverbial head-dress for a fool (Tilley H 585), but the precise meaning is unclear. See LN.

89.1–7] This action has some of the characteristics of a procession, a popular spectacle in the theatre. In the private playhouses, processions were often coupled with masques, as here.

89.1. three or four] possible authorial ambiguity; see 'Printing', 304–5.

89.3–4. another door] The Jones playhouse has three stage entrances; see Figure 1.

89.5. salute] greet each other with a courteous show of recognition (*OED* v. 2).

89.6. rank themselves] arrange themselves in rows or in file, probably with regard for social position (*OED rank* v.[1] 1; sb.[1] 2, 8, 9).

90. *vittailes*] obsolete form of 'victuals', food (contemptuous).

91. *wormwood*] medicinal plant proverbial for its bitter taste; an emblem of grief and bitterness (*OED* 1, 2; cf. *LM* 2.2.82, *PW* 1.2.20–3).

3.4.0.2. as from supper] A very common form of instruction. Dramatists 'knew that the actors could act out such a signal simply yet effectively for their spectators' (Dessen, *Conventions*, 31). Cf. *'Tis Pity* 2.1.0.

1. *on rising*] i.e. about to rise from his meal.

Within. All ready.

Nibrassa. Then, Petruccio, arm thyself with courage and resolution, and do not shrink from being stayed on thy own virtue.

Petruccio. I am resolved.—Fresh lights, I hear 'em coming.

Enter some with lights; the DUKE, ABBOT, BIANCA, FIORMONDA, FERNANDO *and* D'AVOLOS.

Duke. Right reverend uncle, though our mind be scanted
In giving welcome as our hearts would wish,
Yet we will strive to show how much we joy
Your presence with a courtly show of mirth.
Please you to sit.

Abbot. Great Duke, your worthy honours
To me shall still have place in my best thanks.
Since you in me so much respect the Church,
Thus much I'll promise: at my next return,
His Holiness shall grant an indulgence
Both large and general.

Duke. Our humble duty.
Seat you, my lords. Now let the masquers enter.

[*Music.*] *Enter in an antic fashion* FERENTES, ROSEILLI *and* MAURUCCIO *at several doors. They dance a little. Suddenly to them enter* COLONA, JULIA, MORONA *in odd shapes, and dance. The men gaze at them, are at a stand, and are invited by the women to dance. They dance together sundry changes; at last*

3.4.11–12.] *W;* Please . . . sit. / *Abbot.* Great . . . me, / Shall . . . thanks: *Q.*
15. an] *Q;* you an *G.* 17.1. *Music*] *not in Q.* *antic*] *Q;* antique *W.*

4–5. *being . . . virtue*] i.e. being 'put on your mettle', made to prove your valour or worth (Lat., *virtus*).

7. *scanted*] straitened, made deficient, and therefore negligent.

9. *joy*] 'take delight in' or 'greet with expressions of joy' (*OED* 4, 5).

12. *still*] always.

13. *in*] by means of, through.

15. *indulgence*] (a) favour, privilege; (b) remission of sin (ironic, in view of what is about to be witnessed).

16. *general*] i.e. benefiting many.

17. *masquers*] performers in a masque, 'a form of amateur histrionic entertainment, popular at Court and amongst the nobility in England during the latter part of the 16th c. and the first half of the 17th c.; originally consist-

[the women] close FERENTES *in,* MAURUCCIO *and* ROSEILLI *being shook off and standing at several ends of the stage, gazing. The women hold hands and dance about* FERENTES *in diverse complimental offers of courtship. At length, they suddenly fall upon him and stab him; he falls down, and they run out at several doors. Cease music.*

Ferentes. Uncase me, I am slain in jest. A pox upon your outlandish feminine antics! Pull off my visor, I shall bleed to death ere I have time to feel where I am hurt. Duke, I am slain. Off with my visor, for heaven's sake, off with my visor.

17.6–7. *the women*] *this ed.; they Q.* 17.12. *Cease music*] *Separate line in Q.*

ing of dancing and acting in dumb show, the performers being masked and habited in character' (*OED masque* 2). The masquers often made a surprise entry, and invited those already present to dance with them (*W. Devil* 5.6.169n). Supervacuo comments on the convention: 'A masque is treason's licence, that build upon; / 'Tis murder's best face when a vizard's on' (*Rev. Trag.* 5.1.181–2; cf. *Antonio's Revenge* 5.5, *WBW* 5.2, *'Tis Pity* 4.1).

17.1. in an antic fashion] 'fantastically dressed' and/or 'with fantastic or grotesque movements'.

17.2. several] different (two or more).

17.4. in odd shapes] as strange characters; in unusual costumes (including 'visors' or masks; *OED shape* 8).

17.5. at a stand] at a standstill through bafflement (cf. *LM* 2.1.5–6; cf. *MerVen.* 5.1.71–9).

17.6. changes] rounds of the dance (*OED* sb. 1c).

17.10. complimental offers] courteous gestures or shows (*OED complimental* 2; *offer* 3).

18–22. *Uncase me . . . visor*] This speech and 48–54 are similar to Mercutio's last words in *R&J* 3.1.96–103 (Oliver, 80). *Uncase* = take off or unfasten some item of clothing, possibly his doublet; but also perhaps 'uncover, lay bare': 'His hypocrisie shall be uncased and laid open to the view of the world' (George Hakewill, *An Apologie or Declaration of the Power and Providence of God* . . . (1630), 520, quoted in *OED uncase* 2). Ferentes' physical exposure further stresses the discovery of his profligacy. Cf. the action in *Cardinal* 3.2.92.1–2, 94.1.

18. *in jest*] i.e. as if it were a joke or prank. Of course Ferentes has been slain 'in earnest'. *Jest* could also = 'a masque or performance' (*OED jest* 8; cf. *Span. Trag.* 1.4.137). See *Haml.* 3.2.223, *Rom. Actor* 4.2.283 for similar word-play.

18–19. *outlandish*] 'bizarre', but perhaps also 'foreign, or of foreign fashion' (*OED* 1, 2). Possibly referring to a visit by French actresses in 1629; see LN, Intro., p. 8.

Duke. Slain? Take his visor off. *They unmask* [FERENTES].
We are betrayed.
Seize on them, two are yonder—hold, Ferentes—
Follow the rest. Apparent treachery!
Abbot. Holy Saint Benet, what a sight is this!

Enter JULIA, COLONA *and* MORONA *unmasked, every one having a child in their arms.*

Julia. Be not amazed, great princes, but vouchsafe
Your audience. We are they have done this deed.
Look here, the pledges of this false man's lust,
Betrayed in our simplicities. He swore,
And pawned his truth to marry each of us;
Abused us all; unable to revenge
Our public shames but by his public fall,
Which thus we have contrived. Nor do we blush
To call the glory of this murder ours:
We did it, and we'll justify the deed.
For when in sad complaints we claimed his vows,
His answer was reproach. Villain, is't true?

23. his] *G*; this *Q*.

---

24. *two are yonder*] i.e. Mauruccio and Roseilli.

hold] probably addressed to Ferentes—'Bear up!'—rather than instructing others to support him. *'Tis Pity* 5.6.61 has a similar crux (see Revels note).

25. *Apparent*] manifest, blatant.

26. *Saint Benet*] one of the several Saint Benedicts; see Attwater.

26.2. every . . . arms] There is no indication that several months have passed since the events of 3.1, but time was often a fluid medium in the drama. Sidney (*Apologie for Poetrie* 52, ll. 26ff) and Jonson (*Every Man In*, Prol., 7–9) complained about this.

27. *amazed*] bewildered, alarmed (*OED amaze* 2, 3; cf. *'Tis Pity* 4.1.40).

princes] used of male *and* female sovereigns or leaders (*OED prince*; cf. *Tempest* 1.2.174).

29. *pledges . . . lust*] Infants were usually considered as *pledges* (tokens, evidence) of parents' *love* (*OED pledge* 2d).

30. *simplicities*] artless sincerity (*OED simplicity* 3).

31. *pawned his truth*] pledged his fidelity, promised (cf. *Luc.* 156; *OED pawn* v.; *truth* 1, 4).

32. *Abused*] 'deceived' or 'wronged, dishonoured' (*OED abuse* 4, 5; Schmidt).

34. *contrived*] 'brought about'; probably hinting at machinations; cf. *MerVen.* 4.1.357–8 (*OED* v.[1] 1b, 6).

35. *glory*] (a) honour; (b) resplendence. Cf. *'Tis Pity* 5.6.21–2.

Colona. I was 'too quickly won', you slave.
Morona. I was 'too old', you dog.
Julia. I—and I never shall forget the wrong—
I was 'not fair enough'. Not fair enough
For thee, thou monster! Let me cut his gall.
She stabs him.
Not fair enough! O scorn! Not fair enough!
Ferentes. Oh, oh, oh!—
Duke. Forbear, you monstrous women, do not add
Murder to lust. Your lives shall pay this forfeit.

Ferentes. Pox upon all codpiece extravagancy! I am peppered—oh, oh, oh—Duke, forgive me. Had I rid any tame beasts but Barbary wild colts, I had not been thus jerked out of the saddle. My forfeit was in my blood, and my life hath answered it. Vengeance on all wild whores, I say—O 'tis true. Farewell, generation of hackneys—ooh! *Dies.*

39. quickly won] *italic in Q.* 40. too old] *italic in Q.* 42. fair enough . . . fair enough] *italic in Q (as at 44).* 43. SD.] *Q; 'Stabs him' at 44 G.* 48–54.] *W; verse Q.*

43. *gall*] The gall-bladder, commonly regarded as the seat of asperity and rancour. But the phrase 'to break one's gall' = to break the spirit, subdue (Hoeniger, 175–7; *OED* sb.[1] 3a, c).

45. *Oh, oh, oh!*] Perhaps a sign for a protracted groan; see *SS* 29 (1976), 123.

47. *forfeit*] offence, or penalty incurred by one's acts (cf. *'Tis Pity* 4.2.3). Ferentes picks up the word in 51, where it = 'offence' (*OED* 1, 2, 4).

48. *codpiece extravagancy*] sexual impropriety, lechery (*OED extravagancy* 2, 3; cf. *Meas.* 3.1.378–9).

48–9. *peppered*] finished, 'done for' (*OED pepper* v. 5). Mercutio: 'I am peppered, I warrant, for this world' (*R&J* 3.1.98–9).

49. *rid*] with double entendre continued throughout the speech (cf. *Changeling* 4.3.86; *OED ride* 3).

50. *Barbary wild colts*] (a) untamed young Arab horses; (b) wantons (*OED colt* 2c, cf. 3.1.120–1).

51. *blood*] the seat of the sensual appetite (*OED blood* 6). At her death, Vittoria Corombona exclaims: 'O my greatest sin lay in my blood. / Now my blood pays for't' (*W. Devil* 5.6.240–1).

52. *answered*] atoned for (*OED answer* 6b).

53. *generation*] Three possible senses: (a) those born in a particular era; (b) offspring (cf. *LM* 5.2.213); or (c) breed (continuing the speech's equine references). Ferentes thus addresses his lovers or women in general; cf. 1.2.35–9 (*OED generation* 3, 5, 6; cf. Matthew 3:7: 'O generation of vipers').

54. *hackneys*] (a) horses kept for hire (thus 'hackney-carriage'); (b) whores (*OED hackney* 2, 4). Cf. 3.1.120–1, *LLL* 3.1.30–1.

Duke. He is dead.
To prison with those monstrous strumpets.
Petruccio. Stay,
I'll answer for my daughter.
Nibrassa. And I for mine.—[*Aside*] O well done, girls!
Fernando. I for yon gentlewoman, sir.
Mauruccio. Good my lord, I am an innocent in the business.
Duke. To prison with him. Bear the body hence.
Abbot. Here's fatal sad presages, but 'tis just:
He dies by murder that hath lived in lust. *Exeunt.*

55–6.] *G; prose Q.* 55. dead.] *W;* dead, *Q.* 56–7. Stay . . . daughter] *lineation as GD; one line Q.* 58. *Aside*] *this ed.*

---

59. *yon gentlewoman*] i.e. Morona.

62–3. *Here's . . . lust*] The Friar makes a similar comment after Hippolita's murderous masque, *'Tis Pity* 4.1.110–11. 'For the wages of sin is death' (Romans 6:23).

Act 4

ACT 4 SCENE I

Enter DUKE, FIORMONDA, *and* D'AVOLOS.

Fiormonda. Art thou Caraffa? Is there in thy veins
One drop of blood that issued from the loins
Of Pavy's ancient dukes? Or dost thou sit
On great Lorenzo's seat, our glorious father,
And canst not blush to be so far beneath
The spirit of heroic ancestors?
Canst thou engross a slavish shame, which men
Far, far below the region of thy state
Not more abhor than study to revenge?
Thou an Italian? I could burst with rage,
To think I have a brother so befooled
In giving patience to a harlot's lust.

D'Avolos. One, my lord, that doth so palpably, so apparently, make her adulteries a trophy, whiles the poting-stick to

4.1.7. engross] *GD;* ingrosse *Q.* shame,] *W;* shame? *Q.* 9. revenge?] *W;* revenge. *Q.*

4.1.4. *great Lorenzo*] Perhaps with a glance at Lorenzo de' Medici (1449–92), head of the Medici family, ruler of Florence, and renowned patron of learning and the arts.

seat] throne or 'chair of state'.

7. *engross*] 'assume, become absorbed with', and perhaps 'monopolise' (*OED engross* 3, 4, 7). Cf. *Bussy* 3.2.280–1, *BH* 3.3.58–60.

slavish] base, ignoble (*OED* a.[1] 3).

8. *region . . . state*] lofty realm of your greatness. *Region* = 'one of the successive portions into which the air or atmosphere is theoretically divided according to height' (*OED* 4a; cf. *MWW* 3.2.67).

13. *apparently*] plainly, blatantly.

14. *trophy*] prize or token displayed like the spoils of a hunt or the plunder of battle (*OED* 1, 2).

poting-stick] either 'a wooden, iron, or bone instrument for crimping linen' (as in *Malcontent* 5.5.22) or 'a stick for stirring clothes when boiling' (*OED pote* v. 4); with a double entendre in either sense. The one instance in *EDD* is in the latter sense, and from Devonshire (*pote* sb. 3).

her unsatiate and more than goatish abomination jeers at and flouts your sleepish, and more than sleepish, security.

Fiormonda. What is she but the sallow-coloured brat
Of some unlanded bankrupt, taught to catch
The easy fancies of young prodigal bloods
In springes of her stew-instructed art?
Here's your most virtuous duchess, your rare piece!

D'Avolos. More base in the infiniteness of her sensuality than corruption can infect. To clip and inveigle your friend, too, O insufferable! A friend? How of all men are you most unfortunate, to pour out your soul into the bosom of such a creature as holds it religion to make your own trust a key to open the passage to your own wife's womb, to be drunk in the privacies of your bed. Think upon that, sir.

Duke. Be gentle in your tortures, e'en for pity,
For pity's cause I beg it.

Fiormonda. Be a prince?
Th'adst better, Duke, thou hadst been born a peasant.
Now boys will sing thy scandal in the streets,

16. sleepish] *Q;* sheepish *conj. D.* 19. bankrupt,] *W;* bankrupt? *Q.* 20. fancies] *Q;* fancy *W.* 21–2.] *W;* In . . . most / Vertuous . . . peece. *Q.* 23–30.] *W; verse Q.* 32. prince?] *Q;* prince! *G.* 33. Th'adst] *GD;* Th'hadst *Q;* Thou hadst *W.*

---

15. *goatish*] 'lustful'; the goat being a type of lechery (Tilley G 167).

16. *sleepish*] somewhat sleepy (*OED*, quoting this instance).

17. *security*] (a) unsuspecting assurance; (b) carelessness (*OED* 2, 3). 'Securitie in the possession of Honor and prosperitie is a headlong running to ruine' (*GM* 308–9).

18. *sallow-coloured*] having a sickly yellow or brownish yellow complexion (*OED sallow* c). Another reference to Bianca's pale complexion; see 2.3.84n.

20. *bloods*] roisterers, rakes (*OED blood* 15).

21. *springes*] snares.

stew-instructed] learnt in a brothel.

22. *rare piece*] paragon (of virtue etc.), or a jewel or painting (*OED piece* 8c, 17b). Cf. *Maid's Trag.* 2.2.32, *Fancies*, 151–4. *Piece* can also = a girl or young woman (e.g. *Changeling* 4.1.54).

24. *clip*] embrace.

29. *privacies*] private matters (*OED privacy* 4).

31–2. *e'en . . . cause*] 'for the sake of pity itself' or 'at least for pity's sake'. For this use of 'even' (*e'en*), cf. *Err.* 5.1.191–2.

Tune ballads to thy infamy, get money
By making pageants of thee, and invent
Some strangely shaped man-beast that may for horns
Resemble thee, and call it Pavy's duke.

Duke. Endless immortal plague!

D'Avolos. There's the mischief, sir. In the meantime you shall be sure to have a bastard—of whom you did not so much as beget a little toe, a left ear, or half the further side of an upper lip—inherit both your throne and name. This would kill the soul of very patience itself.

Duke. Forbear: the ashy paleness of my cheek
Is scarletted in ruddy flakes of wrath,
And like some bearded meteor shall suck up,
With swiftest terror, all those dusky mists
That overcloud compassion in our breast.
You have roused a sleeping lion, whom no art,
No fawning smoothness shall reclaim, but blood.
And sister thou, thou, Roderico, thou,

37. man-beast] *italic in Q.* 47. meteor] *W.;* meteo *[or* 'metco'*?] Q.* 50. You have] *Q;* You've *GD.* 52. sister] *italic in Q.*

---

35. *Tune*] sing.
ballads] See 3.1.2 LN.

36. *pageants*] Theatrical shows, perhaps presented on a carriage or temporary stage. The civic and royal pageants held in London and elsewhere incorporated elements of the morality plays, folklore, scripture and classical mythology, and might well have included a character such as the *man-beast* of 37. Impersonations of royalty were also a fairly common feature (Chambers, *ES* I, 132, 138).

37. *strangely . . . man-beast*] Reminiscent of Actaeon; see 2.3.113n. *Shaped* = costumed or disguised.
for] on account of (its).

42. *further*] 'front' or 'far'.

45–9. *the ashy . . . breast*] He first likens himself to a dormant (*ashy*) fire stirred into burning fragments (*ruddy flakes*) by his *wrath.* The fire of his anger then becomes a *bearded* (tailed) *meteor* that will draw off (*suck up*) the clouds of *compassion.* Meteors were thought to be formed from vapours 'exhaled' or drawn up from the earth by the sun (see John Maplet, *The Diall of Destiny*, 1581, fol. 35; *R&J* 3.5.13). Thus *overcloud compassion in our breast* seems to = 'overcloud my breast with compassion', a rather strained reading, but one that is hard to avoid, since *compassion* must be removed, rather than manifested, by Caraffa's anger. *Dusky* could = 'melancholy, gloomy' (*OED* 1–3).

50. *sleeping lion*] 'Wake not a sleeping lion' (Tilley L 317).

51. *reclaim*] 'subdue' (*OED* 3) and/or 'call back from a mistaken or evil course' (cf. 3.1.35n).

From whom I take the surfeit of my bane,
Henceforth no more so eagerly pursue
To whet my dullness. You shall see Caraffa
Equal his birth, and matchless in revenge.

Fiormonda. Why, now I hear you speak in majesty.

D'Avolos. And it becomes my lord most princely.

Duke. Does it? Come hither, sister. Thou art near
In nature, and as near to me in love.
I love thee; yes, by yon bright firmament,
I love thee dearly. But observe me well:
If any private grudge, or female spleen,
Malice, or envy or such woman's frailty
Have spurred thee on to set my soul on fire
Without apparent certainty, I vow,
And vow again, by all my princely blood,
Hadst thou a double soul, or were the lives
Of fathers, mothers, children or the hearts
Of all our tribe in thine, I would unrip
That womb of bloody mischief with these nails,
Where such a cursèd plot as this was hatched.
But, D'Avolos, for thee—no more. To work
A yet more strong impression in my brain,
You must produce an instance to mine eye
Both present and apparent—nay, you shall, or—

Fiormonda. Or what? You will be mad? Be rather wise:
Think on Ferentes first, and think by whom
The harmless youth was slaughtered. Had he lived
He would have told you tales. Fernando feared it,
And to prevent him, under show, forsooth,
Of rare device, most trimly cut him off.

67. all my] *W;* all *Q;* all our *G.* 70. tribe] *GD;* Tribes *Q.* 72. cursèd] *GD*; cursed *Q.* 77. wise] *Q;* wiser *W.*

---

53. *bane*] 'woe'; but *surfeit* hints at another sense: 'poison' (*OED* 2b, 5).

54. *pursue*] proceed, endeavour (*OED* 5, 9).

63. *spleen*] malice, ill humour. Cf. 1.1.89.

66. *apparent certainty*] clear and certain knowledge.

70. *tribe*] family or race.

unrip] tear open and expose. A favourite word of Ford's; cf. *'Tis Pity* 3.6.2.

76. *present*] ready at hand (*OED present* 5). Reverting to the *Othello*-like theme of 3.3.71 (see note).

82. *trimly*] neatly (ironic).

Have you yet eyes, Duke?
Duke. Shrewdly urged—'tis piercing.
Fiormonda. For looking on a sight shall split your soul,
You shall not care. I'll undertake myself
To do't some two days hence; for need, tonight,
But that you are in court.
D'Avolos. Right. Would you desire, my lord, to see them exchange kisses, sucking one another's lips, nay, begetting an heir to the dukedom, or practising more than the very act of adultery itself? Give but a little way by a feigned absence, and you shall find 'em—I blush to speak doing what. I am mad to think on't; you are most shamefully, most sinfully, most scornfully cornuted.
Duke. D'ee play upon me? As I am your prince,
There's some shall roar for this. Why, what was I,
Both to be thought or made so vile a thing?
Stay—madam Marquess. Ho, Roderico, you, sir.
Bear witness that if ever I neglect
One day, one hour, one minute, to wear out
With toil of plot or practice of conceit
My busy skull, till I have found a death
More horrid than the bull of Phalaris,

84. soul,] *W;* soul; *Q.* 85. care.] *this ed.;* care, *Q;* care; *W;* care: *GD.* 95. D'ee] *Q;* D'ye *W.* 97. vile] *W;* vild *Q.* 98. madam Marquess] *italic in Q.*

---

85. *care*] 'trouble yourself' (in arranging); *OED* 4.
86. *for need*] if necessary. A good example of her brusque expression.
91. *Give . . . way*] allow (them) a little free scope.
94. *cornuted*] horned, cuckolded.
95. *play upon*] make sport of.
96. *roar*] cry out or weep. *OED* does not record the latter sense, but it is clearly intended at 142.
101. *conceit*] (a) (scheming) imagination; (b) device, trick (*OED* 7b, 8b).
102. *a death*] (presumably for Bianca and/or Fernando).
103. *bull of Phalaris*] Phalaris was a tyrant of Acragus (Agrigentum) in Sicily, sixth century BC. Perillos of Athens had invented a brazen bull in which criminals were to be roasted alive: a fire was lit under the belly, and the victim's cries from within were supposed to sound like the bellows of the bull. Phalaris admired the device and tested it on Perillos himself (Brewer). The many references to Phalaris include: Ovid, *Ibis*, 439–40; Machiavelli, *Discourses* I.10.3; *J. Malta*, Prol., 246.

Or all the fabling poets, dreaming whips;
If ever I take rest, or force a smile
Which is not borrowed from a royal vengeance,
Before I know which way to satisfy
Fury and wrong—nay, kneel down—let me die
[*They kneel.*]
More wretched than despair, reproach, contempt,
Laughter, and poverty itself can make me.
Let's rise on all sides, friends; now all's agreed.
If the moon serve, some that are safe shall bleed.

Enter FERNANDO, BIANCA, *and* MORONA.

Bianca. My lord the Duke.
Duke. Bianca! Ha, how is't?
How is't, Bianca? What, Fernando! Come,

104. poets,] *W;* poets; *Q;* poets *S;* poets' *G.* whips;] *G;* whips: *Q.* 108. SD.] *W, G (after* 'kneel down'*); not in Q.* 111.] *SD, 'They rise', after* 'friends'*, G.* 112. moon] *Q;* morn *W.*

---

104. *dreaming whips*] i.e. 'with their imagined whips'; probably referring to the whips of snakes or scorpions used by the Furies, the three 'merciless goddesses of vengeance' (Brewer), in punishing the wicked. See Seneca, *Hercules Furens*, 88; *Thyestes*, 23ff; cf. *Sejanus* 3.20–1, *Span. Trag.*, 3rd Addn, 40–2. Gifford's punctuation, 'poets' dreaming whips', obscures the sense by making *dreaming* modify *whips* rather than *poets*.

107. *which way*] how.

108. *wrong*] i.e. the offence or injury done to me.

108.1. They kneel] The action here is close to *Oth.* 3.3.333ff, 4.1.1–207; see Intro., p. 59. Honigmann (note to *Oth.* 3.3.454, Arden[3] edition) cites other 'revengers who kneel' in *Tit.* 4.1.87ff, *Faversham* 9.37.1, *Edw. II* 3.1.128, *J. Malta* 1.2.165.

110. *Laughter*] laughter of *contempt* (?).

poverty itself] An appropriate nadir, in view of Caraffa's preoccupation with wealth (cf. 1.1.189–93, 1.2.261–2).

112.] Referring (with a grim pun) to the common practice of blood-letting or phlebotomy. Certain aspects of the moon were deemed more suitable for this treatment; see LN.

serve] is favourable—in its astrological aspect, and perhaps also in giving light. Cf. *Tim.* 5.1.43–4.

safe] (a) secure; (b) complacent. Sense (b) is not recorded by *OED*, but cf. 4.2.117–18.

Shall's shake hands, sirs? Faith, this is kindly done.
Here's three as one. Welcome dear wife, sweet friend!

D'Avolos. [*Aside*] I do not like this now, it shows scurvily to me.

Bianca. My lord, we have a suit. Your friend and I—

Duke. [*Aside*] She puts my friend before most kindly still.

Bianca. —Must join—

Duke What, 'must'?

Bianca. My lord?

Duke. Must join, you say.

Bianca. That you will please to set Mauruccio
At liberty. This gentlewoman here
Hath, by agreement made betwixt them two,
Obtained him for her husband. Good my lord,
Let me entreat; I dare engage mine honour
He's innocent in any wilful fault.

Duke. Your honour, madam? Now beshrew you for't,
T'engage your honour on so slight a ground.
Honour's a precious jewel, I can tell you;
Nay, 'tis, Bianca, go to!—D'Avolos,
Bring us Mauruccio hither.

D'Avolos. I shall, my lord. *Exit* D'AVOLOS.

116. dear . . . friend] *italic in Q.* 117. *Aside*] *H; aside to Fior. G; no aside Q.* 119. I—] *W;* I. *Q.* 120. *Aside*] *W; not in Q.* 121. —Must join—] *this ed.;* Must join. *Q;* Must join—*G.* What, 'must'?] *W (subst.);* What must? *Q.* My lord?] *this ed.;* My lord! *Q.* 131. Bianca . . . D'Avolos,] *G;* Biancha.—Goe too, D'auolos, *Q.*

---

115. *sirs*] The plural was used in addressing both men and women; cf. *A&C* 4.16.87.

kindly] (a) affectionately, congenially; (b) in a natural or proper manner (*OED* adv. 1, 2). Perhaps ironic; cf. 120.

119. *a suit*] Cf. *Oth.* 3.3.1–90 and 3.4.48–97, in which Desdemona urges her husband to reinstate Cassio.

120. *still*] always.

121. *join*] 'enjoin' or 'join together in our suit' (*OED* v.[2] 2; cf. *Queen*, 3831–2). Perhaps Caraffa picks up the word's sexual or romantic connotations. At 174–5, Bianca and Fernando '*join*' the hands of Mauruccio and Morona in a marriage pledge. See 175n, Intro., p. 60.

126. *engage*] pledge.

128. *beshrew*] probably a mild reproof, like 'go to' (131).

129. *ground*] cause.

Morona. I humbly thank your grace.
Fernando. And, royal sir, since Julia and Colona,
Chief actors in Ferentes' tragic end,
Were through their ladies' mediation
Freed by your gracious pardon, I, in pity,
Tendered this widow's friendless misery,
For whose reprieve I shall in humblest duty
Be ever thankful.

Enter D'AVOLOS [*with*] MAURUCCIO *in poor rags, and* GIACOPO *weeping.*

Mauruccio. Come you, my learnèd counsel, do not roar;
If I must hang, why then, lament therefore.
You may rejoice, and both, no doubt, be great
To serve your prince when I am turned worms' meat.
I fear my lands and all I have is begged,
Else, woe is me, why should I be so ragged?
D'Avolos. Come on, sir, the Duke stays for you.
Mauruccio. O how my stomach doth begin to puke
When I do hear that only word, 'the Duke'!
Duke. You sir, look on that woman. Are you pleased,
If we remit your body from the jail,
To take her for your wife?
Mauruccio. On that condition, prince, with all my heart.

141.1. *with*] *W; not in Q.* *poor rags Q;* rags *G.* 143. therefore.] therefore: *Q;* therefore? *S.* 153. wife?] *G;* wife. *Q.*

136. *actors*] 'participants' and 'performers'.
139. *Tendered*] 'took pity on' or 'attended to' (*OED tender* v.[2] 3c, d).
142. *roar*] weep loudly. Cf. 5.3.44. *OED* does not record this sense.
143. *lament therefore*] See LN for discussion of the possible sources of this clichéd phrasing.
144. *You . . . great*] 'you may both rejoice and, no doubt, be great' (?).
146. *begged*] Forfeiture of goods was a common punishment for crimes under the degree of felony (see E. W. Ives, 'The Law and the Lawyers', *SS* 17, 1964, 82). Mauruccio, who appears here in '*poor rags*' (141.1), perhaps imagines that his confiscated possessions have already been requested (*begged*) by others. Cf. *Meas.* 5.1.419–22.
148. *stays*] waits.
150. *only*] single.

Morona. Yes, I warrant your grace, he is content.
Duke. Why, foolish man, hast thou so soon forgot
The public shame of her abusèd womb,
Her being mother to a bastard's birth?
Or canst thou but imagine she will be
True to thy bed, who to herself was false?
Giacopo. [*To Mauruccio*] Phew, sir, do not stand upon that; that's a matter of nothing, you know.
Mauruccio. Nay, an shall please your good grace, an it come to that, I care not. As good men as I have lien in foul sheets, I am sure. The linen has not been much the worse for the wearing a little. I will have her with all my heart.
Duke. And shalt. Fernando, thou shalt have the grace
To join their hands; put 'em together, friend.
Bianca. Yes, do, my lord, bring you the bridegroom hither,
I'll give the bride myself.
D'Avolos. [*Aside*] Here's argument to jealousy as good as

157. abusèd] *GD;* abused *Q.* 161. *To Mauruccio*] *G; not in Q.* Phew] *Q;* Foh *W.* 163. an shall] *this ed.;* and shall *Q;* an't shall *W.* an it] *GD;* and it *Q.* 171. *Aside*] *G; no aside Q.*

155. *warrant*] assure.

157. *abusèd*] 'misused, violated' and (of Morona herself) 'deceived' (*OED* 2, 3).

161. *stand upon*] attach importance to. The *Phew*, the probable bawdy pun on *a matter of nothing* (i.e. virginity? see Williams, s.v. *nothing*), and the bluntly imperative mood of the speech all suggest that he is addressing Mauruccio rather than the Duke; but it would be dramatically effective for Caraffa to overhear Giacopo's comment; cf. 165n. *Stand* is bawdy at 1.2.14.

163. *an shall*] if (it) shall.

165. *sheets*] often mentioned in allusion to sexual intercourse (e.g. *Haml.* 1.2.157; *OED sheet* sb.[1] 3b). Caraffa must surely apply Mauruccio's unfortunate remark to himself.

167–75.] A rather perfunctorily observed spousal or 'handfasting' ceremony. Any such exchange of vows before witnesses, and followed by cohabitation, was recognised by English common law (and popular opinion) as a binding contract. In some remote areas, oral betrothal was regarded by many of the poor as sufficient ceremony without marriage in church. (See Lawrence Stone, *The Family, Sex and Marriage in England 1500–1800*, Oxford: Oxford University Press, 1977, 31–2; Mendelson and Crawford, 118–19; *TwN* 5.1.154–57; *Meas.* 4.1.69–70.)

171. *argument to*] cause for.

as good as] i.e. as strong a cause as.

drink to the dropsy. She will share any disgrace with him. I could not wish it better.

Duke. Even so. Well, do it.

Fernando. Here, Mauruccio:
Long live a happy couple.

[BIANCA *and* FERNANDO] *join their hands.*

Duke. 'Tis enough.
Now know our pleasure henceforth. 'Tis our will,
If ever thou, Mauruccio, or thy wife
Be seen within a dozen miles at court,
We will recall our mercy. No entreat
Shall warrant thee a minute of thy life.
We'll have no servile slavery of lust
Shall breathe near us. Dispatch, and get ye hence.
Bianca, come with me.—[*Aside*] O my cleft soul!

Exeunt DUKE *and* BIANCA.

Mauruccio. How's that? Must I come no more near the court?

Giacopo. O pitiful! Not near the court, sir!

D'Avolos. Not by a dozen miles indeed, sir. Your only course I can advise you is to pass to Naples and set up a house of carnality. There are very fair and frequent suburbs, and

174–7.] *W;* Euen . . . it. / *Fer.* Here . . . couple. / D*uke.* 'Tis . . . henceforth. / 'Tis . . . wife, *Q.* 175. SD.] *G (subst.); ioyne their hands Q.* 178. at] *Q;* o' th' *G.* 183. *Aside*] *GD; not in Q.* 183.1. *and*] *W;* et *Q.*

172. *dropsy*] or hydropsy, a disease in which watery fluid accumulates in the body, characterised by an insatiable thirst.

175. *'Tis enough*] i.e. to complete the betrothal; but the sight of Bianca participating with Fernando in a tainted match is also 'enough' to confirm Caraffa's jealous fears. See 121n, Intro., p. 60.

176. *pleasure*] will, command.

178. *at*] probably 'near' (*OED* 1).

179. *entreat*] entreaty (perhaps echoing Bianca's request at 126).

182. *breathe*] (a) exist; (b) speak.

187. *Naples*] Notorious for its vice; also the location of events in the Gesualdo story; see Intro., p. 30, App. 3.

188. *frequent*] 'crowded, well frequented' or 'numerous' (*OED* 1b, 2).

suburbs] Residential parts lying immediately outside a city's walls or boundaries. '*London*,' wrote Nashe, 'what are thy Suburbes but licensed Stewes?' (*Christs Teares*, 148, 16).

you need not fear the contagion of any pestilent disease,
for the worst is very proper to the place.

Fernando. 'Tis a strange sentence.

Fiormonda. 'Tis, and sudden, too;
And not without some mystery.

D'Avolos. Will you go, sir.

Mauruccio. Not near the court!

Morona. What matter is it, sweetheart? Fear nothing, love. You shall have new change of apparel, good diet, wholesome attendance, and we will live like pigeons, my lord.

Mauruccio. Wilt thou forsake me, Giacopo?

Giacopo. I forsake ye? No, not as long as I have a whole ear on my head, come what will come.

Fiormonda. Mauruccio, you did once proffer true love
To me, but since you are more thriftier sped,
For old affection's sake, here, take this gold.
Spend it for my sake.

Fernando. Madam, you do nobly.
And that's for me, Mauruccio.

D'Avolos. Will ye go, sir?

Mauruccio. Yes, I will go; and I humbly thank your lordship and ladyship. Pavy, sweet Pavy, farewell. Come wife, come Giacopo:
Now is the time that we away must lag,
And march in pomp with baggage and with bag.
O poor Mauruccio, what hast thou misdone,
To end thy life when life was new begun?
Adieu to all, for lords and ladies see

195. sweetheart?] *W;* sweetheart, *Q.* 204.] *SD, 'Gives him a purse', after* 'sake' *W.* 205.] *SD, 'They give him money' after* 'Mauruccio' *G.* 207. and I humbly] *Q;* and humbly *G.*

---

189. *disease*] perhaps syphilis, the 'Neapolitan disease'.

190. *proper*] (a) in keeping, typical; (b) (ironic) seemly, becoming.

197. *pigeons*] emblems of romantic harmony.

199–200. *a whole . . . head*] See LN.

202. *more thriftier sped*] more prosperously dispatched (ironic). Comparatives were often doubled (Abbott 11). 'Thrifty' = 'thriving, prosperous' (*PW* 3.2.186, *BH* 3.1.53; cf. *LS* 5.3.22) or perhaps 'respectable, proper, decent' (*LOL*, Pref., 46; Glossary, *Nondram. Wks*).

210. *lag*] i.e. leave slowly and reluctantly.

My woeful plight, and squires of low degree.
D'Avolos. Away, away, sirs.
Exeunt all except FIORMONDA *and* FERNANDO.
Fiormonda. My lord Fernando.
Fernando. Madam.
Fiormonda. Do you note
My brother's odd distractions? You were wont
To bosom in his counsels: I am sure
You know the ground on't.
Fernando. Not I, in troth.
Fiormonda. Is't possible? What would you say, my lord,
If he, out of some melancholy spleen,
Edged on by some thank-picking parasite,
Should now prove jealous? I mistrust it shrewdly.
Fernando. What, madam, jealous?
Fiormonda. Yes, for but observe,

215. degree.] *W;* degree: *Q;* degree! *G.* 216. SD.] *W; Exeunt, manent Flor. et Fer. Q.* 217–20.] *W;* My . . . *Fernando.* / *Fer.* Madam. / *Fior.* Doe . . . distractions? / You . . . Counsailes; / I . . . on't. / *Fer.* Not . . . troth. *Q.* 220. on't] *Q;* of it *G.*

---

215. *squires . . . degree*] In the medieval metrical romance *The Squire of Low Degree*, the squire falls in love with a king's daughter, who consents to marry him if he can prove himself a worthy knight (*degree* = social rank). Unlike Mauruccio, the squire wins his noble lady. Cf. 2.1.94n, LN, *H5* 5.1.35.

219. *bosom in*] have familiar intercourse with. A rare usage of *bosom*; *OED*'s earliest instance.

220. *ground on*] reason for.

222. *spleen*] fit or humour. Melancholy (often thought to be caused by a disorder in the spleen) was associated with a suspicious or jealous disposition; see Burton, I.2.5.5, p. 380; I.3.1.2, p. 391.

223. *Edged on*] urged on, incited, provoked. Cf. the phrase 'egged on' (the two verbal forms are etymologically identical; *OED edge* v.[1] 2b; *egg* v.[1] 2).

thank-picking] sycophantic, flattering. *OED*'s only recorded instance (*thank* sb. 12). A 'pickthank' = one who 'picks a thank', i.e. curries favour, especially by informing against someone else (*OED pickthank* A). She probably refers to D'Avolos.

224. *mistrust it shrewdly*] have serious suspicions about it. A doubt or suspicion is said to be 'shrewd' when it is felt to come 'dangerously' close to the truth or is of grievous concern (*OED shrewd* 14; *shrewdly* 5a, 6a). Cf. Iago's 'shrewd doubt', *Oth.* 3.3.434, and *JC* 3.1.146–7.

A prince whose eye is chooser to his heart
Is seldom steady in the lists of love,
Unless the party he affects do match
His rank in equal portion, or in friends.
I never yet, out of report, or else
By warranted description, have observed
The nature of fantastic jealousy,
If not in him. Yet on my conscience now,
He has no cause.

Fernando. Cause, madam? By this light,
I'll pledge my soul against a useless rush.

Fiormonda. I never thought her less; yet trust me, sir,
No merit can be greater than your praise,
Whereat I strangely wonder, how a man
Vowed, as you told me, to a single life,
Should so much deify the saints from whom

226–9. *A prince . . . friends*] *GM* refers to 'the unevennesse of match amongst great personages with partners, whose wantonnesse is sometimes the cause that many Noble houses runne to decay' (1267–9; see *LS* I.I.119n.).

227. *lists*] enclosed area for tilting matches or tournaments. This conventional metaphor presents lovers as combatants, perhaps with a pun on *lists* = 'desiring' (see *VA* 595n., New Cambridge edition, *The Poems*, 1992).

229. *portion*] (a) estate; (b) dowry (*OED* 2, 3).

230. *report*] rumour, common talk, account.

231. *warranted description*] authoritative discussion. Perhaps referring to Burton's *Anatomy of Melancholy* (1621), which chronicles the many causes and symptoms of jealousy (Ewing, 70).

232. *fantastic*] proceeding merely from the 'fantasy' or imagination; irrational (*OED* A1). Burton observes that the imagination is 'misaffected' through jealousy (III.3.4.1, p. 288). Cf. Caraffa's dream, 4.2.30–41.

233. *on my conscience*] Once again a common asseveration (= 'in truth, indeed' or 'on my word') is given a new twist by its peculiar relevance to the speaker (cf. 1.2.177n). The moral sense of the noun was well established by this time (*OED* 4).

235. *rush*] a type of something of no value or importance (*OED* sb.[1] 2a).

236. *I . . . less*] i.e. less than faithful (?). Presumably responding to Fernando's avowal that Bianca has given Caraffa no cause for jealousy, but the comment seems inappropriate. T.W. Craik (private correspondence) suggests that the latter part of Fernando's previous speech—in which he may have exonerated or praised Bianca, or lauded women generally—has been accidentally omitted. This would make better sense of Fiormonda's reference to Fernando's 'praise' (237).

You have disclaimed devotion.
Fernando. Madam, 'tis true:
From them I have, but from their virtues, never.
Fiormonda. You are too wise, Fernando. To be plain,
You are in love—nay, shrink not, man, you are.
Bianca is your aim. Why do you blush?
She is, I know she is.
Fernando. My aim?
Fiormonda. Yes, yours.
I hope I talk no news. Fernando, know
Thou run'st to thy confusion, if in time
Thou dost not wisely shun that Circe's charm.
Unkindest man! I have too long concealed
My hidden flames, when still in silent signs
I courted thee for love, without respect
To youth or state; and yet thou art unkind.
Fernando, leave that sorceress, if not
For love of me, for pity of thy self.
Fernando. Injurious woman, I defy thy lust.
'Tis not your subtle sifting shall creep

256. *SD '[walks aside]' G.* 257. shall] *Q;* that shall *G;* e'er shall *conj. W.*

242.] He seems to present himself as an enlightened Neoplatonist who has freed himself from the 'false opinion' engendered by 'the longing of sense', and who beholds 'no more the particular beautie of one woman, but an universall, that decketh out all bodies' (*Courtier* IV, 304–5, 318; cf. Ficino, *Commentary* VII, xv).

243. *wise*] 'clever', perhaps mocking his pretence to Neoplatonic wisdom (see 242n).

244. *shrink*] draw back, recoil.

247. *hope*] trust, suspect (ironic; *OED* 4).

248. *confusion*] ruin.

249. *Circe*] goddess who beguiles a band of Odysseus's men and turns them into swine. When Odysseus goes to Circe's palace to rescue his comrades, the goddess attempts to work her spell on him (*Odyssey* X, 133–347).

251. *hidden flames*] They have hardly been hidden; see 1.2.139ff. Cf. Petrarch, *Rime* 207, l. 66, 'Chiusa fiamma', 'A hidden flame'.

still] constantly.

253. *state*] social rank.

256. *Injurious*] 'dangerous' or 'offensive' (in her references to Bianca).

257.] Strictly speaking, a hypometrical line. Gifford supplies the missing syllable by emending to '*that* shall creep'. But omission of the relative pronoun is characteristic of Ford (cf. 4.2.45–6). And, as Philip Hobsbaum

Into the secrets of a heart unsoiled.
You are my prince's sister, else your malice
Had railed itself to death; but as for me,
Be record all my fate, I do detest
Your fury or affection. Judge the rest. *Exit.*

Fiormonda. What, gone? Well, go thy ways. I see the more
I humble my firm love, the more he shuns
Both it and me. So plain! Then 'tis too late
To hope; change peevish passion to contempt.
Whatever rages in my blood I feel,
Fool, he shall know I was not born to kneel. *Exit.*

ACT 4 SCENE 2

Enter D'AVOLOS *and* JULIA.

D'Avolos. Julia mine own, speak softly. What, hast thou learned out anything of this pale widgeon? Speak soft, what does she say?

Julia. Foh, more than all. There's not an hour shall pass
But I shall have intelligence, she swears.

261.] *Omitted W.*

4.2.1–3.] *W; verse Q.* 1. What,] *this ed.; G;* What? *Q;* What! *W.*

points out to me, *subtle sifting shall* is sibilant: a prompt for the actor to 'snail it out or spit it out'. Thus spoken, the line would not *sound* hypometrical.

sifting] prying (see 1.1.258n).

261. *record*] testimony, proof (of his assertion); *OED* 3.

262. *Judge the rest*] i.e. form your own opinion about what else I might have said—or about the rest of the matter.

263. *go thy ways*] go on; go away (said in reproach). *Ways* = the old genitive form (*OED way* sb.[1] 23a, b).

266. *peevish*] perhaps 'childish, silly'. Sometimes has a purely deprecatory function (*OED* 3).

267. *rages*] violent passion or desire. Cf. 2.2.13n.

4.2.2. *of*] 'about', or perhaps 'from'; see next note.

pale widgeon] fool. A *widgeon* = a kind of wild duck proverbial for its stupidity (*OED* 1, 2; cf. *LM* 4.2.182). Gifford thinks this refers to Colona, Bianca's attendant, but the other allusions to Bianca's pale complexion (e.g. 2.3.84, 4.1.18) suggest that it may refer to her, with the subject shifting in the following sentence (and perhaps in Julia's response) to Colona.

5. *intelligence*] information gained from spying.

Whole nights; you know my mind. I hope you'll give
The gown you promised me.

D'Avolos. Honest Julia, peace. Th'art a woman worth a kingdom. Let me never be believed now, but I think it will be my destiny to be thy husband at last. What though thou have a child, or perhaps two?

Julia. Never but one, I swear.

D'Avolos. Well one, is that such a matter? I like thee the better for't: it shows thou hast a good tenantable and fertile womb, worth twenty of your barren, dry, bloodless devourers of youth. But come, I will talk with thee more privately. The Duke has a journey in hand, and will not be long absent. See, 'a is come already, let's pass away easily. *Exeunt.*

Enter DUKE *and* BIANCA.

Duke. Troubled? Yes, I have cause. O Bianca,
Here was my fate engraven in thy brow,
This smooth, fair, polished table. In thy cheeks
Nature summed up thy dower. 'Twas not wealth,
The miser's god, nor royalty of blood
Advanced thee to my bed, but love, and hope
Of virtue that might equal those sweet looks.
If then thou shouldst betray my trust, thy faith,

18. 'a] *Q* ('a); he *W.* 21. in] *Q;* on *W.* 24. nor] *Q;* or *G.*

6. *Whole nights*] obscure, and rendered more so by (a) uncertainty as to whether *she* (5) = Bianca or Colona, and (b) the possibility of textual corruption. Weber's emendation to 'she swears / Whole nights' gains some support from 5.3.111, 'weep whole nights', but substitutes one mystery for another. If text was lost between 5 and 6, *whole nights* may originally have been part of a claim that 'the Duchess and Fernando have passed such together' (Gifford); or perhaps Julia is promising that she will spend 'whole nights' with D'Avolos.

14. *tenantable*] capable of being tenanted or inhabited (*OED* 1).

19. *easily*] quietly, quickly.

19. SD] No need for a new scene; the action is continuous.

22. *table*] tablet. Cf. *HT* 556–7.

23. *summed up*] (a) reckoned up; (b) encapsulated, displayed (*OED sum* v.[1] 1, 3). 'Beauty is a dower of itself' (*Anatomy* III.2.2.2, p. 68).

To the pollution of a base desire,
Thou wert a wretched woman.

Bianca. Speaks your love
Or fear, my lord?

Duke. Both, both. Bianca, know,
The nightly languish of my dull unrest
Hath stamped a strong opinion; for methought—
Mark what I say—as I in glorious pomp
Was sitting on my throne, whiles I had hemmed
My best beloved Bianca in mine arms,
She reached my cap of state, and cast it down
Beneath her foot, and spurned it in the dust.
Whiles I—O 'twas a dream too full of fate—
Was stooping down to reach it, on my head,
Fernando, like a traitor to his vows,
Clapped in disgrace a coronet of horns.
But by the honour of anointed kings,
Were both of you hid in a rock of fire,
Guarded by ministers of flaming hell,
I have a sword—'tis here—should make my way
Through fire, through darkness, death and all,
To hew your lust-engendered flesh to shreds,
Pound you to mortar, cut your throats and mince
Your flesh to mites. I will—start not—I will!

Bianca. Mercy protect me, will ye murder me?

34. whiles] *Q;* whilst *W.* 38. Whiles] *Q;* While *W.* 46. death and all] *Q;* death, and hell, and all *G.*

31–41. *The nightly . . . horns*] Imagination 'rageth in melancholy persons' (*Anatomy*, I.2.3.2, p. 253).

31. *dull*] listless, sluggish.

34. *hemmed*] Suggesting confinement or restraint, and perhaps emphasising his possessiveness (*OED hem* v.[1] 3, *hemmed*).

36. *cap of state*] hat worn as insignia of his rank.

38. *too . . . fate*] imbued with all too strong a sense of inevitability.

43. *rock of fire*] burning rock, like the brimstone of hell.

46.] Not a deficient line, as Gifford supposes (see Coll.), if Q's two instances of *through* disguise the common variant 'thorough' (Cercignani, 357).

47. *lust-engendered*] conceived in lust.

50. *Mercy*] A mere expression of surprise, fear etc., from 'May God have mercy' (*OED* 4).

Duke. Yes—Oh, I cry thee mercy. How the rage
Of my undreamt-of wrongs made me forget
All sense of sufferance. Blame me not, Bianca;
One such another dream would quite distract
Reason and self humanity. Yet tell me,
Was't not an ominous vision?
Bianca. 'Twas, my lord:
Yet but a vision; for did such a guilt
Hang on mine honour, 'twere no blame in you
If you did stab me to the heart.
Duke. The heart?
Nay, strumpet, to the soul, and tear it off
From life, to damn it in immortal death.
Bianca. Alas, what do you mean, sir?
Duke. I am mad—
Forgive me, good Bianca. Still methinks
I dream and dream anew. Now prithee chide me.
Sickness and these divisions so distract
My senses that I take things possible
As if they were; which to remove, I mean
To speed me straight to Lucca, where perhaps
Absence, and bathing in those healthful springs
May soon recover me. Meantime, dear sweet,

52. undreamt-of] *Q (vndreamt of); own dream'd of G; e'en dream'd of conj. G.* 55. self humanity] *Q*; self-humanity *G.* 59. heart?] *Q;* heart! *GD.*

51–2. *rage Of*] fury caused by.

52. *undreamt-of wrongs*] perhaps 'inconceivable offences' (Hoskins; cf. 87n).

53. *sufferance*] patient endurance, forbearance (*OED* 1; cf. *BH* 2.3.44–5).

55. *self humanity*] 'humanity itself', or 'my very humanity' (*OED self* 1b; cf. 3.3.10). *Self* was sometimes equivalent to Latin *ipse*, 'the same'; see *Malcontent* 2.3.43n.

61. *immortal*] everlasting.

65. *divisions*] 'disagreements, breaches' (*OED division* 4; cf. *Oth.* 4.1.228) or 'mental disturbances'. The latter sense is not recorded by *OED*, but is almost certainly intended in *BH* 5.3.9n (Revels).

68. *Lucca*] city in northern Italy, 40 miles west of Florence, famous for the mineral springs in its vicinity; they are mentioned in *Malfi* 2.1.62, 3.2.315 (Sugden).

Pity my troubled heart; griefs are extreme.
Yet, sweet, when I am gone, think on my dream.
Who waits without, ho?

Enter PETRUCCIO, NIBRASSA, FIORMONDA, D'AVOLOS, ROSEILLI, [*disguised as before,*] *and* FERNANDO.

Is provision ready
To pass to Lucca?

Petruccio. It attends your highness.

Duke. Friend, hold; take here from me this jewel, this:
Gives him Bianca.
Be she your care till my return from Lucca,
Honest Fernando. Wife, respect my friend.
Let's go—but hear ye, wife, think on my dream.
Exeunt all but ROSEILLI *and* PETRUCCIO.

Petruccio. Cousin, one word with you. Doth not this cloud
Acquaint you with strange novelties? The Duke
Is lately much distempered. What he means
By journeying now to Lucca is to me
A riddle. Can you clear my doubt?

Roseilli. O sir!
My fears exceed my knowledge; yet I note
No less than you infer. All is not well;
Would 'twere. Whosoever thrive, I shall be sure
Never to rise to my unhoped desires.

73. SD.] *placed as in GD; after* 'Lucca?' *(74) in Q.* 73.2. *disguised as before*] *GD; not in Q.* 78. SD.] *W; Exeunt omnes, but Ros. et Petr. Q.* 86. Whosoever] *Q;* whoever *G;* whosoe'er *GD.*

71. *extreme*] distressing in the extreme (*OED* 4a, f). Grief was thought to be a cause of madness; cf. Burton, I.2.3.4, p. 259.

73. *provision*] food or other necessaries for the journey (the singular form was common; *OED* 6, 7).

74. *attends*] awaits.

81. *distempered*] troubled, out of humour (perhaps suggesting imbalance in bodily humours; *OED* ppl.a.[1] 2).

83. *doubt*] uncertainty, misgiving (*OED* sb.[1] 1, 3).

85. *infer*] mention, report (*OED* 2).

87. *unhoped*] probably 'not entertained with any serious hope of fulfilment'; cf. 52n., *CBS*, 1030.

But cousin, I shall tell you more anon.
Meantime, pray send my lord Fernando to me,
I covet much to speak with him.

Enter FERNANDO.

Petruccio. And see,
He comes himself. I'll leave you both together. *Exit.*
Fernando. The Duke is horsed for Lucca. How now, coz,
How prosper you in love?
Roseilli. As still I hoped.
My lord, you are undone.
Fernando. Undone? in what?
Roseilli. Lost, and I fear your life is bought and sold.
I'll tell you how. Late in my lady's chamber,
As I by chance lay slumbering on the mats,
In comes the lady Marquess, and with her,
Julia and D'Avolos, where sitting down,
Not doubting me, 'Madam,' quoth D'Avolos,
'We have discovered now the nest of shame.'
In short, my lord—for you already know
As much as they reported—there was told
The circumstance of all your private love
And meetings with the Duchess; when at last
False D'Avolos concluded with an oath,
'We'll make,' quoth he, 'his heart-strings crack for this.'
Fernando. Speaking of me?
Roseilli. Of you. 'Ay,' quoth the Marquess,
'Were not the Duke a baby, he would seek
Swift vengeance, for he knew it long ago.'

90. SD.] *Q; 'Re-enter* FERNANDO*' after 91.1 GD.* 100. Not . . . 'Madam,'] *W;* Not doubting me, Madam *Q.*

93. *As . . . hoped*] as I always expected.

95. *bought and sold*] (a) forfeited, beyond reprieve; (b) betrayed for a bribe (*OED buy* v. 11b; cf. *R3* 5.6.35).

97. *mats*] Rush mats were a common floor-covering.

100. *Not doubting me*] i.e. not suspecting my true identity.

101. *nest*] 'lair, haunt, bed' or 'faction, clique'; with suggestions of procreation.

107. *heart-strings*] 'in old notions of Anatomy, the tendons or nerves supposed to brace and sustain the heart' (*OED* 1).

Fernando. Let him know it. Yet I vow
She is as loyal in her plighted faith
As is the sun in heaven. But put case
She were not, and the Duke did know she were not,
This sword lift up, and guided by this arm,
Shall guard her from an armèd troop of fiends,
And all the earth beside.
Roseilli. You are too safe
In your destruction.
Fernando. Damn him, he shall feel—
But peace, who comes?

Enter COLONA.

Colona. My lord, the Duchess craves a word with you.
Fernando. Where is she?
Colona. In her chamber.
Roseilli. Here have a plum for ie'ee.
Colona. Come fool, I'll give thee plums enow, come fool.
Fernando. [*Aside*] Let slaves in mind be servile to their fears;
Our heart is high in-starred in brighter spheres.
Exeunt FERNANDO *and* COLONA.

114. not, and] *W.*; not; and *Q.* 115. lift] *Q;* lifted *E.* 125. *Aside*] *this ed.; not in Q.* 126. SD. *and*] *W; et Q.*

---

112. *plighted faith*] pledged fidelity (in marriage). Cf. the phrasing of the marriage ceremony: 'I plight thee my troth' (*BCP*).

113. *As . . . heaven*] probably alluding to the constancy of the sun in giving light, or to the regularity of its daily transit of the heavens; cf. *Countess* 3.4.103.

put case] suppose (see 1.1.72n).

115. *lift*] 'lifted': obsolete form of the participle.

117. *the earth*] 'humankind' (cf. Genesis 11:1).

safe] secure, complacent (cf. 4.1.112n).

123. *plum*] Has various sexual associations, including 'male genitals' (e.g. *Chaste Maid* 3.2.63). In Killigrew's *1 Thomaso* (1654) 1.4, 'giving thee Plums' is sexually suggestive. Plums are also among the foods a pregnant woman might crave (Williams).

ie'ee] probably a fool's version of 'ee', a colloquial contraction of 'ye' (Hoskins).

124. *enow*] plural of 'enough'.

126. *Our*] including Roseilli—or a cavalier appropriation of the royal plural?

high . . . spheres] i.e. set like a star in the concentric, transparent *spheres* thought to carry the sun, moon, planets and fixed stars. Perhaps also

Roseilli. I see him lost already.
If all prevail not, we shall know too late,
No toil can shun the violence of fate. *Exit.*

---

referring to the notion that the great were transformed upon death into stars (cf. *Metamorphoses* XV, 948–52, *1H6* I.I.55–6).

128. *all*] i.e. all our efforts (?).

129.] 'It is impossible to avoid fate' (Tilley F 83).

Act 5

ACT 5 SCENE I

Enter above FIORMONDA.

Fiormonda. Now fly, revenge, and wound the lower earth,
That I, ensphered above, may cross the race
Of love despised, and triumph o'er their graves
Who scorn the low-bent thraldom of my heart.

A curtain drawn, below are discovered BIANCA, *in her night attire, leaning on a cushion at a table, holding* FERNANDO *by the hand.*

Bianca. Why shouldst thou not be mine? Why should the laws,
The iron laws of ceremony, bar
Mutual embraces? What's a vow? A vow?
Can there be sin in unity? Could I
As well dispense with conscience as renounce

5.1.0. SD.] *W, G, GD, E conflate with 4.1–3 for opening SD.* 1.] *aside GD.*
2. ensphered] *Q;* inspher'd *W.*

5.1.] Cf. Corona MS (App. 3), ll. 206–18; *Rom. Actor* 4.2.99ff; *Milan* 4.3.261ff. See Intro., pp. 63–5, for further comment on borrowings in this scene.

0.1. above] i.e. on the upper stage. She observes the tragic action 'like an avenging goddess' (Farr, 72).

2. *ensphered above*] placed like a star in a celestial sphere. Thus *cross* = 'thwart', as an unfavourable star was thought to hinder human endeavours; cf. *R&J*, Prol., 6. Perhaps echoing Fernando's 'in-starred', 4.2.126.

race] breed, group of people (referring to Bianca and Fernando).

4. *low-bent*] (a) bowing low; (b) showing deference to those of lower rank. Not recorded in *OED*, but cf. *BH* 3.5.88.

4.1. curtain] perhaps drawn over the large central entrance in the Jones theatre; see Figure 1.

5–14. *Why . . . years*] Cf. Giovanni in *'Tis Pity* 1.1.24–27.

6. *ceremony*] formality (*OED* 3b).

8. *unity*] concord, harmony (*OED* sb.[1] 3).

The outside of my titles, the poor style
Of Duchess, I had rather change my life
With any waiting-woman in the land
To purchase one night's rest with thee, Fernando,
Than be Caraffa's spouse a thousand years.
Fiormonda. [*Aside*] Treason to wedlock. This would make you swear.
Fernando. Lady of all what I am, as before,

* * *

To survive you, or I will see you first
Or widowèd or buried. If the last,
By all the comfort I can wish to taste,
By your fair eyes, that sepulchre that holds
Your coffin shall encoffin me alive.
I sign it with this seal. *Kisses her.*
Fiormonda. [*Aside*] Ignoble strumpet!
Bianca. You shall not swear. Take off that oath again,
Or thus I will enforce it. *She kisses him.*
Fernando. Use that force
And make me perjurèd; for whiles your lips
Are made the book, it is a sport to swear,

11. Duchess] *italic in Q.* 15. *Aside*] *GD; not in Q.* 16–18.] *As W; lacuna not indicated in Q.* 22. encoffin] *Q;* incoffin *W.* 23. *Aside*] *GD; not in Q.* 26. perjurèd] *GD;* periur'd *Q.*

---

10. *style*] title. Her declaration points up the culturally determined nature of her role as well as drawing on the *theatrum mundi* trope.

12. *any waiting-woman . . . land*] Popular literature 'contrasted the matrimonial slavery of the daughters of the aristocracy with the relative freedom of choice enjoyed by poor women' (Mendelson and Crawford, 107; see their quotation from the ballad *Loves Downfall*, 108–9).

16–18. *Lady . . . first*] Probably lacking a line or more. The phrase *as before* may have introduced a renewal of a vow similar to that at 2.4.87. 'Fernando has not threatened to murder the Duke but to wait until Bianca is a widow in the natural course of events before he attempts to consummate his love' (Ure, 101).

23.1, 25.1. Kisses] The subject of controversy in the play as well as in contemporary culture; see LN.

23. *Ignoble strumpet*] Contemporary morality 'differentiated sharply between women and men': 'Women's sexual misconduct had implications for the whole honour of a marriage; blame for men's misconduct, though, was diverted on to the women involved' (Gowing, 112).

27. *the book*] oaths were sworn by kissing 'the book', i.e. the Bible. Hoskins notes echoes of *R&J* 1.5.106–9: '[*Romeo.*] Thus from my lips, by

And glory to forswear.

Fiormonda. [*Aside*] Here's fast and loose,

Which, for a ducat, now the game's on foot.

Whiles they are kissing, enter DUKE *with his sword drawn,* D'AVOLOS *in like manner;* PETRUCCIO, NIBRASSA *and a Guard.*

Colona. [*Within*] Help, help! Madam, you are betrayed. Madam, help, help!

D'Avolos. Is there confidence in credit now, sir? Belief in your own eyes? Do you see? Do you see, sir? Can you behold it without lightning?

Colona. [*Within*] Help, madam, help!

28. *Aside*] *GD; not in Q.* loose,] *this ed.;* loose; *Q;* loose! *G.* 29. Which,] *W;* Which *Q.* foot.] *Q;* foot? *W.* 29.] *Exit from above W.* 29. SD.] *Q; Whilst they are kissing, enter, in the back-ground, the Duke and D'Avolos, with their swords drawn, Fiormonda, Petruchio, Nibrassa, and a Guard. W; Whilst . . . kissing, the Duke and D'Avolos, with their swords drawn, appear at the door. G; Whilst . . . the door [as G], followed by Petruchio, Nibrassa and a Guard. GD.* 32.] *aside to Duke GD.* 33. Do you see?] *Q; omitted W.*

---

thine my sin is purged. *Juliet.* Then have my lips the sin that they have took. *Romeo.* Sin from my lips? O trespass sweetly urged! / Give me my sin again. *He kisses her. Juliet.* You kiss by th' book'. Cf. 5.3.36–8n.

28. *fast and loose*] Literally, 'A cheating game widely patronised by the gypsies in the time of Shakespeare. A leather belt was made up into a number of intricate folds and set edgeways upon a table; one of the folds being made to represent the middle of the belt, so as to lead one to believe that a skewer thrust into it would affix it to the table, whereas it might be drawn away by both ends being taken up' (Brand, 544). Figuratively, to play *fast and loose* is to be 'slippery' or inconstant' (*OED fast and loose*; cf. *A&C* 4.13.25–9, Tilley P 401).

29. *Which*] Previous editors take this as an interrogative pronoun (see Coll.). I think it is probably a loose connective, perhaps = 'as to which' (see Abbott 272).

on foot] started, in action. Cf. 2.3.83.

29.3. a Guard] probably a body of two or more guards.

30–1.] In the Corona MS, Colona's counterpart 'was on the point of shouting, but her life being threatened by the Prince, she withdrew more dead than alive' (App. 3, ll. 213–14).

32. *credit*] 'credence, belief' (in Bianca's fidelity, or D'Avolos's reports of her infidelity); or Bianca's 'good reputation' itself (*OED* 1, 5). Perhaps a sarcastic echo of 3.3.71.

32–3. *your own eyes*] i.e. the proof of your own eyes.

34. *without lightning*] without the aid of lightning (?).

Fernando. What noise is that, I heard one cry.
Duke. [*Coming forward*] Ha! Did you?
Know you who I am?
Fernando. Yes, th'art Pavy's duke,
Dressed like a hangman. See, I am unarmed,
Yet do not fear thee. Though the coward doubt
Of what I could have done hath made thee steal
Th'advantage of this time, yet, Duke, I dare
Thy worst, for murder sits upon thy cheeks.
To't, man!
Duke. I am too angry in my rage
To scourge thee unprovided. Take him hence,
Away with him. [*The Guard*] *take hold on him.*
Fernando. Unhand me!
D'Avolos. You must go, sir.
Fernando. Duke, do not shame thy manhood to lay hands
On that most innocent lady.
Duke. Yet again!
Confine him to his chamber.
Exeunt D'AVOLOS *and Guard with* FERNANDO.
Leave us all,
None stay, not one, shut up the doors.
Exeunt all but DUKE, BIANCA
[*and* FIORMONDA, *above*].
Fiormonda. Now show thyself my brother, brave Caraffa.
Duke. Woman, stand forth before me. Wretched whore,
What canst thou hope for?
Bianca. Death; I wish no less.

36–7.] *W;* What . . . cry. / *Duke*. Ha . . . am? / *Fer.* Yes . . . Duke, *Q.* 36. *Coming forward*] *comes forward W; no SD Q.* 45. SD.] *GD (subst.); They take hold on him Q.* 47. Yet again!] *G;* Yet again: *Q.* 49. SD.] *W; Exeunt omnes, but Du. et Bia Q.* 51. me.] *this ed.;* me,—*Q.*

---

38. *Dressed*] perhaps 'equipped', referring to Caraffa's drawn sword (*OED dress* v. 8).

hangman] executioner (*OED* 1).

39. *coward doubt*] cowardly apprehension, fear (*OED* sb.[1] 3).

43–5. *I . . . him*] Cf. *Rom. Actor* 4.2.150–2.

44. *unprovided*] (when you are) 'not provided with a weapon' or 'unprepared' (*OED* 1, 2).

52ff] Bianca becomes another Evadne (*Maid's Trag.* 2.1.194ff) or Marcelia (*Milan* 3.3.120–31, 4.3.261ff); see Intro., pp. 64–5.

You told me you had dreamt, and, gentle Duke,
Unless you be mistook, you are now awaked.
Duke. Strumpet, I am, and in my hand hold up
The edge that must uncut thy twist of life.
Dost thou not shake?
Bianca. For what? To see a weak,
Faint, trembling arm advance a leaden blade?
Alas, good man, put up, put up; thine eyes
Are likelier much to weep than arms to strike.
What would you do now, pray?
Duke. What? Shameless harlot!
Rip up the cradle of thy cursèd womb,
In which the mixture of that traitor's lust
Impostumes for a birth of bastardy.
Yet come, and if thou think'st thou canst deserve
One mite of mercy, ere the boundless spleen
Of just-consuming wrath o'er-swell my reason,
Tell me, bad woman, tell me what could move
Thy heart to crave variety of youth?

54. you are] *Q;* you're *GD.* 61. What?] *W;* What! *Q.*

---

53. *gentle*] (implying timidity or weakness).

56. *twist*] In classical mythology, a human life was pictured as a thread (*twist*) spun by the three Parcae or Fates. Cf. *'Tis Pity* 5.6.71, *FM*, 302, *Fancies*, 1735–6.

58. *leaden*] heavy, as if made of lead (implying that he has difficulty wielding his sword).

59. *put up*] i.e. sheathe your sword.

63. *mixture*] semen, seed. Perhaps so-called because: (a) it is a product of their 'mixing' ('mix' and 'mixture' being used of sexual intercourse: *OED mix* v. 4b, *mixture* 1e); (b) it is impure. Cf. 5.2.44–5 and quotation in next note.

64. *Impostumes*] gathers into an impostume or abscess. Used substantively in reference to moral corruption (*OED* sb. 1, 2a; v. 1; cf. *Edmonton* 4.2.128, a scene sometimes ascribed to Ford). See also *CBS*, 1641, and *Queen*, 1220–4: 'Mix with some hot vein'd letcher, whose prone lust / Should feed the rank impostume of desires, / And get a race of bastards'.

66. *spleen*] anger, rage.

67. *just-consuming*] *just* is adverbial: 'justly consuming or destructive' (*OED just* a. 13a).

69. *variety of youth*] the first definite sign that Caraffa is an older man. Cf. 73–7. Iago claims that Desdemona 'must change for youth' (*Oth.* 1.3.349).

Bianca. I tell ye, if you needs would be resolved.
I held Fernando much the properer man.
Duke. Shameless intolerable whore!
Bianca. What ails you?
Can you imagine, sir, the name of Duke
Could make a crooked leg, a scambling foot,
A tolerable face, a wearish hand,
A bloodless lip, or such an untrimmed beard
As yours fit for a lady's pleasure? No.
I wonder you could think 'twere possible,
When I had once but looked on your Fernando,
I ever could love you again. Fie, fie!
Now by my life, I thought that long ago
Y'had known it, and been glad you had a friend
Your wife did think so well of.
Duke. O my stars!
Here's impudence above all history.
Why, thou detested reprobate in virtue,
Durst thou, without a blush, before mine eyes,
Speak such immodest language?
Bianca. Dare? Yes, 'faith,
You see I dare. I know what you would say now.
You would fain tell me how exceeding much
I am beholding to you, that vouchsafed
Me, from a simple gentlewoman's place,
The honour of your bed. 'Tis true, you did;
But why? 'Twas but because you thought I had
A spark of beauty more than you had seen.
To answer this, my reason is the like.

70. I] *Q;* I'll *G.* 77. pleasure?] *W;* pleasure, *Q.* 80. again.] *this ed.;* again? *Q.* 82. Y'had] *Q;* You'd *W.* 86. Durst] *Q;* Dar'st *G.* 87. 'faith] *W;* faith *Q.*

---

71. *properer*] (a) more complete; (b) more handsome (*OED proper* 6, 8).

74. *crooked leg*] Vulcan—the husband of Venus (to whom Bianca is compared at 2.2.109), and the 'special patron of cuckolds' (Brewer)—was lame.
scambling] shambling, shuffling. *OED*'s earliest instance (ppl.a. 4); cf. *Fancies*, 448.

75. *wearish*] feeble, sickly, wizened (*OED* 2).

87. *'faith*] in faith.

89. *fain*] gladly, willingly.

The selfsame appetite which led you on
To marry me, led me to love your friend.
O he's a gallant man. If ever yet
Mine eyes beheld a miracle composed
Of flesh and blood, Fernando has my voice.
I must confess, my lord, that for a prince
Handsome enough you are, and no more;
But to compare yourself with him, trust me,
You are too much in fault. Shall I advise you?
Hark in your ear: thank heaven he was so slow
As not to wrong your sheets; for as I live,
The fault was his, not mine.

Fiormonda. [*Aside*] Take this, take all.

Duke. Excellent, excellent, the pangs of death
Are music to this.
Forgive me, my good genius, I had thought
I matched a woman, but I find she is
A devil worser than the worst in hell.
Nay, nay, since we are in, e'en come, say on,
I mark you to a syllable. You say
The fault was his, not yours. Why, virtuous mistress,

102. and no more] *Q;* and—and no more *G.* 107. *Aside*] *this ed.* 108–9.] *G; one line Q.* 115. virtuous mistress] *italic in Q.*

96–7. *The . . . friend*] Domitia tells Caesar: 'Thy lust compell'd me / To be a strumpet, and mine hath return'd it / In my intent, and will, though not in act, / To cuckold thee' (*Rom. Actor* 4.2.135–8).

96. *appetite*] desire. The appetites and passions were thought to be 'powers of the sensitive soul that prompt and direct motion (or action)' (Hoeniger, 162).

100. *voice*] vote.

105. *Hark . . . ear*] a stock phrase, often used to mock or annoy (e.g. *1 Honest Whore* 1.5.105).

106. *sheets*] See 4.1.165n.

107. *Take . . . all*] perhaps = 'if you endure this without complaint, you will endure anything'. Cf. *AYL* 4.3.15.

109. *to*] compared to.

110. *good genius*] good angel or guardian spirit. See 1.1.126n, *'Tis Pity* 5.1.31.

111. *matched*] married.

113. *are in*] i.e. have entered upon the subject.

e'en] even; modifies *come*: 'indeed . . .' (*OED even* adv. 8b).

115. *virtuous mistress*] italic in Q, perhaps to stress his irony.

Can you imagine you have so much art
Which may persuade me you and your close markman
Did not a little traffic in my right?

Bianca. Look what I said, 'tis true. For know it now,
I must confess I missed no means, no time,
To win him to my bosom; but so much,
So holily, with such religion,
He kept the laws of friendship, that my suit
Was held but in comparison a jest.
Nor did I ofter urge the violence
Of my affection, but as oft he urged
The sacred vows of faith 'twixt friend and friend.
Yet be assured, my lord, if ever language
Of cunning servile flatteries, entreaties,
Or what in me is, could procure his love,
I would not blush to speak it.

Duke. Such another
As thou art, miserable creature, would
Sink the whole sex of women. Yet confess
What witchcraft used the wretch to charm the art
Of the once spotless temple of thy mind.
For without witchcraft it could ne'er be done.

117. markman] *italic in Q.* 125. ofter] *Q;* often *W.* 134. art] *Q;* heart *W.*

---

116. *art*] cunning, craft.

117. *close markman*] secret lover. A 'mark' = (a) target in archery; (b) sexual target at which men aim: the vulva (Partridge). *Close* may also imply that Fernando has shot all too near the 'mark'.

118. *traffic . . . right*] '(sexual) commerce which is due to me' (Partridge, *traffic*).

119. *Look what*] an intensifying phrase: 'whatever' (as in *R2* 1.1.87).

122. *religion*] devotion, conscientiousness (*OED* 6a); quadrisyllabic here.

123. *kept*] adhered to.

125. *ofter*] oftener.

urge] dwell emphatically upon.

133. *Sink*] bring to ruin; weigh down with guilt; debase (*OED* 21, 22).

134. *charm the art*] gain control by magic charms. Despite editors' doubts (see Coll.), the sense is clear: he thinks Fernando has mastered the 'art' or skill required to control her mind. *Art* is often associated with magic (e.g. *Temp.* 1.2.1).

136. *without . . . done*] Brabanzio says Desdemona could not have been 'corrupted' 'Sans witchcraft' (*Oth.* 1.3.60–4, the F reading; Q has 'Since [or "Saunce"] witchcraft'; cf. *LS* 3.3.57–9n).

Bianca. Phew! an you be in these tunes, sir, I'll leave.
You know the best, and worst, and all.
Duke. Nay then,
Thou tempt'st me to thy ruin. Come, black angel,
Fair devil, in thy prayers reckon up
The sum in gross of all thy veinèd follies.
There, amongst other, weep in tears of blood
For one above the rest: adultery,
Adultery, Bianca. Such a guilt
As were the sluices of thine eyes let up,
Tears cannot wash it off. 'Tis not the tide
Of trivial wantonness from youth to youth,
But thy abusing of thy lawful bed,
Thy husband's bed, his in whose breast thou sleep'st;
His that did prize thee more than all the trash
Which hoarding worldlings make an idol of.
When thou shalt find the catalogue enrolled
Of thy misdeeds, there shall be writ, in text,
Thy bastarding the issues of a prince.

137. Phew!] *G;* Phew—*Q.* an] *W;* and *Q.* I'll leave] *Q;* I'll leave you *W.* 139. black angel] *italic in Q.* 143–4. adultery] *both italic in Q.* 149. sleep'st] *Q;* slept'st *GD.*

---

137. an] if.
leave] 'depart' or 'leave off speaking'.

139. *black angel*] inverting the word-play on her name (= 'white'; see 2.3.84, 4.1.18); cf. *W. Devil.*

141. *veinèd*] borne in the blood, the supposed seat of sensual desire (*OED* 3).

142. *tears of blood*] (expressing anguish).

146. *tide*] 'momentary welling up of passion' (cf. 1.2.89n, 2.3.88–90, *Fancies*, 383–4); or 'excess' (*GM* 1231–2).

151. *worldlings*] unspiritual, avaricious people (*OED worldling* 1; cf. *J. Malta* 5.5.49).

152. *enrolled*] recorded. 'Enrol' was used of making an entry among the rolls, or records, of a court of justice (*OED* 5, 6). Perhaps conflating the individual's 'book of conscience', 'wherein are written all our offences' (*Anatomy*, 3.4.2.3, p. 400), and God's 'book of life', containing the names of those who were to be saved (Revelation 20:12–15; Kiefer, 113–15). Cf. Jonson Elegy, 16, *Mariam* 4.3.131, *Elegy by W.S.*, 239, 179ff.

153. *text*] 'Capitals' or 'text-hand', a large formal script used for the text of a book, a smaller or more cursive hand being reserved for glosses and commentary (*OED text*[1] 5; *text-hand*). Cf. *LOL*, 585–6.

Now turn thine eyes into thy hovering soul,
And do not hope for life. Would angels sing
A requiem at my hearse but to dispense
With my revenge on thee, 'twere all in vain.
Prepare to die.

Bianca. I do, and to the point
Of thy sharp sword with open breast I'll run
Halfway thus naked. Do not shrink, Caraffa,
This daunts not me; but in the latter act
Of thy revenge, 'tis all the suit I ask,
At my last gasp, to spare thy noble friend,
For life to me without him were a death.

Duke. Not this, I'll none of this, 'tis not so fit.
Casts away his sword.
Why should I kill her? She may live and change,
Or—

Fiormonda. Dost thou halt? Faint coward, dost thou wish
To blemish all thy glorious ancestors?
Is this thy courage?

Duke. Ha! Say you so too?
Give me thy hand, Bianca.

Bianca. Here.

Duke. Farewell.

157. hearse] *GD;* hearse? *Q;* hearse! *W;* hearse, *G.* 159.] *'opens her breast' before speech W.* I do,] *this ed.;* I, do; *Q;* I do; *W.* 166. SD.] *aligned with 166–7 in Q.*

---

155. *hovering*] (a) floating near; (b) lingering, on the verge of flying off at the moment of death (*OED hover* v.[1] 2, 3). Cf. 5.3.38.

156–8. *Would . . . vain*] 'Could I secure a happy immortality by sparing thy life, I would not forgo my revenge' (Gifford).

157. *but*] simply.

159. *I do*] Responding to his 'Prepare to die'. Alternatively, Q's 'I, doe;' could = 'Ay, do;', i.e. 'do your worst!'.

162. *latter*] final, concluding. Often refers to the end of a life, an age etc. (*OED* 3; *Dido* 2.1.256).

164. *last gasp*] Ecclesiasticus 7:9, Apocrypha; cf. Drayton, *Idea* LVI, l. 9.

166. *Not . . . fit*] The probable echo of *Rom. Actor* 4.2.138–52 creates false expectations.

170. *blemish*] disgrace (*OED* 4c). A blemish = 'a moral defect or stain' (sb. 3), with a compelling suggestion of physical (and therefore public) deformation (Opie, 239).

Thus go in everlasting sleep to dwell.
Draws his poniard and stabs her.
Here's blood for lust and sacrifice for wrong.

Bianca. 'Tis bravely done. Thou hast struck home at once.
Live to repent too late. Commend my love
To thy true friend: my love to him that owes it,
My tragedy to thee, my heart to—to—Fernand—oh,
oh! *Dies.*

Duke. Sister, she's dead.

Fiormonda. Then whiles thy rage is warm,
Pursue the causer of her trespasses.

Duke. Good;
I'll slake no time whiles I am hot in blood.
Takes up his sword and exit

173. SD.] *aligned with 173–4 in Q.* 178. My] Ny *Q.* Fernand—oh, oh!] *Fernand*-oo-oh. *Q.* 179. whiles] *Q;* while *W.* 180. trespasses] *Q;* trespass *GD.* 181. slake] *Q;* slack *G.* whiles] *Q;* whilst *W.* SD.] *aligned with 180–1 in Q.*

173.1. poniard] dagger.

174. *Here's . . . wrong*] Perhaps echoed in Shirley's *Love's Cruelty* (a Queen Henrietta's Men play, licensed 14 Nov. 1631). When Bellamente finds his wife with another man, he is 'won with foolish pity': 'Your fears thus vanish; I delight not in / The bloody sacrifice; live both. [*Throws down the pistol*' (4.2, p. 244) This play remained in the Phoenix repertory, with *LS*, until at least 1639. After the Restoration, it was performed by Sir Thomas Killigrew's company, who may also have produced *LS* (see Intro., p. 23).

blood for lust] Cf. Perigot in Fletcher's *The Faithful Shepherdess* (as he wounds the chaste Amoret): 'Death is the best reward that's due to lust' (3.1, p. 72).

sacrifice] See Intro., pp. 65–7.

175. *bravely*] ironic: 'valiantly' (perhaps echoing Fiormonda's 'courage', 171), and 'splendidly, in fine fashion'.

177. *owes*] possesses.

178. *Fernand—oh, oh!*] 'Ford's attempt to make the stabbed heroine expire pathetically with an "O" of pain and anguish . . . goes bathetically wrong because the hero's name ends in "o"' (Madeleine, 43).

181. *slake no time*] lose or waste no time (cf. 'Slack no time'; *OED slack* v. 1c, *slake* v.[1] 14b).

hot in blood] (a) in the heat of passion, alluding to the blood as the seat of emotion; (b) in full vigour ('in blood' was applied to hounds); (c) steeped in (still-warm) blood (*OED blood* 7; cf. *1H6* 4.2.48–51).

Fiormonda. Here's royal vengeance. This becomes the state
Of his disgrace, and my unbounded fate. *Exit.*

ACT 5 SCENE 2

Enter FERNANDO, NIBRASSA *and* PETRUCCIO.

Petruccio. May we give credit to your words, my lord?
Speak on your honour.
Fernando. Let me die accursed
If ever, through the progress of my life,
I did as much as reap the benefit
Of any favour from her, save a kiss.
A better woman never blessed the earth.
Nibrassa. Beshrew my heart, young lord, but I believe thee. Alas, kind lady, 'tis a lordship to a dozen of points but the jealous madman will in his fury offer her some violence.
Petruccio. If it be thus, 'twere fit you rather kept
A guard about you for your own defence,
Than to be guarded for security
Of his revenge. He's extremely moved.
Nibrassa. Passion of my body, my lord, if 'a come in his odd

183. fate] *Q;* hate *G.* 183. SD. *Exit*] *W; recedet Fior. Q.*

5.2.7–10.] *W; verse Q.* 14. He's] *Q* (he's); he is *W.* 15, 16. 'a] *Q* ('a); he *G.*

182. *becomes the state*] is appropriate to—and ennobles—the circumstances (Schmidt, *state* 4).

183. *unbounded fate*] endless suffering (?). Perhaps hinting at '*unbounded* by marital ties' (Hoskins).

183.1. Exit] Q's '*recedet Fior.*', apparently directing Fiormonda to remain on the upper stage but withdraw a little, seems wrong because: (a) the scene location changes with the entry of Fernando and the others; (b) Fiormonda has no lines in 5.2; (c) she is required for a fresh entrance at 5.3.0.1.

5.2.2–5. *Let . . . kiss*] See 5.1.23.1 LN.

7. *Beshrew my heart*] common asseveration, here expressing kind favour. Ironic at 116.

8. *'tis . . . points*] i.e. 'I would wager a lord's estate and title against a dozen points or tagged laces' (used to attach the hose to the doublet, to lace the bodice etc.; of trifling value; *OED point* sb.[1] B5).

9. *offer*] try to inflict (on) (*OED* 5).

13–14. *for . . . revenge*] i.e. to ensure Caraffa's revenge (cf. 5.1.48).

14. *moved*] angry, agitated.

15. *Passion . . . body*] common asseveration referring to Christ's Passion but applied to the speaker (*OED passion* 1b).

fits to you, in the case you are, 'a might cut your throat ere you could provide a weapon of defence. Nay, rather than it shall be so, hold, take my sword in your hand. 'Tis none of the sprucest, but 'tis a tough fox, will not fail his master. Come what will come, take it, I'll answer't, I. [*He gives Fernando his sword.*] In the meantime, Petruccio and I will back to the Duchess' lodging.

Petruccio. Well thought on; and in despite of all his rage,
Rescue the virtuous lady.

Nibrassa. Look to yourself, my lord, the Duke comes.

Enter DUKE, *his sword in one hand, and in the other a bloody dagger.*

Duke. Stand, and behold thy executioner,
Thou glorious traitor. I will keep no form
Of ceremonious law to try thy guilt.
Look here, 'tis written on my poniard's point,
The bloody evidence of thy untruth,
Wherein thy conscience and the wrathful rod
Of heaven's scourge for lust at once give up
The verdict of thy crying villainies.
I see th'art armed; prepare, I crave no odds
Greater than is the justice of my cause.
Fight, or I'll kill thee.

Fernando. Duke, I fear thee not;
But first I charge thee, as thou art a prince,

20–1. SD.] *after* 'lodging.' *(22) Q, other eds.* 23. and in despite] *Q;* and in despight *G;* and, despite *GD.* 25.] *Q; omitted W.* 27. glorious traitor] *italic in Q.* 34. th'art] *Q;* thou'rt *W;* thou art *G.*

---

16. *case*] '(unarmed) condition' (Hoskins).

19. *fox*] kind of sword. The name may have arisen 'from the figure of a wolf, on certain sword-blades, being mistaken for a fox' (*OED* 6).

20. *answer't*] answer for it.

22. *will back*] (ellipsis of the verb of motion).

25.1–2] Reminiscent of Giovanni's entrance with '*a heart upon his dagger*' in *'Tis Pity* 5.6.9.1.

27. *glorious*] proud, vainglorious (*OED* 1).

keep no form] observe no formal procedure (*OED form* 11).

32. *at . . . up*] both (or immediately) render (or reveal); *OED give* 64e, g.

33. *crying*] flagrant, egregious; calling loudly for redress (*OED* ppl.a. 3).

34. *odds*] advantage.

37. *charge*] exhort (*OED* 14).

Tell me, how hast thou used thy Duchess?
Duke. How?
To add affliction to thy trembling ghost,
Look on my dagger's crimson dye, and judge.
Fernando. Not dead?
Duke. Not dead? Yes, by my honour's truth. Why fool,
Dost think I'll hug my injuries? No, traitor,
I'll mix your souls together in your deaths
As you did both your bodies in her life.
Have at thee!
Fernando. Stay, I yield my weapon up.
He lets fall his weapon [*and kneels*].
Here, here's my bosom; as thou art a duke,
Dost honour goodness, if the chaste Bianca
Be murdered, murder me.
Duke. Faint-hearted coward,
Art thou so poor in spirit? Rise and fight,
Or by the glories of my house and name,
I'll kill thee basely.
Fernando. Do but hear me first.
Unfortunate Caraffa, thou hast butchered
An innocent, a wife as free from lust
As any terms of art can deify.
Duke. Pish, this is stale dissimulation,
I'll hear no more.
Fernando. If ever I unshrined
The altar of her purity, or tasted

46. SD.] *this ed.; he lets fall his weapon. Q.* 48. chaste] *italic in Q.* 49.] *'Kneels' after* 'me' *W.*

---

38. *used*] treated.
39. *ghost*] soul; perhaps with a threatening hint of the now more familiar sense.
43. *hug*] cherish, cling to (*OED* 1d).
46. *Have at thee*] 'watch out', 'I'm for you'.
46.1. and kneels] Echoing Bianca's gesture in 5.1.159–61.
48. *chaste Bianca*] italic in Q.
53. *Unfortunate*] The Moor is thus described in *Oth.* 5.2.289.
55.] as any skilfully worded or poetic speech can exalt (cf. *OED term* 13, 14a; cf. *LLL* 5.2.406–7).
56. *stale*] vapid, worn-out; cf. 66.
57. *unshrined*] literally, 'cast from its shrine'.

More of her love than what without control
Or blame a brother from a sister might,
Rack me to atomies. I must confess
I have too much abused thee; did exceed
In lawless courtship, 'tis too true, I did.
But by the honour which I owe to goodness,
For any actual folly I am free.

Duke. 'Tis false. As much in death for thee she spake.

Fernando. By yonder starry roof, 'tis true. O Duke!
Could'st thou rear up another world like this,
Another like to that, and more, or more,
Herein thou art most wretched: all the wealth
Of all those worlds could not redeem the loss
Of such a spotless wife. Glorious Bianca,
Reign in the triumph of thy martyrdom.
Earth was unworthy of thee.

Nibrassa and Petruccio. Now on our lives we both believe him.

Duke. Fernando, dar'st thou swear upon my sword
To justify thy words?

Fernando. I dare. Look here: *Kisses the sword.*
'Tis not the fear of death doth prompt my tongue,
For I would wish to die; and thou shalt know,
Poor miserable Duke, since she is dead
I'll hold all life a hell.

67. O Duke!] *italic in Q.*

---

59. *control*] restraint (*OED* sb. 2).
60. *brother . . . sister*] Cf. *Rom. Actor* 4.2.100–1.
61. *Rack . . . atomies*] tear me into tiny pieces (*OED rack* v.[3] 2b; *atomy*[2] 1).
62. *abused*] taken advantage of, deceived, wronged (*OED abuse* v. 2, 4, 5).
exceed] intransitive: 'pass the bounds of propriety' (*OED* 4).
63. *lawless*] unbridled, licentious.
65. *For*] of, regarding.
folly] lewdness, wantonness (*OED* sb.[1] 3; cf. *Oth.* 5.2.141).
66. *As . . . spake*] Could support rather than undermine Fernando's case—perhaps Caraffa begins to falter.
68–72. *Could'st . . . wife*] Cf. *Oth.* 5.2.150–3.
68. *rear up*] construct (*OED rear* v.[1] 7).
70–2. *all . . . wife*] Compelling, since Caraffa has often praised Bianca thus (1.1.191–3, 4.2.22–3, 5.1.150–1).
76. *upon my sword*] i.e. using the sword's handle as a cross.
77. *justify*] attest to (*OED* 5).
81. *hold*] consider.

Duke. Bianca chaste!
Fernando. As virtue's self is good.
Duke. Chaste, chaste, and killed by me! To her
I offer up this remnant of my—

Offers to stab himself and is stayed by FERNANDO.

Fernando. Hold,
Be gentler to thyself.
Petruccio. Alas my lord,
Is this a wise man's carriage?
Duke. Whither now
Shall I run from the day, where never man
Nor eye, nor eye of heaven, may see a dog
So hateful as I am? Bianca chaste.
Had not the fury of some hellish rage
Blinded all reason's sight, I might have seen
Her clearness in her confidence to die.
Your leave—

Kneels down, holds up his hands, speaks a little and riseth.

'Tis done. Come, friend, now for her love,
Her love that praised thee in the pangs of death,
I'll hold thee dear. Lords, do not care for me,

Enter D'AVOLOS.

85–6. Be . . . carriage] *W;* Be . . . selfe. / *Petr.* Alas . . . carriage. *Q.* 86. Is this . . . carriage?] *G*; this is . . . carriage.*Q;* This is . . . carriage? *W.* 93. Your leave—] *G;*——your leaue——*Q.* 96. SD.] *Q; after* 'O Bianca!' *(97) W.*

83.] The shortfall in syllables leads Dyce to suspect textual corruption. But sense, phrasing and the long 'a' sounds of *Chaste, chaste,* encourage the actor to linger over (and/or pause after) each utterance of this crucial word. The audience would hear metrical variation rather than deficiency.

84. *offer*] with sacrificial overtones; cf. 5.3.42.

84.1. Offers] attempts.

84.2. stayed] restrained.

86. *carriage*] conduct (*OED* 15b).

86–7. *Whither . . . run*] 'Where should Othello go?' (*Oth.* 5.2.278).

90. *fury*] tumult of mind approaching madness (*OED* 1, 3).

92. *clearness*] purity, innocence (*OED* 4; cf. *GM*, 471).

confidence to die] i.e. assurance, fearlessness in dying.

94. *'Tis done*] Perhaps making the 'vows' here that he enacts in the next scene; see 5.3.105n.

I am too wise to die yet.—O Bianca!

D'Avolos. The Lord Abbot of Monaco, sir, is in his return from Rome lodged last night late in the city, very privately; and hearing the report of your journey, only intends to visit your Duchess tomorrow.

Duke. Slave, torture me no more. Note him, my lords.
If you would choose a devil in the shape
Of man, an arch-arch-devil, there stands one.
We'll meet our uncle.—Order straight, Petruccio,
Our Duchess may be coffined. 'Tis our will
She forthwith be interred, with all the speed
And privacy you may, i'th' college church
Amongst Caraffa's ancient monuments.
Some three days hence we'll keep her funeral.
Damned villain, bloody villain.—O Bianca,
No counsel from our cruel wills can win us,
But ills once done, we bear our guilt within us.

Exeunt all but D'AVOLOS.

D'Avolos. God boyee! 'Arch-arch-devil'? Why, I am paid. Here's bounty for good service. Beshrew my heart, it is a right princely reward. Now must I say my prayers that I have lived to so ripe an age to have my head stricken off. I cannot tell, 't may be my lady Fiormonda will stand on my behalf to the Duke. That's but a single hope: a

105. arch-arch-devil] *italic in Q.* 109. i'th'] *W;* 'ith' *Q.* 114. But] "But *Q.* 114. SD.] *W; Exeunt omnes, manet D'auolos. Q.* 115. God boyee] *Q;* Good b'ye *W;* Good b'wi'ye *GD.* 'Arch-arch-devil'?] *W;* 'Arch-arch-devil': *Q.* 119. 't may] *Q* ('tmay), *GD;* it may *W.*

98. *Abbot*] But see 3.2.10–11.
104. *choose*] probably 'discern, distinguish'.
105. *arch-arch-devil*] Othello calls Iago a 'demi-devil', *Oth.* 5.2.307.
106. *straight*] straight away.
109. *college*] community of clergy (*OED* 3).
110. *monuments*] tombs.
111. *keep*] observe with due formality (*OED* 12).
114. *But . . . us*] Q marks this sententia with initial inverted commas.
115. *God boyee*] like 'goodbye', a contraction of 'God be with you/ye'; here ironic.
117. *say my prayers*] i.e. in thanks (ironic).
120. *single*] solitary, meagre (*OED* 12b).
120–2. *a disgraced . . . him*] 'In time of prosperity friends will be plenty, in time of adversity not one among twenty' (Tilley T 301; cf. *Haml.* 3.2.198–200).

disgraced courtier oftener finds enemies to sink him when he is falling than friends to relieve him. I must resolve to stand to the hazard of all brunts now. Come what may, I will not die like a coward, and the world shall know it. *Exit*

ACT 5 SCENE 3

Enter FIORMONDA *and* ROSEILLI, *discovered.*

Roseilli. Wonder not, madam, here behold the man
Whom your disdain hath metamorphosèd.
Thus long have I been clouded in this shape,
Led on by love, and in that love, despair.
If not the sight of our distracted court
Nor pity of my bondage can reclaim
The greatness of your scorn, yet let me know
My latest doom from you.
Fiormonda. Strange miracle!
Roseilli, I must honour thee. Thy truth,
Like a transparent mirror, represents

124. coward, and] *GD;* Cow, and *Q;* Coward; the *S.*

5.3.0. SD *discovered*] *Q; discovering himself W.* 2. metamorphosèd] *GD;* metamorphosed *Q.*

---

123. *stand . . . brunts*] i.e. take my chances and face up to all onslaughts. *Hazard* = 'chance' (often referring to the dice game called 'Hazard') or 'danger' (*OED hazard* 2, 3; *brunt* sb.[1] 2).

124. *coward, and*] Dyce's emendation of Q's 'Cow, and'. Substitution of 'n' for 'r' would be an easy mistake in reading (or writing) secretary hand. The true 'and', or '&', may then have been overlooked or disregarded.

5.3.0.1. discovered] i.e. his true identity revealed. He may still wear part of the fool's costume, since D'Avolos instantly recognises him as 'the supposed fool' at 17–18. Previous editors have Roseilli 'discovering himself' as he enters—a plausible but arbitrary alteration of Q's SD.

3. *shape*] (a) disguise; (b) (fool's) costume (*OED* 7, 8).

6. *reclaim*] amend (*OED* 2d).

8. *latest doom*] final (adverse) fate, sentence or judgement (*OED doom* 2, 4).

9. *truth*] (a) constancy; (b) worth, righteousness.

10. *transparent*] (a) crystal clear; (b) manifest, clearly recognised (*OED* 1, 2b).

mirror] can = 'an exemplar, paragon' (e.g. *FM*, 1031).

10–11. *represents . . . errors*] brings my errors before my rational judgement.

My reason with my errors. Noble lord,
That better dost deserve a better fate,
Forgive me. If my heart can entertain
Another thought of love, it shall be thine.

Roseilli. Blessèd forever, blessèd be the words.
In death you have revived me.

Enter D'AVOLOS.

D'Avolos. [*Aside*] Whom have we here? Roseilli the supposed fool? 'Tis he. Nay then help me a brazen face.—My honourable lord.

Roseilli. Bear off, bloodthirsty man, come not near me.

D'Avolos. Madam, I trust the service—

Fiormonda. Fellow, learn to new-live. The way to thrift
For thee in grace is a repentant shrift.

Roseilli. Ill has thy life been, worse will be thy end:
Men fleshed in blood know seldom to amend.

Enter Servant.

Servant. [*To Fiormonda*] His highness commends his love to you, and expects your presence. He is ready to pass to the church, only staying for my lord Abbot to associate him. Withal, his pleasure is that you, D'Avolos, forbear to rank in this solemnity in the place of Secre-

15. Blessèd . . . blessèd] *Q* (Blessed foreuer, blessed*);* blessèd, forever blessèd *W.* 17. *Aside*] *GD; not in Q.* 17–19.] *W; verse Q.* 20. not near me] *Q;* not thou near me *GD.* 22. live. The] liue the *Q;* like: the *G;* liue; the *S.* 26. SD *To Fiormonda*] *this ed.*

---

16. *revived*] literally 'brought back to life' (Lat. *vivere*, live).
20. *Bear off*] go away, keep off.
22. *thrift*] thriving, prosperity (*OED* sb.[1] 1).
23. *grace*] i.e. the grace of God.
shrift] shriving, confession of guilt. This anticipates her own sentence; see 156–60 (Hoskins). The episode is reminiscent of Ferdinand's rejection of Bosola (*Malfi* 4.2).
25. *fleshed in blood*] inured to bloodshed (*OED* ppl.a. 2a).
28. *staying*] waiting.
29. *associate*] join, accompany (*OED* 5).
Withal] in addition.
30. *rank*] take a place, or take part (*OED* v.[1] 6b; cf. 3.3.89.6n).
solemnity] ceremonial occasion or procession (*OED* 2).
place] official capacity.

tary, else to be there as a private man. [*To Fiormonda*] Pleaseth you to go?

Exeunt all but D'AVOLOS.

D'Avolos. As a private man! What remedy? This way they must come, and here I will stand to fall amongst 'em in the rear.

A sad sound of soft music. The tomb is discovered. Enter four with torches, after them two Friars; after, the DUKE *in mourning manner; after him the* ABBOT, FIORMONDA, COLONA, JULIA, ROSEILLI, PETRUCCIO, NIBRASSA *and a Guard,* D'AVOLOS *following behind. Coming near the tomb they all kneel, making show of ceremony. The* DUKE *goes to the tomb, lays his hand on it. Music cease.*

Duke. Peace and sweet rest sleep here. Let not the touch
Of this my impious hand profane the shrine
Of fairest purity which hovers yet
About those blessèd bones inhearsed within.
If in the bosom of this sacred tomb,

31. SD *To Fiormonda*] *this ed.* 32. go?] *W;* goe.—*Q.* SD] *W; Exeunt. manet D'auolos. Q.* 35. SD.] *Q; Exit. Scene IV.—The Church, with the Tomb in the back of the Scene.—Mournful Music W; A solemn strain of soft Music. The Scene opens, and discovers the Church, with a Tomb in the back ground G.* 35.1. *A sad . . . discovered*] *on separate lines before main SD Q.* 35.8. *Music cease*] *separate line in Q; before 'The* DUKE *goes . . .' W.* 39. those] *Q;* these *W.*

31. *else*] 'other than', not 'or' (see 33).

35.1–8] See pp. 69–70 for comment on staging.

35.3. mourning manner] Male mourners usually wore 'mourning cloaks', and often black hats; aristocrats donned suits of 'solemn black' (Gittings, 120). Since the use of mourning garb distinguished those 'who were considered to be the most important participants in the [funeral] ritual' (Gittings, 120), Caraffa's sombre clothing would emphasise the irony of his presence here. *Manner* may also = mode of behaviour.

35.5. a Guard] a body of two or more guards; see 83–5.

36–8. *Let . . . purity*] 'If I profane with my unworthiest hand / This holy shrine' (*R&J* 1.5.92–3). Sforza asks the spirit of Marcelia to 'pardon me, / That I presume dyde o're with bloody guilt . . . To touch this snow-white hand' (*Milan* 5.2.60–3).

37. *shrine*] The meaning may shift: from 'the tomb' to 'Bianca's spirit'. Or perhaps 'fairest purity' is itself an abstract reference to Bianca (cf. 'the life of innocence and beauty', 48).

Bianca, thy disturbèd ghost doth range,
Behold, I offer up the sacrifice
Of bleeding tears, shed from a faithful spring,
Roaring oblations of a mourning heart.
To thee, offended spirit, I confess
I am Caraffa, he, that wretched man,
That butcher who in my ragèd spleen
Slaughtered the life of innocence and beauty.
Now come I to pay tribute to those wounds
Which I digged up, and reconcile the wrongs
My fury wrought and my contrition mourns.
So chaste, so dear a wife was never man
But I enjoyed; yet in the bloom and pride
Of all her years, untimely took her life.
Enough; set ope the tomb, that I may take
My last farewell, and bury griefs with her.

One goes to open the tomb, out of which ariseth
FERNANDO *in his winding-sheet, only his face*

43. spring,] *GD;* spring; *Q.* 44. Roaring] *Q;* Pouring *G.* heart.] *Q;* heart *W.* 45. spirit,] *Q;* spirit. *W;* spirit! *G.* 48. life . . . beauty] *italic in Q.* 51. wrought] *GD;* wrought; *Q.*

41. *range*] wander (because not at peace; *OED* v.[1] 7).

43. *bleeding tears*] tears of anguish (cf. 5.1.142); but *bleeding* is also prompted by *sacrifice*, 42 (*OED bleeding* 2a). Cf. *Burning Pestle* 4.270, and *Candy* 5.1, p. 291: 'My tears, the Sacrifice of griefs unfeigned'.

44. *Roaring oblations*] weeping offerings. I take *Roaring* to be the continuous form of the verb rather than the participle. Gifford's popular emendation to 'Pouring' overlooks Ford's use of 'roar' to mean 'shout' or 'weep' at 4.1.96 and 142. *Oblations* is often applied to religious offerings. The Prayer of Consecration in the Holy Communion Service refers to Christ's 'sufficient sacrifice, oblation, and satisfaction, for the sins of the whole world' (*BCP*). Cf. Leviticus 1:13 (Geneva Bible).

47. *spleen*] (fit of) anger or ill humour.

48. *the life . . . beauty*] italic in Q. *The life* = 'living model' or 'essence, "soul"' (*OED* 5, 7).

53. *bloom and pride*] prime, heyday (*OED* sb.[1] 9).

56. *bury griefs*] perhaps with a hidden secondary sense: 'end my life (which is nothing but grief) in her tomb'.

56.2. winding-sheet] sheet in which corpse was wrapped (see Gittings, 111–14). The entrance draws on the mainly comic tradition of the seeming resurrection (see *The Knight of Malta* 4.2, p. 179; *Mad Lover* 5.4; *Burning Pestle* 4.275.1; *Law Tricks* 5.1; *Chaste Maid* 5.4.29.1; *A&M* 5.2.246; *J. Malta* 5.1; *1H4* 5.4.109.1; *R&J* 5.3.146.1). See pp. 71–3 for further comment.

discovered. As CARAFFA *is going in he puts him back.*

Fernando. Forbear! What art thou that dost rudely press
Into the confines of forsaken graves?
Has death no privilege? Com'st thou, Caraffa,
To practise yet a rape upon the dead?
Inhuman tyrant!
Whats'ever thou intendest, know this place
Is pointed out for my inheritance;
Here lies the monument of all my hopes.
Had eager lust intrunked my conquered soul,
I had not buried living joys in death.
Go, revel in thy palace, and be proud
To boast thy famous murders; let thy smooth,
Low-fawning parasites renown thy act:

59. Has] *Q;* Hath *W.* 62. intendest] *W;* intend'st *Q.*

56.3. discovered] revealed.

he puts him back] i.e. Fernando repulses Caraffa (not neces-sarily with physical force).

57–70. *Forbear . . . here*] Cf. Govianus's words to the Tyrant in *SMT* 5.2.126–31: 'O thou sacrilegious villain! / Thou thief of rest, robber of monuments! / Cannot the body after funeral / Sleep in the grave, for thee? Must it be raised / Only to please the wickedness of thine eye? / Does all things end with death, and not thy lust?' (5.2.126–31). Also Paris's warning as Romeo opens the Capulets' tomb: 'Stop thy unhallowed toil, vile Montague! / Can vengeance be pursued further than death?' (5.3.54–5).

59. *privilege*] special distinction; immunity.

63. *pointed out*] (a) 'ordained, fixed' (where *pointed* = an aphetic form of 'appointed', *OED point* v.² 2, *pointed* ppl.a.²); see *PW* 4.3.30–1n on possible confusion with 'point out' in the sense of 'indicate'; (b) 'written down' (*OED* v.¹ 2; see 1669 quotation). Perhaps he imagines that his occupation of Bianca's tomb is recorded in the book of destiny.

64. *monument*] In 1.2.274, Bianca is a 'goodly shrine' in which his heart is 'entombed'.

65–6. *Had . . . death*] *Elegy by WS* refers to the 'former joys' which 'now with thee are leapt into thy tomb' (548–9). See p. 73 for comment on Fernando's lines.

65. *intrunked*] enclosed as in a trunk (*OED*).

68. *famous*] notorious (*OED* 3).

69. *Low-fawning*] (a) bowing low; (b) servile, flattering. Cf. *Candy* 3.1.

Thou com'st not here.

Duke. Fernando, man of darkness,
Never till now, before these dreadful sights,
Did I abhor thy friendship. Thou hast robbed
My resolution of a glorious name.
Come out, or by the thunder of my rage,
Thou diest a death more fearful than the scourge
Of death can whip thee with.

Fernando. Of death? Poor Duke,
Why that's the aim I shoot at. 'Tis not threats,
Maugre thy power, or the spite of hell,
Shall rent that honour. Let life-hugging slaves,
Whose hands imbrued in butcheries like thine,
Shake terror to their souls, be loath to die.
See, I am clothed in robes that fit the grave;
I pity thy defiance.

Duke. Guard, lay hands
And drag him out.

Fernando. Yes, let 'em, here's my shield,

78. or] *W;* of *Q.* 79. rent] *Q;* rend *G.*

---

70. *darkness*] (a) 'want of spiritual light, evil', as in 'the Prince of Darkness'; (b) 'death, deathliness' (*OED* 4a, b), as suggested by his garb; (c) the literal darkness of the tomb. The mourning Petrarch frequents 'shadowy dark places, seeking in my thought the high delight that Death has taken' (*Rime* 281, ll. 6–8).

71. *before*] 'in the presence of' or 'prior to'.

dreadful] inspiring dread or fear (*OED* 2).

73. *resolution*] 'intention; fixed determination' (as in *BH* 1.1.24, *PW* 2.3.43–4). Cf. *'Tis Pity* 5.6.15.

glorious name] renown, fame.

77. *aim*] target (*OED* sb. 6).

78. *Maugre*] in spite of.

79. *rent*] rend, tear apart.

slaves] abject wretches dominated by a specified influence; here, the desire for life (cf. 1.1.184n).

80. *imbrued*] probably '(are) bloodstained'. Ford refers thus to the Earl and Countess of Somerset, convicted of the murder of Sir Thomas Overbury: 'Behold how Justice swaies the sword of Law, / To weed out those, whose hands imbrew'd in blood, / Cropt of thy youth' ('A Memoriall', 24–6).

81. *Shake . . . souls*] probably 'shake their souls with terror' (if the subject of *Shake* is *hands*).

Here's health to victory—
As they go to fetch him out
he drinks off a phial of poison.
Now do thy worst.
Farewell Duke, once I have outstripped thy plots.
Not all the cunning antidotes of art
Can warrant me twelve minutes of my life.
It works, it works already, bravely, bravely!
Now, now I feel it tear each several joint.
O royal poison, trusty friend! Split, split
Both heart and gall asunder. Excellent bane!
Roseilli, love my memory. Well searched out,
Swift, nimble venom, torture every vein.
I come, Bianca—cruel torment, feast,
Feast on, do. Duke, farewell. Thus I—hot flames!—
Conclude my love—and seal it in my bosom—oh! *Dies.*

Abbot. Most desperate end!

85.1. *him*] *him him Q.* 87. antidotes of art] *italic in Q.* 95. I come,] *W;* I, come *Q.* 96–7. hot . . . Conclude] *W;* hot flames / Conclude *Q.*

86. *once*] once and for all (*OED* 3; cf. *Rom. Actor* 2.1.372).

outstripped] Cf. *Lerma* 4.2.2.

87. *cunning*] ingenious.

art] (medical) skill or knowledge.

90. *several*] individual (*OED* 3a).

91. *royal . . . friend*] Cf. Romeo in *R&J* 5.3.119–20. Both *royal* and *friend* remind us of Caraffa.

92. *gall*] See 3.4.43n.

bane] poison (*OED* sb.[1] 2b).

95. *I come, Bianca*] Dying stage lovers often address their dead beloved thus (e.g. *Cardinal* 5.3.291, *A&C* 5.2.282).

96–7. *hot . . . love*] In Q's reading (see Coll.) the poison's *hot flames* conclude his love (with a possible allusion to the practice of authenticating and sealing documents with heated wax). But the present pointing is supported by phrasing in Hippolita's death-speech (she also dies by poison): 'Heat above hell-fire!— / Yet ere I pass away—cruel, cruel flames!— / Take here my curse amongst you' (*'Tis Pity* 4.1.92–4). A sensation of 'burning inside' is the usual effect of Elizabethan stage-poisons (*WBW* 5.2.139n). The Phoenix (symbol of chastity and immortality) dies in flames.

98. *desperate*] (a) reckless, violent; (b) despairing, without hope of salvation. The notion that 'love-suicide' was an ennobling act derived from the courtly love tradition, and was at odds with Christian morality (MacDonald and Murphy, 98–100). In the Church's view, 'Self-murder resulted from giving way to the diabolical temptation of despair' (Houlbrooke, 210).

Duke. None stir.
Who steps a foot steps to his utter ruin.
And art thou gone, Fernando, art thou gone?
Thou wert a friend unmatched, rest in thy fame.
Sister, when I have finished my last days,
Lodge me, my wife, and this unequalled friend
All in one monument. Now to my vows:
Never henceforth let any passionate tongue
Mention Bianca's and Caraffa's name,
But let each letter in that tragic sound
Beget a sigh, and every sigh a tear.
Children unborn, and widows whose lean cheeks
Are furrowed up by age, shall weep whole nights,
Repeating but the story of our fates;
Whiles in the period, closing up their tale,
They must conclude how for Bianca's love,
Caraffa, in revenge of wrongs to her,
Thus on her altar sacrificed his life.— *Stabs himself.*
Abbot. O hold the Duke's hand!
Fiormonda. Save my brother, save him!
Duke. Do, do; I was too willing to strike home
To be prevented. Fools! why, could you dream

101. gone, Fernando,] *this ed.;* gone, Fernando? *G;* gone? Fernando, *Q.* 106. henceforth let] *Q;* let henceforth *W.* 113. Whiles] *Q;* Whilst *W.* 119. why, could] *W;* why could *Q.*

105. *vows*] perhaps simply the 'earnest wishes, desires or prayers' (*OED vow* 4) he utters here, but more likely referring to the 'resolution' he mentions at 73, and the vows or prayers he appears to offer in 5.2.93.1–2. (See Huebert, *Baroque*, 93–4.)

106–16. *Never . . . life*] Recalling Othello's final speech: 'in your letters, / When you shall these unlucky deeds relate, / Speak of me as I am' (5.2.349–65).

106. *passionate*] 'sad, sorrowful' or 'moved with pity' (*OED* 5).

113. *period*] 'conclusion', perhaps playing on another sense: 'death' (*OED* 5, 5d; cf. *Oth.* 5.2.366).

closing up] concluding.

116. *Thus . . . altar*] See Intro., p. 76, for comment on staging. The Andronici 'sacrifice' the flesh of Alarbus 'before' their family tomb (*Tit.* 1.1.96–147).

116.1. Stabs himself] Perceived as a more honourable method of suicide than poisoning (MacDonald and Murphy, 185–6, 226–7).

I would outlive my outrage? Sprightful flood,
Run out in rivers! O that these thick streams
Could gather head and make a standing pool,
That jealous husbands here might bathe in blood.
So; I grow sweetly empty. All the pipes
Of life unvessel life. Now heavens wipe out
The writing of my sin. Bianca, thus
I creep to thee—to thee—to thee, Bi—an—ca. *Dies.*

Roseilli. He's dead already, Madam.

D'Avolos. [*Aside*] Above hope, here's labour saved. I could bless the Destinies.

Abbot. Would I had never seen it.

Fiormonda. Since 'tis thus,

120. outrage? Sprightful] *W;* outrage Sprightful *Q.* flood,] *G;* flood *W.* 121. rivers!] *W*; Riuers? *Q.* 127. Bi—an—ca] *Q;* Bianca *W.* 129. *Aside*] *G; not in Q.*

---

120. *outrage*] violent injury (to Bianca); gross offence (*OED* 3).

Sprightful] (a) lively; (b) imbued with spirit or life (*OED* 3, quoting Helkiah Crooke, *Microcosmographia: A Description of the Body of Man*, 1615, p. 238: 'sprightfull blood'). Levinus Lennius observes that, when a vein is opened, at first the blood 'doth shewe and represent to the eye, an ayry & fomy spirite' (Thomas Newton's 1565 translation of *The Touchstone of Complexions*, quoted by Hoeniger, 105). Cf. 124–5, *BH* 5.2.122, *PW* 1.1.128.

121–3. *O . . . blood*] Perhaps referring to the belief that a bath in warm blood was 'a very powerful tonic in great debility from long-continued diseases' (*OED blood* sb. 21; cf. *A&C* 4.2.5–7, *Discoveries*, 1058–61). Blood also had redemptive significance in Hebrew sin-offerings (see Leviticus 9:9). The blood of the sacrificed Christ (the *idée fixe* of *CBS*) was a powerful symbol of humanity's salvation: 'For this is my blood of the new testament, which is shed for many for the remission of sins' (Matthew 26:28).

122. *gather head*] collect.

124. *sweetly empty*] Blood-letting, widely employed at this time, was believed to purge the excess of a corrupt bodily humour, and was a principal treatment for love-melancholy (Hoeniger, 238–42; *Anatomy* III.2.2.1, p. 58, 3.2.5.2, p. 194). More generally, Caraffa's *pipes / Of life* drain him of a life which has become synonymous with grief. Sforza finds a similar release in death (*Milan* 5.2.257–8).

124–5. *pipes Of life*] veins; cf. *Cor.* 5.1.54.

126. *The . . . sin*] Cf. 5.1.152n.

126–7. *thus . . . thee*] Perhaps he crawls into or towards her tomb; see Intro., p. 76.

129. *here's . . . saved*] Echoing Ambitioso at the death of the Duke, *Rev. Trag.* 5.3.51–2.

130. *Destinies*] the Fates, the three goddesses of classical mythology who determined the course of human life (*OED destiny* 5).

My lord Roseilli, in the true requital
Of your continued love, I here possess
You of the dukedom, and with it, of me,
In presence of this holy abbot.

Abbot. Lady, then
From my hand take your husband.

He joins their hands.

Long enjoy
Each to each other's comfort and content.

Omnes. Long live Roseilli!

Roseilli. First, thank to heaven, next, lady, to your love,
Lastly, my lords, to all; and that the entrance
Into this principality may give
Fair hopes of being worthy of our place,
Our first work shall be justice. D'Avolos,
Stand forth.

D'Avolos. My gracious lord?

Roseilli. No, graceless villain,
I am no lord of thine. Guard, take him hence,
Convey him to the prison's top. In chains
Hang him alive. Whosoever lends a bit
Of bread to feed him dies. Speak not against it,
I will be deaf to mercy. Bear him hence.

D'Avolos. Mercy, new duke? Here's my comfort: I make but one in the number of the tragedy of princes.

Exit [Guard with D'AVOLOS*].*

Roseilli. Madam, a second charge is to perform
Your brother's testament. We'll rear a tomb

136. SD.] *Q aligns with 136–7; after* 'enjoy' *W.* 139. thank] *Q;* thanks *W.* 147. Whosoever] *Q* (whosoeuer), *W;* whosoe'er *GD;* whoever *G.* 151. SD.] *S; exit Q; He is led off W.*

135. *Lady*] perhaps a hypermetrical vocative.

139. *thank*] the obsolete singular form.

141. *principality*] position of prince; sovereignty (*OED* 2).

142. *our*] He slips easily into use of the royal plural.

150–1.] D'Avolos's prototype, Iago, also remains defiant to the last (5.2.309–10), as does Lodovico in *W. Devil* 5.6.293–7.

152. *charge*] task, responsibility (*OED* 12).

153. *testament*] declaration of final wishes (referring to Caraffa's request at 103–5).

rear] build. Montague and Capulet vow to raise statues of the lovers in *R&J* 5.3.298–303.

To those unhappy lovers which shall tell
Their fatal loves to all posterity.
Thus, then, for you: henceforth I here dismiss
The mutual comforts of our marriage bed.
Learn to new-live; my vows unmoved shall stand;
And since your life hath been so much uneven,
Bethink in time to make your peace with heaven.

Fiormonda. O me, is this your love?

Roseilli. 'Tis your desert,
Which no persuasion shall remove.

Abbot. 'Tis fit:
Purge frailty with repentance.

Fiormonda. I embrace it.
Happy too late, since lust hath made me foul,
Henceforth I'll dress my bride-bed in my soul.

Roseilli. Please you to walk, lord Abbot?

Abbot. Yes, set on.
No age hath heard, nor chronicle can say,
That ever here befell a sadder day. *Exeunt.*

FINIS

167. nor] *Q;* no *W.*

158. *Learn to new-live*] An exact, ironic echo of Fiormonda's own advice to D'Avolos at 22.

159. *uneven*] intemperate.

160. *Bethink*] resolve.

163. *frailty*] moral weakness. Sounds like a euphemism, but used thus in *GM*, 1270–1.

165. *dress . . . soul*] prepare or adorn my spiritual marriage bed. Perhaps referring to the custom of strewing the nuptial bed with flowers. *Bride* = 'wedding' (cf. *'Tis Pity* 4.1.111).

167. *chronicle*] historical record such as Holinshed's *Chronicles*. A conventional final couplet; cf. *Span. Trag.* 4.4.202, *R&J* 5.3.308–9.

Longer Notes

Epistle Dedicatory

17–21. *The contempt . . . herein*] Neill argues that the discerning audiences of the Caroline theatre, for whom appreciation of plays was an accomplishment as essential as taste in music or fashion in clothes, were liable to be 'hypercritical': 'The difficulty of pleasing the new generation, to which the dramatists so often refer, may have been a flattering exaggeration; but the querulous tone of some prefaces [to plays] suggests that it was no mere fiction' ('Wits', 346–7). Ford's cousin, to whom this preface is dedicated, complained of the same problem in his commendatory verses to *PW* (10; Neill, 'Wits', 349). Ford could also be referring here to William Prynne, whose attack on stage plays, *Histriomastix*, was published late in 1632, the year before *LS* (*JCS* III, 451). Shirley almost certainly refers to Prynne in his commendatory verses to *LS*. (See next LN, and Intro., p. 6, for discussion of these allusions in connection with the play's date.)

'To my friend Mr John Ford'

James Shirley (1598–1666) and Ford were fellow dramatists at the Phoenix between 1624/5 and 1636 (*JCS* V, 1068). Ford contributed commendatory verses to Shirley's *The Wedding* (1629), while Shirley's *Love's Cruelty* (licensed 1631) may have been influenced by *LS* (see 5.1.174n). Shirley probably addresses William Prynne in the second stanza of this poem. Prynne's publications were indeed 'voluminous' (7); *Histriomastix*, his attack on stage plays, is a massive work. Moreover, Shirley addresses a scathing epistle to Prynne in the *The Bird in a Cage*, printed in the same year as *LS*. While the present verses respond to Prynne's criticism of the drama, the royalist Shirley must also have been annoyed by Prynne's apparent attack on the Queen (see *Lady of Pleasure*, 3). His contempt here 'suggests that he wrote at a time when he was aware of the probability of severe punishment for Prynne' (*JCS* III, 452). This could mean that these verses were composed in about January 1632/3, when Prynne first appeared before the Star Chamber, or in February, when he was committed to the Tower (*JCS* III, 451). See p. 6 for further comment.

Weber's claim (after Steevens and Malone) that Shirley addresses Ben Jonson was refuted by Gilchrist, who points out (29) that Prynne had already displayed his 'malice to the stage' in works such as *The Perpetuitie of a Regenerate Mans Estate* (1626), and *A Briefe Survay and Censure of Mr Cozens his Couzening Devotions* (1628).

1.1.233. *Their . . . quicksands*] A further comment on the deceitfulness of women (cf. *3H6* 5.4.26). But, as Gifford notes, there also seems to be a reference to the ancient story of the discovery of glass. In *Naturalis Historiae*, Bk XXXVI, 26, 65, Pliny relates that some merchants once moored their ship on a sandy stretch of the Phoenician coast at the mouth of the river Belus. The merchants were unable to find any rocks to support their cooking pots, so they used lumps of natron from their own cargo. Natron, or hydrated sodium carbonate, is used in glass-making. Heated by the cauldrons, it fused with the sea-sand to produce a translucent stream of glass. Ford may have read the story in Philemon Holland's translation of Pliny, *The Historie of the World* (1601, p. 597).

1.2.54. *half-turns instead of bevers*] Obviously a bawdy quibble, but the precise meaning is uncertain. A 'bever' is 'a potation, a drinking; a time for drinking' or 'a small repast between meals; a "snack," nuncheon or lunch; especially one in the afternoon between mid-day dinner and supper' (*OED* sb. 2, 3). The word has the latter sense in *Queen* 1769–70; cf. *Faustus* A 2.3.142. *Half-turns* is probably related to 'turn', a spell of work, a feat or bout, which was often susceptible to lewd interpretation (e.g., *A&C* 2.5.59: 'the best turn i'th' bed'). Ferentes is perhaps claiming, then, that Julia brings him from his meals or snacks with her demands for brief amorous sessions.

1.2.59. *how shay by that*] Q's obscure 'shey' is not recorded by *OED*, nor, in any applicable sense, by *EDD*, and all previous editors of the play have emended it to 'say' or 'say ye' (see Coll.). But 'shey' also occurs in the quartos of two other Ford plays (*Fancies* 843, 'What's that you mumble, Gelding, shey'; and *'Tis Pity* 4.3.15, 'Shey, must I?'—1633 Q, H1r, emended to 'Why must I?' in the Revels edition). Instances of 'shay' and 'sha' are also found in Chapman's *The Gentleman Usher* (1606), H2r; *The Second Maydens Tragedy* (1610–11), fol. 44b; and *The Welsh Embassador* (c. 1623) fol. 15a, the last example occurring in a scene which may have been written by Ford (see Bertram Lloyd, 'Two Notes on Elizabethan Orthography', *RES* II, 1926, 204–6, and 'The Authorship of the Welsh Embassador', *RES* XXI, 1945, 192–201). In each case the sense of the word is almost certainly 'say' or 'say ye'. As I argue in '"Shey" in Jacobean and Caroline Drama', *N&Q* 238 (June 1993), 228–9, 'the presence of these forms in six independent play-texts, and the clear semantic relation between the various examples, strongly suggests that "shey", "shay", and "sha" are representations of an idiom overlooked by *OED* and *EDD*. Possibly the initial ʃ arose through anticipation of "ye"—a change in pronunciation which has precedence in the formation of some dialect words'. 'Shey' would be difficult to explain as a graphic error for 'say' or 'say ye'. The long s-h ligature and the single long s are usually quite distinguishable, even in a cursive secretary hand.

1.2.72. *in conjunction*] When the moon seems close to, or in the same zodiac as, the sun—in other words, when there is a new moon. 'If the Moon be in conjunction or opposition at the birth-time . . . many diseases are signified, especially the head and brain is like to be misaffected with pernicious humours, to be melancholy, lunatic, or mad' (*Anatomy* I.2.1.4, p. 207). Perhaps Ferentes' lust is one such 'pernicious humour'. 'The fleeting moon' (*A&C* 5.2.236), as a type of changeableness and inconstancy, is also a suitable emblem for him. *Conjunction* can = copulation (*OED* 2b, 3; cf. *Queen*, 1036; *2H4* 2.4.265–6; *Widow's Tears* 5.1.45–7).

2.1.0.1–2.] Demosthenes (often cited as a model for later sixteenth-century gentlemen; Bryson, 174) was said to have possessed 'a great Glasse in his house, in the sight whereof he used to stand, till he had ended suche

Orations as he minded to utter before the people' (*The Three Orations of Demosthenes, Chiefe Orator among the Grecians, in Fauour of the Olynthians*, translated by Thomas Wylson, 1570, 112). The title-page of John Bulwer's *Chironomia: The Art of Manual Rhetorique* (1644) shows Demosthenes making gestures with his hands before a mirror. Mauruccio's preoccupation with his appearance, speech and gesture has many echoes in the compliment books and other literature instructing gallants in wooing and courtly conduct (Bryson, Ch. 5, 6; see notes below).

2.1.36. *rapt with fury*] Chapman, after Ficino, distinguishes between two kinds of rapture: '*Insania*, a disease of the mind, and a meere madnesse', and '*Diuinus furor*', 'a perfection directly infused from God'. He cites Homer as the 'first and last *Instance*' of divine '*Furie*' (*Odysseys*, Dedication to the Earl of Somerset, prose ll. 76–89; see *The Poems of George Chapman*, ed. Phyllis Brooks Bartlett (New York: Russell, 1962), 486; also *Ion*, 533–6). For the audience, *fury* is perhaps a further signal (cf. 22n) that Mauruccio is given to 'the scenical strutting and furious vociferation' which Jonson saw as characteristic of 'the Tamerlanes, and Tamer-Chams of the late age' (*Discoveries*, 789–91). In *The Discovery of the Knights of the Post* (1597), C2v, a character is described as acting with 'such furious Iesture as if he had beene playing Tamberlane on a stage' (quoted by Gurr, 'Strutted', 98). Furor Poeticus, a character in *The Return to Parnassus*, Part II, personifies poetic fury as well as being 'a vehicle for the parody of Marston's style' (J. B. Leishman, ed., *The Three Parnassus Plays*, London, 1949, 82). For *rapt*, cf. 1.1.128.

2.1.62. *crystal*] At 76 Mauruccio compares this heart-shaped mirror to a 'prospective' or 'prospective glass', a sort of magic telescope (see note). As if by magic, then, Fiormonda will be able to see what is in his heart: her own image (*OED crystal* 5, 6; *prospective* B1). In his commentary on Plato's *Symposium* (*Commentarium in Convivium*), Ficino observes that 'a lover imprints a likeness of the loved one upon his soul, and so the soul of the lover becomes a mirror in which is reflected the image of the loved one' (2.8, 146; similarity noted by Neill, 'Riddle', 179, n. 47). Lovel appears to echo Ficino's conceit in *The New Inn*, 3.2.98–101 (see notes in Revels edition). In Petrarch the image of the beloved's face penetrates 'through my eyes to my deepest heart' (*Rime* 94; cf. Donne, 'Witchcraft by a Picture', 13–14; *Son.* 24); and the heart is depicted as a mirror in the final emblem of Henry Hawkins's *The Devout Hart* (1634). In thus giving absurd form to serious ideas about the nature of love, Mauruccio's 'souvenir' (see *Private Life*, 232–3) can be viewed as a comic expression of the play's dialectic on love and infatuation.

2.1.94 *Angelica . . . for me*] Taken almost verbatim from Greene's *The Historie of Orlando Furioso* (c. 1591), an adaptation of Ariosto's poem. In the first scene of the play, Marsillus, Emperor of Africa, asks five 'victorious Princes' to present their suits for the hand of his daughter, 'the fair Angelica'. Soldane, Rodamant, Mandrecard and Brandemart all expatiate on their heroic feats and rich possessions, each concluding with the words, 'I loue, my Lord, let that suffice for me'. When it is Orlando's turn, he admits that he is 'no king, yet am I princely borne' (100), refrains from boasting of his 'acts of Chiualrie' (126), and caps the others' speeches with the final words, 'I loue, my Lord; / Angelica her selfe shall speake for me' (134–5). Angelica then chooses Orlando for her husband (147–68). Mauruccio thus compares himself with a great romantic hero and Fiormonda with a princess of 'matchles beautie'. Q lacks a syllable and an auxiliary verb, and most editors emend to 'doth plead' (see Coll.). But it seems better to adopt the reading of what is surely the source of Mauruccio's remark. Mauruccio may echo Greene's play again at 2.2.233. He mentions Ariosto at 35, above.

2.2.31.2 Enter . . . two pictures] Butler (215) compares this episode to Bosola's exposure of the Duchess's pregnancy in *Malfi* 2.1.129ff. (D'Avolos is later cast off by Fiormonda in much the same way as Bosola is rejected by Ferdinand; see *LS* 5.3.22–3, *Malfi* 4.2.288ff.) Fernando's fascination with Bianca's portrait is also reminiscent of the episode in the *New Arcadia*, I, in which Palladius falls in love with a portrait of Philoclea; see 98n below. (Ford drew on the *New Arcadia* for the story of Ferentes and his lovers; see Intro., p. 32.) In general, this scene is related to the many Renaissance stories describing how clever physicians discover the secrets of their lovesick patients. The most popular of these was the tale of Antiochus, derived from Galen, Plutarch (*Demetrius* XXXVIII), and other classical sources, which tells how the physician Erasistratus discovered a lover's secret by observing his reaction upon the appearance of his beloved. The story also occurs as the twenty-seventh novel in William Painter's *The Palace of Pleasure* (1566). (See Babb, 137–8, n. 77; 151–2.)

2.2.32–8. *Now . . . extremest*] Fernando's behaviour here reflects conventional literary and theatrical notions of the melancholy or 'pining' lover. He displays a number of the symptoms of love melancholy. Babb enumerates the symptoms expounded in works such as Burton's *Anatomy of Melancholy*, Ferrand's *Erotomania* and Coeffeteau's *A Table of Humane Passions*: lovers are often found weeping and sighing, standing 'as if they were either in some deepe contemplation, or else were earnestly fixt in beholding something or other that much delighted them'; their 'words are short & scarce intelligible'; they are heedless of 'all practical concerns'; they prefer solitude; they 'have their imagination depraved, and their judgement corrupted' (Babb, 135—6). 'The prevalence throughout the period, indoors and out, of dumbshows and other forms of wordless action that frequently convey complex narrative and character detail, confirms that actors needed well-developed gestural skills' (White, 69). Here, the continuous forms of D'Avolos's verbs—'reading', 'striking', 'Tearing'—indicate that his commentary is simultaneous with the described action, which perhaps tends to underscore the formality of Fernando's gestures (see White's discussion of *H8* 3.2.114–20, pp. 72–3).

2.2.109. *feigned*] *OED*, citing this passage, glosses Q's 'fain'd' as 'enshrined', from 'fane', a temple (*faned* ppl.a.; *fane* sb.^{2}). The same reading is offered by Weber, Sutfin and Hoskins, while all other editors follow Gifford in emending to 'famed' (see Coll.). Possibly Ford was thinking of the passage in the *Anatomy* in which Burton relates that 'Charicles, by chance espying that curious picture of smiling Venus naked in her temple, stood a great while gazing, as one amazed' (III.2.2.2). However, the Q reading is not 'fan'd', as *OED* suggests, but 'fain'd', a significant difference. 'Fain'd', meaning 'imagined', is used in the quarto of *Fancies*, 772–3, 'the ancients, / Who chatted of the golden age, fain'd trifles'; and again in the quarto of *LM*, B3r (1.1.98–9): 'the Tales / Which Poets of an elder time haue fain'd'. Since none of *OED*'s quotations for the substantive 'fane' uses the 'ai' spelling, and, moreover, since the present passage provides *OED*'s only example of 'fan'd', it must be doubted whether the latter word ever existed. In any case, it seems unlikely that Ford would have written 'fan'd' when the audience would hear only the more familiar *feigned*. Also note Q's spelling of 'vnfainedly' at 2.4.27, and 'fained' (meaning 'pretended') at 4.1.92 (F2r, H3v).

2.2.148–51] Q gives these lines to Ferentes, but most editors regard them as more suited to Mauruccio, and reassign them to him. However: (a) Fernando would be more likely to ask Ferentes to speak in his 'own mother tongue' (152–3) than to ask the irredeemably orotund Mauruccio to amend his speech; (b) as Oliver suggests (81), Ferentes is probably parodying Mauruccio's last extravagant utterance; (c) there may be comedy in the fact that Ferentes is immediately pulled up for his momentary affectation, while Mauruccio's continual offences are never censured. Sutfin points out that Fernando directly addresses Mauruccio at 153–4, which perhaps indicates that he does not recommence conversation with him until this point.

2.3.99–101. *there . . . lines*] Q's italicisation of this passage (probably deriving from Ford's own MS) points up the words which Bianca is to echo at 2.4.93–5 (also italicised in Q), and highlights a favourite, though conventional, conceit: 'Rip up my bosom, there thou shalt behold / A heart in which is writ the truth I speak' (Giovanni to Annabella, *'Tis Pity* 1.2.210–11; cf. *Gypsy* 3.3.48–9; Petrarch, *Rime* 5; Donne, 'The Dampe', 1–4; Proverbs 3:3). See Rosemary Freeman, *English Emblem Books* (London: Chatto & Windus, 1948), 148, on examples from emblem books. Mary Tudor claimed to die with Calais engraved upon her heart (Neill, 'What Strange Riddle', 178, n. 33). The *bloody lines* perhaps recall the very common notion of documents or letters written in blood; cf. *Faustus* 2.1.49–75, 5.1.72–5 (A-Text); *Bussy* 2.2.284–8; *Span. Trag.* 3.2.24ff. Christ spoke of 'the new testament in my blood', Luke 22:20, 1 Corinthians 11:25. See Kiefer for further discussion.

2.4.] In *Monsieur Thomas*, Francisco falls in love with Cellidè, mistress of his friend Valentine. Francisco becomes ill and is at risk of dying of a broken heart, when Valentine vows that he will give 'all I have' to restore him (2.5, p. 341). He persuades Cellidè to offer herself to his friend (2.5, pp. 342–5). Cellidè goes to Francisco's bedside and administers the 'cordial' of her kisses (3.1, p. 347). But the faithful Francisco swears that he would rather die than triumph in his friend's misery (p. 348). Cellidè tempts him further, but to no avail. In the meantime, Valentine has been watching this encounter. He exits (p. 351) before Cellidè reveals to Francisco that she only wishes him to fortify his 'honesty' against a 'thousand foes, / Besides the tyrant Beauty' (p. 351). Yet Francisco's resistance has impressed her deeply, and she reveals in an aside that she now loves him with all her soul (p. 352).

3.1.2. *ballad singers*] Henry Chettle's *Kind-Hartes Dreame* (1592, 15) describes 'a company of idle youths' who 'betake them to a vagrant and vicious life, in euery corner of Cities & market Townes of the Realme singing and selling of ballads and pamphletes full of ribaudrie'. A *ballad* = a popular song relating an amatory tale or story of topical interest, often supposedly told by a protagonist of the story (e.g. no. LVII in *The Shirburn Ballads*). The fate of the woman in 'A lamentable ballad called The Ladye's fall' (*Shirburn* no. XLIX) is not dissimilar to that of Julia. To be 'Traduced by odious ballads' (*AWW* 2.1.172) was regarded as a particularly grave misfortune; cf. 4.1.34–5; *A&C* 5.2.210–12; *1H4* 2.2.44–5; *Queen*, 910–15; Philip Stubbes, *Anatomy of the Abuses in England*, 1583, 171. 'Prescriptive literature, dramatic plots, popular pamphlets and ballads all communicated a vision of morality in which women, not men, bore the load of guilt for illicit sex, and in which women's virtue was premised entirely on sexual chastity' (Gowing, 2).

3.2.31. *fit ye*] Hoskins (61) notes an echo of Hieronimo's ominous assurance that he will be able to provide a 'show' to entertain the Viceroy of Portugal: 'Why then I'll fit you, say no more' (4.1.70). Although the darker secondary meaning of Hieronimo's phrase is appropriate to Fiormonda's overall intentions, it has no bearing on her promise to provide a fool for the masque. There are other echoes of Kyd's play here. Both scenes feature a discussion of the planned entertainment, with recollections of a previous performance (*LS* ll. 15–22; *Span. Trag.* ll. 60–2). Both performances are to be staged before distinguished visitors. Both Fernando and Hieronimo ask male and female members of the court to take part (l. 19, 28–34; ll. 81–3, 95–7). Both men envisage that the performances will seem 'strange' as well as pleasant to the audience (l. 22; 84–5). Later in each play, the revenge taken 'in earnest' under cover of 'fabulous counterfeit' is explained to the bewildered on-stage audience by one of the revengers (3.4.27–38; 4.4.73–152).

3.2.155. *privilege of coxcombs*] A *coxcomb* = (a) 'cap worn by a professional fool, like a cock's comb in shape and colour'; (b) fools themselves (*OED coxcomb* 1, 3). Roseilli thus seems to think of his assumed role as that of a clown rather than a natural fool. Enid Welsford, *The Fool: His Social and Literary History* (London: Faber, 1935), 160–79, cites contemporary accounts of the privileged positions enjoyed by professional fools at court and in noble households. In *Archie Armstrong's Banquet of Jests* (1630), Archie, court jester to James I, speaks of the 'privilege' of his fool's coat (Welsford, 178). There is also a play on 'privilege of clergy' and similar phrases (*OED privilege* 4; cf. *BH* 1.3.48–9).

3.3.88. *yellow hood*] Perhaps the joke is that Caraffa will wear a hood to hide his cuckold's horns. The same jest occurs in a ballad by Ralph Smart: 'take heed lest that you see: / The cokscōbe knockt about your pate, / then hoods no more wyll seeme / Your hornes to hyde, but al men shall / a monster thee esteeme' (1565–6; no. 27 in Herbert L. Collmann, ed., *Ballads & Broadsides chiefly of the Elizabethan Period and Printed in Black-Letter*, 1912, repr. New York: Franklin, 1971). Or perhaps D'Avolos is suggesting that Caraffa has been 'hoodwinked', as in the game of 'hoodman blind' or blindman's bluff. Cf. *Malcontent* 1.3.93–101, where the cuckold is said to be 'hoodwinked with kindness'. Caraffa's imagined hood may be *yellow* because that is the traditional colour of jealousy; see Peele, *Araygnement of Paris* 1.3, ll. 108–9, *Fatal Dowry* 3.1.201–3.

3.4.18–19 *outlandish*] = 'foreign' on the title-page of *A Hundreth Sundrie Flowres Bounde vp in one small Poesie* (1573); in Nashe, *Christs Teares Over Iervsalem*, 142, 18–20; and in *Poetaster* 5.3.537. *GM* describes banishment as 'but a journey of pleasure into some outlanding country' (975–7). Actresses were hardly a familiar sight on the English stage (the word 'actress', as used in reference to a female stage player, is not recorded in English before 1626; see Howe, 21). But in 1629 a troupe of French actresses caused a great stir when they appeared at several London theatres, including Ford's own Phoenix. Perhaps *outlandish* glances at them (see Intro., pp. 7–8, on the play's date).

4.1.112] The almanacs often specified the astrological aspects of the moon that were considered to be most favourable for blood-letting. In P. Moore's *A Fourtie Yeres Almanack* (1567–1606), a chapter of 'Rules concernyng Bloudlettyng' advises surgeons to 'let no bloud, nor open any veine, excepte the Moone be either in Aries, Cancer, the first halfe of Libra, the laste halfe of Scorpio, or in Sagittarius, Aquarius, or Pisces. Remembryng also, that you ought not to dooe it, in the daie of the chaunge, nor in the daie next before, or next after the same'. Cf. *R2* 1.1.157: 'Our doctors say this is no time [Qq. "month"] to bleed'.

4.1.143. *lament therefore*] The emphatic use of 'therefore' is usually traced to Marlowe's 'Cry out, exclaim, howl till thy throat be hoarse, / The Guise is slain, and I rejoice therefore!' (*Massacre* (1593), 21.148–9). But it is also found in an earlier play by Robert Greene, *The Comicall Historie of Alphonsus, King of Arragon* (1587) 3.2, l. 1077: 'For if you do, you both shall die therefore'. The expression 'clearly struck Elizabethans as histrionic' (Gary Taylor, Oxford Shakespeare edition, *H5*, 3.6.51n). Pistol ridicules the phrasing thrice, in *H5* 2.3.5–6 and 3.6.50, and in *2H4* 5.3.108–9. It seems to be the latter passage which Ford has in mind: '*Shallow.* Honest gentleman, I know not your breeding. *Pistol.* Why then, lament therefor' (*sic*). The echo points up possible links between Pistol and Mauruccio; perhaps they were played with a similar verbal and gestural extravagance.

4.1.199–200. *a whole . . . head*] It is tempting to see this as a reference to the punishment of William Prynne, who had his ears cropped for political libel after the publication of *Histriomastix* (late 1632; *JCS* III, 451). Ford and Shirley seem to refer to Prynne's attack on the theatres in their preliminary matter to *LS* (see Intro., p. 6, LN to Shirley's poem). But ear-cropping was not an uncommon punishment, and Prynne was not sentenced to have his ears cropped until 17 February 1633, nearly a month after *LS* was licensed for the press (Gardiner, 17). Giacopo may simply refer to some comic business—perhaps Mauruccio has a habit of holding him by the ears (cf. 2.1.52–3, 'Give me both thy ears').

5.1.23.1, 25.1. Kisses] Peter Bembo sets out the 'Platonic' view that a woman may 'lawfully and without blame come to kissing', for 'the reasonable lover woteth well, that although the mouth be a parcell of the bodie, yet it is an issue for the wordes, that be the interpreters of the soule, and for the inwarde breath, which is also called the soule'. Thus 'all chaste lovers covet a kisse, as a coupling of soules together' (*Courtier*, IV, 315). In the variety of *amour courtois* outlined by Andreas Capellanus, the 'pure' lovers may go so far as 'the kiss and the modest embrace with the nude lover, omitting the final solace, for that is not permitted to those who love purely' (*The Art of Courtly Love*, translated by J. J. Parry, New York, 1941, 184; quoted by Hoskins, 30). Yet the two kissing scenes in *LS* (this and 2.4) 'give prominent dramatic importance to the act' (*Nondram. Wks*, 388, n. 237–42). And in *HT* Ford argues that 'although in the eyes of some more Stoicall censures, Kissing seems but a needlesse ceremonie, yet in the feeling of love, it is the first tast of love, the first certaintie of hope, the first hope of obtaining, the first obtaining of favour, the first favour of graunt, the first graunt of assurance, the first and principallest assurance of affection; the first shadow of the substance of after contented happinesse' (236–42). Cf. 5.2.2–5.

Appendix 1: the text

THE 1633 QUARTO

Like many plays of the period, *Love's Sacrifice* made its first appearance in print in the form of a play quarto: a small and (by our standards) roughly printed volume about the height and width of this edition, but with only forty-odd pages. This quarto was printed in 1633, and, as its title-page informs us, was available for sale at the bookseller Hugh Beeston's premises in Cornhill. More than 360 years later, it remains the only true authority for the text of *LS*, and is therefore of utmost importance to students of the play. I hope the following discussion of the printing of the Quarto (or Q) will give the reader a clear impression of the character and reliability of this text. The present discussion is necessarily brief. Readers who would like a more detailed account of the printing of Q should refer to my article 'The Printing of John Ford's *Love's Sacrifice*', *The Library*, 6th series, 14, 4 (December 1992), 299–336.

LS was entered in the Register at Stationers' Hall on 21 January 1632/3. The entry reads as follows:

> Hugh Beeston. Entred for his Copy vnder the hands of Sir HENRY HERBERT and master Aspley warden a Tragedy called *Loues sacrifice* by JOHN FORD ....vj^{d}.[1]

The play was printed for Beeston by John Beale in the same year. Beeston, who seems to have had a very brief career as a bookseller and publisher, also brought out *BH* and *PW*. *LS* was his first registered publication. In contrast, John Beale's career lasted from 1612 till about 1643.[2] Among the many plays produced by his presses are the first quarto of *A King and No King* (1619), *The Maid of Honour* (1632), *B. Fair* (1631), *J. Malta* and *BH*, the last two appearing in the same year as *LS*. The bibliographical relation between *LS* and *J. Malta* is especially interesting. The two quartos must have been printed around the same time, and have important similarities (see 'Printing', 328–9).

Beale's quarto of *LS* has 42 unnumbered leaves, collating $\pi 1$(= L4) A^2 B–K^4 L^4(–L4). Thirty-five copies are extant, and these are listed below. The play proper is preceded by Ford's '*Epistle Dedicatory*' and commendatory verses by James Shirley—two indications that Ford himself was involved in publishing the play. Another indication of this is the presence in the text of emphasis italic, i.e. italic type used to point up certain words or phrases, as in the following lines from Bianca's speech to Fernando at 2.3.75–81 (E4v in Q):

couldst thou dare to speake
Againe, when we forbad? no, *wretched thing*,
Take this for answer; If thou henceforth ope
Thy leprous mouth to tempt our eare againe,
We shall not onely certifie our Lord
Of thy *disease in friendship*, but reuenge
Thy boldnesse with the forfeit of thy life.[3]

Such use of italic emphasis has a distinctly authorial stamp, and is an outstanding feature of several early texts of Ford's works.[4] It is the mark of a dramatist who gave some thought to the literary form of his plays. Like other professional playwrights who seem to have had no contractual relation with their acting companies, Ford showed little restraint in allowing his plays to be printed,[5] and there are many signs that he participated in the business of publication: he provided prefatory matter for most editions of his works; he apparently insisted that a dedication and commendatory poem be included in some copies of the 1638 edition of *Fancies*, even after others had already been bound;[6] he wrote (or at least requested) an apology for printer's errors at the end of the *'Tis Pity* quarto and appended a similar note to the 1613 edition of *CBS*;[7] he provided a list of 'Speakers names, fitted to their Qualities' for the benefit of readers of *BH*; he apparently embellished his manuscripts with emphatic italic script in the expectation that printers would reproduce his emphases in the printed editions; and he introduced a few new examples of emphasis italic to the second edition of *GM* (1614), along with other changes to the original 1613 text.[8] Such attention to printed detail on Ford's part may help to explain why Q presents a fairly reliable version of *LS*.

There are only two definite disruptions in Q's text. The first occurs on B2v:

Petr. Now Nephew, as I told you, since the Duke
Hath held the reines of state in his owne hand,
Much altered from the man he was before,
(As if he were transformed in his mind)

To sooth him in his pleasures, amongst whom
Is fond *Ferentes*

(ll. 13–18; 1.1.91–7)

These lines show no serious metrical irregularities, but the sense is obviously disjointed. The subject, corruption at court, raises the possibility that the passage may have been censored.[9] Again, at I4v, 8ff (5.1.16ff), the confused wording in the opening of Fernando's speech suggests that a line or so has been omitted, though I see no reason to suspect censorship in this instance. There is also a possibility of lost material in 4.1 (236n) and 4.2.6 (see note). The text features the usual scatter of literal errors—omissions, inversions, transpositions etc. But generally, Beale's compositor(s) did a reasonable job. There are relatively few cruces, and an editor is not obliged to make many substantive emendations. Q's punctuation is clear but not systematic: it rarely clouds the meaning of the dialogue or disrupts the metre of verse lines.

Very cursory press-correction (not unusual in Beale's shop[10]) produced a handful of variants in three of the twenty formes. Only one of these alterations, in which 'We's me' was amended to 'vd's me' at C1r (1.1.259), gives any suggestion that the manuscript was consulted after the printing of the sheets had begun. Thirty-four of the thirty-five extant copies of Q were collated by Herbert W. Hoskins for his unpublished thesis edition of the play (Columbia University, 1963). My own collation of the four Bodleian Library copies as well as those at the University of Texas and Haverford College turned up just two previously unnoticed press-variants. All variants are recorded below.

The printer's copy

The Quarto's provision of prefatory matter, its use of emphasis italic for certain key words and phrases (see 'Printing', 303–8) and the general clarity and coherence of its narrative, dialogue and stage directions (the only significant flaw is the inconsistency about Baglione's title, see 3.2.11n) all point to the likelihood that the manuscript supplied to the printer was a fair copy. It is probable that this manuscript was in Ford's own hand. The sensitive punctuation in particular is unlikely to have originated wholly from a scribe or compositor (see 'Printing', 303–4). The Quarto's Latin act-headings and Latin and part-Latin stage directions—'*recedet Fior.*' (K3r, 14; 5.1.183.1n), '*Exit Duke cum suis*' (D3r, 4; see Coll. 2.1.108),

'*Exeunt omnes, but Ros. et Petr.*' (I3r, 31; 4.2.78.1), and '*Exeunt omnes, but Du. et Bia*' (K1r, 14–15; 5.1.49.1–2)—also look Fordian,[11] as do the handful of permissive entry directions: '*Enter Duke, Lords and Ladies aboue*' (D1v, 16; 2.1.13.1–2), '*Enter 3. or 4. with Torches*' (H1r, 2; 3.3.89.1), '*Enter some with lights*' (H1r, 17, 3.4.6.1). But the evidence for authorial copy is by no means conclusive.

Consideration of Q's stage directions suggests that the exemplar for this edition would have presented few obstacles to its use in the theatre. Disparities between the directions and stage movements, which could count against theatrical influence, are quite rare, and are exceptions to a general consistency not incompatible with the preparation of the copy-manuscript as prompt-book. At first blush, Q's long, descriptive SDs (e.g. 3.4.17.1–12, 5.3.35.1–8) might seem to betray a manuscript that was 'closer to the study than the stage'. But there is hardly a word in these SDs which would not provide valuable guidance to performers. There is no obvious reason why such directions could not have been left intact by a book-keeper annotating the text for use in the theatre. The same may be said of the other authorial-looking features mentioned above. A few SDs look as if they may have entered the text as a direct result of its preparation for the Phoenix stage—e.g. the several short cues for music ('*Sound of Musicke*', G4v, 32, 3.3.83.1; 'Loud Musicke', H1r, 1, 3.3.89.1; 'Cease Musicke', H1v, 6, 3.4.17.12; and '*Musicke cease*', L1v, 13; 5.3.35.8), the few mentions of stage-properties ('*he draws a letter*', D4r, 20, 2.2.31.1; '*Enter D'au[o]los with two Pictures*', D4r, 21, 2.2.31.2), and 'costume notes' like '*Enter Petruchio, and Roseilli like a foole*' (E2r, 22, 2.2.179.1). These features raise the possibility that Ford prepared a fair copy for the printer, working from the manuscript he had originally supplied to the theatre and incorporating some or all of the theatrical annotations it had accumulated. On the other hand, none of the 'theatrical' features noted above would have been beyond an experienced playwright such as Ford in the first place.

The printing of the quarto

My examination of the headlines in Q (described in detail in 'Printing', 308–9) established that two sets were used in most sheets, one for inner formes and one for outer, presumably in association with two skeletons. This pattern indicates that, in the majority of sheets, printing and composition/distribution were carried on concurrently—a finding which received ample support from my analysis of recurring types ('Printing', 310–17). Study of spacing practices and distribution patterns of distinctive types revealed strong indications that copy for at least five of Q's ten sheets (F, G, H, I and K) was cast off and set by formes, and this may well have been the case throughout Q. If so, it seems to have created little need for the compositor to tamper with Ford's lines, for only a small proportion of Q's mislineation can be traced to spacing problems. At least in the five sheets named, inner formes were composed before outer formes, and in all sheets but B they were printed and distributed before the setting of one or both formes of the following gathering. Outer formes of most sheets were not distributed until after the setting of the next gathering. Evidence from the patterns of distributed type-pieces shows there was a delay in the composition or printing of the I Outer forme, and this may be connected with the loss of one or more lines in the last page of I Outer, I4v (the lacuna at 5.1.16–18); see note and 'Printing', 312.

It proved difficult to establish the number of compositors who worked on the Quarto. R. J. Fehrenbach cites variations in the distribution of emphasis italic, full SDs, and mis-setting of prose as evidence of more than one compositor.[12] But there must be doubts about this analysis. In the first place, it is unlikely that the copy would have been shared out amongst the compositors in acts; and, as we have seen, there is good evidence that the text was set by formes. Furthermore, Fehrenbach's three criteria cannot be considered as comprehensive or reliable compositor determinants in Q. At least two of them, emphasis italic and treatment of SDs, are not obviously influenced by the differing habits of two compositors. Emphasis italic, in particular, is never very dense, and its variations do not seem to be governed by any bibliographical division. Variation in the setting of prose is stronger evidence, only because of a marked concentration of mislining in sheets B and C; but when one looks for a reliable correlation between the occurrences of italic, full SDs and correctly set prose, the picture looks very hazy indeed.

For all this, the handling of prose in sheets B and C is distinctive. All prose in these sheets, except that at C1r, is mis-set. The prose is usually set like long verse-lines without any approximation to the iambic pentameter, line-breaks seldom falling at syntactical pauses. The mislineation in D'Avolos's speech at B4v, 15–24, is particularly interesting. Here, several of the prose lines are set as verse, while others are justified and provided with initial capital letters. This last practice (referred to as 'verse-cum-prose' setting in my collation) seems to be a trademark of one of the compositors in Beale's shop, for it also appears in the quarto of *J. Malta*, printed by Beale in the same year as *LS* (see 'Printing', App. 1). But while the passages of mislineation in these sheets deserve consideration, it is far from certain that they betray the hand of a second compositor. Like the ordinary mislined prose, the prose set as justified, capitalised lines is seen at a number of places in the text, including pages Fehrenbach attributes to the reliable compositor (e.g. E3r, 34, E4v, 13–15, F3r, 19). Moreover, my analysis of patterns of spelling, punctuation, abbreviation, capitalisation, elision, spacing and many other features of the Q text (see 'Printing', 323–7) showed an overall consistency in compositorial practices. In the absence of more telling evidence, it seems best to regard the variations in prose-setting as the work of a single workman who, for any number of reasons,[13] was capable of treating prose correctly or incorrectly.

OTHER EDITIONS

After 1633, no part of *LS* was reprinted until 1808, when Charles Lamb reproduced the discovery scene, 2.4, in his *Specimens of English Dramatic Poets, who lived about the Time of Shakspeare* (London, 1808). Lamb cuts Q's opening SD, with its description of Bianca with '*her hair about her ears, in her night-mantle*'. He omits the SD for Fernando to kiss Bianca at 60, and removes references to their final kiss at 91. He also leaves out 91–6 ('All mine . . . faithful servant'), presumably because Bianca's repetition of Fernando's vow at 2.3.98–101 would seem mystifying out of context.

It was not until 1811 that *LS* was reprinted in full. That year saw the publication of *The Dramatic Works of John Ford* (2 vols, Edinburgh, 1811), edited by Henry William Weber. This, the first collected edition of Ford's plays, was not well received. Foremost among its many critics was William Gifford,[14] who called Weber's edition 'a facsimile of blunders' (480). Certainly, Weber's commentary on *LS* displays little understanding of Ford's language, and is heavily reliant on the Variorum Shakespeare, as Gifford observed (477–8). In his text of the play, several words and phrases are left out (e.g. 2.1.62–3, 65, 2.2.178, 5.1.33); at least two whole lines disappear (4.1.261, 5.2.25); obsolete forms are needlessly retained (e.g. 'president', Ep., 27); and emendations are introduced to no obvious benefit ('without' for 'above', 1.1.134; 'and' for 'or', 1.1.186; 'my most earnest' for 'my earnest', 1.2.7; 'too' for 'so', 1.2.215,

'Frinulzio' for 'Trinultio', 2.2.116; and 'loves' for 'joys', 3.3.36, are typical). Yet not all of Weber's emendations were otiose, and a good many of his changes in wording and punctuation have been adopted by later editions, including the present endeavour. In many instances, too, Weber is heedful of the wording and import of the Quarto SDs (apart from the usual nineteenth-century '*A Room in the Palace*' scenic prescriptivism). Probably his most damaging interference with staging is at 5.3.35.1–8, where a scene-break is introduced at a point where the action is clearly continuous.

Weber's great detractor, William Gifford, adopted scores of his predecessor's emendations of the text of *LS* for his own edition of *The Dramatic Works of John Ford* (2 vols, London, 1827); e.g. 'he has', 3.1.56; 'pericranium', 3.3.87–8; 'an't', 4.1.163; '*discovering himself*', 5.3.0.1; and 5.3.35.1–8. Indeed, since Gifford also took on more than a few of Weber's errors (e.g. 'fancy', 4.1.20; 'leave you', 5.1.137; 'these', 5.3.39; 'Hath', 5.3.59, and the omission of 'lady', 2.1.65), it is conceivable that he prepared his own text of *LS* by marking up a copy of Weber's edition.[15] Gifford does show more understanding of the text than Weber, but he introduces a large number of fresh errors through cavalier emendation of difficult lines (e.g. 'Lady, I do' for 'I do, Lady', 1.1.176; 'you' for 'thee', 1.2.62; omission of 'noble', 1.2.81; omission of 'I', 4.1.207; 'hate' for 'fate', 5.1.183; 'death, and hell, and all' for 'death, and all', 4.2.46; 'Good b'wi'ye' for 'God boyee', 5.2.115; 'Pouring' for 'Roaring', 5.3.44). Too frequently he elides or expands the text to increase metrical regularity. Alexander Dyce rectified a fair number of Gifford's verbal errors when he re-edited the text forty years later (*The Works of John Ford, with Notes . . . by William Gifford, Esq. A New Edition, Carefully Revised . . . by the Rev. Alexander Dyce*, 3 vols, London, 1869). But many more inaccuracies were allowed to stand. Dyce also introduced some questionable emendations of his own (e.g. 'slep'st' for 'sleep'st', 5.1.149, 'trespass' for 'trespasses', 5.1.180), as well as augmenting Gifford's metrical regularisation. The Gifford-Dyce edition nevertheless remains the standard collection of Ford's plays. It was reprinted by Hartley Coleridge in his edition of *The Dramatic Works of Massinger and Ford* (London, 1839–40), by A. H. Bullen in *The Works of John Ford* (3 vols, London, 1895), and (in part) by Havelock Ellis in his popular selection of Ford's plays, *John Ford* (Mermaid series, London: Fisher Unwin, 1888). Thus the most widely known text of *Love's Sacrifice* is an amalgam of nineteenth-century editorial practices in scenic stage-direction and metrical regularisation, preserving numerous substantive and accidental distortions of the Quarto text.

Herbert Wilson Hoskins's unpublished thesis edition of *LS* (Columbia University, 1963) consists of a page-for-page xerographic reproduction of a Library of Congress copy of the 1633 Quarto, accompanied by a light textual apparatus. Punctuation 'is left unchanged wherever a reader familiar with seventeenth-century usage would not be unduly confused . . . Interference with the quarto has been kept to a minimum' ('Abstract', 1). Joe Andrew Sutfin prepared another thesis edition of the play in the following year ('Ford's *Love's Sacrifice*, *The Lady's Trial*, and *The Queen*, Critical Old Spelling Editions of the Texts of the Original Quartos', unpublished Ph.D. dissertation, Vanderbilt University, 1964).

THIS EDITION

This edition presents a modern-spelling text of *Love's Sacrifice* based on the only authoritative edition of the play, the 1633 Quarto. The text was prepared from a collation of six copies of the Quarto. All but two of the seventeeen British copies and photocopies of most of the eighteen quartos held in the United States were consulted to verify the accuracy of the transcript. (See below for details of copies.)

As we have seen, the Quarto is a relatively well-printed text which appears to derive from a fair-copy manuscript possibly in Ford's own hand. A number of features suggest that the manuscript reflected the requirements of performance in quite detailed ways—a sign of influence from the prompt-book, perhaps, or simply proof of Ford's experience and capability as a professional playwright. Of course, we have no certain knowledge of the lost copy manuscript, and all arguments concerning the 'authenticity' of the surviving text are at best conjectural. But the Quarto's coherence and general freedom from corruption do seem to justify the conservative editorial approach adopted here. My close adherence to the 1633 text has entailed frequent departure from the readings of other editions. Quarto readings excluded by other editors have been re-examined, and in many instances reinstated (e.g. 'prescribed', Ep. 19; 'correspondence', 1.1.137; 'shay', 1.2.59; 'follows', 1.2.273; 'syllable', 2.1.13; 'out my', 2.1.100; 'Kneeled', 2.1.151; 'feigned', 2.2.109; 'Narbassa's', 2.2.145; 'That he should be the man!', 3.3.65; 'God boyee', 5.2.115; see notes). I have also tried to free the play's poetic language from the constraints of nineteenth-century metrical regularisation.

Ellipses are restored (e.g. 'd'ee', 2.3.35, 'He's', 5.2.14, 'th'art', 5.2.34), and forms contracted by previous editors are expanded to reproduce Q's readings ('To impart', 1.1.85, 'in the', 1.1.112, 'thou art', 1.1.191 etc.).

In this edition, spelling and punctuation are silently modernised according to the general principles set out for the Revels Plays series. Thus archaic spellings such as 'murther', 'Counsailes', 'phantasticke', 'then' (for 'than'), 'bin' (been) and 'vild' are modernised. Modernisation is resisted only in those instances where the orthography appears to represent a distinct linguistic form, or where emendation would affect the metre. Obsolete forms such as 'stover', 'bever', 'Ud's me', the pronoun 'a' and the conjunction 'and' (i.e. 'if') are either transcribed as they appear in the Quarto or slightly regularised. In many places it has been possible to retain Q's sensitive but unsystematic punctuation. Q's practice of using dashes to indicate changes in tone or direction of speech (possibly an authorial habit) has been made more uniform. Alterations of pointing which affect meaning are always recorded in the Collation, and sometimes discussed in the Commentary. Half-lines of verse spoken by different characters, usually set against the left-hand margin in Q, are rearranged to show their metrical relation. Minor printer's errors such as turned or raised letters are silently corrected; literal errors which may have some bearing on the sense of the lines are recorded in the Collation. The Quarto's abbreviations have been expanded ('et cetera' for '&c', 'Saint' for 'S.', and so forth), and seventeenth-century practices in capitalisation and italicisation have generally been modernised. Since it is far from clear that Ford's emphasis italic would have the effect he intended in a modernised text, this feature has (with considerable reluctance) been edited out. All instances of emphasis italic are recorded, however, in the Collation. The play's act-divisions have been retained, and the scene-divisions introduced by Weber are indicated (except at 5.3.35, where Weber unnecessarily began a new scene). Speech prefixes have been silently regularised. Most of Q's SDs are reproduced verbatim; slight corrections or modifications are indicated by square brackets. Since the play's action is generally unlocalised, there is no need to indicate a fictional setting. In those scenes where the action is more precisely located (e.g. 2.4), Q's SDs and dialogue adequately convey a sense of place.

Editions of Ford's works consulted in preparing the collation are shown in 'Abbreviations and References', part 2. Three Ford editions are not included in the collation: *The Dramatic Works of John*

Ford, anonymous ed., 2 vols (New York: Harper, 1831); *The Works of John Ford*, ed. A. H. Bullen (3 vols, London, 1895); and *John Fordes dramatische Werke*, ed. W. Bang, *Materialien zur Kunde des älteren Englischen Dramas*, vol. 23 (Louvain: Uystpruyst, 1908). The first two are reprints of Gifford's text, while the last gives a typographical reprint of Q.

THE 1633 QUARTO: PRESS-CORRECTIONS AND EXTANT COPIES

Five, possibly six, press-variants have been found in the Quarto. They occur in three formes: C Outer (three, all on C1r); F Inner (one); and H outer (two). It will be noted that most occur at the top or bottom of the page. If the proportion of corrected and uncorrected sheets in the thirty-five surviving copies is any guide, most of the corrections were not made especially early in the press-work. An exception here is the 'But' catchword on C1r, which only copy 1 omits. It is possible, though, that the catchword simply failed to print in this copy. The 'l' in 'lemnity', L1v, 1, seems to have fallen out at some stage in the printing; it is present in the Haverford and Texas copies. The variants labelled a, b, d and e were located by Hoskins, but the following list is based on my own collation and examination, and corrects a number of his errors. I collated six quartos—numbers 1, 2, 3, 4, 23 and 24—and examined all British copies. I examined ten of the eighteen American quartos by microfilm or xerox, and am grateful to staff at the libraries holding the other copies for providing information about their variants. In the first list, each variant is followed by the reference numbers of the copies in which it occurs. The second list gives all extant copies, together with their reference numbers.

Location	*Variant form*	*Copies*
(a) C1r, line 10	We's me foole,	1, 14, 15, 18, 19, 22, 35
	vd's me,foole	2–13, 16, 17, 20, 21, 23–34
(b) C1r, signature	D	1, 14–16, 18, 19, 22, 30, 35
	C	2–13, 17, 20, 21, 23–9, 31–4

(c)	C1r, catchword	[missing]	1
		But	2–35
(d)	F3v, line 1	(thou whore |)	2–16, 20–4, 26–34
		(thou whore)	1, 18, 19, 25, 35
(e)	H2v, line 33	tience	4, 8, 9, 11, 19, 21, 25, 28, 29
		ence	1–3, 5–7, 10, 12–18, 20, 22–4, 26, 27, 30–5
(f)	H4v, line 4	fergot	4, 8, 9, 11, 19, 21, 25, 28, 29
		forgot	1–3, 5–7, 10, 12–18, 20, 22–4, 26, 27, 30–5

List of copies

1. Bodleian Library, Mal B164
2. Bodleian Library, Mal 238
3. Bodleian Library, Mal 203.6
4. Bodleian Library, Douce F209
5. British Library, 644.b.36
6. British Library, C12.g.3(3)
7. Magdalen College, Oxford
8. Wadham College, Oxford
9. Liverpool University
10. John Rylands University Library, Manchester
11. Trinity College, Cambridge
12. King's College, Cambridge, C.7.4
13. National Library of Scotland, Bute 231
14. National Library of Scotland, H.28.e.12
15. Eton College
16. Dyce Collection, Victoria & Albert Museum
17. University College, London
18. Harvard University
19. Pierpont Morgan Library
20. Huntington Library
21. Newberry Library
22. Clark Library, University of California
23. University of Texas
24. Haverford College
25. Library of Congress
26. Chapin Library, Williams College
27. University of Illinois
28. Boston Public Library
29. Folger Shakespeare Library #1
30. Folger Shakespeare Library #2
31. Folger Shakespeare Library #3
32. University of Chicago
33. Yale University, 1h F753 6331
34. Yale University, 1977 2709
35. Columbia University

Notes: Copy 1 lacks L1. Copy 9 lacks π1 and L1, both replaced by hand-written transcripts. Copy 10 wants K2–L3, replaced by reprint (perhaps nineteenth-century). Copy 17 lacks sheets B, D, E and F. Sutfin (p. 15) reports a non-conjugate blank before π1 in 26. See Greg, II, 626, for additional remarks.

NOTES

1 Arber, IV, 291. Herbert, *de facto* Master of the Revels from 1623 until 1642 (Richard Dutton, *Mastering the Revels: The Regulation and Censorship of English Renaissance Drama*, Houndmills: Macmillan, 1991, 229), licensed plays for printing from early 1624 until 1638 (Bawcutt, 47) The bookseller William Aspley was a Warden of the Stationers' Company 1632–3. Books had to be 'allowed' by a Warden before they could be printed, sixpence (vj[d]) being the standard fee for this.
2 Cyprian Blagden, *The Stationers' Company: A History, 1403–1959*, 2nd ed. (Stanford, California: Stanford University Press, 1977), 125–9; entry on Beale in Henry R. Plomer, *A Dictionary of Booksellers and Printers . . . 1641–67* (London: The Bibliographical Society, 1907). See also 'Printing', 300–1.
3 Quoted from Q. Only long s has been modernised.
4 'Printing', 299, 304, 307–8; R. J. Fehrenbach, 'Typographical Variation in Ford's Texts: Accidentals or Substantives?', in *Concord in Discord*, 265–94.
5 G. E. Bentley, *The Profession of Dramatist in Shakespeare's Time, 1590–1642* (Princeton: Princeton University Press, 1971), 264–92.
6 Fehrenbach, 284
7 On Ford's authorship of this work, see G. D. Monsarrat, 'John Ford's Authorship of *Christes Bloodie Sweat*', *ELN* IX, 1 (Sept. 1971), 20–5.
8 Fehrenbach, 270–1.
9 Principal subjects of censorship by the Master of the Revels included 'critical comments on the policies or conduct of the government', 'unfavourable presentations of *friendly* foreign powers or their sovereigns, great nobles, or subjects', and 'personal satire of *influential* people' (Bentley, *Profession*, 167). See Bawcutt, 90–3, for discussion of some relevant instances of censorship by Sir Henry Herbert; also Clare, 158–65, 154, 202; *LM* 1.1.76–7n.
10 See Revels editions of *J. Malta*, 38–9; *BH*, 4–5; *Staple*, 5.
11 Cf. the Latin SDs in *PW*, D1v, E1v, G1v; *BH*, B4r, C1r, D1v, I3r.
12 Fehrenbach, 278.
13 For example, perhaps Ford himself exerted some (less than consistent) pressure on the printer in getting his prose and emphasis italic rendered accurately. See 'Printing', 322–3.
14 *The Quarterly Reivew*, 'Article IX', 6 (1811), 462–87. See Intro., n228, for details of other reviews of Weber's edition.
15 T. J. B. Spencer makes the same claim regarding Gifford's text of *BH* (7).

Appendix 2: the Inigo Jones drawings and the Phoenix Theatre

D. F. Rowan searched in vain for evidence linking Inigo Jones's drawings with any known theatre of the period (Rowan[1], Rowan[2], Rowan[3]). Glynne Wickham suggested that they could be related to the Salisbury Court Theatre (*Early English Stages 1300 to 1660*, 4 vols, London: Routledge & Kegan Paul, 1959–72, II, Part 2, 144–7). But this was built in 1629, and, as Rowan showed, the watermarks of the paper used for the drawings indicate a date closer to 1616 (Rowan[3], 127). The possibility that Jones's drawings could be connected to the Phoenix Theatre was first entertained in print by Iain Mackintosh in 'Inigo Jones—Theatre Architect', *TABS* 31 (1973), 101–4. The first scholar to offer a detailed argument for the Phoenix connection was John Orrell ('Inigo Jones'). Orrell expanded on his findings in *Theatres*, and again in his chapter on the private theatre at the London Globe project in *Rebuilding*.

John Harris and Gordon Higgott reject the Phoenix attribution, arguing that the drawings' 'style, technique and architectural detail' indicate a date in the late 1630s (*Inigo Jones: Complete Architectural Drawings*, London: Zwemmer/Wilson, 1989, 266). Harris and Higgott suggest that the designs should instead be connected with William Davenant's abortive plan for a theatre in Fleet Street in 1639 (268). I am not qualified to comment on these scholars' stylistic analysis of the drawings. However, I note that they make no reference to Rowan's dating of the watermarks; and generally, the arguments linking the drawings with the Phoenix, though far from decisive, seem to me more convincing. The evidence for the Phoenix attribution (for the most part derived from the scholarship of John Orrell) can be summarised as follows.

1. *The drawings represent a serious theatrical project.* As D. F. Rowan and Richard Leacroft have observed,[1] Jones's drawings contain many confusions and unfinished details. The doorway leading from the staircase to the back of the first gallery shown on the plan does not appear in the elevation of the auditorium. The doors from the tiring house to the lower galleries, visible in the plan, are missing in

the interior drawing of the stage-end of the theatre. The ground-level entrance to the auditorium shown in the elevation cuts awkwardly into the tiers of seats above. On the other hand, John Orrell notes the care with which the drawings have been prepared. They are on high-quality paper, rendered in a neat, attractive ink-and-wash finish. Meticulous attention has been paid to many details of the theatre's structure and appearance, from the cartouche above the central stage entrance to the careful arrangement of the tiered seats and the positions of the roof trusses. The overall impression is of a serious project, not just an architectural flight of fancy. Orrell thinks the drawings show every sign of being presentation copies of a planned theatre (*Rebuilding*, 139; cf. Rowan³, 125). Perhaps Jones, as Royal Surveyor, prepared them for the King himself?

2. *The drawings may date from around the time of the construction of the Phoenix.* A decade before his work with Gordon Higgott, John Harris dated the drawings on stylistic grounds to the period between about 1616 and 1618.[2] This tallies with Rowan's dating of the watermarks. Apart from the Phoenix, the only other theatre project known to have been undertaken around this time was the Puddle Wharf or Porters Hall theatre, which Philip Rosseter and others had begun building around 1615. Very little is known about this theatre, but other links between Jones's drawings and the Phoenix tend to rule out Porters Hall as a possible subject for the designs.

3. *The drawings suggest a conversion of an already existing structure.* John Orrell's ingenious analysis of the proportions of the theatre shown in the drawings suggests that the width of the theatre 'was a datum from which Jones began, and not something he arrived at by his usual methods' ('Inigo Jones', 160.). This points to the possibility that the drawings relate to the conversion of an already existing building rather than to a completely new construction.

4. *Jones's round auditorium looks like a modified cockpit.* The round auditorium in Jones's design no doubt owes something to the design of the popular, open air theatres, but it is very easy to imagine how this part of the building might have begun life as a cockpit. This impression is given substance by the fact that the width of the auditorium is 40 feet, the same as the (estimated) average diameter of a cockpit. If the basic structure of John Best's cockpit was retained as the auditorium end of the house, the extension for the stage and tiring-house end would not have been much more than the one-third of the original size allowed by King James's building restric-

tions. As Royal Surveyor, Inigo Jones would have been quite familiar with these constraints on new building work (Gurr, *Companies*, 123). It is worth noting, too, that there are possible allusions to a rounded auditorium in at least three plays performed at the Phoenix.[3]

5. *A detailed study of staging practices in plays performed at the Phoenix provides much support for the Phoenix identification.* Markward's 'A Study of the Phoenix Theatre in Drury Lane, 1617–1638' presents a very useful survey of staging practices in eighty-seven plays associated with the Phoenix Theatre. Many of his conclusions—for example that the Phoenix auditorium was 'amphitheatrical', that the stage façade featured two flanking doors with a central 'inner stage', that at least one of the stage doors was large enough to permit the entrance of processions and large properties, and that there was at least one upper playing space which might also have housed the musicians (Markward, 661–8)—correspond with the evidence of Jones's drawings.

6. *An extant stage-design for the Phoenix fits the dimensions of the stage in the Jones theatre.* The final piece of evidence is perhaps the most convincing. Sir William Davenant's *The Siege of Rhodes* was performed at the Phoenix theatre in 1658–9. Orrell demonstrates that John Webb's accurately drawn design for scenery to be used in performances of Davenant's work almost exactly fits the dimensions of the stage and stage frontage of Jones's theatre. (See Orrell's chapter on 'The Inigo Jones Designs' in *Rebuilding*, 138, 146–8.)

NOTES

1 Rowan, 'The English Playhouse: 1595–1630', *RenD*, n.s., IV (1971), 43, 49; Rowan[2], 71; Rowan[3], 128; Richard Leacroft, *The Development of the English Playhouse* (London and New York: Methuen, 1973, rev. 1988), 73.

2 John Harris, Stephen Orgel and Roy Strong, *The King's Arcadia: Inigo Jones and the Stuart Court*, Catalogue for a quatercentenary exhibition held at the Banqueting House, Whitehall, in 1973 (London: Arts Council, 1973), 109.

3 There is an apparent reference to a round auditorium in *Love's Mistress* (1636) 1.1, B2r: 'Seest thou this spheare spangled, with all these starres'. Similar allusions occur in *Darling* and *The Coronation* (*JCS* VI, 50).

Appendix 3: the Gesualdo Story and the Corona Manuscript

The two principal sources of information concerning the best-known episode in Carlo Gesualdo's life are: (1) the account contained in the seventeenth-century *Successi tragici et amorosi di Silvio et Ascanio Corona*, or Corona Manuscript; and (2) the *Informatione presa dalla Gran Corte della Vicaria. Die 27 Octobris, 1590, in quo habitat Don Carolus Gesualdus*, a verbatim report of the proceedings of the Grand Court of the Vicaria, which preserves the observations of court officials and the statements of two servants who were present in Gesualdo's house on the night of the murders. Of the two documents, it is the more fanciful version of the story presented in the Corona MS which is the most likely source of certain details in *Love's Sacrifice*. This appendix presents a discussion of Ford's possible borrowings from the Corona MS, followed by a translation of the section of the MS dealing with the Gesualdo tragedy. Line numbers for the Corona MS cited in my discussion are keyed to the extract from the MS.

Hopkins ('Coterie Values', n82, pp. 300–2; 'A Source') argues that many details of the Gesualdo tragedy recur in *LS*. She points out that Donna Maria's surname, D'Avalos, may have provided Ford with the name of his male villain ('A Source', 66), and notes that the name Carafa occurs thrice in the Gesualdo story: it was the name of Donna Maria's lover, of her first husband and, later, of the husband of her daughter by her first marriage. Hopkins speculates that 'If Ford had heard only a garbled version of the story, and had not had access to the Italian manuscript account of the affair, that might explain the transferring of the name Caraffa to Bianca's husband, while the name D'Avolos, with its echo of "devil", was clearly a name more fitted to the diabolic secretary than to the heroine' ('A Source', 66). Hopkins also points out that both Maria and her lover Fabrizio are described as being exceptionally attractive, while Gesualdo seems to have been comparatively plain ('Coterie Values', 300). In the Princess's case, at least, this is unlikely to be a matter of mere *politesse* or narrative convention, for the

Venetian ambassador to Naples at the time of the murders remarked that Donna Maria was 'considered the most beautiful lady in Naples' (Watkins, 14). Unlike the trio in *LS*, however, the real-life lovers and husband seem to have been about the same age.

The Corona MS relates that among the first to learn of the affair was Don Giulio Gesualdo, Don Carlo's uncle, who was himself 'fiercely enamoured of Donna Maria's beauty' (l. 101). Hopkins ('A Source', 66–7) compares Donna Maria's threat to tell her husband of Don Giulio's advances (ll. 104–8) to Bianca's warning to Fernando in *LS* 2.3.77–81. Don Giulio's realisation that 'neither through gifts nor prayers nor through tears had he been able to make [Donna Maria] pliant to his will' (ll. 108–11) also seems close to Fernando's description of Bianca's apparent invulnerability to his 'tears, and vows, and words' (2.1.150–2). Again, Hopkins notes that Don Giulio's exposure of Maria and Fabrizio is similar to the jealous Fiormonda's revelation to Caraffa. Fiormonda has herself been rejected by Fernando (cf. 2.3.127–8, 4.1.256–62; 'A Source' 66–7). Another similarity is the audacity of both wives in the face of danger ('Coterie Values', 301; cf. Corona MS, ll. 133ff, *LS* 5.1.52ff).

Caraffa's pretended journey to Lucca is reminiscent of Gesualdo's feigned hunting trip. Both men are accompanied by a band of followers (Corona MS, ll. 187–8; *LS* 4.2.67–74). The detail of Gesualdo's hunting trip occurs only in the Corona Manuscript's account of the murders; the eye-witness reports preserved in the *Informatione presa dalla Gran Corte della Vicaria* agree that Don Carlo remained at home on the night of the murder (see Watkins, 18–22). Cecil Gray therefore judges the hunting trip to be an erroneous detail, 'reminiscent of the device of the Sultan Schahriar in the "Arabian Nights"' (Gray and Heseltine, 20). But a possible source of this ploy is found in the testimony of one of the eye-witnesses, Gesualdo's personal servant Pietro Malitiale. Malitiale recounts that, on being called to the Prince's bedchamber in the early hours of the night of the murder, he discovered Don Carlo up and dressed. The servant asked him where he was going at that hour, and the Prince replied that he 'wanted to go hunting': 'When said witness said to him that it was not the time to go hunting, Don Carlo replied, "You will see the kind of hunting I am going to do!"' (Watkins, 21).

Hopkins notes that, according to the Corona MS, Donna Maria's wounds were 'all in her belly and especially in those parts which most ought to be kept honest' (ll. 239–41). She suspects that this is recalled in Caraffa's threat to Bianca to 'Rip up the cradle of thy cursèd womb, / In which the mixture of that traitor's lust / Impostumes for a birth of bastardy' (5.1.62–4). Hopkins remarks: 'so far as we know Bianca is not pregnant, and there are no other references in the play to an actual pregnancy, although Fiormonda and D'Avolos taunt the Duke with the possibility of one [see 4.1.40–3]. Maria D'Avalos, however, had had a baby shortly before her death, and the child, in some versions of the story, was also murdered by Gesualdo. Perhaps the "phantom pregnancy" of Bianca has wandered in from Ford's source' ('A Source', 67). The suggestion is plausible but not compelling. It does not seem unusual that the jealous Duke should accuse Bianca of carrying a bastard. In 'the language of insult', pregnancy and bastardy were often cited as 'proofs of whoredom' (Gowing, 88); and Alphonso accuses his wife in very similar terms in *The Queen*, ll. 1214–26. Nor is it surprising that the conniving Fiormonda and D'Avolos should remind Caraffa of this possibility.

Hopkins also suggests that Caraffa's anguish after the murder of Bianca recalls Gesualdo's own guilt ('Coterie Values', 301–2). There is no lack of evidence that Gesualdo suffered from guilt. Among other acts of contrition, he constructed a Capuchin monastery and church, the Santa Maria delle Grazie, at Gesualdo in the province of Avellino, in Irpinia. In the church there is a large painting by the Florentine artist Giovanni Balducci. This picture, *Il perdono di Carlo Gesualdo* (1609), shows the Prince himself suing for absolution from Christ at the Last Judgement.[1] Gesualdo's later music conveys similar feelings of 'sin and expiation'.[2] Yet if Ford knew of Gesualdo's contrition, it must have been from a source or sources other than the Corona MS, for the MS has nothing to say of the Prince's later conduct. Overall, I see no special reason for connecting the repentant Caraffa with the Gesualdo whose sombre face is seen in Balducci's painting.

A few other details offer better support for Hopkins's theory. In *LS* 1.2.249–51, D'Avolos claims that Roseilli has 'departed towards Benevento' on his way to Seville. This is an extremely unlikely route to take from the northern city of Pavia, for Benevento is 95 miles south-east of Rome, half the length of the country away. Benevento is, however, in the region of Naples, and it is not inconceivable that Ford was thinking at this point of the Neapolitan setting of the Gesualdo story. Moreover, Benevento figures prominently in the history of the Gesualdo family. The town of Gesualdo received its name when a Cavaliere Gesualdo was given control of the castle estate by Duke Romualdo of Benevento. This Gesualdo afterwards distinguished himself in defence of Benevento during the seige by Constans II, Emperor of Byzantium (Gray and Heseltine, 3–5; Watkins, 3). Perhaps Ford came across the place-name in reading an account of Gesualdo's ancestry. Another possible link is found in the Corona Manuscript's reference to Donna Maria and Don Fabrizio's meeting 'in the garden of Don Garzia ofToledo' (ll. 66–7). In *LS* 1.2.251–2, D'Avolos claims that Roseilli intends to visit 'his cousin Don Pedro de Toledo in the Spanish court'. Also, the episode in which the courageous Donna Maria elicits from Don Fabrizio a declaration of unswerving loyalty might be compared to the scene in which Bianca scorns 'the iron laws of ceremony' and receives Fernando's pledge of enduring love (MS, ll. 133–77, cf. *LS* 5.1.5–23).

Caraffa's entrance with a few armed followers in 5.1.29.1–3 is similar to Gesualdo's sudden intrusion into his wife's bedchamber 'accompanied by a troop of armed cavalieri' (MS, ll. 206–7). The MS relates that Donna Maria's maid, hearing the noise made by Gesualdo and his companions, 'was on the point of shouting, but her life being threatened by the Prince, she withdrew more dead than alive' (ll. 212–14). In *LS*, Colona's cries are heard offstage: 'Help, help! Madam, you are betrayed' (5.1.30–1, 35). Perhaps the audience is meant to assume that Bianca's attendant, like Donna Maria's, was surprised in her duties as sentinel. The situation is archetypal, however, and *The Roman Actor*, a probable dramatic source of *LS* (see pp. 63–4), also has an entrance for Caesar '*and Guard*' at a very similar point in its action (4.2.112.1).[3]

Hopkins concludes that while some details of the Corona MS seem to be closely followed by Ford, 'the relationship is not so close as to suggest that he had access to it' ('A Source', 67). This may underestimate the evidence. Nearly every detail of the Gesualdo story considered here would have been available to Ford in the Corona MS. Of all the parallels, only the mention of Benevento is not to be found there. It is noteworthy, too, that many of the details of the Gesualdo story which are apparently echoed in *LS* could not have been derived from the more accurate version of the story presented in the report of the Grand Court of the Vicaria. The relative plainness of Don Carlo, the story of Don Giulio Gesualdo's jealousy and subsequent revelation to the Prince, the feigned hunting trip, Donna Maria's courage in the face of danger, Don Fabrizio's declaration of loyalty to the Princess, Donna Maria's pregnancy and the details of her wounds 'in her belly', the verbal echoes of Benevento and Don Garzia of Toledo—none of these details could have come from the verbatim report. Where the Corona MS and the Vicaria report are contradictory—on the question of Gesualdo's pretended hunting trip, and on the method of murder (the Vicaria report shows that Gesualdo used an arquebus as well as a sword)—it is the Corona Manuscript's version which is apparently favoured in *LS*. The MS also imparts a dual awareness of the lovers as both heroic and sinful which may have influenced Ford's equivocal presentation of Bianca and Fernando (see MS, ll. 1–13, 95–8, 133–74). A similar ambivalence is evident in other contemporary Italian references to the Gesualdo story.[4] But these other accounts deal with the tragedy in far less detail than the Corona MS. None of them, as far as I have been able to determine, could have provided a significant source for Ford's play.[5]

Like other such fictionalised historical accounts, the Corona MS was frequently copied. There are thirty-six extant MSS, dating from the seventeenth to the nineteenth century (Watkins, 7). It is quite possible that Ford saw one of the early copies. Italian MSS may have provided source material for other English plays of the period (see *WBW*, xliii–xliv; *W. Devil*, xxvii–xxxi; *Malfi*, xxxiii). Moreover, the list of dedicatees for Ford's dramatic and non-dramatic work suggests that he had 'a large yet intimate circle of friends, lawyers, playwrights, gentlemen and wits' focused on the Inns of Court and the private playhouses (Butler, 204)—precisely the kind of company in which there may have been opportunities to view MSS recently acquired in Italy. Ford's membership of the Middle Temple would also have provided contacts with those interested in foreign literature, for the Inns of Court were an acknowledged centre of literary production and consumption, with a strong tradition in translation.[6] It is also worth noting that Ford's fellow students at the Middle Temple may have included Sir John Stradling, one of the Welsh Stradlings to whom Ford was related on the mother's side of his family. Hopkins suggests that Ford may have obtained knowledge of Italian affairs through his connection with the Stradlings.[7] Sir John and his father, Sir Edward, 'had numerous links with Italy' (Hopkins, 'Incest', 1–2). In particular, they were friends of Humphrey Llwyd, 'who travelled to Italy in 1566, and may have met Dr Gruffydd Robert' ('Incest', 2). The latter was confessor to Saint Carlo Borromeo, the maternal uncle of Carlo Gesualdo who is shown with him in the painting in Santa Maria delle Grazie.

Amongst the several aristocratic dedicatees of Ford's printed works, perhaps the most likely to have been able to supply him with an Italian MS of amorous and tragic tales is Thomas Howard, Earl of Arundel, one of the dedicatees of *Honour Triumphant* (1606). Hopkins argues that Ford's association with Arundel continued after 1606, and that it may have furnished the playwright with source material for *Edmonton* and *PW* (*Political Theatre*, 19). Arundel, a renowned collector of Latin and Greek antiquities, paintings, statues and inscriptions, books and manuscripts, travelled to Italy in 1612 and again in 1613/14. During the second visit he spent several weeks, from early March to mid-May, in Naples.[8] Gesualdo was still alive at that time (he died in September 1614), and probably resident in Naples or nearby Gesualdo (Watkins, 79–80). Arundel's protégé, Henry Peacham, also visited Italy in 1613/14, perhaps as part of Arundel's train (Hervey, 171). Peacham's *The Compleat Gentleman* (1622) contains the first mention of Gesualdo in English (see p. 99; Hopkins, 'Coterie Values', 191, 302).

Of course, many of the similarities between *LS* and the Gesualdo story concern situations and events that are hardly unique, in literature or in life. But one cannot wholly dismiss the possibility that Ford was aware of the parallel between his play and Gesualdo's real-life tragedy. Perhaps the small cluster of recurring names (Caraffa, D'Avolos, Benevento, de Toledo) is a deliberate signal of the general resemblance. If Ford *had* heard or read a version of Gesualdo's story, it is most likely to have been that presented in the Corona MS—a debt possibly recorded in the name of Bianca's maid-servant, Colona.

NOTES

1 Zarrella, 35, who gives a reproduction of the painting on 34.
2 Denis Arnold, *Gesualdo* (London, 1984), 9.
3 Edwards and Gibson's SD, '*Enter* CAESAR *and Guard*', does not appear in the 1629 edition, but it is required by dialogue at 4.2.138–41.
4 One anonymous poem from the period has Donna Maria declaring from the tomb: 'Questo (ahi lassa!) mi avvenne / per troppo amar ed io ne son contenta, / che, s'alta colpa l'alma mia tormenta, / io vo' ch' il mondo senta / che per il mio Fabricio infamia e interno / reputò gloria e paradiso eterno.' ('This, alas, befell me because of having too much loved. And I am content with it. For if great sin torments my soul I wish the world to know that for my Fabrizio's sake I hold infamy and hell to be glory and eternal paradise.'—Watkins's translation, 30–1.) A sonnet which Tasso addresses to the dead lovers claims that heaven is 'adorned' by their sin ('Anzi è di vostra colpa il Cielo adorno', l. 9).

5 Pierre de Bourdeilles, in *Vies des Dames Galantes*, and Spaccini, in *Cronaca Modenese*, give only brief outlines of the story, and omit nearly all of the details echoed in *LS*. A report by the Venetian ambassador to Naples mentions only the most obvious circumstances, and is mainly concerned with the effects and implications of the shocking events. The numerous poems by Tasso, Giambattista Marino, Ascanio Pignatelli, Camillo Pellegrino, Horatio Comite and others provide lyrical comment on the lovers' fate but add little or nothing to circumstantial knowledge of the tragedy (see Watkins, 14, 23–5, 28). Watkins, 3, mentions four principal authorities on Gesualdo's ancestry. Two of these, Aldimari's *Historia genealogica della Famiglia Carafa* and Lellis's *Discorsi delle famiglie nobili del regno di Napoli*, were not published until the second half of the seventeenth century. Of the other two, Scipione Ammirato's *Delle Famiglie nobili Napoletane* (Florence: Part I, 1580; Part II, 1651) contains only a brief notice of Gesualdo in its first part (p. 7), while Giovanni Antonio Summonte's *Historia della città e regno di Napoli* (Naples, 1601–43) is unlikely to have provided Ford with any details for *LS*.

6 Philip J. Finkelpearl, *John Marston of the Middle Temple* (Cambridge, Massachusetts: Harvard University Press, 1969), 19–31.

7 'Incest and Class: *'Tis Pity She's a Whore* and the Borgias', forthcoming in Elizabeth Barnes, ed., *Thicker Than Water*; also see Hopkins, *Political Theatre*, 8.

8 Mary F. S. Hervey, *The Life, Correspondence and Collections of Thomas Howard, Earl of Arundel* (Cambridge: Cambridge University Press, 1921), 64–7, 74–88.

THE CORONA MANUSCRIPT

The following is a translation of an extract from the early seventeenth-century Italian manuscript, the *Successi tragici et amorosi di Silvio et Ascanio Corona* (or Corona Manuscript). This section of the MS relates the story of the illicit affair between Don Fabrizio Carafa and Donna Maria, wife of Don Carlo Gesualdo, Prince of Venosa. It concludes with a detailed, if sensationalised, description of Gesualdo's murder of the lovers.

This translation, based on a copy of the MS held in the Biblioteca Brancaccia in Naples, is taken from Glenn Watkins's *Gesualdo: The Man and His Music* (London: Oxford University Press, 1973), 7–13. I am grateful to Oxford University Press for permission to reproduce it here. I have given the relevant section of the MS in full, except for two brief cuts of extraneous material; these are indicated by ellipses. Where similarities with *LS* seem especially pronounced, I have provided references to the play, marked by asterisks and in italic, in the right-hand margin. Line numbers for the translation are given in roman type.

How much ruin lust has brought to the world is evident for the pages of writers are filled with it, and there is no doubt whatsoever that it brings along with it all sorts of evils and discords, and weakens the body and does harm to all virtues and goodness of the soul. It is lust for which men debase themselves in order to submit the body and soul to the inconstant will and unbridled desire of an unbalanced and vain woman; for we see a man, at a mere nod from her, place himself in danger of losing his soul, honour, and life, and often struck by the just anger of God serve as a wretched spectacle to a whole people, as we shall hear in the present story.

To Don Carlos d'Avalos, Prince of Montesarchio and to Donna Severina Gesualdo, first families of greatness and nobility in the city and kingdom of Naples, there was born, among others, Donna Maria, who, having reached the age of fifteen and being no less celebrated for her name than famous for her beauty, was married *1.1.113 to Federigo Carafa, Marchese of San Lucido. They sired two children, a male named Ferrante who died a few months after his birth and a daughter who, brought up in a noble manner, and whose parents being dead, married Marcantonio Carafa. The Marchese of San Lucido having engendered these two children, as has been said, passed from this to a better world, Donna Maria remaining a widow. The year of mourning having scarcely passed, she was again married by her parents, with the dispensation of the Pope, to D. Carlo Gesualdo, Prince of Venosa, her cousin. The marriage was celebrated with royal magnificence in the house of this Prince, situated near the church of San Domenico, in which house there were festivities for several days. This marriage for the space of three or four years was a happy one, whence, living more like lovers [than husband and wife], there was born as the fruit of their conjugal love a son named D. Emmanuele, who in the course of time succeeded Don Carlo, his father, in the principality. But the enemy of human nature not being able to endure the sight of such great love and such conformity of tastes in two married people, implanted in the bosom of Donna Maria unchaste and libidinous desires, and an unbridled appetite to enjoy the beauties of a certain cavaliere. He was Don Fabrizio Carafa, Duke of Andria, *5.1.71, 98–100* perhaps the most handsome and graceful cavaliere in the city, vigorous and flourishing and not yet thirty years of age, so delicate and yet so irascible in his manner that at one moment you would have esteemed him an Adonis for his beauty and at another a Mars for his fury. He was joined in marriage to Donna Maria Carafa, daughter of Don Luigi, Prince of Stigliano, by whom he fathered five children [. . .]

The lovers' uniformity of minds, the occasions presented by dances during festivities, the equal desire of both to enjoy the beauty of the other through their gazes were all so much fuel which burnt in their breasts. The first messages of their desires were their glances which with the tongue of the heart of love betrayed the fire which burnt in each other's breast. From glances of love they proceed to written messages, given to and received by faithful messengers, in which they invited each other to battle on the fields of love. This Archer, although blind, was most adept at bringing the lovers together, and knew well how to find an appropriate place for their meeting.

They met alone for the first time in the garden of Don Garzia of Toledo, in the town of Chiaia, in the pavilion *1.2.251–2* whereof the Duke did lie concealed, awaiting his mistress and beloved, who, on the pretext of diversion and entertainment, started off with a simple retinue of a faithful maid named Laura Scala and some gentlemen of hers. While she was going about in the garden, pretending that she was afflicted with a pain in her body, she betook herself from the group of those waiting on her, entering, guided by the wife of the gardener who had been well paid by the Duke, into the house where he was hiding. Seeing her approach, he came without wasting time, and taking her in his arms, kissed her a thousand times—as she did him—and with the greatest ardour they were moved to enjoy together the ultimate amorous delight.

This was not the last time that they were together in their pleasure, but many, many times for months on end such usance continued in the said house of Don Garzia as well as in other secret places according as their wit and fortune provided the opportunity. Many times in the very bedroom of the Princess, with the maid as a sentinel, did they dally amorously together, and as evil, amorous meetings became habitual, it was no longer possible to keep their love secret, especially from him who with most jealous eyes gazed on the proceedings and actions, although private, of Donna Maria. Their sins were first disclosed and then punished in their body—and perhaps would have been similarly punished even in their souls, if at the extreme moment God out of his mercy had not enjoined them to make an act of true contrition and thereby made the whole population a laughing stock.

The first who noticed their mutual love was Don Giulio Gesualdo, blood uncle of the Prince, who being fiercely enamoured of Donna Maria's beauty, and not heeding the fact that she was the wife of his nephew, had left no stone unturned in order to effect his intent. But he had not only been rebuffed by her, but sharply **2.3.76–81* reproved for his mad love, even to the point of her threatening him that, should he persist in such thought and device, she would inform her husband that he was a plotter against her honesty. For which reason, realiz- **2.1.150–2* ing that neither through gifts nor prayers nor through tears had he been able to make her pliant to his will, and believing truly that she was a chaste Penelope, poor Don Giulio resigned himself and ceased to importune her. But when whispers came to his ears of her loves and pleasures with the Duke, and having perceived them by more than one indication with his own eyes, so great was the anger which assailed him on seeing that she was another's whore, that, without losing a moment's time, he went to report the matter to the Prince. At such grievous news Don Carlo remained more dead than alive. But in order not to be too prone to belief on the basis of the reports of others, he determined that that which had come to his ears should be **3.3.71,* evident, too, to his eyes. *4.1.73–6*

In the meantime, the lovers having been informed

that their crimes were already known, the Duke put an end to their pleasures; but Donna Maria not being able to bear such respite urged him to reinstate the interrupted delights. The Duke, however, explained to her how he knew that their love had been revealed, and pointed out the danger to their honour and their life as well, unless they abstained from their amorous excesses.

To these salutary reasonings the Princess replied to the Duke that if his heart was capable of fear, he had better become a lackey, since nature had made an error in creating a cavalier with the heart of a woman, and had erred in making her—a woman—with the heart of a cavalier. It was not worthy of him to show such plebeian virtue, for, if he was capable of harbouring fear, then should he chase from his breast any love of her and nevermore appear before her.

At this angry reply, which touched him to the very quick, the Duke hastily went to his beloved and unhappy lady, and said to her: 'Fair lady, you wish that **5.1.16–23* I should die? Then let me die. For love of you, this soul of mine will be happy to leave its body, a victim of such beauty. I have the strength to meet my death, but not the fortitude to suffer yours. For if I die, you will not continue alive, and this is the fear which makes a coward of me. I have no heart for this. If you have no eyes to foresee this calamity, give me assurance that the Duke of Andria alone will be the victim of your husband, and I shall show you whether I can bear the thrust of a sword. You are cruel, not to me, who have found you greatly merciful. But cruel you are to your own beauty which, still fresh, you risk allowing to rot in the tomb.'

To this the Princess replied: 'My Lord Duke, more **5.1.52ff* deadly to me is a moment when you are away from me than a thousand deaths that might result from my crime. If I die with you, I shall never be far from you; but if you leave me, I shall die alone far from all my heart holds dear, which is you. Resolve, then, either to show yourself disloyal by going away, or to show yourself faithful by never abandoning me. As for the reasons which you have expressed, you should have given con-

sideration to them before, and not now when the arrow
has sped to its mark. I have the courage necessary to **5.1.159–61*
suffer the wound of cold steel but not your zeal in going
away. You should not have loved me, nor I you, if such
fears were to present themselves. In short, I so wish and
so command, and to my wish let there be no opposition unless you would lose me forever.'

To the above-mentioned speech the Duke, bowing **5.1.16–23*
humbly, replied: 'Lady, since you want to die, I shall die
with you. Such is your wish; so be it.' And he left, pursuing still his accustomed pleasures.

The Prince, now alert and attentive to every action,
having with great speed had all the locks of all the doors
of the palace removed and put out of working order so
that the Princess should not suspect anything, spread **4.2.67–70*
the news one day that he was going to go hunting, as it
was his custom to do, and that he would not return that
evening but, rather, the following day. The day when he
was to go hunting having arrived, and accompanied by **4.2.73.1–3*
many kinsmen and friends who were aware of the ruse,
all dressed as hunters, he mounted his horse pretending to go to a place called Astruni, eighty-two miles
from Naples.

In the meantime he left orders with several of his
most trusted servants that during the night they should
leave all the necessary doors open, that they
should pretend that the doors were shut, and that they
should watch and see if the Duke were to come. The
Prince then left and went to hide himself in the home
of a relative of his until it was time to leave.

The Duke, having been informed that the Prince had
gone a-hunting and that he would not return that
evening, betook himself at four hours of the night to his
accustomed pleasures. Having been received by Donna
Maria with her wonted affection, both, having disrobed,
got into bed where several times they gave each other
solace, and overcome by fatigue from such supreme
pleasure both soul and body drifted into sleep.

Towards midnight the Prince returned to the palace *5.1.29.1ff
accompanied by a troop of armed cavalieri who were
relatives of his. Having entered the house, he betook

himself with dispatch to the bedroom of the Princess in front of which was stationed a careful sentinel, Laura *5.1.30–1, Scala, her faithful maid, who was half asleep on a bed. 35 The maid, hearing the noise made by these people, was on the point of shouting, but her life being threatened by the Prince, she withdrew more dead than alive, and the Prince, breaking down the door of the bedroom with a blow of his foot, and entering therein ablaze with anger with his companions, found his wife lying naked in bed in the arms of the Duke. (In the meantime, all having gone into the bedroom, the good maid seized the opportune moment and took to her heels, nor was anything more heard of her.)

At such a sight one can well imagine how dumbfounded the poor Prince was, who, nevertheless, shaking himself loose from the stunned state which such a scene had precipitated in him, slew the sleepy lovers with many dagger thrusts before they could catch their breath.

This happened on the night which followed the day of 16 October, 1590. The bodies were dragged outside the room and left on the stairs, the Prince ordering the servants not to move them from that place; and having made a placard which explained the cause of the slaughter which they affixed to the door of the palace, he went with some of his relatives to his state of Venosa.

The bodies of the wretched lovers remained exposed all the following morning in the middle of the stairs, and the entire city ran thither to view such a spectacle. *5.1.62–4 The Princess's wounds were all in her belly and especially in those parts which most ought to be kept honest; and the Duke gave evidence of having been even more grievously wounded than she [. . .]

The body of the Duke was taken away to be buried that same evening and the body of the Princess the following day. Such was the end of their unchaste love.

Appendix 4: *Love's Sacrifice* and *Mirandola*

The knowing 'friend' who wrote the Prologue for Bryan Waller Procter's tragedy *Mirandola*[1] has good cause to compare the play to the works of the 'mightier masters' who flourished 'two hundred years' since (p. vii). However, Davril (478) and Hoskins (12) believe that Procter's play, one of the hits of the 1821 season, reveals a specific debt to *LS*. *Mirandola* could perhaps be read as a disguised version of *LS* which takes the central figures of Ford's play—the unstable Duke, his young and beautiful wife who was 'not born to princely pomp' (1.2, p. 10), the younger man (here the Duke's own son) whose relationship with the Duchess arouses her husband's jealousy, the Duke's scheming sister and her machiavellian offsider—and remoulds them for the refined sensibilities of nineteenth-century playgoers. Isidora, in particular, might be seen as a nineteenth-century version of Bianca, the object of rival lovers yet guilty of no impropriety. A handful of verbal echoes offer slight support for this reading. Mirandola resembles Caraffa in his possessive joy: 'I have my wife here, and my son, / The one is beautiful, the other brave' (3.1, p. 51; cf *LS* 1.1.132–4). His 'meteors' (3.3, p. 65) may remind one of Caraffa's 'bearded meteor' (*LS* 4.1.47). Isabella's words to Guido as she discovers him alone—'What study's this' (p. 56)—are reminiscent of her counterpart Fiormonda's greeting to the solitary Fernando (*LS* 1.2.94). And Mirandola's dead wife was named Bianca (2.2, p. 37). But I can find no unequivocal evidence of a link between the plays.

NOTE

1 Barry Cornwall (pseud. of Bryan Waller Procter), *Mirandola, A Tragedy*, 2nd edn (London: Warren, 1821). The play was acted at Covent Garden in January 1821. For further details about the composition and performance of *Mirandola*, see Henry Saxe Wyndham, *The Annals of Covent Garden Theatre from 1732 to 1897*, 2 vols (London: Chatto and Windus, 1906), II, 12; Nicoll, IV, 283; Sir Frederick Pollock, ed., *Macready's Reminiscences, and Selections from his Diaries and Letters*, 2 vols (London: Macmillan, 1875), I, 222–3; Alan S. Downer, *The Eminent Tragedian, William Charles Macready* (Cambridge, Massachusetts: Harvard University Press, 1966), 85–6; and Telford Moore, 199–201.

Index to the Introduction and Commentary

The following index lists: (a) words and phrases discussed in the Commentary; (b) proper names and topics referred to in the Introduction. An asterisk indicates that a glossarial note contains information supplementing that in *OED*. Note: 'n.' after a page reference indicates the number of a note on that page. Literary works are listed under authors' names.